Studying Peoples in the People's Dem
Socialist Era Anthropology in East-Central Europe

The contributors to this volume describe the theorie, teaching practices, and influential personalities of various strands of anthropology in the German Democratic Republic, Czechoslovakia, Hungary, and Poland during the socialist era. While the distinctiveness of national traditions in the human and social sciences has long been recognised, in all of these countries the history of anthropology has been tightly bound up with the history of nation-building. In the German case, *Völkerkunde*, the comparative study of non-European peoples, was institutionally separate from *Volkskunde*, the study of one's own people. In the other countries of this region the two were intertwined, but the latter dominated. Anthropology was everywhere associated with history rather than with the social sciences.

After the Second World War both strands in Germany lay in disrepute, and all the nation-centred anthropologies were confronted by the universalising doctrines of Marxism-Leninism: 'scientific socialism' in its most dogmatic, Stalinist variant. Yet the authors of this book show that the established national schools of anthropology survived this encounter, and indeed, the discipline was generally strengthened institutionally. Some new fields opened up, such as the study of the industrial working classes, but the home variant of the discipline continued to focus primarily on the peasant folk culture, identified in the nineteenth century as the essence of national identity. Distinctions between Völkerkunde and Volkskunde were not transcended, even though the GDR, made a determined effort to forge a unified discipline called *Ethnographie*.

It is impossible to reach blanket conclusions about the accomplishments of the anthropologists of this era, some of whom present their own accounts in this volume. The elements of long-term planning introduced in the 1950s led to some solid achievements, such as ethnographic atlases that needed decades to prepare. Socialism did not stifle theoretical or methodological innovation. Condemnation of the relations between 'bourgeois anthropology' and imperialism anticipated similar critique in Western countries by decades. Yet the scholars of East-Central Europe were subject to severe ideological constraints and isolated internationally. With access to literature and fieldwork limited, they had few opportunities to develop the discipline in new directions. Some of the most innovative work took place in the GDR, empirically in the domain of Volkskunde, which adopted new styles of socio-cultural history, and theoretically in Völkerkunde, where 'primitive communism' and the stages of social evolution received attention. Yet at the end of the socialist era the anthropologists of the GDR, unlike their eastern neighbours, were subjected to a scholarly evaluation—and in many cases found to be inadequate by the new, Western standards.

Halle Studies in the Anthropology of Eurasia

General Editors:

Chris Hann, Richard Rottenburg, Burkhard Schnepel, Shingo Shimada

Volume 8

LIT

Chris Hann, Mihály Sárkány and Peter Skalník (eds.)

Studying Peoples in the People's Democracies

Socialist Era Anthropology in East-Central Europe

LIT

Cover Design: Gerd-Roland Müller and Judith Orland

Bibliographic information published by Die Deutsche Bibliothek
Die Deutsche Bibliothek lists this publication in the Deutsche
Nationalbibliografie; detailed bibliographic data are available in the
Internet at http://dnb.ddb.de.

ISBN 3-8258-8048-6

A catalogue record for this book is available from the British Library

© LIT VERLAG Münster   2005
Grevener Str./Fresnostr. 2   D- 48159 Münster
Tel. +49/(0)251-62 03 20   Fax +49/(0)251-23 19 72
e-Mail: lit@lit-verlag.de   http://www.lit-verlag.de

Distributed in the UK by:
Global Book Marketing
38 King Street, London WC 2E 8JT
Phone: +44 (0) 207 240 6649 – Fax: +44 (0) 20 7497 0309
http://www.globalbookmarketing.co.uk

Distributed in North America by:

Transaction Publishers
New Brunswick (U.S.A.) and London (U.K.)

Transaction Publishers   Tel.: (732) 445 - 2280
Rutgers University   Fax: (732) 445 - 3138
35 Berrue Circle   for orders (U. S. only):
Piscataway, NJ 08854   toll free (888) 999 - 6778

Contents

Preface

This volume marks a new departure in the series Halle Studies in the Anthropology of Eurasia. Whereas previous volumes comprised investigations
of anthropological topics concerning society in Eurasia, here the spotlight is
turned on the discipline of anthropology itself. Why?

The answer is partly personal. When I moved to Halle in 1999 as one
of the directors of the Max Planck Society's newly established Institut für
ethnologische Forschung, I had little awareness of the German-language
traditions in our discipline. I knew almost nothing about recent developments in the former German Democratic Republic (GDR), where our institute is situated. Almost all of my colleagues here, both at the institute and in
the universities in our vicinity, have been recent arrivals from the West.
Naive curiosity turned into something more pressing when I began to hear
stories of East German colleagues who had lost their posts after the *Wende*
of 1989. This situation contrasted sharply with professional continuity elsewhere in the region, a pattern with which I was familiar through my contacts
with anthropologists in Hungary and Poland. For help in exploring this
puzzle I turned to my old friends Mihály Sárkány in Budapest and Peter
Skalník in Prague, both of whom were thoroughly familiar with the GDR.
Together we organised a workshop in Halle in August 2003, at which most
of the papers gathered in this volume were first presented.

It was an exceptionally stimulating meeting. At the end of two intensive days I no longer felt guilty about having convened a meeting merely to
satisfy my personal interests. The participants agreed unanimously that this
recent history needed to be documented and disseminated as a matter of
urgency. I hope they will forgive me if I suggest that the motivation might be
compared to that which lies behind projects of 'salvage anthropology',
where it is imperative to record as much as possible while the last members
of a tribe can still tell their stories.

Although some of the papers were originally written and presented in
German, English dominated at the workshop. There was a general wish to
publish in what has become, even in East-Central Europe, the lingua franca
of the modern discipline. (Prior to socialism, German was the most important language of anthropology and of intellectual life generally in these parts;
attempts under socialism to impose Russian were not very successful.) We
make no strong claim for the unity of this particular group of countries—the
GDR, Poland, Hungary, and the former Czechoslovakia—either in the past
or today. This restriction was determined primarily by pragmatic factors. It

would be interesting to repeat the venture for the countries of South-East Europe. Of course the history of anthropology in the Soviet Union lies continuously in the background in these chapters. That history, too, is still insufficiently known, at least to non-Russian speakers such as myself. In other words, there is a need for further salvage intellectual history of this kind.

It remains for me to thank everyone who helped in organising the workshop and producing this book. In addition to my co-convenors and all contributors, Michał Buchowski in Poznań and my Max Planck Institute colleagues John Eidson and Tilo Grätz gave support and many useful suggestions. For permission to republish Tamás Hofer's concluding chapter from his 1968 contribution to *Current Anthropology* we are indebted to the University of Chicago Press. Andreas Hemming (Chapters 9, 10 and 18), Diana Quetz (Chapters 12 and 16), and Marit Keil (Chapter 11) prepared translations, Britt-Marie Öberg helped to polish both these and other chapters, Jane Kepp was our expert copy editor, and Berit Westwood and Tobias Köllner coordinated the volume with great efficiency and patience.

Chris Hann
November 2004

Chapter 1
Introduction: Continuities and Contrasts in an Essentially Contested Field

Chris Hann, Mihály Sárkány, and Peter Skalník

We are anthropologists, not historians. Although we are concerned in this volume with the history of anthropology, we have in a way approached the task ethnographically: our aim is to combine critical analysis with a sympathetic understanding of the context in which this history was made. Some chapters may be read as the statements of key informants, though others draw on careful archival research. In any case, the history of anthropology in the group of countries that we term East-Central Europe (*Ostmitteleuropa*)— Poland, Hungary, Czechoslovakia, and the German Democratic Republic (GDR)—during socialism is a history which almost all the contributors to this volume experienced personally in one way or another. Their assessments are inevitably influenced by many factors, including 'worldview' and personal experiences of socialism. Consequently, just as it is usual in anthropological monographs nowadays to say something about the nature of the fieldwork and address the problem of reflexivity, so it seems important to emphasise the element of subjectivity in exploring a disciplinary history which has come to an end but which is still very much alive in memories and is at multiple levels 'essentially contested'.[1] A brief introduction to the editors of this volume can also serve to alert readers unfamiliar with the scene in East-Central Europe to the diversity of disciplinary developments and anthropological career paths during the socialist era, details of which are explored in the succeeding chapters.

Hann is very much the outsider—which of course renders his perspective no less subjective. He had no knowledge of anthropology in the region until 1975, when he purchased at Foyles bookshop in London a copy of *Proper Peasants: Traditional Life in a Hungarian Village*, by Edit Fél and Tamás Hofer. Later that year he went to Budapest as a British Council exchange scholar. For two years he was affiliated with the Anthropology

---

[1] This is a loose extension of the notion of 'essentially contested concepts' (Gallie 1956).

Institute (then known as the Néprajzi Kutatócsoport) at the Hungarian Academy of Sciences, where his principal adviser was Mihály Sárkány. In the relatively relaxed political climate which prevailed in Hungary at the time, it was not too difficult to obtain permission to spend the entire second year in a village on the Great Plain and to apply the methods of participant observation to investigate its changing economic and political structures.

Hann's project grew out of a simple conviction that anthropologists could play a role in demystifying living conditions behind what most people in the West, including the majority of social scientists, still conceived of as an 'iron curtain'. Contacts with colleagues at the Academy of Sciences and in other institutions exposed Hann to the different theoretical approaches and methods of Hungarian anthropologists, but he did not address these in his work. He went on to undertake a postdoctoral project in provincial Poland, where his main scholarly ties were not to anthropologists but to the rural sociologists Bogusław Gałęski and Zbigniew Tadeusz Wierzbicki, whose work corresponded to the contemporary focus and socio-economic orientation of his project

In later years, as a junior lecturer in the Department of Social Anthropology in Cambridge, Hann was much influenced by Ernest Gellner's numerous publications on Soviet anthropology (e.g. Gellner 1980, 1988). Gellner, by then the head of the department in Cambridge, read the work of Soviet colleagues through at least two lenses. He was, on the one hand, respectful of an evolutionist theoretical framework based on Marxist-Leninist historical materialism, because he was increasingly convinced that the Malinowskian paradigm, with its emphasis upon the synchronic collection of ethnographic data, had outlived its theoretical usefulness for the discipline. On the other hand, Gellner read Soviet texts in the spirit of a faithful Malinowskian. He wanted to understand their function in the present, not only in the context of Soviet ideology but also in relation to the social realities of that system, which Gellner himself came to know well during the year he spent in Moscow in the *perestroika* period. In preparing for the workshop in Halle in 2003 on which this book is based, Hann suggested that participants approach the corpus of East-Central European anthropology in a similar spirit. The incitement to speculative detective work was not generally taken up, because it was no longer necessary. The chief difference with Gellner's work in the 1970s and 1980s was of course that, with the demise of socialism, the anthropologists of that era could now speak for themselves, freed from the constraints under which they had worked previously.

Sárkány and Skalník are near contemporaries whose academic careers exhibit certain similarities. Both combined an Africa specialisation with an interest in Western social anthropology. They were able to apply the latter when they collaborated in fieldwork projects in their native countries (Hungary and Czechoslovakia, respectively). This collaboration took place within the framework of a comparative project on the future of rural communities in industrialised societies, directed by Henri Mendras in the early 1970s. Sárkány worked in the north Hungarian village of Varsány between 1971 and 1975, in a team led by Tibor Bodrogi. His particular focus was the transformation of the village economy and changing social stratification. From 1970 to 1976, Skalník worked with social anthropological methods in two adjacent northern Slovak villages, Nižná Šuňava and Vyšná Šuňava (in 1974 they merged to form a single community, Šuňava).

There, however, the similarities end. Sárkány's career has been based all along in Budapest. He studied anthropology (néprajz) in the 1960s, was appointed to a position at the Institute of Ethnography of the Hungarian Academy of Sciences in 1968, and became the head of its Department of Non-European Studies in 1988. Since 1975 he has lectured on British and American anthropological theory, economic anthropology, and African anthropology within the Department of Néprajz at the Eötvös Loránd University of Budapest (ELTE). In 1990 he was one of the founders of a Department of Cultural Anthropology (*kulturális antropológia*) at the same university, assuming an increased leadership role after 1997. As an active academic throughout these decades, particularly in his role as editor of the foreign-language journal *Acta Ethnographica* between 1981 and 1990, Sárkány had many opportunities to observe and work with some of the most influential personalities of anthropology in all the countries covered in this volume. He was also exposed to international scholarship in several Western countries, spending five months in Cambridge in 1979 and taking part in many international conferences.

These experiences, together with his theoretical inclination towards studying contemporary social and cultural phenomena in their structural and functional relations and in the process of social change (rather than for their own sake, as cultural objectifications), distanced him from mainstream Hungarian néprajz. He was quietly critical of this discipline, to the extent that one colleague classified him as a 'vertical dissident'. Despite his Africanist training and his holding of a secure position in the Academy of Sciences, he was unable to make extended field trips to other continents in the socialist era (the only exception was a private expedition to East Africa, organised with a group of geographers in 1987–88). Only in the 1990s was he able to carry out a fieldwork project in economic anthropology in Kenya. Recently he has been engaged in a restudy of Varsány, this time in collaboration with Hann, who has also been restudying the Hungarian community of his first fieldwork.

Skalník's career has been punctuated by almost continuous upheavals and shifts of direction, not all of them voluntary. The son of Olga Skalníková, herself a leading anthropologist in the socialist period and a contributor to this volume, he was familiar from his childhood with most of the leading Czech and Slovak representatives of národopis (the equivalent of néprajz), including some of the leading figures of the pre-socialist era. Inspired by the examples of his mother, who in 1961 was able to undertake fieldwork in Guinea, and of Ladislav Holý, who worked in Sudan in the same period, Skalník enrolled in Prague for African Studies (rather than etnografie and folkloristika, the combination chosen by his friend Josef Kandert). In 1963 he went to Leningrad, where he studied African anthropology under Dmitriy Alekseevich Ol'derogge and became acquainted with the history and major living protagonists of Soviet anthropology (etnografiya). After returning to his native Prague, he spent some years teaching 'general ethnology' in Bratislava.

Then, like so many others, including Holý and Milan Stuchlík, he was forced into exile by the intellectual repression which followed the Soviet military invasion of 1968. He fled to the Netherlands in 1976 and, after holding posts there and in South Africa, he returned to Prague in 1990. Following a stint as ambassador to Lebanon (first of Czechoslovakia and then, after the 'velvet divorce,' of the Czech Republic), in recent years Skalník has been tireless in his efforts to promote new models for teaching and research in anthropology in his native country—although, as elsewhere in the region, the academic landscape is complex and the task facing innovators is far from straightforward. In 2000 he accepted an invitation to join the newly established Faculty of Humanities at the University of Pardubice, where social anthropology (sociální antropologie) has been awarded disciplinary recognition for the first time in the Czech Republic. In Pardubice his main research project is a restudy of the nearby village of Dolní Roveň, first documented by a Czech rural sociologist in 1939.

Though we have been friends and colleagues for decades, and working together on this book has strengthened these ties, our contrasting backgrounds and career paths no doubt help to explain why we hold different views on many of the subjects covered in this volume.

The Anthropological Field in East-Central Europe

One of the points on which we have had difficulty in reaching agreement is the very terminology for our field. The problems may already be apparent to the reader. Hann's institute in Halle, Germany, is known in English as the

Max Planck Institute for Social Anthropology (simply because this was the designation preferred by the two founding directors). But the official German name, bestowed by the Max Planck Society, is Max-Planck-Institut für ethnologische Forschung. To most contemporary British social anthropologists, 'ethnological research' sounds mysterious and somehow antiquated. The term ethnology has more recognition in North America, for good historical reasons. There are equivalents in many European languages. In Germany nowadays Ethnologie is usually a synonym for Völkerkunde. Both terms have traditionally referred to the study of non-European peoples, whereas Volkskunde is the study of one's own *Volk*. The consolidation in recent decades of departments of *Europäische Ethnologie* has by no means resolved all the ambiguities. In the German title of our 2003 workshop we attempted to get around the problem by referring to die *Ethnowissenschaften*, but 'the ethnosciences' still appears strange and potentially bewildering to English-speaking readers.[2] These naming confusions are an indication of the contested nature of the field, in which both substantive intellectual agendas and control over resources are at issue.

Ultimately we have opted for anthropology as the best available 'umbrella' term for this English-language publication. The umbrella shelters a range of subjects, which together make up a single disciplinary field. The alternative would be to argue that subjects such as néprajz in Budapest and národopis in Prague are quite different disciplines from anthropology. Several contributors do indeed lean towards this view. For example, Josef Kandert (chapter 13) opposes 'home anthropology' (národopis) to comparative social anthropology, and Tamás Hofer (chapter 20) contrasts 'national ethnography' (néprajz) with American cultural anthropology. In each case it is clear from the context how the author is using the term anthropology. We nonetheless suggest that anthropology (without qualification) is the best available overarching designation; this usage should not be understood as an act of Anglo-American imperialism and it does not preclude a full airing of important differences within the field.

Of course many problems remain, not least because the connotations of anthropology in other languages are liable to mislead. For example, the German *Anthropologie* relates primarily to two fields which do not fall under our umbrella at all: philosophical anthropology, on the one hand, and biological anthropology, on the other. The terms *Kultur-* and *Sozialanthropologie* currently have little recognition in the German-speaking world, though

---

[2] The late Croatian scholar Dunja Rihtman-Auguštin (2004) proposed the term *ethnoanthropology* to label the discipline as it passed through a transitional stage between Volkskunde and sociocultural anthropology.

this is beginning to change in a few places.[3] Related terms, however, have become widespread in recent years in the other countries covered in this volume. We return to this point at the end of this introduction.

As we apply the term in this volume, anthropology still embraces a broad field. With some simplification we can identify two poles in this field. One is the pursuit of social or cultural anthropology as an explicitly comparative enquiry on a global basis. This pole is associated particularly with the European states which ruled over far-flung empires. The other pole is an understanding which focuses attention on one's own people or nation.[4] In Germany both poles—that is, Völkerkunde and Volkskunde—were well developed historically, but both were casualties of the world wars of the twentieth century. Elsewhere the disciplinary name with greatest public recognition in this region is the equivalent of Volkskunde: Polish, ludoznawstwo; Czech and Slovak, národopis; Hungarian, néprajz. Each of these means more or less 'a description of the people' and it was initially conceived more as an artistic portrait than as a rigorous scientific analysis. These terms are sometimes translated as 'ethnography', while 'ethnology' is reserved for the generalising science. Unfortunately, there is little consistency in the renderings. In some cases the contents have been subject to significant change while the name has remained the same (e.g. Hungarian néprajz in the 1950s); in other cases a change of name (e.g. from etnografia to etnologia in socialist Poland, or the partial supplanting of Volkskunde by Europäische Ethnologie in Germany) does not necessarily correspond to substantive change in theoretical orientation or in methods. Numerous shifts and relabellings are documented in this volume. The Volkskunde pole is often divided into more or less autonomous subfields such as folklore, material culture, and museum studies. All of these fall in the contested field of anthropology in our 'umbrella' sense.

A full exploration of the origins and development of anthropology in East-Central Europe in the pre-socialist era is beyond the scope of this volume. But it is important to stress that this intellectual history is tightly intertwined with other aspects of the history of East-Central European societies since the Enlightenment. German-language contributions played a major role in setting the academic agenda in the middle of the eighteenth century. The most important terms, Ethnographie, Ethnologie, Volkskunde, and Völkerkunde, were all coined between 1767 and 1783 in Göttingen and Vienna. One leading figure in this creative process was August Ludwig

---

[3] The case of *historische Anthropologie* raises additional issues, too complicated to pursue here.
[4] Cf. George Stocking's (1982) distinction between 'nation-building' and 'empire-building' anthropologies.

Schlözer, who was directly responsible for introducing the term Völkerkunde as a synonym for Ethnographie in 1771 (see Vermeulen 1995, 1996; Stagl
1998). Even before this, German scholars (including those based in St.
Petersburg) were concerned with documenting the customs and *Lebensart* of
remote, 'exotic' peoples, above all in Siberia. Explorers such as Gerhard
Friedrich Müller drew up detailed 'instructions' (*Anweisungen*) for the
systematic collection of ethnographic data to represent what later anthropologists would come to call the 'culture' of the other (Bucher 2002). But it
was Schlözer and his associates who pioneered a systematic comparative
critique of knowledge concerning both ancient and contemporary peoples.

    Johann Gottfried Herder, a pupil of Kant, also has a strong claim to
being considered a major ancestral figure in the development of German
anthropology, even though he did not actually employ the terms Ethnologie
or Ethnographie. The key unit in his philosophy of history was the *Volk* or
the *Nation*, which he sometimes identified with *Cultur* (*sic*). His was the
most powerful pluralising counterpoint to the new universalism emerging
from Enlightenment France. Whereas the Parisian *philosophes* agitated for a
general emancipation based upon human rights, Herder urged recognition of
the unique spirit of each people, conceived of as a separate organism, developing according to its own specific trajectory. This early variant of cultural
relativism had a lasting effect on scholarship in East-Central Europe as the
era of romanticism led into an era of nationalist mobilisation. Herder's direct
impact on the consolidation of academic research and teaching in German
Volkskunde and Völkerkunde in the nineteenth century seems to have been
rather small: others, such as the Grimm brothers and the Humboldt brothers,
were more influential. But his ideas were enthusiastically embraced in the
course of the nineteenth century in the neighbouring Slavic nations, whose
intellectuals played key roles in national movements and paved the way for
the new world of nation-states which dominated in East-Central Europe after
the collapse of the Habsburg Empire in 1918.

    By this time the subject of 'people-science' was already firmly estab-
lished on a national(ist) basis. Its specialists were concerned with documenting contemporary regional and local diversity but also with reconstructions—that is, the identification of original, archaic forms of the nation. This
discipline was concerned to look back to the roots of the 'national' culture in
a pre-industrial age, and its contemporary research agenda concentrated on
alleged 'survivals' of that past. It had an affinity with the researches of Sir
James Frazer, who was widely read in East-Central Europe (most famously
by Malinowski); the main difference (apart from the political) was that East-
Central European rural societies offered rather more opportunities than
industrialised Britain for empirical research into these survivals. Compari-

sons, if they were made at all, were typically limited to peoples of the same close 'family', such as Western Slav or Finno-Ugric.

The links to nationalism must not be exaggerated. In the multi-ethnic imperial powers of Austria-Hungary and Russia, the differences between comparative Ethnologie or Völkerkunde and the Volkskunde orientation were less sharp than they were in Germany. Within Germany itself, increasing knowledge of the cultural traits of European peoples and the spread of diffusionist interpretations of cultural changes undermined nationalist simplifications around the turn of the twentieth century and led to greater recognition of the importance of cultural interpenetration. The German school of cultural history in anthropology is well known (Zwernemann 1983). It is less commonly recognised that similar developments took place in research within Europe, particularly in the study of folktales. But the language of the disciplines did not change, and it often sounded as if nationality (ethnicity) was the ultimate and sole *explanandum* for the existence of a cultural feature. This shortcoming was exposed with the emergence of national socialist ideology, which had a disastrous influence on both the Volkskunde and Völkerkunde branches of anthropology in Germany. Elsewhere in the region, 'people-science' maintained its orientation towards the cause of the nation, but without being tainted by Fascism.

In the more rural states of East-Central Europe, especially in Hungary, another trend was prominent in the 1930s. A new generation of scholars, some of whom called themselves 'sociographers', set out to describe actual social conditions in the countryside, rather than glorifying the peasant in terms of national characteristics and a magnificent culture of the past. The extent to which these rural researchers had an effect on the new discipline of varied. Even in Hungary the long-term consequences of this radical, 'populist' scholarship were arguably more significant for sociology than for néprajz.

These are some of the features of the intellectual and socio-political context which help us to understand the convulsions which transformed the anthropological field following the end of the Second World War. Quite suddenly, in 1945 the victory of the Red Army rendered the Soviet Union the dominant power in East-Central Europe. Marxism-Leninism was, at least ostensibly, an internationalist movement oriented towards building a communist utopia. How would it affect anthropology, a disciplinary constellation associated at one pole with foreign imperialism and at the other with a celebration of the exclusivity of one's own nation? Both poles emphasised investigations of the primitive or the rustic, in contrast to the futurist modernism exhorted by the Soviets. Whereas in the eighteenth century German scholars had spread anthropological ideas in Russia, now the ideas and practices of Soviet etnografiya were exported to East-Central Europe. Their reception varied greatly, primarily in line with local political circumstances. In the following section we outline the general political context of Soviet domination. We then review the problematic imprint of Marxist ideas, especially the theory of historical materialism, on East-Central European anthropology. We conclude with a brief outline of the structure of the volume and some general reflections.

The Political Framework

Politics shaped the destinies of anthropology in socialist East-Central Europe in countless ways, official and unofficial. The repercussions of Soviet domination can be traced at several levels. First, scholarly endeavours were directly affected by international conditions. The superpower rivalries of the Cold War era greatly restricted the contacts that anthropologists of Eastern and Central Europe were able to maintain with their colleagues in the West. More bridges were built from the 1960s onwards, but even in the years of détente the Russian language enjoyed privileges not enjoyed by English or French. Even if more Western literature had been available, relatively few scholars in the region were in a position to read and profit from it.

At the national level, however, conditions varied significantly. In Hungary and Poland the political liberalisation which was gradually consolidated after 1956 also opened up more spaces for scholarly creativity. By contrast, in Czechoslovakia and the GDR the regimes retained a more repressive character to the very end.

It is also important to consider the mechanisms by which political control was exercised in the research institutes and universities. At this level certain general similarities obtained among the four countries, such as in the organisation of the Communist Party and in the role of politics in the recruitment and promotion of staff and the granting of privileges and permission to travel abroad. But here, too, practices varied, and even in the more repressive phases in the more repressive countries, individuals were sometimes able to create the space they needed to continue their work unhindered.

Very few anthropologists were oriented towards left-wing politics in East-Central Europe before the advent of socialism. Most variants of anthropology were marginal to the progressive trends of European culture, and some variants had strongly nationalist or narcissistic elements. Volkskunde, for example, celebrated race ideology and the mysticism of the German Volk, while the exaltation of local heritage in *Heimatkunde* was paralleled by *vlastivěda* among Czechs and Slovaks. With the exception of German Völkerkundler, few anthropologists had contact with theoretical trends in French, British, or American anthropology. Before the Second World War, practically no contacts took place between East-Central European anthropologists and their Soviet counterparts in etnografiya. Although artists, writers, and social activists from Germany and Czechoslovakia were frequent visitors to the USSR, anthropologists did not cultivate such contacts. This accentuated their difficulty in adapting to Soviet influences after 1945.

In East-Central Europe both the form of the state and its ideological claims were significantly different from those of the USSR. The states which concern us in this volume, the GDR included, were classified as People's Democracies. They were committed to a path that would only gradually lead to socialism, while the USSR, according to its politicians and party theorists, was already moving beyond socialism towards communism. Of course the Communist Party was no less fully in control.[5]

Before the death of Stalin in March 1953, the Soviet example was emulated emphatically in virtually all fields, an emulation that included the grandiose reorganisation of scientific life. New research institutes were founded and university education was substantially extended. The natural sciences and engineering and technical knowledge were favoured at the expense of the humanities and the social sciences. The latter were generally replaced by Marxism-Leninism. For more than a decade sociology was abandoned and the discipline of economics was altered fundamentally by the shift to the socialist, centrally planned economy (though market relations never disappeared entirely).

The relatively liberal atmosphere of the later 1950s and 1960s was conducive to a diversification of interests and also to more pluralism in theoretical orientations, although Soviet Marxism remained dominant. Sociology was rehabilitated in both the USSR and Eastern Europe, at least in its 'empirical' form, and it began to exert influence on some anthropologists. Only in the GDR were the years 1956-68 still beset with political tensions, especially following the erection of the Berlin Wall. Any positive reference to the Federal Republic was highly unwelcome. On the other hand, borders with other socialist states (Bulgaria, Romania, etc.) opened up even for the GDR. Experts were sent to help with their know-how in the world's newly independent colonies, mostly in African and Asian countries. This contributed to lively scientific exchanges among scholars of the Soviet satellite countries and to an activation of non-European studies within anthropology, especially in the GDR (see van der Heyden, this volume).

The most liberal developments took place in Hungary and Poland, both of which experienced revolutionary protest in 1956. Paradoxically,

---

[5] Only in Czechoslovakia was the Communist Party known officially by this name. Elsewhere it was the Party of Socialist Unity (GDR), the Socialist Workers' Party (Hungary), and the United Workers' Party (Poland).

reprisals by pro-Soviet forces were short-lived, and within a few years the atmosphere became more tolerant, both economically and socially. This enabled greater contact with Western scholars, anthropologists among them. Western anthropological literature became more accessible, and it was also reviewed and translated. In Poland, the suppression of the Solidarity movement and the imposition of a state of emergency in 1981 cast inevitable shadows. Yet it was nonetheless possible in these years to consolidate a unit for social anthropology (*antropologia społeczna*) within the Institute for Sociology of the Jagiellonian University in Cracow. This initiative had a special genealogy. Andrzej Waligórski had studied with Malinowski in prewar London, and his pupil Andrzej Paluch managed to obtain support for recovering Malinowski's intellectual legacy. In addition to an ambitious programme to publish the classics of Malinowski in Polish translations, Paluch and his group organised an international conference to mark the centenary of his birth in 1984 (Ellen et al. 1988). Leading figures of British social anthropology such as Ernest Gellner, M. G. Smith, Ladislav Holý, Edwin Ardener, Maurice Bloch, and Esther Goody were regular visitors to seminars in Cracow and Zakopane during the last decade of socialism (Mach and Paluch 1992). Yet these visitors did not establish contacts with the mainstream of Polish anthropology (etnografia/etnologia; see Posern-Zieliński, this volume).[6]

One sign of the more relaxed situation in both Poland and Hungary was the relative ease with which foreigners such as Hann could undertake fieldwork in those countries. Polish and Hungarian scholars were able to visit the West more frequently, and a few of the latter became known internationally when they published their work in German and English (e.g. Hofer 1968; Fél and Hofer 1969). Although the Hungarian anthropologists could not boast an émigré compatriot of the stature of Malinowski, they contributed actively to the (re)discovery of Karl Polanyi (whose birth centenary was commemorated in Budapest in 1986, only two years after the Malinowski centennial celebrations in Cracow).[7] The main difference be-

---

[6] Hann came to know some of the scholars around Paluch quite well during this period, but these contacts did not extend to etnografowie in the neighbouring institute. Some etnografowie (notably Michał Buchowski in Poznań) were themselves pursuing foreign ties and absorbing influences from Western anthropology during these years (see Posern-Zieliński, this volume; Sokolewicz, this volume).

[7] Sárkány was the leading anthropologist to participate in the reappropriation of Polanyi in the city where he spent his youth. In a somewhat different way, the attention later paid to Ernest Gellner in Prague, the city where he grew up, can be compared to the cases of Malinowski and Polanyi: in each case a distinguished émigré scholar could serve as a symbol, an alternative source of inspiration to those promoted by the regime. (There seems to be no comparable figurehead in the case of the GDR.)

tween Hungary and Poland in the last decades of socialism was the former's success in promoting new forms of mixed economy and private enterprise, developments which some scholars of a social anthropological bent, such as Sárkány, documented through fieldwork.

In contrast, in the GDR and Czechoslovakia anthropology of the Volkskunde variety still attracted some suspicion in some quarters as a bourgeois science, while the global, comparative pole of the field remained an anathema. GDR scholars were able to maintain contact with colleagues in other German-speaking countries, but these were strictly monitored by the authorities and did little to counter the country's international isolation. Czechoslovak anthropology experienced a short upswing in the relatively liberal 1960s, when leading international figures such as Meyer Fortes and Jack Goody gave lectures in Prague. This came to an end in the aftermath of the 1968 invasion, which had the effect of strengthening traditional národo-dopis and led to the departures of the most dynamic figures engaged in comparative anthropology.

Anthropology and Marxism-Leninism

Before the Second World War hardly any anthropologists in East-Central Europe were aware of the work of their Soviet colleagues or of what the implementation of Marxism might mean for the discipline. For example, in Hungary, Gyula Ortutay (1937) took note of Malinowski's functionalism in his pre-war theoretical work but not of the Marxism of the new Soviet school in etnografiya. The same was true in Slovakia of Andrej Melicherčík's theory of národopis (Melicherčík 1945) and of the Czech theorist Josef Voráček as well (Voráček 1936, 1940, 1941). Only in Germany was it possible to find traces of Marxism—for example, in the pre-war works of Julius Lips (Lips 1951 [1936]).

After 1945 the works of Marx, Engels, Lenin, and Stalin were promptly translated into the languages of the region, as were other works deemed to be close to Marxism or materialism, such as Lucretius's *De rerum natura*, Morgan's *Ancient Society*, Childe's *Man Makes Himself*, and Lips's *Vom Ursprung der Dinge*. Sergey Pavlovich Tolstov's pamphlet on the Soviet anthropological school (1949), Mark Osipovich Kosven's book on the matriarchate (1952), and collections such as *Anglo-American Ethnography in the Service of Imperialism* (Potěchin 1953) and *Lineage Society* (*Rodová spoločnosť* 1954, with a foreword by Andrej Melicherčík) were among the works translated from Russian. However, the entire programme of constructing socialism on the basis of a Marxist-Leninist concept of social development had ambiguous consequences for anthropology in East-Central Europe.

Socialism was first and foremost an attempt to transform traditional relations, forms of social organisation, and notions about what was good and desirable in society. Because the development of science was considered a necessary precondition for successful modernisation, science in general was supported. However, the prioritising of particular branches of science, including anthropology, was determined by considerations derived from Marxist-Leninist ideology, often with additional inspiration from the specific circumstances of the Soviet Union. Between 1948 and 1953 the Stalinist interpretation of Marxism-Leninism enjoyed a domination that could not be questioned. Marxism pervaded all disciplines, and so-called scientific socialism became a discipline in its own right, a sort of Marxist political science. Older academics were required to familiarise themselves with Marxism through various forms of retraining and adult education.

In retrospect it seems surprising that anthropology was able by and large to survive this onslaught. The discipline was endowed promptly with new research institutes at the academies (except in Hungary, where this was delayed until 1967). Of course researchers were now expected to be critical of earlier intellectual traditions. The renewal of aims and methods was supposed to find its inspiration in the Marxist-Leninist theory of social development. Of these two expectations, the first was easier to fulfill than the second. Renewal in the spirit of Marxism-Leninism was a more complicated issue, because it struck at the very roots of anthropology as it had been practised in this part of the world. The key concepts of 'culture' and 'peoples' (later 'ethnic groups') had little relevance for Marx and Engels, and certainly not in combination. Marx himself represented a kind of philosophical anthropology, in the sense that he had a distinctive image of 'man' which could be contrasted with other philosophical assumptions (including the Malinowskian). He envisaged the human actor as a social product who creates his existence in nature by transforming that nature through labour, that is, through purposeful activity within social relations, which are reproduced in the process. The social processes of reproduction, including knowledge and training, the means of production, and the relations in which the production is carried out, form the 'base' (*Grundlage*) of social life and determine its 'superstructure' (*Überbau*). It follows from this perspective that the ideas which direct and legitimise social relations—in other words, the culture, as it is expressed in law and religion—are no more than social forms of the mind. In a class-divided society this culture, too, is bound to be differentiated.[8] There is a dialectical relationship between base and super-

---

[8] This idea was elaborated by Lenin as the double theory of culture of capitalist society, in which a bourgeois culture and a workers' culture develop separately (see Kroeber and Kluckhohn 1952). This argument echoes the dominant German concept of culture in the nineteenth

structure, and ideas can therefore have an effect on elements of the former. Social changes of historical significance, however, such as the emergence of new socio-economic formations, can come about only through changes in the mode of production, that is, in the forces of production and relations of production. This entire intellectual apparatus left little room for an atomistic approach to cultural traits as interesting objects of research in their own right. In short, Marxism was a universalistic approach to human social life in which neither ethno-nationalist inclinations nor ethnographic 'butterfly collecting' had a place.

Given these difficulties, it is all the more fascinating to see how anthropologists adopted the ideas and concepts that they were not free to ignore. Some solved the problem by token citations, preferably not only of the Marxist classics but also of Soviet scholarship. Others took the challenge much more seriously. The most sophisticated engagement was to be found in the GDR, above all in the works of Irmgard Sellnow and Günter Guhr (see Noack and Krause, this volume). The GDR was a special case, not only because of the strength of Soviet political influence there but also because of attempts to draw together the legacies of Volkskunde and Völkerkunde to form a new discipline, Ethnographie, resembling in both its name and its scope Soviet etnografiya. The so-called formations debate proceeded on the premise that historical materialism was the only possible social theory for understanding 'pre-capitalist socio-economic formations'. German scholars followed their Soviet counterparts in taking a strong interest in primitive communism, a topic of self-evident relevance in countries in which a new, mature variety of communism was supposed to be within reach.[9]

Although the practitioners of this Marxist-Leninist anthropology drew on a wide range of empirical data, including fieldwork data, to support their analyses, they did not themselves do fieldwork; they were in this sense 'armchair' theoreticians. Their continuing preoccupation with 'ethnos' reveals the implicit, persisting power of a nationalist worldview hardly compatible with the views of the founders of socialism. In any case, these theoretical debates tended to engage only the Völkerkunde side of anthropology, even in the GDR, where Völkerkunde and Volkskunde had supposedly been united. It was much easier for the Volkskundler to undertake

---

century, which viewed it as an ennobling process: the expansion of 'cultivation' was a process of adding value. See Markarjan 1969; Peacock 2002; Noack and Krause, this volume.

[9] The theory of historical materialism also needed archaeological support, and archaeologists were very influential, especially in the 1950s. In the USSR the long serving director of the Institute for Ethnology at the Academy of Sciences was Sergey Pavlovich Tolstov, famous for his excavations in Khorezm. In Czechoslovakia the archaeologist Jaroslav Böhm was instrumental in the establishment of *etnografie* as the progressive replacement for the discredited *národopis* (see Skalníková, this volume).

fieldwork, and in some cases their adaptations of Marxism reflect this clearly. Thus the GDR Volkskundler were able to develop the concept of 'demos' in the course of developing new approaches in social and cultural history—approaches which have stood the test of time rather well (Jacobeit, this volume; Mohrmann, this volume). In other words, it was the 'home anthropology' branch of the discipline which seems to have adapted more successfully, at any rate from the vantage point of contemporary debates and the literature that is still read nowadays, as socialism recedes into the past.

Outside the GDR, Otakar Nahodil in Czechoslovakia made significant theoretical contributions, and Tadeusz Moszyński in Poland and Tibor Bodrogi in Hungary also pursued a Marxist-Leninist agenda to some extent. But in these countries the enthusiasm for intellectual pyrotechnics within a Marxist framework was never really strong among anthropologists. It was stronger in adjacent disciplines, notably philosophy. The Budapest Orientalist Ferenc Tőkei was a significant contributor to international debates on the concept of the Asiatic mode of production, and the rigorous materialism of the Poznań philosopher Leszek Nowak also won many admirers in Western countries, but neither of these scholars attracted a significant following among mainstream anthropologists.

For four decades the anthropologists of East-Central Europe were expected to work within a Marxist-Leninist framework and to supply data which would confirm the doctrines of historical materialism. In spite of this rigid constraint, some innovations were implemented. Workers were studied for the first time, as was the socialist village and the social integration of migrant groups. The reintroduction of sociology had some positive effects in the 1960s, and at approximately the same time the possibility of working in newly liberated Third World states helped to foster an interest in the comparative discipline. Despite these new directions, it has to be concluded that the core of anthropology in East-Central Europe proved highly resistant, almost immune, to all attempts at Marxist fructification.

Towards an Assessment

The main goal of the Halle workshop was to elicit papers offering new insights into a corner of recent disciplinary history which remains poorly understood even in the countries concerned. The papers documented differences within as well as between the countries examined, but also recurring similarities. If we had widened the geographical framework, the diversity would have been even greater, but certain common influences and tensions would probably be visible wherever socialism of the Marxist-Leninist variety was imposed.

Most of the contributions which follow are based on the original workshop papers, in some cases much revised. We have divided them into four sections. Part One comprises four chapters, each providing an overview of a single country (Czechoslovakia qualifying as one entity for the socialist period). Part Two focuses on the early period of socialist rule and shows that even under Stalinism, in which new institutions and research orientations were imposed, often in highly repressive ways, not everything could be changed 'overnight'. The division of the remaining papers expresses one of the outstanding continuities we recognised among the four countries: even when a contrary goal was explicitly adopted, anthropology at home (Volks- kunde, národopis, etc.) remained largely separate from 'universal', compara- tive anthropology. The latter was weaker, and this is reflected in the cover- age provided in this volume.

The chapters do not allow comprehensive, inter-country comparisons of the schools and practices documented. For example, Vidacs's chapter, comparing her anthropological education in socialist Hungary with the training she received later in the United States, is the only one which en- gages directly with teaching. The work of museum-based anthropologists is discussed in detail only in Neuland-Kitzerow's chapter on the Museum für Volkskunde in East Berlin. Some important topics are neglected or alto- gether overlooked. There is little discussion of how anthropology was dis- seminated through publications for the general public, though such works of popularisation were significant under socialism, nor is there any discussion of the ways in which anthropology of the Volkskunde-folklore variety fed into the public sphere through the activities of local and regional history associations. On the other hand, we have deliberately sought to maintain a mix of contributions. They range from highly personal statements by schol- ars who created this anthropology to more distanced appraisals by members of a new generation. No unified interpretations emerge, but we conclude this introduction by offering a few general reflections.

First, the conditions which shaped the production of anthropological knowledge in East-Central Europe were often difficult, sometimes extremely so. The Stalinist years were oppressive everywhere. While Hungary and Poland could liberalise after 1956, scholars in Czechoslovakia and the GDR remained subject to further waves of ideologically inspired interference and dogmatism. A few scholars were driven into reluctant emigration. But they were the exceptions: the great majority were neither radical opponents nor enthusiastic supporters of their governments, and they managed by one means or another to find enough personal room to manoeuvre. Thanks to their efforts, anthropology did more than just survive: it was successfully consolidated within new institutional and intellectual frames.

Second, what can we say of the quality of this anthropology? The record is of course uneven, and no blanket judgements are possible. Socialism did not stifle intellectual innovation: one needs only to think of numerous Polish and Hungarian sociologists and economists who achieved world fame in the later decades of socialism (some of them in exile, it has to be added). Alongside the solid achievements of collective prestige projects such as atlases, difficult research conditions could also stimulate individual anthropologists to pursue ingenious new lines of research. Is it possible that scholars in the West were blinded or otherwise hindered by the politics of the Cold War from recognising path-breaking contributions by their counterparts in East-Central Europe? It is clear that the Cold War hindered the reception of works by East-Central European scholars in Western countries. While Marxism became extremely influential in international anthropology in the last decades of state socialism, ironically it was a variety grown on the banks of the Seine and the Thames, not the Spree, Vltava, Vistula, or Danube—let alone the Moscow. However, contacts with the West were never broken off completely: the Wenner-Gren Foundation for Anthropological Research and its journal, *Current Anthropology*, distributed throughout East-Central Europe, did a great deal to facilitate communication in both directions from the 1960s onwards. It seems improbable, then, that any towering figures have suffered undeserved neglect. The contributions of East-Central European anthropologists who adopted Marxism are of minor significance when set alongside the works of Soviet authors.

Third, it would seem that, on the whole, Marxism-Leninism had surprisingly little influence on a discipline which was largely able to continue along the paths laid down by national movements in the pre-socialist generations. Even in the GDR, where the old Volkskunde was the most discredited, it proved possible to maintain a great deal under the new protective banner of Ethnographie. We suggest that the socialist regimes of this region allowed this continuity with the traditions of 'anthropology at home' as an element in their own legitimation strategies. In terms of the ideology, both poles of anthropology were a suspect bourgeois science, but socialists never became sufficiently cosmopolitan to dispense with local, regional, and national rootedness. This was what enabled the 'native ethnographers', as Tamás Hofer calls them in his essay of 1968, which we republish at the end of this volume, to regroup and continue the established disciplinary traditions.

This is not to suggest that every practitioner of 'home anthropology' sympathised politically with a nation-centred agenda. Some undoubtedly held strong allegiances to particular groups, local and regional as well as national, and this could lead to tensions with socialist powerholders. But others identified strongly with the goals of the socialist movement and saw no inconsistency between party membership and advancing knowledge in the discipline, such as through pioneering documentation of working-class cultures. Overall we might, from today's perspective, view the anthropologists themselves, greater in number than ever before, with their diverse motivations and ideological persuasions, as a distinctive 'subaltern group' in socialist society, no different in principle from the peasant and proletarian groups which they investigated. Their labours, both individually and collectively, produced much solid work and left many resources that are now available for use by their successors.

With the exception of those who found genuine inspiration in the Marxist classics, socialist anthropologists had little to gain from pursuing the big questions of human social evolution and the comparative analysis of peoples on a global scale. Political anxieties about borders and foreign travel, not to mention scarce finances, rendered fieldwork abroad difficult. The upshot was that throughout East-Central Europe, the Volkskunde pole received more attention and resources than did Völkerkunde. This uneven legacy is one of the factors which has contributed to tremendous controversies over the future of the discipline in the postsocialist years. Some have argued that 'anthropology' has to be brought in from outside, that no indigenous products qualify for this designation, owing to the isolation and political distortions caused by socialism. We cannot enter into these discussions here (see Godina 2002; Sárkány 2002; Skalník 2002), but we suggest that some of the participants in today's debates are insufficiently aware of the complexities of the recent past. They oversimplify the positions with which they disagree, and this cannot be good practice for anthropologists. Even those most anxious to press ahead vigorously in adopting the discourses and methods of 'global anthropology' need a close-up understanding of their local intellectual landscape, of what happened in the era which came to an end around 1990.

There can be no tabula rasa in the specialised communities of the academic world, any more than there can ever be a completely fresh start in the life of any human society. Most studies of postsocialism reinforce this basic point (which in essence is the same point that emerges when we examine carefully the impact of Stalinism). The accounts which follow should increase awareness of both continuities and breaches in a specific intellectual field in a difficult period. They help us to acknowledge deficits but also many reputable achievements and to recognise the ultimate contingency of this disciplinary history, not least of the term anthropology and the many other names that have been applied.

References

Bucher, G. 2002. „*Von Beschreibung der Sitten und Gebräuche der Völcker"*: *Die Instruktionen Gerhard Friedrich Müllers und ihre Bedeutung für die Geschichte der Ethnologie und der Geschichtswissenschaft*. Stuttgart: Steiner.

Ellen, F., E. Gellner, G. Kubica, and J. Mucha (eds.). 1988. *Malinowski between Two Worlds: The Polish Roots of an Anthropological Tradition*. Cambridge: Cambridge University Press.

Fél, E., and T. Hofer. 1969. *Proper Peasants: Traditional Life in a Hungarian Village*. Chicago: Aldine.

Gallie, W. G. 1956. Essentially Contested Concepts. *Proceedings of the Aristotelian Society* (n.s.) 56: 167–98.

Gellner, E. (ed.). 1980. *Soviet and Western Anthropology*. London: Duckworth.

——. 1988. *State and Society in Soviet Thought*. Oxford: Blackwell.

Godina, V. V. 2002. From Ethnology to Anthropology and Back Again. In P. Skalník (ed.), *A Post-Communist Millennium: The Struggles for Sociocultural Anthropology in Central and Eastern Europe*, pp. 1–22. Prague: Set Out.

Hofer, T. 1968. Anthropologists and Native Ethnographers in Central European Villages: Comparative Notes on the Professional Personality of Two Disciplines. *Current Anthropology* 9 (4): 311–15.

Kosven, M. O. 1952. *Matriarchát*. Praha: Melantrich.

Kroeber, A. L., and C. Kluckhohn. 1952. *Culture. A Critical Review of Concepts and Definitions*. Cambridge: The Museum.

Lips, J. 1951. *Vom Ursprung der Dinge. Eine Kulturgeschichte des Menschen*. Leipzig: Brockhaus.

Mach, Z., and A. Paluch (eds.). 1992. *Sytuacja mniejszościowa i tożsamoośc: Zeszyty naukowe Uniwersytetu Jagiellońskiego MXXIX*. Cracow: Jagiellonian University.

Markarjan, E. 1969. *Ocherki teorii kul'tury*. Jerevan: Izd. An Armjanskoj SSR.

Melicherčík, A. 1945. *Teória národopisu*. Liptovský sv. Mikuláš: Tranoscius.

Ortutay, Gy. 1937. *Magyar népismeret*. Budapest: Magyar Szemle Társaság.

Peacock, J. 2002. Action Comparison: Efforts towards a Global and Comparative Yet Local and Active Anthropology. In A. Gingrich and R. G. Fox (eds.), *Anthropology, by Comparison*, pp. 44–69. London: Routledge.

Potěchin, I. (ed.). 1953. *Anglo-americká etnografie ve službách imperialismu*. Praha: Nakladatelství československo-sovětského institutu.

Rihtman-Auguštin, D. 2004. *Ethnology, Myth and Politics: Anthropologizing Croatian Ethnology.* Aldershot: Ashgate.

Rodová spoločnosť: Národopisné materially a výskumy. 1954 Bratislava: SAV.

Sárkány, M. 2002. Cultural and Social Anthropology in Central and Eastern Europe. In M. Kaase, V. Sparschuh, and A. Wenninger (eds.), *Three Social Science Disciplines in Central and Eastern Europe: Handbook on Economics, Political Science and Sociology (1989–2001),* pp. 558–66. Berlin and Budapest: Social Science Information Centre (IZ) and Collegium Budapest.

Skalník, P. (ed.). 2002. *A Post-Communist Millennium: The Struggles for Sociocultural Anthropology in Central and Eastern Europe.* Prague: Set Out.

Stagl, J. 1998. Rationalism and Irrationalism in Early German Ethnology: The Controversy between Schlözer and Herder, 1772–1773. *Anthropos* 93: 521–36.

Stocking, G. W. 1982. Afterword: A View from the Center. *Ethnos* 47 (1–2): 172–86.

Tolstov, S. P. 1949. *Sovětská škola v národopisu.* Praha: Umění lidu.

Vermeulen, H. F. 1995. Origins and Institutionalization of Ethnography and Ethnology in Europe and the USA, 1771–1845. In H. F. Vermeulen and A. A. Roldán (eds.), *Fieldwork and Footnotes: Studies in the History of European Anthropology,* pp. 39–59. London: Routledge.

———. 1996. *Taal-, Land- en Volkenkunde in de achtiende eeuw.* Leiden: Oosters Genootschap in Nederland, nr. 23.

Voráček, J. 1936. *Počátky vlastnictví a práva ve světle ethnologie a sociologie.* Praha: Melantrich.

———. 1940. *Úvod do studia člověka, společnosti a civilisace.* V Praze: Česká grafická unie.

———. 1941. *Primitivní rodina: Rozprava o theoriích a methodách ethnologické sociologie.* Praha: Česká akademie věd a umění.

Zwernemann, J. 1983. *Culture History and African Anthropology.* Uppsala: Almquist and Wiksell.

PART ONE

COUNTRY OVERVIEWS

Each of the four chapters in this opening section gives a wide-ranging per-spective on the history of anthropology under socialism in one of the four countries we cover. There is no doubt that the state framework was—and remains—of fundamental importance in shaping the development of the discipline.

The first country we consider was entirely the creation of socialism. As Karoline Noack and Martina Krause show, the anthropology of the German Democratic Republic always had its distinctive features. The legacy of German history ensured that scholars had to rebuild their discredited disciplines on new foundations after the Second World War. Soviet power meant that the paradigms of Soviet Marxist etnografiya were ever-present in the background. However, several GDR anthropologists made original and independent contributions to the 'formations debate', which explored issues of social evolution whose importance was by no means restricted to Marx-ism. Others pursued new agendas in empirical research 'at home' (there were few opportunities to carry out fieldwork abroad). Volkskunde was transformed into a lively branch of cultural-social history which, despite political restrictions, was increasingly able to include present-day socialist society within its purview. Noack and Krause focus on the most ambitious feature of GDR anthropology, the attempt to forge a unified discipline of Ethnographie out of the historically distinct traditions of Volkskunde and Völkerkunde. This goal proved to be unattainable in practice, even before the experiment was terminated with the end of socialism.

In comparison with anthropology in the GDR, the discipline in each of the other countries showed much more continuity with pre-socialist tradi-tions. In his chapter on Czechoslovakia, Peter Skalník notes that there, too, a new etnografie (etnografia in Slovak), based on Soviet etnografiya, was introduced in the Stalinist years by a young elite, among whom the dominant personality had studied in the USSR. Yet only one scholar lost his position for political reasons in the 1950s. The great majority continued to publish on the traditional topics of folk culture, and the introduction of the new name etnografie never fully displaced the older term národopis. It was impossible to document the socialist transformation of the countryside as it took place, though it was possible to launch pioneering investigations of industrial communities, notably those involved in mining. The 1960s brought ideological relaxation, and a few younger scholars were able to carry out fieldwork in Africa and elsewhere. However, the repression which followed within a few years of the Soviet invasion of 1968 put an end to most positive developments. The discipline remained theoretically and methodologically moribund. Skalník shows that the socialist approach to culture hardly differed in principle from the essentalist approaches of traditional 'nation-drawing'.

In contrast to the GDR and Czechoslovak cases, anthropology in Hungary and Poland was able in the later decades of socialism to develop in a much more liberal political climate. In the Hungarian case the traditional name, néprajz, was never challenged. Mihály Sárkány emphasises a discrepancy between the radical goals outlined for the discipline in 1949 and the high degree of continuity which ensued in practice. Soviet influences were strong in the early 1950s but, later on, Hungarian scholars made their own creative contributions to Marxist anthropology, notably concerning the Asiatic mode of production. Marxism had less influence on mainstream studies of Hungarian folk culture. Western anthropological influences were apparent in several village studies, which came to include detailed research into the impact of socialist transformation; but fieldwork abroad was never easy to organise. Sárkány concludes by drawing a careful balance: the stability of the later socialist period was conducive to significant accomplishments, such as dictionaries, encyclopaedias and monographs, all executed to a high standard; but the innovative developments of the 1960s and 1970s were not consolidated until after 1990.

Finally, Aleksander Posern-Zieliński sets out a number of theses concerning Poland, some of which apply equally well to the other countries of the region. From the point of view of the powerholders, anthropology (etnografia) was a marginal discipline, and in the academic division of labour it was cast as a subsidiary branch of history. Sociologists led the way in appropriating innovative developments in Western anthropology, though the practitioners of etnografia, methodologically eclectic, did eventually embark upon successful modernisation of their subject. Political considerations influenced the topics to be addressed and, equally importantly, the topics on which researchers were well advised to remain silent. Thus, many researchers investigated new processes of rural integration, where sociological influences made themselves felt, but official portrayals did not always correspond to reality, especially concerning groups suspected of German sympathies. Ethnic factors within the country were too sensitive to be examined in detail, but studies of the Polish diaspora were supported. There was considerable continuity with pre-socialist intellectual traditions, and Soviet influence appears to have been even weaker in Poland than in Hungary. Despite the fact that it had only weak links to adjacent social sciences, the end of international isolation helped to ensure a favourable evolution for anthropology. This was symbolised in the gradual rejection in the last years of socialism of the term etnografia and the readoption of the discipline's old name, etnologia.

Although the anthropologists of the German Democratic Republic were on the whole perhaps more innovative than their contemporaries in other socialist states, after German unification many of these scholars lost their positions. Nothing comparable happened in the other countries considered. The impact of Western cultural and social anthropology has been considerable in all three cases, in some places beginning well before 1990, but the legacies both of socialism and of earlier generations of 'nation-drawing' remain strong.

CH

Chapter 2
Ethnographie as a Unified Anthropological Science in the German Democratic Republic

Karoline Noack and Martina Krause

Our aim in this chapter is to explore the development of Ethnographie in the German Democratic Republic, where it was understood to mean a unity of Völkerkunde (the study of peoples outside of Europe) and Volkskunde (the study of the German people). This conception of anthropology—which drew no theoretical or methodological distinctions between the study of social structures and human culture outside and inside of Europe—was new in post-war Germany. It was adopted in the GDR as the key to reorganising the disciplines along non-racist, non-nationalist lines. Implementation began in 1953–54 at the Humboldt University's Institut für Völkerkunde und deutsche Volkskunde, which in 1968 gave way to the Department (*Bereich*) of Ethnographie. This fusion of Volkskunde and Völkerkunde into a single anthropology gave the Humboldt University a unique place in the German academic landscape, both eastern and western.[1]

The destiny of GDR science after 1989 was determined by evaluations carried out by committees of the Scientific Advisory Board (*Wissenschaftsrat*) of the Federal Republic. Ethnographie, like many other subjects, experienced almost complete liquidation. It is clear that this process was not always guided by objective, scientific criteria but was shaped also by political and ideological factors (see Lee 2001: 75). In total, 79 per cent of all academic staff in higher education lost their jobs after 1989. In the humanities the figure was 85 per cent.[2] All humanities institutes of the GDR Academy of Sciences were closed. The only exception was the Institute for Sorbian Studies (Institut für Sorbische Volksforschung) in Bautzen. The evaluators of the Wissenschaftsrat recognised the significance of retaining research

---

[1] Regional differentiation was retained within this new conception. Thus, German Ethnographie was taught alongside Latin American Ethnographie, African Ethnographie, Australian Ethnographie, and so forth.

[2] Only 5 per cent of this group belonged to the 'nomenclature' (Hecht 2002: 36, 60). See also van der Heyden 1999: 13–14.

expertise concerning the GDR's only ethnic minority and therefore recommended retention of this institute in Saxony, albeit on a new organisational
footing.[3]

The Department of Ethnographie at the Humboldt University was
transformed into the Institut für Europäische Ethnologie. Four members of
the old department, all of them specialised in Germany, were given temporary contracts (Beck and Scholze-Irrlitz 2001: 187). These transformations
stimulated some to recall the struggles which had surrounded Ethnographie—among them such leading figures as Ute Mohrmann (1991, 2001),
Wolfgang Jacobeit (1997, 2000), and Hermann Strobach (1991).[4] Given the
importance attached in the GDR years to the unified conception of Ethnographie ('Einheit von Volks- und Völkerkunde'), it is surprising that none of
these leading Volkskundler discussed this aspect in any detail in their relatively recent publications. It is also worth noting that the Berlin Völkerkundler—those who specialised in ethnographic regions other than Germany—
have been markedly less assiduous in appraising the history of the discipline
during GDR times.[5]

At this point it seems appropriate to insert some words about our-
selves, since our backgrounds no doubt influence our perspectives and our
arguments. Both of us graduated in Ethnographie at the Humboldt University
in 1988 and continued our academic careers by studying topics we had
already begun to work on during the GDR period, but now we were enjoying
a much wider range of research possibilities. Each of us was able to leave
Germany and discover the 'real' Mexico (Krause 2003) or Peru (Noack
2003, 2005). To revisit GDR Ethnographie after absorbing very different
theoretical and methodological approaches over the last 15 years is to re-
enter a field which has become unfamiliar. Nonetheless, given our experiences before and after the unification of Germany, we feel well placed to
'translate' the scientific language of Ethnographie and make this experiment
comprehensible to contemporary anthropologists who never knew it at first
hand. We focus upon the aspiration to create a new unity of Volkskunde and

---

[3] Unlike other institutes of the academy and the university sector, the Sorbian institute had
been distinguished since its establishment in 1951 by strong interdisciplinarity. Apart from
language and literature, Volkskunde and history were also covered; this range enabled the
institute to match up to the 'requirements of the modern humanities' (see Nowotny 1992: 21;
Scholze 1992: 15). It seems likely, however, that political considerations also played a role:
the institute's unique minority focus had also helped it to maintain its profile and autonomy in
GDR times.
[4] See also Lee 1998; Scholze and Scholze-Irrlitz 2001; Krause, Neuland-Kitzerow, and Noack
2003.
[5] Mohrmann and Rusch 1991 is the only publication to emphasise the unity of Volkskunde
and Völkerkunde. Ulrich van der Heyden has addressed the deficit on the Völkerkunde side,
but only with respect to Africa; see van der Heyden 1999, this volume

Völkerkunde, and we concentrate on the Humboldt University, not only because it is the institution we know best but also because it was one of the most significant centres of anthropology in the GDR and the only one to bring Volkskunde and Völkerkunde together into one institutional frame.[6] This makes it the best place in which to examine how far the programme to create 'one out of many' was successfully implemented in research.[7]

Volkskunde, Völkerkunde, and Ethnographie

To appreciate the significance of the GDR project one must go back to the beginnings of anthropology in Germany. Unlike in other European (and non-European) countries, the discipline was from the beginning of its institutionalisation divided between Volkskunde and Völkerkunde. This was due to the distribution of political power at the global level as well as local levels and to the late emergence of the German nation-state in 1871. Beginning in the 1830s, but accelerating after unification in 1871, two distinct profiles developed, each with its own theoretical conceptions and institutional anchorings. Volkskunde acquired socio-political significance at the national level in the quest to bind together the country's previously fragmented regions. In alliance with *Altertumskunde* (archaeology), the Volkskundler were charged with proving common 'archaic German' origins, the evidence for which they sought in folk culture (*Volkskultur*), that is, among the peasantry. Folk culture itself they elevated to the status of 'the soul of the people' (*Volksseele*).

Völkerkunde, on the other hand, defined itself in the context of Germany's emergence as a great power in Europe with new colonial ambitions. In this sense Völkerkunde, too, was caught up with national interests. Colonial conquests abroad were accompanied by intensive anthropological investigations of the local societies, theorised by the Völkerkundler as 'natural

---

[6] For further detail on Volkskunde institutions, see Mohrmann, this volume. Regarding Völkerkunde, besides the institute in Berlin, the developments at Leipzig University were especially significant; see Treide, this volume. Völkerkunde was also taught in Departments of Regional Sciences at the Universities of Berlin (African and Asian Studies), Leipzig (Near East and African Studies), and Rostock (Latin American Studies). In addition, two major museums (Museum für Völkerkunde) in Leipzig and Dresden had the status of research institutes (see Neuland-Kitzerow, this volume). All these institutions collaborated closely in research and in teaching. This close cooperation is documented in the series of colloquia 'Ethnographentreff', initiated and organised by the Berlin institute since 1978. On these occasions, Volkskundler and Völkerkundler came together to discuss topical research problems and present research results.

[7] We draw on interviews with Günter Guhr, Wolfgang Jacobeit, Ute Mohrmann, Dietrich Treide, Ursula Willenberg, and Ingeburg Winkelmann. We have consulted a wide range of publications by these and other scholars, but we have not undertaken archival research.

peoples' (*Naturvölker*) and 'tribal cultures' (*Stammeskulturen*). They thereby contributed to natural science conceptions of the global development of human types (*menschliche Arten*) by giving these a concrete form (Kaschuba 1997: 6, 1999: 51–53).

The mobilisation of both branches of anthropology for reactionary political ends peaked with their distortion to provide 'scientific' support for the racist policies of the Nazis, as a result of which they stood in grave disrepute after 1945. Both disciplines were obliged to submit themselves to a new beginning, which encompassed changes not only in personnel and institutions but also in theoretical orientations. GDR scholars attached priority to jettisoning those positions which had led to the academic separation of Volkskunde and Völkerkunde. Ethnographie was advanced as a way to overcome nationalist and racist legacies, as an instrument to promote 'peace … understanding and the bonds between peoples'.[8] The new name was intended from the beginning, even before the GDR was formed in 1949, to indicate a new programme, taking its inspiration from Soviet etnografiya. Previously, German scholars had used this term in much the same way that anthropologists in other Western countries had used it from the nineteenth century on: it referred to the *description* of a society, as distinct from its comparative analysis, which was the task of Ethnologie. After 1945 the word Ethnographie acquired a primarily political significance, and Marxism was the theory supposed to be able to unite the anthropological disciplines. It was a dramatic rupture, shaped not only by Soviet influences but also by the inputs of numerous scholars who returned from exile after 1945. As we shall see, however, despite the theoretical commitment to this unified programme, differences between Volkskunde and Völkerkunde did not entirely evaporate in the decades which followed.

Definitions and Debates in the Early Period

Disciplinary developments after the war cannot be understood only as the effects of political decisions. They must also be considered in the context of particular biographies, although these, too, were of course related to the political situation. One of the most important personalities to shape GDR Ethnographie was Wolfgang Steinitz, a Völkerkundler and specialist in Finno-Ugrian languages (PhD Berlin, 1932). He was Jewish and took an active part in the anti-fascist resistance movement. A year after being fired from his job at the Friedrich Wilhelm University in Berlin in 1933 because

---

[8] Sergey Aleksandrovich Tokarev, cited by Kothe (1954: 80). Tokarev was the first Soviet ethnographer to teach in the universities of Berlin and Leipzig (in 1951–52). See also Jacobeit, this volume; Treide, this volume.

of his membership in the Communist Party, he emigrated with his family to the Soviet Union. For some years he taught at the Institute of Northern Peoples in Leningrad. Differences of opinion with some of his Soviet colleagues concerning state policy toward ethnic minorities led to political problems with the authorities, and from 1938 until the end of the war Steinitz lived with his family in Stockholm.[9]

After returning to Berlin in 1946 he became a professor of Finno-Ugrian languages at the Humboldt University. In 1952 he was nominated as director of the Institut für deutsche Volkskunde at the German Academy of Sciences, replacing Adolf Spamer, who had fallen ill.[10] It is possible that the beginnings of Ethnographie in Berlin owe much to contacts Steinitz made during his years of emigration, notably those with Sergey Aleksandrovich Tokarev, who came in 1951 as a guest at the Finno-Ugrian Institute. Tokarev also taught students of anthropology (still in 1951–52 called Völkerkunde in the syllabus), history, and Slavonic languages.

It is uncertain exactly how Tokarev came to be posted to the GDR, and this uncertainty is indicative of a more general confusion over the quality and strength of relations between Soviet and German anthropologists in this early period.[11] Steinitz warned against too one-sided an orientation towards the Soviet model: he saw no alternative, but it would take time for German-Soviet relations to mature (Nötzoldt 2001: 134). While Wolfgang Jacobeit and Dietrich Treide both tend to play down the intensity of Soviet links in the first two decades of the GDR, Ute Mohrmann attaches greater weight to borrowings from Soviet etnografiya in this period, together with the adoption and further refinement of Soviet approaches in the 1970s and 1980s, albeit unevenly.[12] The apparent truism that close professional relations with Soviet anthropologists were an abiding feature of the GDR scene needs to be explored more carefully in the archives.

---

[9] For more details see Nötzoldt 2001: 125–27.

[10] For more biographical details see Nötzoldt 2001 and http://www.fraenger.net/per_steinitz.html.

[11] Though none of our interview partners can be certain, it seems likely that the dispatch of Tokarev to Berlin was arranged by Steinitz, who would have met him in Siberia in the 1930s. Tokarev was discharged from Moscow University in 1930. He then 'taught in a number of Siberian universities and did a lot of fieldwork ..., published many historiographical studies, and never discussed any "sharp" questions' (Artemova 2002: 5, 7). Wolfgang Jacobeit (personal communication, 23 August 2004) supposes that the lectures of Tokarev, by now professor of etnografiya at Moscow's Lomonosov University, were arranged by Soviet culture officers. Zwerenz (2002) emphasises that the culture officers were frequently Jewish communists who had escaped Stalin's regime of terror; see also Hartmann and Eggeling 1994.

[12] Jacobeit, personal communication, 23 August 2004; Treide, this volume; Mohrmann, this volume and personal communication, 8 July 2004.

What is certain is that Tokarev's presence in Berlin and Leipzig influenced Ethnographie in its formative years by supporting the progressive directions outlined by Steinitz. Tokarev emphasised the importance of Ethnographie in addressing actual social problems, both in the countryside and in the city. He was aware of the possibility for conflict between older ways of life (Russian, *byt*; German, *Lebensweise*) and social practices of more recent origin (Tokarev 1954: 18, cited in Jacobeit 1986: 18; Tokarev 1951: 657, cited in Kothe 1954: 83).[13] He found the Western term *acculturation* inappropriate for analysing such conflicts. Even today Tokarev is esteemed in Russia as 'the most respected and beloved Soviet scholar', a man of remarkable erudition whose students were among the first 'to try to get rid of Morgan and Engels's official scheme' (Artemova 2002: 7). He helped to pave the way for innovative discussions in the 1970s and 1980s, by which time the proper object of the discipline no longer revolved solely around the *ethnos* theory of Yulian Bromley (see Bromley 1974). In any case, for Tokarev's students in Germany the task was the creative application of theory to the particular social and political situation of the GDR.

In comparison with the limited contacts between GDR and Soviet colleagues, Wolfgang Jacobeit recalls much closer cooperation with Czech, Slovak, Polish, and Hungarian colleagues.[14] This is well demonstrated in the journal *Demos*, published for the first time in 1960 by the Institut für deutsche Volkskunde at the GDR Academy of Sciences. Günter Guhr (1961)

---

[13] Günter Guhr (1976: 122–23) pointed out that the concept of Lebensweise came to have a much wider significance in GDR Ethnographie, in comparison with the original Russian term (sometimes translated as 'folklore'). See also note 39. For further reflection on Tokarev's significance for the GDR, see Jacobeit 1986. The beginnings of GDR Ethnographie were undoubtedly influenced to some degree by other Soviet anthropologists as well. However, it would be misleading to give the impression that a Soviet school exerted systematic influence; rather, influence was felt in particular research spheres and reflected the special topics of particular Soviet colleagues.

[14] This took the form of organising international conferences and joint publications, especially in the field of folklore (e.g. a series of folktales and legends), and a joint research project investigating folk music in Albania. In addition, exhibitions from Hungary and Poland were displayed at the Volkskunde museum in East Berlin, which in turn cooperated with the Hungarian and Polish cultural institutes in the city and put on exhibitions there (Jacobeit, personal communication, 1 September 2004). On the other hand, the Sorbian institute in Bautzen maintained close links with colleagues in the USSR, as well as in Poland and Czechoslovakia, on the basis of common interests in Slavistics. The interdisciplinary profile of this institute was also conducive to multiple international contacts, which resulted not only in discussions of theory and methods but also in practical empirical cooperation. Dialectologists from Poland, the Soviet Union, and Czechoslovakia all participated in field research in the 1960s in villages in the Lausitz region as part of the preparation for a 'Sorb linguistic atlas'. A further example of such cooperation was the major undertaking 'Ethnographie of the Slavic Peoples', led by the academy institute in Moscow (Nowotny 1992: 20, 23).

welcomed it as an important medium for communicating the results of anthropological research in the European socialist countries to scholars in other European and in non-European countries. Besides 'traditional' topics such as agriculture, crafts production, and settlement structures, he drew attention to the new topics addressed in the journal, such as the 'socialist village' and the 'industrial working class'. GDR anthropologists also had limited contacts with French and British colleagues through international organisations such as the International Union of Anthropological and Ethnological Sciences, of which Steinitz was vice-president between 1960 and his death in 1967.[15]

Following an initiative taken by Steinitz, in spring 1954 the Humboldt University's recently established Institut für Völkerkunde was expanded to become the Institut für Völkerkunde und deutsche Volkskunde. This was the moment when the subject (*Fachrichtung*) was labelled Ethnographie for the first time. From this point onwards Volkskunde was taught within the same institutional frame as Völkerkunde.[16] Richard Thurnwald, who held a chair at the Humboldt University from 1946 until his retirement in 1949, had derived a link between Volkskunde and Völkerkunde from a general sociological point of view (Scholze-Irrlitz 1991: 44). Now, however, the challenge was posed by Steinitz in terms of its special 'significance for German research' (Steinitz 1955: 274). He saw the task of Ethnographie in explicitly political terms: in future the discipline was to bind peoples together instead of separating them (*völkerverbindend* and not *völkertrennend*) (Rusch and Winkelmann 1987: 298; see also Nötzoldt 2001: 125).

The unity that had been achieved in terms of a programmatic challenge and an institutional base still needed a substantive theoretical foundation on which all parties could agree. It is important in this context to recognise that, in spite of Soviet influence, no one at this stage anticipated a long-term fragmentation of German anthropology along the political lines of 'East' and 'West'. Participants in common discussions were always in search of one German anthropology, but it was called Ethnographie in the East and

---

[15] See also the papers from the second congress of the International Society for European Ethnology and Folklore, held in Suzdal in 1982. The topics discussed on that occasion were wide ranging, and urban themes were prominent. Numerous scholars from Western Europe participated (USSR Academy of Sciences 1982). The form and extent of foreign contacts, especially those with Western colleagues, depended on a certain internal hierarchy. This was determined not only by scientific qualification but also by one's position in the political hierarchy, in particular membership in the Communist Party, which often entailed specific responsibilities inside the institute.

[16] Only in the university reform of 1968 was the name of the institution changed to Bereich Ethnographie. The reason for this delay is unclear. In the lecture lists of the mid-1950s the terminology remains muddled: Völkerkunde, Ethnologie, Ethnographie, and deutsche Volkskunde are used alongside each other.

Ethnologie in the West. The task of defining a new anthropological science after the war was disrupted by a conservative fraction within West German Volkskunde, which still retained some sympathy with fascist ideologies. Such tendencies were always rejected in GDR Volkskunde.[17] These discussions continued long after the political separation of the two German states, and they were broken off only when the Berlin Wall was constructed in 1961.[18]

The substantive agenda and theoretical arguments developed in these key years of reorientation in the 1950s continued to mark the subject over the following decades. They were connected to sweeping changes in cultural politics in general. The Stalinist era had threatened cultural heritage in all fields, proletarian and bourgeois, left-wing avant-garde and mass culture alike. Now the task was 'to forge the structures of a new culture' (Mühlberg 1999: 55). Against this background, the socio-political significance of Steinitz's definition of the subject matter of Ethnographie in 1953 is clear.

---

[17] Jacobeit, personal communication, 2 October 2004. A workshop addressing the sensitive theme of displaced persons (*die Vertriebenen*) was organised under the title 'Ostforschung in Westdeutschland' in 1962 by the Institut für deutsche Volkskunde of the Academy of Sciences and the Institut für Völkerkunde und deutsche Volkskunde of the Humboldt University. Anthropologists from other GDR institutes as well as from Prague and Poznań participated (see Referate und Diskussionsbeiträge der Arbeitstagung in Berlin vom 27. und 28. Februar 1962, Archiv der Landesstelle für Berlin-Brandenburgische Volkskunde). Paul Nedo advocated a more intensive process of facing up to what had happened under fascism. This became a reality only from the mid-1960s, and then the process unfolded independently in the two German states (Bausinger 1965; Jacobeit 1965). These discussions of the German past were accompanied by a distinct articulation of the new Ethnographie perspective, which explicitly included contemporary developments within its field of study (Jacobeit, personal communication, 2 October 2004).

[18] Steinitz and his colleagues emphasised up to the early 1960s that Volkskunde had to study both East and West (*gesamtdeutsche*) German 'popular culture' (Nötzoldt 2001: 140–41). In the case of Völkerkunde, differences as well as resemblances were accentuated. The conference of the German Society for Völkerkunde in Stuttgart in 1959 was attended by eight Völkerkundler from the GDR. When the West German Paul Trappe called for the development of a Völkerkunde oriented towards present-day social, economic, and cultural predicaments in colonial and ex-colonial states, which would connect German Völkerkunde with American and English anthropology, he was supported by the GDR scholars Helmut Reim and Wolfgang König (who later became director of the Museum für Völkerkunde in Leipzig). The GDR anthropologists drew attention to the threatening new forms of capitalist exploitation which accompanied the expansion of West German industries into what was soon to be known as the Third World. They also supported Hermann Trimborn, from Bonn, when he criticised the presentation of another West German, Josef Haekel, concerning the origins of civilisation (*Hochkultur*): the GDR scholars emphasised that the most important feature of an early 'civilisation' was the invention of exploitation. Generally, participants expressed their discontent with the conventional topics of Völkerkunde and its preoccupation with the Naturvölker as the 'traditional' subject matter of the discipline in Germany (Reim and König 1960: 67–68).

By 'investigating the German working people, in its material and spiritual culture', the academic discipline would contribute to the building of the 'new culture' (Kunze 1955: 262; see also Mohrmann 1991: 105).

Although Steinitz emphasised the importance of material culture for Ethnographie, from 1964 to 1966 the Academy of Sciences was the stage for a methodological controversy over how best to define popular culture (*Volkskultur*). Steinitz and his ally Hermann Strobach, supported by almost all of their colleagues who studied mental or spiritual culture (*geistige Kultur*), defined popular culture principally in terms of orally transmitted memories and traditions ('folklore'); this approach excluded other forms shaped directly by literacy. Jacobeit and his ally Paul Nedo opposed this concept and advocated a widening of the subject to include the working classes and the study of contemporary society in general.[19] In particular, Jacobeit's emphasis upon popular culture was intended to counter the privileging of either material or spiritual culture (Mohrmann 1991: 112; Lee 2001: 79–84). This controversy was the moment which enabled Jacobeit and Nedo to lay the foundations for a new Ethnographie of the nineteenth and twentieth centuries, influenced by both social history and the German humanities tradition of Kulturwissenschaft, and explicitly including the study of the working classes (see Mohrmann, this volume).[20]

The early period of GDR Ethnographie was shaped by the international situation and by the fact that a significant proportion of its founders, those who formed a new generation of anthropologists, came to the GDR from abroad: from the USSR, Sweden, the USA, Australia, and above all West Germany (van der Heyden 1999: 281–82). The main topic at the first conference organised by the Völkerkunde institute at the Humboldt University, in 1951, was Ethnographie, the effort to promote a fusion with Volks-

---

[19] Nedo's ideas were based on his empirical work on culture and politics at the Institut für Volkskunstforschung.

[20] To demarcate themselves from Steinitz and Strobach, Jacobeit and Nedo put forward the terms *sinnliche Wahrnehmung* and *Lebensweise*, though neither was precisely formulated at the beginning (Lee 2001: 80). Jacobeit and Nedo presented their ideas to an international congress on contemporary anthropological research in Bad Saarow in 1967, with colleagues from Eastern Europe as well as from West Germany in attendance (Jacobeit and Nedo 1969). The volume resulting from this congress was at first ignored by colleagues at the Academy of Sciences and was not reviewed until much later (Ute Mohrmann, personal communication, 8 July 2004). (English-speaking readers should be aware that the German traditions of Kulturwissenschaft are much older than the field of 'cultural studies' which has developed recently in the Anglo-Saxon world. But—for understandable reasons—neither nineteenth-century foundations in Germany nor contemporary bourgeois scholarship was explicitly cited by these GDR scholars.)

kunde.[21] Heinz Kothe, at this time still very close to Steinitz, emphasised 'that there could be no differences of principle, for example in theoretical questions or in research methods, between the two disciplines, still separated today' (Kothe 1954: 81).[22] New spheres of investigation were envisaged as cooperative 'experiments' between Volkskunde, Völkerkunde, and prehistory. The anthropological study of agriculture and agricultural implements was given particular priority.[23] At the Volkskunde conference of the Academy of Sciences in the following year, attended by scholars from both Germanies and also by Czechoslovak colleagues, Steinitz emphatically defended the notion of Volkskunde and Völkerkunde as a unity. In doing so he particularly inveighed against an argument put forward by Ingeborg Weber-Kellermann of the German Academy of Sciences, to the effect that the investigation of one's own people could reach 'much deeper than the investigation of another people', as in Völkerkunde (Steinitz 1955: 270).[24] Such statements can still be found in German anthropology today (Krause and Noack 2003: 38–39).

Ethnos and Ethnogenesis

In accordance with Soviet etnografiya, Heinz Kothe, one of the leading voices of the new, progressive Ethnographie in the 1950s, defined its main object as the study of 'ethnogenetic' processes, which meant the evolution from 'tribe to nation' and therefore a primary emphasis upon long-term history. The German *Volk* was replaced by the Greek term *ethnos*, defined as 'a historically developing community with distinctive linguistic, economic-

---

[21] Participants at this conference included Wolfgang Jacobeit, Heinz Kothe, Günter Guhr, and Hans Damm.

[22] Kothe (PhD Göttingen, 1946–47) came to the Academy of Sciences in East Berlin in the early 1950s. Like Jacobeit, he had studied with Will-Erich Peukert and specialised in the study of agricultural implements. After completing his habilitation, promoted by Steinitz, he assumed the Völkerkunde chair at the university institute. Shortly afterwards he moved back to the academy. He resigned his position after a break with Steinitz at the end of the 1950s (Wolfgang Jacobeit, personal communication, 23 August 2004).

[23] Hoe cultivation was one of the main subjects of Richard Thurnwald's pupil Sigrid West-phahl-Hellbusch, who taught at the Humboldt University until 1953 before moving to the Anthropology Museum in (West) Berlin–Dahlem. Günter Guhr wrote his dissertation on 'Hoes in New Guinea', and Hans Damm studied hoes in Oceania (Guhr, personal communication, 23 October 2001).

[24] This statement could just as well have been made by Adolf Spamer, with whom Weber-Kellermann had close ties (Jacobeit, personal communication, 2 October 2004). Weber-Kellermann was a junior lecturer (*Assistentin*) at the Institut für deutsche Volkskunde from 1946 to 1959. She then served briefly as vice-director of the institute. In 1960 she moved to the Institut für mitteleuropäische Volksforschung in Marburg, West Germany, later renamed the Institut für Europäische Ethnologie.

cultural and psychic features' ('eine historisch entstandene und sich entwickelnde Gemeinschaft in ihrer sprachlichen, wirtschaftlich-kulturellen und psychischen Eigenart') (Kothe 1954: 78–79). This term had been used in Russian anthropology since the early twentieth century in the sense of 'people' (Bromley 1977: 24, 1980: 33).[25] It was also used to refer to pre-national structures—to societies which were not well demarcated and were 'lagging behind' in an evolutionary sense, such as the Hopis, Botocudos, and Aleuts (examples cited by Bromley 1980: 33). Both Western and Eastern anthropologists used the word in this manner (Bromley 1977: 26–27, 1980: 33).

The adaptation of the concept of ethnos in the early years of East Germany does not imply that all scholars shared a common definition. On the contrary, both the word *ethnos* and the very subject of the discipline were contested throughout the existence of GDR Ethnographie; different aspects were emphasised in different periods by practitioners of Völkerkunde and Volkskunde, respectively. One conflict, unforeseen in the 1950s but increasingly evident from the 1960s onwards, was the conflict between ethnos and *demos*. The latter tended to find favour among the Volkskundler, whereas Völkerkundler aspired to defuse the legacy of the term *Volk* by promoting ethnos as the key concept for a coherent anthropological science throughout Eastern Europe. Volkskundler typically insisted that the main subject of anthropology was the study of the working or lower classes of the population, the demos, situated for the first time within a long-term historical framework.

The death of Stalin on 5 March 1953 had an immediate effect on the debates about social evolution in general and ethnogenesis in particular, both in Soviet etnografiya and in the new GDR Ethnographie. Instead of dogmatic adherence to the rigid scheme of social evolution in five stages, it became possible to explore alternative approaches to evolution, both at the level of universal regularities and at the level of more local patterns in particular periods. These questions struck at the heart of Marxist historical theory. The early Soviet anthropologists of the 1920s had already had to face this problem in practical terms, notably through their involvement in the classification of the many diverse peoples of Siberia and the Russian North. The multinational Soviet Union had to be squeezed into the Marxist scheme of historical evolution even as it moved into a new historical 'stage'. Yet Marxist theory hardly seemed adequate to the task. For instance, there was uncertainty concerning the stages following primitive communism. Both the 'Asiatic mode of production' (attributed to Marx) and 'military democracy'

---

[25] Bromley pointed out that the influential ideas of Sergey Shirokogorov were published in London in 1935 but were not immediately noticed. Only at the end of the 1930s did Western anthropology begin to reflect on the term *ethnos*.

(Engels) were understood as transitional stages in progress towards the 'ancient oriental mode of production', the first class-based society. Early Soviet Marxist anthropologists were especially interested in the field of primeval history and in opening up comparative studies of stateless societies (Artemova 2002: 3–4). Stalin put an end to these debates by imposing the five-stages scheme as ideological dogma.[26] He did not, however, suppress all analytic investigation of ethnogenesis, 'the origin and the early history of various ethnic groups' (Artemova 2002: 6). It was perhaps thanks to this circumstance, due in turn to the historical moment in which the past, present, and future of Siberian peoples demanded a new theoretical frame, that ethnos and ethnogenesis became key topics of GDR Ethnographie from its inception.[27]

The post-Stalin liberalisation thus allowed a resumption of earlier Marxist debates about evolution, which focused once again on the transition from primitive communism to class society—precisely the topic repressed by Stalin's orthodox theory. The historical dynamics were rendered in ethnic terms; in other words, this fateful moment of historical transition was said to coincide with the origin of the later ethnos, a 'people' beginning its trajectory from 'tribe to nation'. A long-lasting debate ensued, played out in a variety of colloquia and conferences and, from 1968, in the journal *Ethnographisch-Archäologische Zeitschrift* (EAZ), published since 1960 by the Departments of Prehistory and Ethnographie at the Humboldt University. In addition to the Völkerkundler, many prehistorians and specialists in ancient oriental history participated in the so-called formations debate (*Formationsdebatte*), which grappled not only with questions of universal evolution but with the evolutionary classification of concrete ethnic and linguistic groups. It is important to note that, although other disciplines were also involved, it was Ethnographie that was expected to play the leading role in resolving methodological and theoretical difficulties. Ethnographie was the master discipline in constructing a *unitary systematisation of human society*, a task perceived to lie at the core of the social sciences (Guhr 1976: 120).

---

[26] The five-stages scheme viewed the social development of both European and non-European societies in terms of progress from 'classical primitive communism' to slavery, feudalism, capitalism, and finally communism.

[27] In the Institut für Völkerkunde at the Humboldt University, the anthropologist Heinz Kothe and prehistorian Karl-Heinz Otto taught a course called 'Problems of Ethnogenesis of the German People' in 1952–53. Ursula Willenberg (1990: 73) emphasised the reductionist error of equating ethnogenesis with studies of the origin and descent of a people and failing to take into account the social and political context.

The Grand Formations Debate

The early phase of the formations debate culminated in the doctoral thesis of Irmgard Sellnow, 'Basic Principles of Periodisation of Primeval History'.[28] This work was one of the few anthropological studies in the GDR that had an influence on international theoretical discussions (van der Heyden 1999: 280). It elaborated, in a way characteristic of its epoch in the GDR, a picture of primitive society based on the 'modern horizon of gentile societies and early class-state societies'—this is, on ethnographic materials. (The term *gentile* referred to societies organised primarily through kinship, *gens* being the term used by Engels, following Morgan, to denote what most early anthropologists termed the clan.) This picture was then set alongside that which emerged from prehistory and archaeology (Guhr 1987: 345). The 'basic principles' Sellnow proposed were derived from anthropological studies of various societies in Polynesia and Africa, but they were claimed to represent regularities in the evolution of all primitive societies. This raised the important issue, quickly taken up in international debates, of the relation between local and universal history. Sellnow herself regarded the historical interpretation of ethnographic materials, to ensure their comparability, as the key methodological question in anthropology (Sellnow 1961b: 124). Showing the 'dialectical unity' of universal and local history, of historical events and general patterns, Sellnow was unafraid to take on all the big names in the discipline.[29]

Her classifications caused much controversy. Günter Guhr argued that the picture that emerged from the concrete history of the societies studied by Ethnographie was better viewed as a complementary appendix to the history known from archaeological sources, rather than the two merely reflecting each other. On this basis he, like other GDR scholars, called for closer cooperation between archaeologists and anthropologists in the specification of evolutionary regularities and generalisations (Guhr 1963: 174). This interdisciplinarity was reflected in the book series *Ethnographisch-Archäologische Forschungen* (EAF) (1953–59) and later in EAZ. The edi-

---

[28] 'Grundprinzipien einer Periodisierung der Urgeschichte' (Sellnow 1961a). Irmgard Sellnow was one of the first graduates in anthropology after the war. She taught introductory courses in anthropology at the Humboldt University in 1954–55. After her graduation (1956) she was appointed to a post at the Institute of Oriental Studies of the Academy of Sciences. From 1970 to 1982 she was the vice-director of that institute (by then known as the Central Institute of Ancient History and Archaeology). For an account of the most important research project under her leadership, 'Universal History Up to the Emergence of Feudalism', see Sellnow 1977.

[29] She analysed the relations between local and universal history in the work of Tylor, Lubbock, White, Rivers, Boas, Radcliffe-Brown, Malinowski, and Thurnwald, among others (Sellnow 1961a, 1961b).

tors of the first volume of the EAF, Kothe and Karl-Heinz Otto, pointed out that since Ethnographie and archaeology were based on different sources, their tasks were necessarily different.[30] Nonetheless, in the case of the history of gentile society, the object of research was the same (Kothe and Otto 1953: vii).[31] The upshot was that, from the beginning, Ethnographie in Berlin was taught in close relationship to archaeology and prehistory.[32]

In the course of the long-running debate, the term *ethnos* was expanded into the concept of 'ethnosocial organism' (Russian, *etnosocial'nyy organism;* German, *ethnosozialer Organismus*) (Bromley 1977: 39, cited in Sellnow 1990: 206). It was assumed that ethnos and social organism coincided; in other words, every socio-economic formation (*Gesellschaftsformation*) produced its specific form of ethnic community as an outcome of the process of ethnogenesis. These forms ranged from tribe, association of tribes, and 'group of people' (*Völkerschaft*) to capitalist and socialist nation. This paradigm was taken from Soviet etnografiya and was applied in novel ways by GDR anthropologists who studied the so-called developing countries of Africa, Asia, and Latin America (e.g. Willenberg 1972; Zell 1973; Lau 1981; Rusch and Stein 1982; Thiemer-Sachse [1983] 1995).[33] The paradigm was not subjected to authoritative critique until 1990, when Sellnow herself (1990: 207) wrote that 'ethnos and social organism are two different things'.[34] There was the *possibility* of coincidence of the two in the formation of states but too little evidence to explain how differences in Gesellschaftsformationen had influenced ethnicity (Sellnow 1990: 208, 212).

The fruitfulness of the formations debate was due to the diverse viewpoints put forward, even if all participants saw themselves as working within the general framework of Marxist social theory. A theoretical systematisation of the debate, relating the Marxist concepts to those of contemporary Western anthropology, was provided by Dietrich Treide in his Leipzig habilitation thesis (1981). But of course this debate was as much political as

---

[30] Otto was a prehistorian who graduated from the Humboldt University in 1954 (habilitation).

[31] Wolfgang Jacobeit, still based in Göttingen at the time, contributed an article titled 'The Question of Primitive Settlement and Economy in Central Europe' (1954).

[32] Before the university reform of 1968, prehistory was taught as part of Ethnographie. Later the tight relationship between the two disciplines continued to be reflected in the syllabus. Ethnographie students were required to study prehistory for one semester, and archaeology students had to study the basics of anthropology. The two departments were located together in the same building, a typical Berlin tenement house quite far from the prestigious centre of the Humboldt University.

[33] For further non-European studies see Rusch and Winkelmann 1987.

[34] In fact Soviet ethnographers such as Yuri Semenov, Michail Illarionovich Artamonov, and Michail Vasil'evich Kryukov, as well as Bromley himself, had already reached similar conclusions as far as contemporary societies were concerned (Sellnow 1990: 207).

it was theoretical, engaging as it did with the fundamental questions of social theory, notably the relationships between economy, power, and social and cultural phenomena. The most controversial and creative discussion concerned the 'Asiatic mode of production', a concept which for some Western critics was 'incompatible with a coherent Marxism' because it linked the idea of primitive communism to that of government, which in the old official version of primitive communism was absent by definition (Gellner 1988: 47, 49).

The formations debate also touched upon the relations between social and biological aspects of reproduction. Günter Guhr, a pupil of Richard Thurnwald and Sigrid Westphal-Hellbusch, made the Marxist concept of social 'production of life' the starting point of his Lebensweise concept, the key instrument by which he sought to anchor Völkerkunde and Volkskunde in one Ethnographie (Guhr 1969, 1976, 1988). He stressed that both Marx and Engels had used the concept of 'production of life' (*Produktion des Lebens*) to address social reproduction in its totality (Guhr 1988: 52). Many later Marxists, from Karl Kautsky and Heinrich Cunow in the first decades of the twentieth century to Lawrence Krader in West Berlin in the 1970s (Krader 1973), had criticised the concept and, associating it with Engels alone, had reduced its field of reference to the production of material goods. In fact, both Marx and Engels used the concept to refer to the production of the lives of people as a whole, and theirs was by no means an economistic theory of social development. It was true, according to Guhr, that some earlier GDR scholars, under the influence of the distortions imposed by Stalin, had repeated the economistic fallacies erroneously attributed to Engels. But by the end of the 1960s it was possible to reassess the concept of Lebensweise and make it the cornerstone of the GDR's unified anthropology. Guhr thereby placed Ethnographie within a solid Marxist sociological framework and opened up new opportunities for cooperation with other social and human sciences, above all with sociology. This initiative evoked an early response from the economic historian Jürgen Kuczynski (1963; see Guhr 1988: 58), one of the most creative of GDR social scientists, who went on to cooperate with Paul Nedo and Wolfgang Jacobeit.[35]

It can be seen that the formations debate provided a platform for ideas which challenged official versions of social development. Anthropologists such as Guhr took political risks with their apparently arcane publications on

---

[35] See Jacobeit, this volume; Mohrmann, this volume. Kuczynski's 'everyday history' anticipated Ethnographie's basic approaches to the proletariat. The publication of his *Geschichte des Alltags des deutschen Volkes* in 1980–82 caused considerable turbulence at the highest level of government in the GDR (Wolfgang Jacobeit, personal communication, 2 October 2004).

the long passage from primitive communism to its eventual re-emergence on a higher level (cf. Gellner 1988: 21). Guhr was in fact obliged to give up his position in the Department of Prehistory at the Humboldt University and move to the Museum für Völkerkunde in Dresden.[36] The entire debate was a creative elaboration of Marxist ideas and a constructive response to the critique of Western Marxists such as Krader. It ranged widely in its theoretical topics, which included anthropological theories of the origin of the state, questions of matri- and patrilineality, the influence of war on social evolution, and the social division of labour.[37] Geographically the range was similarly wide, since historical comparisons were made for almost all regions of the world. Methodological and theoretical discussions fed into international discussions of the evolutionary process, including continuing discussions in Western anthropology. The culmination of three decades of scholarly ferment was the conference held at the Museum für Völkerkunde in Dresden in 1984 to mark the centenary of the publication of Engels's *The Origin of the Family, Private Property and the State*. It was a highly interdisciplinary meeting: in addition to anthropologists, it included historians, philosophers, legal historians, linguists, literary scholars, and regional studies specialists from 15 countries who debated human social evolution from primitive communism to the present day. The ensuing publication (Herrmann and Köhn 1988) is a rich compendium reflecting the vitality of the entire debate.

Lebensweise

Whereas Guhr and his co-participants in the formations debate succeeded in constructing a common theoretical framework for Ethnographie, methodological problems could not be adequately addressed at this level. Each historical community (or ethnosocial organism) had its specific social features, not only according to its Gesellschaftsformation but also according to 'ethnic specific features'. According to Iris Tschöpe (1988: 137, 139), the latter were the 'fundamental moments' (*grundlegende Momente*) ensuring the social integration of specific communities in time and space. The 'ethnic

---

[36] There he continued his path-breaking reappraisals of the work of Marx and Engels, which culminated in his habilitation thesis at the Martin Luther University of Halle-Wittenberg in 1986 (Guhr 1987).

[37] The topic of genealogical kinship principles and gentile organisation was the subject of an important critique by Frederick Rose (1960). Rose was born in the United Kingdom and had done fieldwork in Australia among the Groote Eylandt Aborigines. As a member of the Communist Party of Australia he was politically hounded, and in 1956 he moved to the GDR. He was the director of the Institut für Völkerkunde und deutsche Volkskunde from 1960 to 1972. In 1974 he moved to the Museum für Völkerkunde in Leipzig. His academic work was driven primarily by the desire to improve the situation of the Australian Aborigines. For more details of his biography and his work see Guhr 1991.

specifics' of a group referred to a people's distinctive way of thinking about the world and its sense of collective identity. This meant in practice that, while ethnicity in the stage of primitive communism was the exclusive preserve of Ethnographie, aspects of ethnic phenomena in succeeding socio-economic formations would have to be studied by neighbouring disciplines; anthropologists were to investigate the residual social field, and this is where the term *Lebensweise* was taken up, to refer to 'one ... part of social life' with its 'ethnic characteristics' (Guhr, Otto, and Grünert 1962: 33–39). In the 1970s and 1980s, Lebensweise in this sense, as the manifestation of 'ethnic characteristics', became the key concept in defining the subject matter of Ethnographie.[38]

It is important to recognise that both Volkskundler (notably Jacobeit and Nedo) and Völkerkundler (notably Guhr and Wolfgang König) contributed to the elaboration of the concept of Lebensweise.[39] During the 1960s it was taken up in investigations of working-class people, in both industry and agriculture, and in addition to historical studies it was also applied in research into contemporary society (Mohrmann 2001: 378). Theoretical foundations of the Lebensweise concept were taken far beyond the Soviet notion of *byt*, thanks to collaboration between Nedo, Jacobeit, Guhr, and the Kulturwissenschaftler Dietrich Mühlberg (Mohrmann, this volume).

In particular, Guhr's theoretical triad of *Lebensweise, Kultur,* and *ethnos* (1976) had a major effect on his colleagues (Jacobeit 1986: 19; Mohrmann 1991: 114). Lebensweise put the emphasis on social relations (*Bezogenheit*); 'social man' was studied in his affiliation with groups of all kinds, including social class, status, or professional group, family, tribe, gens, community, territory, locality, town, village, region, and ethnos. This approach resembled that of Western social anthropology and sociology; the focus was on the intersection between living conditions and actual social

---

[38] This adaptation of Lebensweise as a central concept of the discipline dates back to the early 1950s and derives from Soviet etnografiya (see note 13). However, it underwent a modification in the course of translation from Russian (*byt* or *obraz zhizni*) into German. Whereas in Soviet etnografiya, *byt* referred to something like 'folklore' and to the mental side of social life, the East German concept acquired a wider sociological sense; it referred both to the *substance* of the life of man in society and to the *form* of that social life in both an abstract and a concrete sense (Guhr 1976: 122–23).

[39] König, the director of the Museum für Völkerkunde in Leipzig from 1970 to 1979 and a specialist in Turkmen studies, had studied etnografiya with Tokarev in Moscow. He had brought Tokarev's concept of *byt* back with him (Wolfgang Jacobeit, personal communication, 2 October 2004.). König was also responsible for translating Bromley's key work (1977) into German. Ute Mohrmann, however, believes it was Paul Nedo who first introduced the concept of Lebensweise to Ethnographie. According to her, he had taken it up from other East European anthropologies but not from Soviet etnografiya in particular (Mohrmann 2001: 378).

activities (Guhr 1976: 122–23, 127).[40] The Volkskundler took over the Lebensweise concept from Mühlberg, who used it as an essential constituent of his culture concept (see Mohrmann 2001: 380–81). Jacobeit focused on the productive *forces* and the way they interacted with the *relations* of production (Jacobeit, personal communication, 2 October 2004; see Scholze and Scholze-Irrlitz 2001: 27). Culture was no longer divided into the 'material' versus the 'spiritual/mental', as it had been by Steinitz; instead, a new distinction between 'objective' and 'subjective' culture was drawn (Jacobeit and Mohrmann 1968–69). The emphasis was placed on the degree to which culture was appropriated by the individual as a member of the 'working people'.[41] Recognition and even accentuation of the fact that a 'common culture' could be shared by all social classes within a society was an important advance on Lenin's insistence that in class societies only cultures dominated by class differences could come into existence. This was known as the 'two cultures' theory (Johansen 1988: 279; Mohrmann 1991: 106).

Although the 'two cultures' theory could not be officially upheld, the closely related concept of demos proved more enduring. Indeed, the more cultural (*kulturwissenschaftliche*) perspective of Volkskunde made demos a more fruitful tool to work with than ethnos (Jacobeit and Mohrmann 1968–69; Mohrmann, this volume).[42] Demos therefore became an obstacle in realising the unity of Volks- and Völkerkunde in one Ethnographie, because the Volkskundler increasingly resisted the attempts of the Völkerkundler to elaborate ethnos as the foundational concept of both disciplines (e.g. Willenberg 1986). As a result, Ethnographie was condemned to use ethnos in the sense of ethnicity as it had evolved in Soviet etnografiya, that is, on the basis of a very different situation with regard to 'nationalities'. The specific national situation of partitioned Germany was reason enough for the Volkskundler to avoid plunging into debates over 'two national cultures' or two 'ethnic identities' (see Mohrmann, this volume).

In short, the Volkskundler took up the concept of Lebensweise and transformed it into a key component of a modern Kulturwissenschaft, with culture itself as its key concept. Whereas in the theoretical foundations laid by Guhr, initially welcomed by the Volkskundler, the Lebensweise concept was understood very broadly, subsuming culture while always interacting with it, increasingly culture became more prominent. Together with the

---

[40] Thus deployed, Lebensweise included the Marxist concepts of 'relations of production' (*Produktionsverhältnisse*) and 'productive forces' (*Produktivkraft*).

[41] The emphasis placed on the individual in the social process by Volkskundler was a step which was soon followed in Völkerkunde. For example, Guhr identified the productive and the self-reproducing individual (1976: 126–27).

[42] Strobach (1976) attempted to synthesise the two, but the relation of the 'two cultures' to the persistence of social class could not be refuted (Mohrmann 2001: 380).

Volkskundler's fondness for the notion of demos, these developments led to growing friction and indeed the separation of Volkskunde from Völkerkunde, both theoretically and methodologically.

For Guhr and for GDR Völkerkunde in general the sociological notion of Lebensweise had included the demos as part of the 'people' in ethnos. Ethnos was understood as one specific form of social organisation: its members were bound together by the 'most specific characteristics' they had in common and that differentiated them from other groups. The details depended upon a host of evolutionary, economic, geographical, political, linguistic, and cultural conditions (Guhr 1976: 127–28). The configuration of Lebensweise, culture, and ethnos determined how the 'ethnic specifics' would change over time. Compared with the concept of 'ethnic specifics' (*etnicheskiye osobennosti*) in Soviet etnografiya, the striking feature of the GDR concept was the emphasis placed on *variability* in the course of social process (Rusch 1986: 87–88). Obviously, ethnos was a concept that was ultimately more important to the Völkerkundler than to the Volkskundler. The fact that demos nonetheless acquired such currency in Ethnographie is to be explained by the history of Volkskunde itself and the determination of its practitioners to demarcate their subject as clearly as possible from the object of the discipline between its emergence in the nineteenth century and the catastrophe of the Nazi period. At the same time, the assertion of demos in this way weakened the new subject of Ethnographie and showed the continued strength of the Volkskunde current within the GDR anthropological field.

By Way of Conclusion

The permanent frictions between the academic world and politics, together with anthropology's continual attempts to legitimate itself and counter its increasing marginality, were abundantly demonstrated in the theoretical and methodological tensions that existed between Volkskunde and Völkerkunde in the GDR. According to Jacobeit, many political conflicts regarding Ethnographie in general were actually expressed as conflicts pertaining to Volkskunde, though Völkerkunde was in some respects more directly affected.[43] The Cold War limited the latter to those regions or states with which the GDR had good foreign political relationships.[44] In comparison

---

[43] Personal communication, 2 October 2004. For further discussion of the conflicts between Volkskunde and the political domain see Mohrmann and Jacobeit, this volume.
[44] In Asia such regions included Vietnam, India, Indonesia, and China. Australia and Papua New Guinea were also studied. The list of possibilities in Africa is discussed by Ulrich van der Heyden (this volume). In Latin America it was possible to work in Cuba, Mexico, Chile, and Bolivia. The GDR also admitted students of Ethnographie from many of these countries;

with Berlin, there were fewer problems at Leipzig University, where from 1968 the Julius Lips Institute formed part of the Regional Sciences Department of Near East and African Studies. The students trained there in Völkerkunde were destined for jobs in fields such as foreign trade or the diplomatic service. At the Humboldt University, by contrast, the reform of 1968 assigned the Department of Ethnographie to history, and Völkerkunde was consequently marginalised. The number of positions for Völkerkunde specialists was cut, and following the death in 1979 of the Latin America specialist Ursula Schlenther, her chair in Ethnographie was left vacant.[45]

In summary, we can distinguish two main fields within the Völkerkunde of the GDR, which varied according to historical framework. While some researchers interested in ethnogenesis investigated the early history of certain regions of the world, others concentrated on the relations between ethnic and social processes in recent times, beginning frequently in the nineteenth century. Both frameworks were encompassed by the formations debate, under which almost any topic could be subsumed. The political difficulties which thwarted fieldwork for many scholars led them instead to invest their energy in discussions of theoretical foundations, without necessarily giving up their interest in contemporary topics. The formations debate among the Völkerkundler was in a sense reflected in the widening of the temporal horizon of the demos studies of the Volkskundler to include the 'capitalist and socialist formations' of the present day.[46] Because of the differences discussed earlier, however, the engagement of Volkskundler in the formations debate did not proceed beyond the level of formality.

Ethnographie was an eminently political discipline, a point Jacobeit always emphasised. It participated self-consciously in a 'dialogue' with Western anthropology, but not in an impartial and objective manner, as was illustrated in exemplary fashion by Ernest Gellner (1980, 1988), who focused on concrete issues and evidence. Rather, GDR anthropology was often

---

they proceeded to graduation in the same framework as other students, and some went on to make professional careers in the discipline in their home countries (see also Treide, this volume).

[45] On Schlenther see Krause 1991 and Thiemer-Sachse 2003. Her student Ursula Thiemer-Sachse taught 'Indian languages and cultures' at the Latin American Institute of Rostock University, which was comparatively well staffed and, like Leipzig, concentrated on training students for jobs in the foreign ministry.

[46] Examples include the publications of the project carried out on the Magdeburg Plain from 1978 to 1987 (see Mohrmann, this volume) and the *Compendium on the History of the Working Classes and Strata of the German People from the Eleventh Century to 1945*, edited jointly by staff of the Academy of Sciences and the Humboldt University under the direction of Weissel, Strobach, and Jacobeit (Adam 1972). The latter served as a kind of manual for generations of students of Ethnographie.

caught up in ideological campaigns.[47] Its scholars had to be skilled at 'reading between the lines', particularly when it came to communication between East and West. It was possible to discuss anthropological work produced in West Germany, but only if it was tackled in a specific way.[48]

At the end of the day, the most solid accomplishments of the Volkskunde wing of GDR Ethnographie lay in the opening to new, emancipatory forms of social history (see Mohrmann, this volume), while those of the Völkerkunde wing are bound up with the formations debate. Ethnographie was based on a coherent theoretical approach to history, and yet the relation to the discipline of history was continuously being modified. Just as Meyer Fortes once pointed out that 'there is clearly no such thing as a unified, let alone monolithic, system of theory or practice in Soviet ethnography', so within a 'basic framework of, loosely speaking, Marxist orientation' (Fortes 1980: xix), GDR Ethnographie was always in flux. From Gellner's point of view, the Marxist idea of a sequence of evolutionary stages presented 'a kind of terribly foreshortened vision of human history, which grossly underestimates the stabilities, circularities, repetitions of actual historical processes' (1980: 7). Yet as Gellner pointed out, 'Western comparative anthropology or sociology possesses no superior typology, or indeed any typology at all' (Gellner 1988: 6). Such schemas are sorely missed in today's debates concerning social evolution. Anthropology cannot do without history, and it is paradoxical that some theoreticians in the West, including West Germany, were emphasising this point, partly under the influence of Marxism, during the last decade in which a Marxist orthodoxy still prevailed in the GDR (Schmied-Kowarzik and Stagl 1981; Szalay 1983; Lau 1986).

The way in which the German unification process unfolded precluded any possibility of the continuation of Ethnographie as a unified anthropological science. The political situation made it impossible to recognise any merits in Marxist theory and even to tolerate significant academic and institutional continuity in the discipline. This can be viewed as a setback for some of the progressive trends in West German anthropology as well. Eth-

---

[47] For example, the same year in which Gellner's edited book *Soviet and Western Anthropology* was published (1980) saw the publication in the GDR of Weissel 1980, a provocative 'stir up volume' (*Scharfmacher-Band*) in the opinion of Ute Mohrmann (personal communication, 8 July 2004). It derived from a conference devoted to the 'critique of bourgeois anthropology' held at the Museum für Völkerkunde in Leipzig in 1976, the same year in which the contributors to Gellner 1980 gathered for their meeting at Burg Wartenstein.

[48] See the review essay by Lau (1986). Communication and even cooperation between East and West German anthropologists was perhaps easier for Volkskundler, particularly after the emergence of a progressive Volkskunde in West Germany, with its focus at Tübingen. In general, GDR anthropologists found it easier to establish ties with Austrian anthropologists— for example, with the groups around Helmut Fielhauer and Karl R. Wernhart (Jacobeit, personal communication, 2 October 2004; see also Wernhart 1986).

nographie has been replaced in Berlin by *Europäische Ethnologie* (European ethnology), which claims to have a distinctive methodological perspective that can be applied both inside and outside of Europe. In fact it derives to a large extent from long-established trends in Volkskunde, common to both East Berlin and Tübingen since the 1960s. Although the new staff have pursued some new approaches, such as in the urban field and in studies of national symbolism, little or no attention has been paid to mutual influences between Europe and the rest of the world. In this sense we are witnessing a return to the German anthropological traditions in which Völkerkunde and Volkskunde remain separate pursuits. The elaboration of a theoretically more coherent, unified model of the discipline has, for the time being at least, been removed from the academic agenda in German anthropology.[49]

References

Adam, U. 1972. *Zur Geschichte der Kultur und Lebensweise der werktätigen Klassen und Schichten des deutschen Volkes vom 11. Jahrhundert bis 1945: Ein Abriss.* Wissenschaftliche Mitteilungen der Deutschen Historiker-Gesellschaft, 1/3. Berlin: Deutsche Historiker-Gesellschaft.

Artemova, O. Y. 2002. *Hunter-Gatherer Studies in Russia and the Soviet Union.* Paper presented at the Ninth International Conference on Hunting and Gathering Societies, 9–13 September, Heriot-Watt University, Edinburgh, Scotland. Electronic version at www. abdn.ac.uk/chags9/1artemova.htm.

Bausinger, H. 1965. Volksideologie und Volksforschung: Zur nationalsozialistischen Volkskunde. *Zeitschrift für Volkskunde* 61: 177–204.

Beck, S., and L. Scholze-Irrlitz. 2001. Berliner Diskussion: Perspektiven Europäischer Ethnologie—Versuch einer Zwischenbilanz. Gespräch zwischen Wolfgang Kaschuba, Peter Niedermüller, Bernd Jürgen Warneken, und Gisela Welz. In T. Scholze and L. Scholze-Irrlitz (eds.), *Zehn Jahre Gesellschaft für Ethnographie: Europäische Eth-*

---

[49] The Society for Ethnographie (Gesellschaft für Ethnographie), which was founded by GDR anthropologists shortly after the fall of the Berlin Wall and which includes members from all parts of Germany and abroad, is today the principal forum for those who have not abandoned the aspiration to unity. In cooperation with the Institut für Europäische Ethnologie, it runs a publication series, *Berliner Blätter: Ethnographische und ethnologische Beiträge.* The Society has also organised numerous conferences designed to cross the boundaries between Europe and the wider world.

nologie in Berlin, pp. 167–90. Berliner Blätter: Ethnographische und ethnologische Beiträge Nr. 23, Jubiläumsheft. Münster: LIT Verlag.

Bromley, Y. V. (ed.). 1974. *Soviet Ethnology and Anthropology Today.* The Hague: Mouton.

——. 1977. *Ethnos und Ethnographie.* Berlin: Akademie-Verlag.

——. 1980. Zur Frage nach dem Gegenstand von Kultur/Sozialanthropologie und Ethnographie: Versuch einer vergleichenden Analyse der angloamerikanischen und der sowjetischen Standpunkte. In B. Weissel (ed.), *Kultur und Ethnos: Zur Kritik der bürgerlichen Auffassungen über die Rolle der Kultur in Geschichte und Gesellschaft,* pp. 23–38. Berlin: Akademie-Verlag.

Fortes, M. 1980. Introduction. In E. Gellner (ed.), *Soviet and Western Anthropology*, pp. xix–xxv. London: Duckworth.

Gellner, E. (ed.). 1980. *Soviet and Western Anthropology.* London: Duckworth.

——. 1988. *State and Society in Soviet Thought.* Oxford: Blackwell.

Guhr, G. 1961. Rezension: Demos. *Ethnographisch-Archäologische Zeitschrift* 1: 85–86.

——. 1963. Rezension: Irmgard Sellnow, Grundprinzipien einer Periodisierung der Urgeschichte. *Ethnographisch-Archäologische Zeitschrift* 4: 173–79.

——. 1969. *Karl Marx und theoretische Probleme der Ethnographie.* Jahrbuch des Museums für Völkerkunde zu Leipzig 26, Beiheft. Berlin: Akademie-Verlag.

——. 1976. Über die Komplexität von Kultur und Lebensweise. *Acta Ethnographica Academiae Scientiarum Hungaricae* 25 (1–2): 119–37.

——. 1987. Marx', Engels' Auffassung zur Ethnographie und Urgeschichte. Thesis, Martin-Luther-Universität Halle-Wittenberg. *Ethnographisch-Archäologische Zeitschrift* 28: 337–45.

——. 1988. 'Production of Life'. In J. Herrmann and J. Köhn (eds.), *Familie, Staat und Gesellschaftsformation: Grundprobleme vorkapitalistischer Epochen einhundert Jahre nach Friedrich Engels' Werk „Der Ursprung der Familie, des Privateigentums und des Staats",* pp. 51–61. Berlin: Akademie-Verlag.

——. 1991. Frederick G. G. Rose (1915 bis 1991) zum Gedenken: Biographisches und Werk. *Ethnographisch-Archäologische Zeitschrift* 32: 511–19.

——, K.-H. Otto, and H. Grünert. 1962. Die Ur- und Frühgeschichtsforschung im Rahmen der Gesellschaftswissenschaften. *Ethnographisch-Archäologische Zeitschrift* 3 (1): 13–58.

Hartmann, A., and W. Eggeling. 1994. Art Patterned on That of the Sister State: Culture Officers in the Soviet Zone. *German Research: Reports of the DFG* 2–3: 15–18.

Hecht, A. 2002. *Die Wissenschaftselite Ostdeutschlands: Feindliche Übernahme oder Integration?* Leipzig: Verlag Faber und Faber.

Herrmann, J., and J. Köhn (eds.). 1988. *Familie, Staat und Gesellschaftsformation: Grundprobleme vorkapitalistischer Epochen einhundert Jahre nach Friedrich Engels' Werk „Der Ursprung der Familie, des Privateigentums und des Staats".* Berlin: Akademie-Verlag.

Heyden, van der, U. 1999. *Die Afrikawissenschaften in der DDR: Eine akademische Disziplin zwischen Exotik und Exempel. Eine wissenschaftsgeschichtliche Untersuchung.* Die DDR und die Dritte Welt, 5. Hamburg: LIT-Verlag.

Jacobeit, W. 1954. Zur Frage der urgeschichtlichen Siedlung und Wirtschaft in Mitteleuropa. *Ethnographisch-Archäologische Forschungen* 2: 159–68.

——. 1965. *Bäuerliche Arbeit und Wirtschaft: Ein Beitrag zur Wissenschaftsgeschichte der deutschen Volkskunde.* Berlin.

——. 1986. Dreißig Jahre Ethnographie an der Humboldt-Universität zu Berlin 1952–1982. *Ethnographisch-Archäologische Zeitschrift* 27: 13–26.

——. 1997. Marginalien eines nachdenklichen Volkskundlers. *Berliner Blätter: Ethnographische und ethnologische Beiträge* 13–14: 23–29.

——. 2000. *Von West nach Ost und zurück: Autobiographisches eines Grenzgängers zwischen Tradition und Novation.* Münster: Westfälisches Dampfboot.

——, and U. Mohrmann. 1968–69. Zum Gegenstand und zur Aufgabenstellung der Volkskunde in der DDR. *Lětopis* Reihe C 11–12: 94–103.

——, and P. Nedo (eds.). 1969. *Probleme und Methoden volkskundlicher Gegenwartsforschung: Vorträge und Diskussionen einer Internationalen Arbeitstagung in Bad Saarow, 1967.* Berlin: Akademie-Verlag.

Johansen, U. 1988. Die Ethnologie in der DDR. In H. Fischer (ed.), *Ethnologie: Einführung und Überblick*, pp. 271–86. Berlin: Dietrich Reimer Verlag.

Kaschuba, W. 1997. Die Europäische Ethnologie und der Raum der Geschichte. *Berliner Blätter: Ethnographische und ethnologische Beiträge* 13–14: 4–22.

——. 1999. *Einführung in die Europäische Ethnologie.* München: Beck.

Kothe, H. 1954. Die vordringlichsten Aufgaben der Ethnographie in der DDR. In, *Völkerforschung: Tagung für Volkskunde 25.-27.4.1952,* pp. 78-91 Veröffentlichung des Instituts für Deutsche Volkskunde 5. Berlin: Akademie-Verlag.

——, and K.-H. Otto (eds.). 1953. Vorwort der Herausgeber. *Ethnographisch-Archäologische Forschungen* 1: vii–viii.

Krader, L. (ed.). 1972. *The Ethnological Notebooks of Karl Marx: Studies of Morgan, Phear, Maine, Lubbock.* Assen: Van Gorcum.

——. 1973. *Ethnologie und Anthropologie bei Marx.* München: Hanser.

Krause, M. 1991. Ursula Schlenther (1919–1979): Ihr Beitrag zur Weiterführung der Tradition der Völkerkunde Lateinamerikas an der Berliner Universität. In H. Bernhardt, *Geschichte der Völkerkunde und Volkskunde an der Berliner Universität* pp. 73–80. Beiträge zur Geschichte der Humboldt-Universität zu Berlin 28. Berlin: Humboldt-Universität.

——. 2003. Der Widerspenstigen Zähmung? Staatliche Schulungskurse für indigene Hebammen in Oaxaca, Mexiko. *Lateinamerika Analysen* 6: 38–69.

——, D. Neuland-Kitzerow, and K. Noack (eds.). 2003. *Ethnografisches Arbeiten in Berlin: Wissenschaftsgeschichtliche Annäherungen.* Berliner Blätter: Ethnographische und ethnologische Beiträge 31. Münster: LIT Verlag.

——, and K. Noack. 2003. Der Berliner Königsweg? Von der Völkerkunde zur Ethnografie an der Humboldt-Universität Berlin. In M. Krause, D. Neuland-Kitzerow, and K. Noack (eds.), *Ethnografisches Arbeiten in Berlin: Wissenschaftsgeschichtliche Annäherungen*, pp. 33–42. Berliner Blätter: Ethnographische und ethnologische Beiträge 31. Münster: LIT Verlag.

Kuczynski, J. 1963. Einige Überlegungen über die Rolle der Natur in der Gesellschaft anläßlich der Lektüre von Abels Buch über Wüstungen. *Jahrbuch für Wirtschaftsgeschichte* 3: 284–97.

——. 1980–82. *Geschichte des Alltags des deutschen Volkes: Studien 1–5.* Berlin: Akademie-Verlag.

Kunze, H. 1955. Bericht über den Volkskunde-Kongreß der Deutschen Akademie der Wissenschaften zu Berlin vom 4. bis 6. September 1953. *Deutsches Jahrbuch für Volkskunde* 1: 260–69.

Lau, U. 1981. *Ethnographisch-historische Untersuchung zu den Vorstellungen altchinesischer Philosophen (5.-3. Jh. v.u.Z.) über die Ur- und Frühgeschichte.* Thesis, Humboldt-Universität zu Berlin.

——. 1986. Zur Standortbestimmung der BRD-Völkerkunde am Beispiel des Sammelbandes 'Grundfragen der Ethnologie'. *Ethnographisch-Archäologische Zeitschrift* 27: 141–51.

Lee, Y. J. 1998. *Volkskunde in der DDR zwischen innovativen Methoden und politischer Einbindung 1963–1973*. Diploma thesis, Fachbereich Geisteswissenschaften der Freien Universität Berlin.

———. 2001. '... als ob die Volkskundler schwarze Schafe wären': Wissenschaft, Politik und Eigensinn in der DDR-Volkskunde 1945–1973. In T. Scholze and L. Scholze-Irrlitz (eds.), *Zehn Jahre Gesellschaft für Ethnographie: Europäische Ethnologie in Berlin*, pp. 75–104. Berliner Blätter: Ethnographische und ethnologische Beiträge Nr. 23, Jubiläumsheft. Münster: LIT Verlag.

Mohrmann, U. 1991. Volkskunde in der DDR während der 50er und 60er Jahre: Ein Überblick. *Wiss. Zeitschrift der Humboldt-Universität zu Berlin, Reihe Geistes- u. Sozialwissenschaften* 40 (11): 103–20.

———. 2001. 'Roundabout 68': Zur DDR-Volkskunde Ende der sechziger und während der siebziger Jahre. In S. Becker et al. (eds.), *Volkskundliche Tableaus: Eine Festschrift für Martin Scharfe zum 65. Geburtstag von Weggefährten, Freunden und Schülern*, pp. 375–84. Münster: Waxmann Verlag.

———, and W. Rusch. 1991. Vier Jahrzehnte Ethnographie an der Humboldt-Universität zu Berlin. In H. Bernhardt, *Geschichte der Völkerkunde und Volkskunde an der Berliner Universität* pp. 61–72. Beiträge zur Geschichte der Humboldt-Universität zu Berlin 28. Berlin: Humboldt-Universität.

Mühlberg, D. 1999. Wann war 68 im Osten? Oder: Wer waren die 68er im Osten? *Berliner Blätter: Ethnographische und ethnologische Beiträge* 18: 44–58.

Noack, K. 2003. Caciques, escribanos y las construcciones de historias: Cajamarca, Perú, siglo XVI. In D. Cahill and B. Tovías (eds.), *Elites indígenas en los Andes: Nobles, caciques y cabildantes bajo el yugo colonial*, pp. 213–27. Quito, Ecuador: Abya Yala.

———. 2005. Negociando la política colonial en el Perú: La perspectiva desde la región norte en los Andes centrales (1532–1569). In N. Böttcher, I. Galaor, and B. Hausberger (eds.), *Los buenos, los malos y los feos: Poder y resistencia en América Latina*, pp. 199–226. Frankfurt a.M.: Vervuert/Iberoamericana.

Nötzoldt, P. 2001. Wolfgang Steinitz: Wissenschaftler und Wissenschaftsorganisator an der Deutschen Akademie der Wissenschaften zu Berlin. In T. Scholze and L. Scholze-Irrlitz (eds.), *Zehn Jahre Gesellschaft für Ethnographie: Europäische Ethnologie in Berlin*, pp. 125–48. Berliner Blätter: Ethnographische und ethnologische Beiträge Nr. 23, Jubiläumsheft. Münster: LIT Verlag.

Nowotny, P. 1992. Zur Geschichte der sorbischen Volksforschung. *Info-Blatt der Gesellschaft für Ethnographie e.V.* 4: 13–30.

Reim, H., and W. König. 1960. Tagung der Deutschen Gesellschaft für Völkerkunde in Stuttgart 1959. *Ethnographisch-Archäologische Zeitschrift* 6: 67–68.

Rose, F. 1960. *Classification of Kin, Age Structure and Marriage amongst the Groote Eylandt Aborigines: A Study in Method and a Theory of Australian Kinship.* Völkerkundliche Forschungen 3. Berlin: Akademie-Verlag.

Rusch, W. 1986. 'Ethnische Besonderheiten' und ihre Bedeutung im Prozeß der Nationenwerdung, namentlich auf dem afrikanischen Kontinent. *Ethnographisch-Archäologische Zeitschrift* 27: 79–95.

———, and L. Stein. 1982. *Siwa und die Aulad Ali: Darstellung und Analyse der soziaökonomischen, politischen und ethnischen Entwicklung der Bevölkerung der Westlichen Wüste Ägyptens und des Prozesses der Integration in den ägyptischen Staat vom Beginn des 19. Jh. bis 1976.* Thesis, Karl-Marx-Universität Leipzig.

———, and I. Winkelmann. 1987. Zur Entwicklung der außereuropäischen Ethnographie in der DDR. *Ethnographisch-Archäologische Zeitschrift* 28: 295–320.

Schmied-Kowarzik, W., and J. Stagl (eds.). 1981. *Grundfragen der Ethnologie: Beiträge zur gegenwärtigen Theorie-Diskussion.* Ethnologische Paperbacks. Berlin: Dietrich Reimer Verlag.

Scholze, D. 1992. Sorbisches Institut/Serbski institut: Tradition und Neubeginn. *Info-Blatt der Gesellschaft für Ethnographie e.V.* 5: 14–20.

Scholze, T., and L. Scholze-Irrlitz (eds.). 2001. *Zehn Jahre Gesellschaft für Ethnographie: Europäische Ethnologie in Berlin.* Berliner Blätter: Ethnographische und ethnologische Beiträge Nr. 23, Jubiläumsheft. Münster: LIT Verlag.

Scholze-Irrlitz, L. 1991. Richard Thurnwald (1869–1954): Einige Aspekte seiner Forschungs- und Lehrkonzeption. In H. Bernhardt, *Geschichte der Völkerkunde und Volkskunde an der Berliner Universität* pp. 37–45. Beiträge zur Geschichte der Humboldt-Universität zu Berlin 28. Berlin: Humboldt-Universität.

Sellnow, I. 1961a. *Grundprinzipien einer Periodisierung der Urgeschichte: Ein Beitrag auf Grundlage ethnographischen Materials.* Völkerkundliche Forschungen 4. Berlin: Akademie-Verlag.

———. 1961b. Zum Problem von Lokal- und Universalgeschichte in der völkerkundlichen Methodik: Referat gehalten auf dem 6. Internationalen Kongress der anthropologischen und ethnologischen Wissenschaften 1960 in Paris. *Ethnographisch-Archäologische Zeitschrift* 2: 124–33.

——. 1990. Das Problem der 'Völkerschaft': Eine völkerkundliche Kontroverse. *Ethnographisch-Archäologische Zeitschrift* 31: 199–214.

Sellnow, I. (ed.). 1977. *Weltgeschichte bis zur Herausbildung des Feudalismus: Ein Abriß.* Berlin: Akademie-Verlag.

Steinitz, W. 1955. Volkskunde und Völkerkunde. *Deutsches Jahrbuch für Volkskunde* 1: 269–75.

Strobach, H. 1976. Lenins Zwei-Kulturen-Theorie und der Begriff der Volkskultur. *Abhandlungen und Berichte des Staatlichen Museums für Völkerkunde Dresden* 35: 33–42.

——. 1991. Forschungen in den achtziger Jahren zur Geschichte von Kultur und Lebensweise des deutschen Volkes. *Zeitschrift für Geschichtswissenschaft* 39 (5): 462–79.

Szalay, M. 1983. *Ethnologie und Geschichte: Zur Grundlegung einer ethnologischen Geschichtsschreibung.* Ethnologische Paperbacks. Berlin: Dietrich Reimer Verlag.

Thiemer-Sachse, U. [1983] 1995. *Die Zapoteken: Indianische Lebensweise und Kultur zur Zeit der spanischen Eroberung.* Beiheft 13. Berlin: Gebr. Mann Verlag.

——. 2003. Ursula Schlenther (1919–1979): Eine Wissenschaftlerin in ihrer Zeit. In M. Krause, D. Neuland-Kitzerow, and K. Noack (eds.), *Ethnografisches Arbeiten in Berlin: Wissenschaftsgeschichtliche Annäherungen,* pp. 134–42. Berliner Blätter: Ethnographische und ethnologische Beiträge 31. Münster: LIT Verlag.

Tokarev, S. A. 1951. Die ethnographische Forschung in der Sowjetunion, ihre neuen Aufgaben und Erfolge. *Sowjetwissenschaften: Gesellschaftswissenschaftliche Abteilung* 4: 645–59.

——. 1954. Die nationale Politik der Sowjetunion und die Aufgaben und Erfolge der sowjetischen Ethnographie. In, *Völkerforschung: Tagung für Volkskunde 25.-27.4.1952,* pp. 7-22 Veröffentlichung des Instituts für Deutsche Volkskunde 5. Berlin: Akademie-Verlag.

Treide, D. 1981. *Zur Methode der Formationsanalyse: Das Erbe der Klassiker des Marxismus-Leninismus und gegenwärtige Untersuchungen zu urgesellschaftlichen Verhältnissen, ihrer Auflösung und der Herausbildung von Klassen unter verschiedenartigen historischen Bedingungen.* Thesis, Karl-Marx-Universität, Leipzig.

Tschöpe, I. 1988. Ethnische Prozesse und Formationstheorie: Einige Bemerkungen. In J. Herrmann and J. Köhn (eds.), *Familie, Staat und Gesellschaftsformation: Grundprobleme vorkapitalistischer Epochen einhundert Jahre nach Friedrich Engels' Werk „Der Ursprung der*

Familie, des Privateigentums und des Staats", pp. 136–39. Berlin: Akademie-Verlag.

USSR Academy of Sciences. 1982. *Problems of the European Ethnography and Folklore, II: Congress of the International Society for European Ethnology and Folklore.* Summaries by the congress participants. Moscow: N. N. Mikloucho-Maclay Institute of Ethnography.

Weissel, B. (ed.). 1980. *Kultur und Ethnos: Zur Kritik der bürgerlichen Auffassungen über die Rolle der Kultur in Geschichte und Gesellschaft.* Berlin: Akademie-Verlag.

Wernhart, K. R. 1986. *Ethnohistorie und Kulturgeschichte: Ein Studienbehelf.* Böhlau-Studien-Bücher: Aspekte der Ethnologie 1. Wien: Böhlau.

Willenberg, U. 1972. Interethnisch-ökonomische Beziehungen in Süd-Viet-Nam: Ihre Bedeutung für den Ethnogeneseprozeß. Veröffentlichungen des Museums für Völkerkunde Leipzig 24. Berlin: Akademie-Verlag.

——. 1986. Ethnische Kulturen, regionale Volkskulturen, Klassenkulturen und das Problem der Ethnogenese: Bemerkungen zur historischen Stellung regionaler Volkskulturen im Ethnogeneseprozeß. *Ethnographisch-Archäologische Zeitschrift* 27: 96–124.

——. 1990. Von der Kulturentwicklung zur Völkerentwicklung. *Abhandlungen und Berichte des Staatlichen Museums für Völkerkunde Dresden* 44: 71–87.

Zell, R. 1973. *Entwicklungsformen der Territorialgemeinschaft in Vietnam im 19./20. Jahrhundert.* Abhandlungen und Berichte des Staatlichen Museums für Völkerkunde Dresden 32. Berlin: Akademie-Verlag.

Zwerenz, G. 2002. Wofür starben Sokrates und Jesus? *Ossietzky, Zweiwochenschrift für Politik/Kultur/Wirtschaft*, http://www.sopos.org/aufsaetze/3caa26290051d/1.phtml.

Chapter 3
Czechoslovakia: From Národopis to Etnografie and Back

Peter Skalník

In twentieth-century East-Central Europe, political upheavals decisively affected developments in the seemingly apolitical scholarly discipline of národopis, which was ostensibly concerned with the study of rural folk culture and society. Before the Second World War, two major paradigmatic shifts took place in anthropology: the Malinowskian revolution, which rejected historical conjectures and stressed the authenticity to be gained through long-term fieldwork, and the related emergence of structural linguistics and its application in studies of folklore, mythology, and literature (Lévi-Strauss did not make his presence felt until the appearance of *The Elementary Structures of Kinship* in 1949). Neither Malinowski's functionalism nor Radcliffe-Brown's structural functional method exerted much influence on leading Czech národopis specialists such as Karel Chotek, Drahomíra Stránská, and Vilém Pražák, but some folklorists in both Slovakia and the Czech lands were inspired by the new theories and ideas of de Saussure, Trubetzkoy, Jakobson, and Bogatyriov (see Toman 1995 for a discussion of the Prague Linguistic Circle). The leading theoretical position, however, was a default positivism which reigned throughout the region.[1] Also strong was a narcissistic 'butterfly collecting' of customs and folklore items akin to German *Heimatkunde.*

We nonetheless have two noteworthy bodies of evidence about the theoretical concerns of Czechoslovak scholars during the pre-communist period (1918–48). One is the work of Josef Voráček (1941) on the primitive family, and the other is Andrej Melicherčík's *Theory of Národopis* (1945). Both men were erudite, talented, hard-working scholars. The former was sacrificed after the communist takeover and had to leave academia. The latter performed a complete *salto academico* towards orthodox communism

---

[1] This was strongly influenced by German historiography, later enriched with cultural historical ingredients. Their most important Czech mediator was Lubor Niederle, the author of *Slav Antiquities* (1953) and *The World of the Slavs* (1909).

and Marxism-Leninism, which enabled him to survive and even to maintain a leading position until his early death at the age of 49 in 1966. Let us look more closely at the careers of these two exceptional theorists.

Josef Voráček

Josef Voráček (1910–80) studied during the 1930s in Prague, Munich, and Paris (Ecole Normale Supérieure, Sorbonne). Originally he specialised in Germanic and Romance philology and sociology, but soon his interest shifted towards ethnology. His first article, published in 1934, dealt with the sociology of the German National Socialist movement. In 1936 he published a short book on the origins of property and law in the light of ethnology and sociology. In 1939, at the age of 29, he presented his habilitation thesis (which was accepted only in 1945) on the primitive family. It was published two years later—that is, after Charles University had been closed by the Nazi occupiers (Voráček 1941).

The subtitle of the book is *A Treatise on Theories and Methods of Ethnological Sociology*. The expression 'ethnological sociology' reflects Voráček's special position in the Czechoslovak scholarly scene. He was a sociologist working on ethnological themes; today we would probably call him a social anthropologist. Although he was interested in the origins of institutions such as clan, family, incest prohibitions, and totemism, he did not stop there. Drawing on the international literature of the period, Voráček used works by members of the functionalist school in Britain (especially those of Malinowski) along with those of American cultural anthropologists (Kroeber, Goldenweiser, Boas, Mead), German diffusionists, and the French Durkheimians (Mauss was his teacher in Paris) to produce a synthesis in which he expressed scepticism towards 'singular' explanations such as evolutionism and diffusionism. A detailed and comprehensive testing of theories of the primitive family led Voráček to conclude that the family among 'present-day primitives' was not a biological unit but a social one. It was so variable, however, that no 'general history of the family' was possible, but 'only a history of the family in this or that whole, tribe, nation, territory, etc.' (Voráček 1941: 193). Neither in this work nor in his textbook (Voráček 1940) is there any reference to Marxism or to Soviet scholarship.

In 1945 Voráček became a reader (*docent*) in ethnology, but in 1950 his lectures were suspended and in 1952 he was compelled to leave Charles University at the age of 42 (Vařeka 1970: 1). He never resumed his academic career but worked instead as a scientific information specialist in the Czechoslovak Ministry of Heavy Machinery (Vařeka 1970: 2). According to one of his former students, Voráček was known as a devout Roman Catholic, which undermined his academic security. Moreover, he was clearly Western-oriented in his anthropological interests. Although acquainted with Soviet theoretical works on the family and other topics, he did not think highly enough of them to mention them in his writings.[2]

Andrej Melicherčík

Andrej Melicherčík (1917–66) studied in Bratislava with Pyotr Grigoryevich Bogatyriov and specialised in 'functionally structural' studies of folklore (*funkčno štrukturálny národopis*) in the late 1930s and early 1940s (Bratislava University was not closed during the war, because Slovakia was formally an independent state under the aegis of Nazi Germany). Melicherčík published several works on Slovak folklore before embarking upon his major theoretical opus, *Theory of Národopis*. This book of 171 pages was written in the summer of 1944, just before the Slovak National Uprising, and published in 1945, at the moment of the final demise of Nazi Germany and its Slovak puppet.

In the book Melicherčík addressed the theory of his discipline with the utmost seriousness. He understood národopis (translated as 'ethnography' in the English summary and as 'etnografiya' in the Russian summary at the end of the book) as a separate discipline, existing quite apart from ethnology (which he viewed as the study of 'cultural manifestations of primitives'). Národopis 'analyzes and explains cultural manifestations in the folklore of a cultured nation'. Melicherčík stressed folklore; to him, the sociology of a village and the ethnography of a village were different, because the former dealt with 'precisions of a social character, it analyzes life', whereas the latter was focused, within a single 'social region', on manifestations fixed by 'essential characteristics of folklore' (*folklornost*) (Melicherčík 1945: 154–55). His entire theory revolved around this 'folkloreness'.

Melicherčík critically reviewed many works of contemporary anthropology, mainly German and Russian. He concluded that národopis could not afford to continue with its 'discovery of curious peculiarities of the village', which would soon disappear. It needed to become 'a science of the present', of the concrete, liberated from 'surviving and pseudoscientific ballast' (1945: 125). Diachronic reconstruction would be possible only when individual phenomena were viewed as a system and studied statically. Melicherčík appealed for the study of function, and not only form, in folk culture phenomena. He also suggested studying new topics, citing in support a Soviet collection on 'old and new ways of life', edited by Vladimir Germanovich Bogoraz-Tan (1924). On the whole, Melicherčík considered 'functionally structural národopis' to be perfectly suitable for the study of

---

[2] Telephone conversation with Professor Ludvík Baran, 5 November 2004.

folklornosť in the entire society. As Gabriela Kiliánová demonstrates in her contribution to this collection, Melicherčik reacted to post-war Soviet hegemony in East-Central Europe with severe self-criticism and a renunciation of the method he developed so carefully in 1945. I shall come back to his role in the post-1948 period.

A New Paradigm? Marxist-Leninist Etnografie/Etnografia versus Národopis

The Czechoslovak case is a good example of the contradictory developments which occurred in East-Central Europe after the Second World War. Many things happened under the force of the victory of the Soviet Union and the celebrated liberation of Czechoslovakia by the army of the world's only socialist state. As early as 1947 a leading representative of positivist národopis published an article calling for a socialist orientation within his discipline (Pražák 1947). Students such as Otakar Nahodil were sent to the Soviet Union and also to Bulgaria (Hana Hynková) to study etnografiya, and Professor Karel Chotek, a Slavophile, apparently wanted to strengthen the comparative strand in Czechoslovak národopis. The communist take-over was completed in February 1948 and led quickly to the imposition of Marxist-Leninist ideology in forms identical or similar to those found in the Soviet Union from the 1920s onwards.

Following his return from studies in Leningrad, Otakar Nahodil initiated the First All-State Conference of 'Nationographers' (*1. celostátní konference národopisců*) in January 1949. All participants received a free copy of Nahodil's translation of Sergey Pavlovich Tolstov's *Soviet School in Ethnography* (Tolstov 1949). The title was translated as *Sovětská škola v národopise;* perhaps out of tactical considerations, Nahodil was still translating the term *etnografiya* as národopis. The conference participants clearly distanced themselves from the discipline's positivist past. Even representatives of the old school such as Chotek and Stránská called for the development of a socialist ethnography (Czech *etnografie*, Slovak *etnografia*) to replace the old národopis. The stress was laid upon transforming the contents of the discipline rather than merely renaming it.

A relatively small 'Marxist Circle' was formed around Otakar Nahodil and Jaroslav Kramařík. With moral and political support from the then Ministry of Information, they managed to convene three all-state conferences of národopis practitioners, in 1949, 1952, and 1953. The Czecho-Slav Národopis Society (Národopisná společnost českoslovanská) and the journal *Český lid* (Czech people), until 1950 in the hands of those who defined 'the people' primarily as countryside dwellers, and first and foremost as rich farmers, were then either marginalised or taken over by the young activists of the Marxist Circle. Karel Chotek and Václav Černý were replaced as the editors of *Český lid* by Olga Skalníková early in 1951, when she was barely 29. She had not yet obtained her doctorate and was not a member of the party at the time, but her closeness to Nahodil and the other members of the Marxist-oriented group accounted for her appointment.

In the first double number of volume 6 (new series) for the year 1951, Skalníková wrote an editorial with the title 'For a New *Český lid*'. Without mentioning Marxism-Leninism, she proclaimed that the task of the editorial board was 'to give the journal a new ideational [*ideový*] content which would entirely correspond to the present tasks of science during the construction of socialism' (Skalníková 1951a: 1). She criticised the previous editors for not realising the 'journal's mission in the epoch of the construction of socialism in our country'. They had 'remained prisoners of the bourgeois view of our national past ... and were unable to detach themselves from bourgeois methodology in historiography' (1951a: 1). In the same issue, the Marxist historian Oldřich Říha discussed the emergence of the Czech nation and bourgeois nationalism, Nahodil wrote with Kramařík about the importance for národopis of Stalin's *On Marxism in Linguistics,* and Skalníková published her notes on národopis research into the construction of socialism in the village. Drahomíra Stránská, who remained on the editorial board, wrote on the patterns of folk blueprints (*sic*).

Nahodil and Kramařík, in their article in the 1951 issue (which soon afterwards appeared as a book), severely criticised the alleged anti-historicism and cosmopolitanism of the 'migration theory' of the origins of Slav folk culture proposed by the Brno národopis professor Antonín Václavík. They wrote: 'Prof. A. Václavík, in his "theory" of národopis, eclectically merged all current bourgeois theories of expressedly reactionary character in a certain 'synthesis'. ... From the arsenal of bourgeois ethnography, Prof. Václavík took over first and foremost migration theory in its crudest form'. Václavík had traced substantial traits of Slav folk culture in south-western Asia, India, and even Micronesia. The critics concluded (1951: 14): 'One can arrive at such a "theory", seeking the "genesis of the phenomena of Slav folk culture" as far as Micronesia, only if the researcher wants at all costs to apply an anti-historical and cosmopolitical viewpoint'.

Nahodil and Kramařík also alleged that Václavík's theories were connected to the 'reactionary bourgeois-clerical' Vienna school of cultural circles (*Kulturkreislehre*):

> Prof. Václavík is thus guided by the directives of that bourgeois 'school' which emerged as a direct reaction to the teaching of Lewis H. Morgan and F. Engels concerning the history of primeval society.

He follows the directives of that 'school', which purports to 'uproot'
Morgan and Engels at the cost of the crudest falsification of historical reality, which endeavours with the help of its 'cultural circles' to
prove that private property, exploitation, classes, an exploitive state,
patriarchal institutions and monotheism have always existed. (Nahodil and Kramařík 1951: 14)

Finally, they accused Václavík of combining the 'cultural historical school'
with the 'so-called 'functional-structural' method'. As they put it: 'In his
entire current work Prof. A. Václavík follows this functional-structural
method, which presently serves the Anglo-American colonisers and instiga-
tors of the new world war. The method of the "school" is "the most disgust-
ing synthesis of all that is backward, reactionary and anti-scientific in anthropology and sociology"' (Nahodil and Kramařík 1951: 15, quoting from
Ivan Izosimovich Potekhin's 1948 article in *Sovetskaya etnografiya*). They
summarised as follows: 'Czechoslovak národopis will not advance unless,
with all decisiveness, it debunks, criticises and eliminates these reactionary
anti-historical tendencies. Etnografie, building consistently on the basis of
Marxist-Leninist methodology, is not a hodgepodge of fantasies, as one finds
in bourgeois anthropology, but a real science. Therefore it has to struggle
mercilessly against non-scientific chimeras' (1951: 15).

Václavík had a chance to repent at the Second All-State Národopis
Conference, which took place on 6 and 7 April 1952. His reply to his critics
was published in *Český lid* that same year. Václavík chose to explain the
conditions under which národopisci like himself were working during the
bourgeois era. He apologised for his 'Czechoslovakism' (i.e. his endorse-
ment of state nationalism), for 'ethnologising' (it is not clear what that was),
and above all for his use of the 'functional-structural method'. He explained
this alleged anti-historicism by reference to his disagreement with historians
who hated everything folkish (*zášť vůči všemu lidovému*), and he declared
his devotion to the salvage of 'those values of folk culture which strengthen
national and class self-confidence' (Václavík 1952: 139). Václavík stressed
that his main research concern was the genesis of phenomena, and so he
could hardly be suspected of neglecting historical approaches: 'If this endeavour to base ethnographical research on history displayed surface traits of
formalism and mechanicism, this was caused by the fact that I was not
acquainted with the theory of Marxism-Leninism, namely, historical materialism, which is the right framework for a real, not merely formal, use of
historical methods, especially in národopis' (1952: 139).

Václavík also denied that he had ever been an adherent of the theory
of cultural circles. For him, folk culture was not derived from the art of the
high 'master culture'. He also asserted that he had not consistently applied

the functionally structural method, which had been introduced to národopis by Jakobson and Bogatyriov only in 1936. He admitted that he valued that method because it had brought a breakthrough in a situation of 'general methodological helplessness'. He nonetheless concluded that 'there is no doubt about my progressivism' and dared to criticise his critics for not taking into account the positive aspects of his work. Interestingly, he rejected 'anti-national definitions from bourgeois sociology and philosophy', according to which 'národopis was only an auxiliary science of ethnology, and they both serve sociology' (1952: 141). He explained methodological deficiencies in národopis in terms of its Western orientation and the 'considerable depend-ence of the whole of Czechoslovak science on foreign sources'. This had led to regrettable classifications, whereby the Czech lands had been allotted to the Central European circle of high culture and Slovakia to the Balkan-Carpathian cultural circle (1952: 142). Václavík also frowned on 'foreign cosmopolitanism' and on political pressure exerted on národopisci by pow-erholders. This was apparently a reference to Chotek, who was close to the establishment of pre-war Czechoslovakia.

At the end of this important article, Václavík described a way to exit the crisis by drawing on the experience and support of Soviet science. It was necessary 'even more than up to now to turn to the study of the people itself, to abandon all remnants of older theories and master thoroughly the theory of historical materialism' (1952: 142). What seems to me remarkable in this article is not so much its self-critical and sometimes self-deprecating con-tents as its constructive conclusion. Václavík not only called for a deep understanding of Soviet science but also advocated an 'evaluation of previ-ous národopis, identifying its progressive traits and developing them fur-ther'. He called for detailed acquaintance with Soviet theory in order to show the negative side of národopis, his own works included. He proposed to build a critical, detailed, and reliable bibliography and to put together a reader of progressive works in národopis. He supported the establishment of a národopis unit at the Czechoslovak Academy of Sciences, with provincial branches. Finally, he advocated the construction of central and regional ethnographic museums and the training of staff to lead them. Whether or not Václavík was compelled to write this document for personal reasons, he managed to deflect attention away from personal matters and toward broadly valid propositions.

Nahodil and Kramařík, in their 1951 article, also criticised a 1949 ar-ticle by Chotek on the periodisation of Czechoslovak folk culture. Although, according to them, Chotek was apparently in agreement with the Marxist historian Václav Husa, he had in fact introduced an 'idealist periodisation' inspired by the pre-war positivist historian Josef Pekař. They also alleged

that the very concept of Czechoslovak folk culture denied the specific national character of Slovak folk culture (cf. Kramařík 1952b).

In her short paper in the same first issue of the new *Český lid,* Olga
Skalníková outlined her ideas concerning how practitioners of národopis
should study the construction of socialism in the village. She called for study
of the folk culture created by small and middle peasants and regretted that
'no národopis study to date has revealed the role of the rich, who dominated
our village and influenced even the folk culture'. She insisted that the contribution of rural workers should not be forgotten (Skalníková 1951b: 24).
Kramařík (1952a) and, in Slovakia, Ján Mjartan (1952), were the first to
react to Skalníková's call. Simultaneously, quite a few works by Abramzon
and other Soviet scholars on kolkhoz peasantry were translated (Abramzon
1952; Kisljakov 1952; Kušner 1952; Robakidze 1952; Vorobjev 1952;
Vorobjov 1952; Vozdviženskaja and Lašuk 1952). Yet in fact no major work
investigating the socialist transformation of the countryside ever appeared
during the entire 41 years of communist rule. Field research into the transformation of the peasantry into cooperative farmers started only after a long
delay in the 1970s and 1980s, when it could be relegated to the past.

Instead, Skalníková (as she explains in her own chapter in this volume), pioneered fieldwork on urban workers and, especially, miners. In 1952
she published a programmatic article titled 'On the Question of Národopis
Research into Working-Class Life'. In it she characterised the work of the
summer 'expedition' to the region of Žďársko, where the participants examined 'the influence of the construction industry on the way of life' in villages
surrounding a new industrial town. More concretely, the task was 'to find
out about the employment of the population in the past [and] to register still
existing old production techniques in agriculture, home production (primarily weaving and the production of small working tools and utensils from
wood) and woodwork, as well as old traditions in iron-working and glass-
working'. Together with research in mining regions begun in 1949, this was
'the first attempt at národopis research in an industrial region in a place
where it is possible to follow the transformation of a region with agricultural
and woodworking production into an industrial region, and the move of
agricultural workers to work in factories and construction sites' (Skalníková
1952: 147). She admitted that the Žďársko research could shed only partial
light on the way of life of the working class, since 'the whole problematic of
this branch of národopis is very broad; it does not have a sufficient theoretical base and cannot rely on sufficient research experience' (1952: 147). Even
Soviet ethnographers, she admitted, had not yet adequately developed the
subject matter and methodology.

In the Czechoslovak case, the lack of interest in the life of workers could be traced back to the Czecho-Slav Národopis Exhibition of 1895, which included no representations of workers and their place in Czech national life. This situation lasted until after 1945. Skalníková and her collaborators knew the work of Will-Erich Peuckert, especially his book *Volkskunde des Proletariats* (1931), but did not refer to it because of Peuckert's alleged involvement with National Socialism. They did not attempt to write a theoretical treatise themselves, to show how to place the study of workers into the theory of ethnography. This class was, by definition, the carrier of a historical mission, according to the canon of Marxism-Leninism, and the only theoretical frame was historical materialism. Nor did they use the term 'proletariat', but instead 'workers' (*dělnictvo*).

Skalníková led a group of researchers in writing the landmark monograph *Kladensko* (Skalníková 1959), dealing with the folk culture of the Kladno coal-mining region to the west of Prague. The book was researched and written as a traditional monograph, without employing any new research methods derived from Marxism, but the choice of the topic and the collective character of the research were new. What was not new was the approach of historical reconstruction, which endeavoured to describe as truthfully as possible the folk culture of the miners as it had existed during the pre-socialist period.

Otakar Nahodil and the Infamous 1950s

Otakar Nahodil (1923–95) was the Czechoslovak champion of the Soviet brand of Marxism in národopis. It remains an open question whether he was an ideologue rather than a scholar. That he was passionate, talented, and hard-working is beyond doubt. Sponsored by Karel Chotek, he immersed himself in the study of non-European materials. He came back from Leningrad State University not only with a thesis on the bear cult in Siberia but also with a prophetic vision of Marxism-Leninism as a method for transforming positivist národopis in his homeland.

In his foreword to the Czech translation of Tolstov's pamphlet on the Soviet school in ethnography, which he completed at his own initiative only a few months after the communist take-over in Czechoslovakia, Nahodil stressed the need for a 'consistently Marxist approach to národopis' (Nahodil 1949: 3).[3] Soviet scholars, he argued, knew the discipline only as an histori-

---

[3] Neither Nahodil nor other proponents of the Marxist approach used the term *etnografie* consistently. They employed *etnografie, národopis,* and *národopisná věda* interchangeably. This usage contributed to the confusion and eventual survival of discredited theories and methods.

cal science, both descriptive and interpretive, which, unlike its bourgeois counterpart, did not classify nations into historical and non-historical (cultural and non-cultural), a dichotomy that contained the germ of racism. According to Nahodil, the concept of etnologie did not occur in Tolstov's work because 'for a Marxist it has no raison d'être, while in our own scientific world it is widespread' (1949: 4). Ethnology was condemned during the following 40 years as a 'bourgeois science'. Nahodil emphasised the need to study primitive-communal society, the 'longest existing socio-economic formation'. The history of this society and its various stages (such as the matriarchate and patriarchate) and the origins of the family, clan order, and law were 'central general questions'. In answering them, Soviet scholars had contributed to the development of historical materialism (Nahodil 1949: 5).

Soon afterwards Nahodil summarised his Marxist views in a booklet entitled *Soviet Národopis and Its Progressive Task* (1950). Having explained why bourgeois theories (e.g. functionalism, anti-historicism) were harmful and what was wrong with the cosmopolitan formalist comparativism of Soviet authors such as Vladimir Propp and Dmitriy Konstantinovich Zelenin, not to mention Bogatyriov's 'functional-structural method', Nahodil revealed the secret of the successes of the Soviet discipline: its historicism and its rejection of the thesis of non-historical peoples. He dwelled on the example of Leonid Pavlovich Potapov, whose *Outline of the History of the Altaians* had won the Stalin prize and was *the* exemplary Soviet monograph. Nahodil's 80-page pamphlet stressed the need to study the works of Soviet scholars and to follow their example in constructing a 'progressive Czechoslovak národopis' by '*a cohesive collective of scientific workers* who love their science and selflessly contribute to its development'.

Nahodil criticised Andrej Melicherčík for arguing that the central problem of modern národopis was the nature and existential condition of the 'folklore fact' (Melicherčík 1946). Instead he suggested that folkloristics should become an independent science (Nahodil 1950: 76). He also criticised Chotek for his 'bourgeois nationalism', which had supported the 'mainly agrarian' ruling circles of pre-war Czechoslovakia. In works such as *Folk Culture and Costumes in Czechoslovakia* (1937), Chotek had, according to Nahodil, remained silent about class struggle in the village and had coined a theory of a 'united' village culture, represented by the rich peasant. This was to idealise backward economic and social conditions and to promote Czech nationalism at the expense of the Slovaks (Nahodil 1950: 70).

Elsewhere Nahodil criticised the formalism and 'functional-structural method' of the Slovak folklorists. His denunciation of 'ethnosociology', which he blamed for 'reactionary anti-Morgan theories, especially the American, English and French schools', could be interpreted as a covert criticism of Voráček's work. He concluded: 'Thus Czechoslovak národopis entered a blind alley. It threw away beautiful traditions of classical Czech národopis and changed into a bourgeois *vlastivěda* [something approximating German *Heimatkunde*] with a very limited horizon' (1950: 71). After the war, he claimed, a new wave of národopis students had witnessed 'a gradual natural dying out of bourgeois národopis', a discipline which 'during the period of construction of socialism no longer has anything to say to the world' (1950: 71).

Whereas real purges and show trials were confined to the upper echelons of political life, nobody, with the notable exception of Josef Voráček, was sacrificed within Czechoslovak národopis (etnografie).[4] Chotek had to step down from the headship of the národopis seminar at Charles University (there was no independent department at that time, národopis being incorporated into the Department of Czechoslovak History).[5] Nevertheless, he remained a professor until his retirement. Otakar Pertold, a communist, a religious studies specialist, and a Czechoslovak diplomat in Ceylon before the war, became the new head of the seminar.

During the period 1948–56, hardly any dissident opinions were tolerated. Národopisci-turned-*etnografové* enthusiastically promoted Marxism in their publications. The alternative was not to publish at all. Chotek, Stránská, and Vilém Pražák, a *soukromý docent* (private reader), did not publish but were able to teach. Chotek refused to supervise theses which, in his view, lay outside the realm of *národopis*. Thus Olga Skalníková's thesis on miners had to be examined by Václav Husa, a Marxist historian at the Faculty of Philosophy, in 1952. Communists such as Nahodil, Kramařík, and Pertold wrote books about Soviet etnografiya, Stalin's contribution to linguistics, the origins of religion, and the culture of primitive society (Nahodil 1950,

---

[4] Voráček was never invited to rejoin, though in the liberal years 1968–70 he assessed general and theoretical articles for the journal *Český lid*. His work was laudably evaluated by Vařeka (1970). After 1950 Voráček's lectures were taken over by Nahodil, who taught theory as a Marxist history of primeval society and used 'extra-European' materials. Characteristically, Nahodil never referred in his writings to Voráček's work, either critically or apologetically. An explanation could be found in Nahodil's oral, but never published, critique of Voráček at the First All-State Conference of Nationographers (Ludvík Baran, personal communication).

[5] The department had seven full members and seven external teachers but was reduced to the status of a section within Václav Husa's Department of Czechoslovak History and Archives Studies in 1958. The section was headed by Nahodil and had only four members; they included Josef Wolf, a biological anthropologist with a keen interest in extra-European societies. In 1960 the section was renamed 'ethnography and folkloristics' (etnografie a folkloristika). It reassumed the status of a department in 1961, when it had eight members, with the folklorist Karel Dvořák as its head. Ladislav Holý and Milan Stuchlík began their careers as external teachers of 'general ethnography' (obecná etnografie) in the years 1962–68 (see Petráňová and Bahenský 2002).

1954a, 1954b, 1956, 1957; Nahodil and Kramařík 1952; Pertold 1956; Nahodil and Robek 1959, 1961; see also Kandert 2001).

In the course of the 1950s a new generation of students was formed by this enforced association with Marxism, including future key protagonists such as Antonín Robek, who worked with Nahodil, and also some of those who became interested in non-European anthropology (variously known as *cizokrajný národopis, obecná etnografie,* and *mimoevropská etnografie).* While Robek complemented Nahodil's contributions to the Marxist theory of religion, Ladislav Holý and Milan Stuchlík acquainted themselves with social anthropological and cultural anthropological literature, both theoretical and that dealing with Africa and Oceania (Holý and Stuchlík 1964).

Nahodil's theoretical interests, however, were not limited to the study of the origins of religion and superstitions. His prime interest lay in 'matricults' *(mateřské kulty),* the study of which he considered his own original contribution to Marxist historical materialism. It was on this topic that he presented his Doctor of Science (DrSc) thesis in the late 1950s.[6] He was the first anthropologist in Czechoslovakia to obtain this highest scientific degree of the Soviet type. He published the essence of the thesis in the journal *Československá etnografie,* which he founded in 1953 (Nahodil 1959–60). Searching for factual confirmation of Marxist historical materialist theory, he found 'evidence' for the existence of a matriarchate in the rich data he knew concerning Siberia. He initiated translations of Mark Osipovich Kosven's *Matriarchate* (1952), Lewis Henry Morgan's *Ancient Society* (1954), and Julius Lips's *Vom Ursprung der Dinge* (1960), and he wrote forewords to these and other 'progressive' works.

His ambition was to prove that the matriarchate had preceded the patriarchate and to document the transition from the one to the other, which he considered a 'substantial rupture in the history of the primeval society' (Nahodil 1959–60: 4). He also wanted to show that 'totemism is substantially an expression of the religious ideology of the matriarchal order', whereas the patriarchate was characterised by 'the emergence of the cult of male spirits-ancestors' (1959–60: 4). Using what he termed the 'comparative historical method', he claimed to have established the 'really existing high social position of women' in early human societies. He formulated this in the overall category of matricults, cults that had originated in the matriarchal epoch and survived due to 'the magnificent power of tradition' (1959–60: 5).

---

[6] Nahodil's academic advancement was spectacular. He received his first degree (the equivalent of an MA) from Leningrad State University in 1948; this was followed by a PhD from Charles University. He became reader *(docent)* and Candidate of Sciences (CSc) in 1956 and Doctor of Sciences (DrSc) in 1959, a rate of progress which kept him well ahead of others in the discipline.

Nahodil displayed a vast erudition, covering not only classical literature dealing with his topic but also recent works in German and Russian. At the same time, his analysis was typical of the period in the way in which he forced the data into the Procrustean bed of Marxism-Leninism.

Soon after the publication of his book on the origins of religion, co-authored with Antonín Robek (1961), Nahodil fell victim to a scandal over an alleged extramarital affair with an East German woman, the wife of a senior academic functionary, and after several years of insecurity he managed to flee to West Germany in 1965. There he tried to pursue an academic career, but with limited success (Mácha 1983). He tried to re-enter the Czech academic scene at the beginning of 1990 but was almost unanimously rejected. He was already seriously ill, and he died in 1995, leaving a self-edited pamphlet as a professional testament in which he tried to defend his Marxist past (Nahodil 1995; see Jeřábek 1998).

Andrej Melicherčík, the outstanding personality in Slovak národopis during this period, was quick to recognise the inevitability of embracing the Soviet Marxist approach, even though it meant rejecting his own previous theorising. In 1950 he introduced a special issue of the *Národopisný sborník SAVU* (Národopis collection of the Slovak Academy of Sciences and Arts), which contained translations of Soviet theoretical works (Melicherčík 1950). Two years later he repeated this exercise, quoting Stalin several times before lauding the Soviet etnografiya school (Melicherčík 1952: 13):

> The foremost characteristic of the Soviet school in národopis is its consistent historicism. In contradistinction to bourgeois scholars, the Soviet researchers view národopis as an *organic part of historical science.* ... Soviet etnografiya, based on the methodology of Marxism-Leninism, studies objects, phenomena and events in the process of their emergence, evolution and disappearance, in concrete historical conditions, as shaped by the mode of production of material values, and the development of productive forces and of the relations of production (authors emphasis).

Like Nahodil, Melicherčík attacked the division between 'cultural' and 'non-cultural' nations, which he attributed to 'West-European bourgeois ethnography'. Citing Tolstov, he asserted that

> *the subject matter of Soviet etnografiya is the people in its historical development. The task of národopis research is the study of the culture and way of life of the peoples of the world, in whatever stage of historical development they are to be found, each in its national and ethnic specificity, its distinct historical origin and evolution. (authors emphasis)*

The task was to explain what was specific to each nation and nationality (meaning an ethnic group that had not yet attained the level of nation) and thereby (citing Tolstov again) 'to reveal its contribution to the common treasury of world culture' (Melicherčík 1952: 13).[7]

Melicherčík attacked the reactionary basis of 'English functionalism' and the 'functional-structural method'. In this context he mentioned Malinowski, Smuts, and Radcliffe-Brown but skillfully avoided his own functional-structural orientation in folklore studies.[8] This could be seen as an echo of the Soviet collection of essays entitled *Anglo-American Ethnography in the Service of Imperialism* (Kramařík and Nahodil 1953). In fact this book indirectly had a positive influence, because it provided some detail about the work of the Western streams it discussed. For me personally, the book was the inspiration to study Malinowski's works, which were described in a long chapter by my future teacher Dmitriy Alekseevich Ol'derogge and his Africanist colleague Ivan Izosimovich Potekhin as follows: 'Malinowski thoroughly rejected the traditional study of culture of the given nationality, which had usually been carried out through systematic description of the individual elements of culture. In contrast to this, Malinowski saw in culture not a set of mechanistically connected parts but a certain organisation, which had its distinctive characteristics' (Ol'derogge and Potekhin 1953: 91–92).

The authors even quoted Malinowski to the effect that the task of the anthropologist was not only to explain the origin and history of institutions but also to point out their meaning in the given society. This was a challenge for a young adept of the discipline who had until then been fed only on the theory of survivals and the (often futile) search for origins. Ol'derogge and Potekhin preceded Talal Asad (1973) in their harsh criticism of the imperialism of the functional school, but they also provided interesting details about the work of the pupils of Malinowski and Radcliffe-Brown and in this way whetted appetites for social anthropology among young Czech readers. At

---

[7] Melicherčík also initiated the translation of Soviet writings on 'lineage society' in which various aspects of Engels's historical materialism (inspired by Morgan) were exemplified in different settings, such as Siberia (for the transition from lineage-tribal to territorial ties), southern Africa ('military democracy'), and Central Asia (forms of lineage and tribal organisation among the nomads). Ol'derogge's article on the Malay kinship system and Kosven's theory of transition from matriarchate to patriarchate and other theoretical questions were also translated (Melicherčík 1954). In his foreword to the 1954 collection, Melicherčík argued that the 'materialist historicism of Soviet ethnographers enabled results which put Soviet ethnography rightfully on the first rung in world ethnographic science' (1954: 10).

[8] The term 'structural-functional' had different meanings in linguistics and folklore studies, as Bohuslav Beneš (1972: 244) pointed out in his appraisal of the life work of Bogatyriov. The phrases used to designate post-Malinowskian anthropology were 'structural functionalism' and 'the structural-functional method', not 'functional structuralism' or 'the functionally structural method' (*funkčně strukturální metoda*).

the same time they demonstrated that it would not be easy to implement this branch of the discipline in socialist countries, as long as it was identified with the imperialist enemy (see also Copans 1975).

The Dynamic 1960s

The relaxation of the political scene in Czechoslovakia after 1956 was only slowly reflected in národopis/etnografie. One of its signs was an expansion of non-European studies. In 1961 Ladislav Holý defended his Candidate of Science thesis on a topic inspired by the theory of Marxist historical materialism, namely, the disintegration of clan order, but he was allowed to address it using data from the East African interlacustrine area, known for the formation of centralised polities such as Buganda, Busoga, Bunyoro, Toro, Rwanda, and Burundi. Holý necessarily relied on data collected by British functionalists, but he interpreted them in such a way that he could not easily be accused of merely emulating the Malinowskians (Holý 1963). His life-long colleague Milan Stuchlík worked with the Dutch and American literature on the Sumatran Bataks and produced his own version of the disintegration of their kinship organisation (Stuchlík 1962).

In 1961 Holý also received a research grant from his employer, the Czechoslovak Academy of Sciences, which enabled him to begin fieldwork among the Berti of Darfur in the Sudan. He continued this fieldwork in 1965 when he was allowed to accept a stipend from the International African Institute. The first version of his first Berti monograph, *Neighbours and Kinsmen* (1974), was written in Czech, though it was never published in the Czech original.

A small group of Africanists formed around this tandem and published in English a library study of social stratification in 'tribal Africa' (Holý 1968). At that time British anthropologists, including Max Gluckman, were also addressing 'tribal' matters (see Gluckman 1965), and this apparently influenced Holý, Stuchlík, and their collaborators. Though it was not their intention to expound Marxist views—indeed, this was the liberalising period leading up to the Prague Spring of 1968—Western critics of the book such as Peter Lloyd could not help finding Marxist dogmatism in it. Holý and his collaborators did not indulge in historical reconstructions but rather treated African societies from the viewpoint of the ethnographic present, relying predominantly on British and French literature. Most of this literature treated 'traditional' and 'tribal' African societies as unchanging traditions, a bias common in Czech národopis from pre-Marxist times. The same tendency can be found in Soviet etnografiya, whose practitioners, in spite of their commitment to historicism, often depicted societies as they were (supposed to be) up until the October 1917 revolution. A peculiar blend of historicism and archaism was the result.

This blend was especially evident in the study of workers and miners, which was marked by slavish historicism. The would-be-Marxist národopisci set out to study miners or collectivised peasants, but instead of concentrating on their lives at the time of research and collecting authentic data about the present which they could observe in the field, they concentrated on life and customs in pre-communist times. They made the same mistake as Soviet researchers, who also reconstructed the pre-revolutionary folk culture and treated the past as an unchanging ethnographic present. The reality before their eyes thus escaped them and remained unexamined.

The adoption of a research strategy for the study of the present, especially in urban settings, became a high priority for the more open-minded Czechoslovak národopisci in the 1960s. In the improved political climate it was now possible to study 'bourgeois' literature, and the pioneering works of Hermann Bausinger, a West German who launched his own revolution of the present within Volkskunde (Bausinger 1961), were especially influential.

A thin booklet entitled *Towards a Theory of the Národopis of the Present* (Skalníková and Fojtík 1971) concluded the quasi-liberal period of 'socialism with a human face' in this discipline. Its authors still quoted Engels and Marx, but only their most pertinent texts. They made numerous references to Western community studies and to the theories of modern social anthropology and sociology. The book opened with a six-page joint introduction, to which Karel Fojtík added a section devoted to the folk and folk culture in the pre-capitalist period. Olga Skalníková, in her section, examined folk culture and its role in urban and industrial regions. The third section dealt with various techniques for researching contemporary folk life. The authors stressed the wider European research context, including Russian *etnografiya sovremennosti*, German *Gegenwartsvolkskunde*, and British 'social anthropology of complex societies'. They noted that Marxist anthropologists had participated actively in formulating the methodology and theory of the study of the present, and they opted for the term etnografie rather than národopis. In practice this was not a significant change, since both národopis and etnografie were based on the concept of the *lid*, or folk, which was taken to mean the working people, in both rural and urban settings. Fojtík therefore began his theoretical discussion by considering folk and folk culture (*lidová kultura*) in both the pre-capitalist period and in the new anthropology of the present.

He argued that 'folk' (*lid*), had to be defined in terms of the 'inner character of a "people" as a social and cultural category' (Skalníková and Fojtík 1971: 11). While the definition of *lid* in the late nineteenth century was already complex, according to Fojtík it was even more difficult to define the term for contemporary research purposes. Older definitions were restricted to specific rural groups, supposedly the carriers of 'peopleness' (*lidovost*), but these definitions were laden with a priori, speculative qualities due to the then overriding task of raising national consciousness. The peasant and country life were 'romantically idealised' as the 'most important composite part of the nation' (1971: 13). If contemporary researchers should also study urban folk (*městský lid*), they would have to 'define more precisely the social and cultural traits of *lid*, so as not to exclude these elements of the urban population' (1971: 14).

Instead of proposing a new positive definition of *lid*, Fojtík discussed a number of definitions put forward from outside anthropology, especially sociology, and accepted the usefulness of the concept of community as originally developed by Ferdinand Tönnies when he coined his Gemeinschaft-Gesellschaft opposition. He also discussed at length Robert Redfield's concept of folk society and proposed applying the 14 main traits assigned by Redfield to 'folk culture' to Central European data. Fojtík stressed the early opening up of the isolated communities to external influences and also their early internal heterogeneity. If there was homogeneity in some villages, this was the result of the conscious strivings of the 'leading layer in the community', who needed such uniformity to succeed in their agricultural enterprise. The striving for conformity was expressed in a local tradition of folk culture, which 'even today marks the internal order of small communities' (1971: 25).

At the end of his part of the book, Fojtík summarised the most important traits of folk culture. First, the cultural tradition of an internally differentiated group appeared on the outside as if it were homogeneous, and all members participated in the imposition of sanctions for breaches of the traditional norms and forms of culture. Second, a group's cultural tradition was increasingly relevant to social integration: cultural tradition was, 'in the consciousness of each individual and in the collective consciousness, an accomplished, inherited set of norms and forms'. Third, the 'suicentristic' relation of the group's members to its cultural tradition made it 'the criterion for assessment of the value of the traditions of other, similar groups'. Fourth, other cultural traditions, such as those of various professions, were tolerated provided they were not in direct conflict with the basic norms of the local cultural tradition. And fifth, the group was relatively flexible in allowing exceptional individuals concessions, which served personal and family representation (Skalníková and Fojtík 1971: 34).

In the second part of the book Skalníková explored folk culture and its functions in urban life and industrial settings. After referring to Tönnies's,

Redfield's, and Wirth's characterisations of urbanism, she stressed that
etnografie defined the workers' community in the light of 'social status
within a separate class', and specifically 'groups of primary informal social
relations such as family, friend and neighbourhood group' (Skalníková and
Fojtík 1971: 37). In these primary groups of the 'so-called folk strata of
industrial society', it was especially important to study 'those elements
which drew on and were continuations of the traditions of the village community or similarly positioned social strata' (1971: 37). The result was that
the folk strata of industrial society were 'defined economically and socially
as exploited strata and classes, culturally not only continuing to transmit
basic features of the folk culture of the village but at the same time creating
new values, whose quality [was] influenced both by their own cultural
capacities (level of education and degree of embeddedness in the national
culture) and by their role as consumers of a qualitatively different urban
culture' (1971: 37).

Skalníková then discussed the character of mediaeval mining communities (her special interest) and proceeded on this basis towards a detailed
analysis of the worker communities of the industrial period, focusing on the
structure and development of workers' families and kin and network relations.

In their 'methodical conclusions', the two authors stressed that the
study of the present made it more urgent to resolve certain problems tabled
by classical anthropologists, but contemporary work also raised new theoretical issues and called for a reconsideration of the position of etnografie in
the social sciences. They also underlined the novelty of studying the present,
since especially in the new cities and their surroundings the population was
'very numerous and diverse in its origins, and therefore also [displayed a]
variety of customs, attitudes, ideas, norms and forms of daily life' (Skalníková and Fojtík 1971: 56). Such complex fieldwork required more precision
in its methods and in the preparation and management of research. This,
according to the authors, had been accomplished in monographs dealing with
the mining regions of Kladensko, Rosicko-Oslavansko, and Žakarovce.
Skalníková and Fojtík added that this work was largely in accord with the
experience of foreign researchers. They considered it important 'to get as
close as possible' to the groups under investigation, to 'gain the trust of the
inhabitants of the studied locality without concealing the reasons for the
researchers' stay. ... Worries that the very presence of a researcher distorts
the recorded phenomena are to be seen as exaggerated. Such an approach
allows the researcher simultaneously to preserve the necessary distance from
the observed realities and groups' (1971: 58).

Back to Square One: 'Normalisation' in the 1970s and 1980s

The Soviet invasion of Czechoslovakia in 1968 had a direct and devastating effect on Czechoslovak národopis/etnografie. Just a few days after the invasion a Czechoslovak delegation travelled to Tokyo to attend the Eighth Congress of the International Union of Anthropological and Ethnological Sciences. They acquainted their colleagues from around the world with the frustration they were experiencing as a result of the Soviet military invasion of their country. They were offered not just sympathy but also jobs, should they decide not to return home. Indeed, a positive echo of 1968 lasted for a few more years, and books prepared during the liberal period were still being published in 1971–72, including translations of Lévi-Strauss. Josef Wolf (born 1927), one of the Czech champions of 'integral' anthropology (Wolf 2002), published a methodological article on cultural and social anthropology in 1969 and followed it with a reader of classic anthropological texts in 1971. The theoretical work of Fojtík and Skalníková, just discussed, was published at the last possible moment, in 1971. After this, even theoretical work based upon Marxist assumptions was viewed with the deepest suspicion.

At this time I received clear signals that I had no career prospects at Prague's Charles University, so I moved to Bratislava's Comenius University. There, under the leadership of Ján Podolák, a tiny, research-oriented Institute of Ethnology published the annual *Ethnologia Slavica: An International Review of Slavic Ethnology.*[9] I was able to teach the foundations of social anthropology under the name 'general ethnology' and to finish my Candidate of Science thesis (Skalník 1973a), which was a prelude to my later work on the early state. However, the thesis could not be defended. In 1971 I was invited to present a theoretical paper at a conference to mark the centenary of the publication of Engels's *The Origin of the Family, Private Property and the State.* I argued that social anthropology had managed to further develop Marxist historical materialism and that scholars such as Jack Goody and Max Gluckman were, 'in principle', Marxists (Skalník 1973b). I also translated Marx's writings on fetishism from the handwritten originals into Slovak; at the time this was the only complete publication of these ethnological notes, which led Marx to his theory of commodity fetishism (Skalník 1976). My Bratislava appointment was discontinued in 1976, after a 'complex evaluation' of my work and political attitudes proved unfavorable (I did not sign the evaluation, which among other points accused me of publishing 'too much'). I managed to escape to the Netherlands to work with

---

[9] The Institute of Ethnology (Kabinet etnológie) was the only Czechoslovak institution to bear ethnology in its official name.

Henri Claessen on early states (Claessen and Skalník 1978). My direct
participation in Czechoslovak academic life was thus forcefully interrupted
for almost 14 years.

As a result of purges in the Communist Party of Czechoslovakia, those
branded counter-revolutionaries for their active opposition to the Soviet
invasion were excluded from the party and sacked from their positions.
Others lost their party membership but could retain their jobs under certain
humiliating conditions. For example, in the Institute of Ethnography and
Folklore of the Czechoslovak Academy of Sciences, the director, Jaromír
Jech, and his deputy, Olga Skalníková, were left in the dark for a long time
and then demoted. Jech was subsequently pensioned off. Skalníková was
stripped of her permanent contract with the academy and then given a temporary contract, which was extended every six weeks. Her salary was reduced substantially. Then, on her fifty-fourth birthday, she too was obliged
to take early retirement. A number of their colleagues were either sacked or
retained on condition that they adopt the new research program. This eliminated non-European materials and almost all traces of a social anthropological approach.[10] It stressed instead the primacy of studying the Czech national
revival, the Czech diaspora, cooperative villages, and workers. Some new
personnel were brought in for the last two topics, but they lacked any background in sociology or social anthropology.

The leading figure in the implementation of this new order was well
known from the infamous 1950s. Antonín Robek was both a staunch communist and an isolationist nationalist. Born in 1931, he was recruited by
Otakar Nahodil at Charles University immediately upon his graduation in the
mid-1950s. He then co-authored with Nahodil a book on folk superstitions
and later a thick volume on the origins of religion, strictly conceived in the
spirit of Marxist anti-religious dogma (Nahodil and Robek 1959, 1961).
After Nahodil left the university, and later the country, Robek never criticised his erstwhile older colleague. The Soviet invasion gave Robek the
chance of his life. He approved of it wholeheartedly and recognised that it
was an opportunity for him to seize the reins of the discipline. As Bohuslav
Šalanda wrote in praise of Robek on the occasion of his fifty-fifth birthday,

---

[10] One qualification should be entered: social anthropology in those unfortunate years did
exert influence on the work of the Social Relations Section in the International Commission
for the Study of the Carpathian Region, led by Soňa Švecová. Švecová was a Slovak who
worked at Charles University but did her fieldwork exclusively in Slovakia. She had studied
in Hungary with István Tálasi and, like her close colleague Ladislav Holý, had good working
relations with Hungarian colleagues such as Tibor Bodrogi and Lajos Boglár. I, too, benefited
from the 'Hungarian connection' in the first half of the 1970s, when I used to visit Bodrogi's
younger colleagues Mihály Sárkány and Csaba Ecsedy in order to break out of the isolation I
experienced in Czechoslovakia.

'in the crisis period 1968–1969 he was one of the leading scholars to represent the healthy core at the Faculty of Philosophy of Charles University. At that time he displayed bravery and deliberation, political skill and firm communist conviction' (Šalanda 1986: 182).

Robek became the director of the institute, was promoted to full professorship, and was awarded the degree of Doctor of Science (DrSc). He knew how to make people dependent on him in a kind of academic serfdom. He invited numerous historians and Slavists as well as národopisci into the academic institute and ensured that his name appeared in almost every publication, either as editor or as contributor, regardless of who actually did the work. As one scholar who owed the substance of her career to Robek wrote in a recent evaluation, Robek was educated in traditional národopis, religious studies, and comparative history. He saw the subject 'as an historical discipline. He therefore saw the task of národopis as a branch of science in the study of the evolutionary connections between cultural and social changes, in the study of their causes and effects' (Moravcová 2003: 147).

According to this apologist, Robek was personally active in all aspects of the discipline as practised in this period: studies of national and social emancipation processes, the transformation of Czech villages in the nineteenth and twentieth centuries, folk origins, beliefs, superstitions, and religion, regionalism as cultural identity, and inter-ethnic relations. He also displayed 'a deeper relation to the problematic of the emancipation of Czech workers' (Moravcová 2003: 148). In this capacity he put himself forward as the senior co-editor of the collection *The Old Prague of Workers* (Robek, Moravcová, and Šťastná 1983). The indisputable merits of the book rested mainly on theoretical achievements of the previous period. Because Robek published in no language other than Czech, he did not go to international conferences unless he absolutely had to (e.g. when he attended a SIEF gathering in Moscow).

Within the inward-looking circle of Czech národopis, with Robek at the helm, two other Prague národopis specialists were awarded Doctor of Science degrees. Mirjam Moravcová wrote a thesis on the unsuccessful attempt to introduce a Czech national costume in the revolutionary year 1848 (Moravcová 1986). In it she made no reference to the literature on theories of nationalism or the cultural construction of tradition. She described details of a potentially fascinating episode, but only in the course of a purely non-theoretical historical reconstruction, without searching for social or semiotic meaning. Josef Vařeka, the second DrSc of the Robek era, was a politically neutral disciple of Chotek's and a life-long specialist in folk architecture. He viewed buildings as expressions of the genius of the folk but studied them without much attention to the people who lived in them. In the careers of both Vařeka and Moravcová we can see the boomerang effect in Czech národopis. The atheoretical positivism of pre-communist národopis had returned even before the demise of communism as such.

In Moravia, where folk traditions were deemed to be more alive than in Bohemia, Václav Frolec of the Purkyně/Masaryk University organised conferences on 'living folk culture' at the Institute of Folk Art (later Folk Culture) at Strážnice. This gave rise to a series of publications called Folk Culture in the Present (*Lidová kultura v současnosti*). By contrast, the study of collectivised villages was never consolidated in this way.

Another aspect of the period of 'normalisation' in the 1970s was the elaboration of the concept of ethnos, based on the publications of the leading Soviet anthropologist of the Brezhnev era, Yulian Bromley. Bromley believed, not quite without reason, that if the name of the discipline was etnografiya, then its basic concept should be the 'ethnos'. Bromley's book *Ethnos and Ethnography* was translated into Slovak (Bromlej 1980), and Robek recruited a research team in the 1980s which produced a series of preparatory texts on ethnos theory, though a full summary of its researches was published only after the change of regime (Brouček et al. 1991).

One of the members of this group was Václav Hubinger, a talented národopisec who had non-European interests and social anthropological inclinations. In 1990 he published a theoretical article on the definition and use of the term 'folk' (*lid*) as the most essential concept of národopis. It was a term used in many disciplines, by politicians, and even by ordinary people. Hubinger wrote his text shortly before the revolutionary changes in his country. 'Folk' for him referred to all those 'culturally, socially and to some extent even ethnically defined parts of a society ... all class-differentiated societies' (Hubinger 1990: 45). His point was that the 'people' were composed of 'working, unprivileged, and exploited layers and groups of population', and this definition could be applied to both European and non-European state societies (1990: 45). The people, often seen as middle peasants, were in the Czech context 'the core of the nation, the carrier of genuine and the best national traditions'. Until the end of the nineteenth century, however, 'proletarianised layers of rural and urban population were not considered (in the národopis sense of the word) as (part of the) people' (1990: 45). Hubinger stressed that 'in the contemporary era it is indisputable that precisely the workers must be the object of serious and multifaceted research interest' (1990: 45). At the same time he aptly remarked that the habit of studying *lid* as representing the past in the present meant that this group 'fulfilled in principle the same function which in the science of some countries was performed by so-called "primitives" or "savages"; ... in both cases a special term is introduced to denote social and cultural realities distinct from the reality of so-called modern civilised society' (1990: 44–45).[11]

Evaluations of the Communist Era after 1989

Fairly soon after the collapse of the communist regime in Czechoslovakia in November 1989, an extraordinary general assembly of the members of the Czechoslovak Národopis Society gathered on 18 January 1990. The participants elected a task force (*pracovní skupina*) which was commissioned to prepare 'a critical evaluation of the development of Czech národopis' and the activities of the society.

Slovak národopis was not evaluated.[12] Ján Podolák published a short commemorative article on the národopis jubilee at the Comenius University, covering the entire period of 70 years since Chotek launched the discipline in Bratislava (Podolák 1991). Podolák was soon afterwards forced to leave the university because of his critical approach: he founded a new department at the University of St. Cyril and St. Methodius in Trnava. This department organised a conference on 'Národopis and Folkloristic Institutions in Slovakia' in 2001. Podolák delivered a keynote paper in which he sketched the stages of development of Slovak ethnology (Podolák 2003). Its depiction of the stability in the staffing of Slovak národopis from pre-war times up to the end of communist rule is striking. The main protagonists, whether communists or not, were flexible enough to ensure that neither the demise of the Slovak fascist state, the communist takeover, nor the purges that followed the Soviet invasion of 1968 caused any major shake-ups. The first Slovak professional národopisci, Ján Mjartan and Ján Bednárik, survived all changes of regime. As I described earlier, the structuralist Andrej Melicherčík became a Marxist within months after February 1948. From 1958 until 1990 the Národopis Institute was directed by the communist Božena Filová. Even

---

[11] Hubinger applied his talents to the cause of introducing social anthropology in Czechoslovakia by organising the Second Biennial Conference of the European Association of Social Anthropologists in 1992 in Prague. From the mid-1990s, however, he became a professional diplomat.

[12] The name of the society included the epithet 'Czechoslovak', but, as with so many other organisations in Czechoslovakia, an asymmetrical model was applied. For example, along with the Czechoslovak Communist Party there was also the Slovak Communist Party; along with the Czechoslovak Academy of Sciences, the Slovak Academy of Sciences; and along with the Czechoslovak Národopis Society, the Slovak Národopis Society. Slovak institutions were largely autonomous, but there were practically no 'Czech' institutions because the epithet 'Czechoslovak' implied a dominant Czech element. Developments in Slovakia, especially after the official creation of the federation in 1969, in many ways followed their own logic. Only after the partition of Czechoslovakia in 1993 did a Czech Národopis Society emerge as a parallel formation to the Slovak Národopis Society.

Ján Podolák (born 1926), an *enfant terrible,* survived the loss of party membership after 1968 and several demotions in both the academy and the university. He was eventually re-admitted to the party, awarded a Doctor of Science degree, and appointed rector (vice-chancellor) of the Catholic university at Trnava after 1989.

The Prague task force presented a short report which began by pointing out that the group had too little data for 'a responsible analysis of ... the post-war history of our disciplines'. It concluded that 'personal evaluation of the moral principles of one's life attitudes and actions should be left to the individual, to each and every one of us, so that we may all analyse our consciences and reach our own conclusions about the ethics of our work' (Jiřikovská and Mišurec 1991: 6).

Nevertheless, the authors did attempt to sketch an evaluation and to propose steps for rectifying past shortcomings ('to attempt to find constructive departure points for further conceptual and scientific work with a view to accelerating the creation of optimal conditions for the development of our národopis in the new socio-historical conditions of the life of our nation'). They began by explaining why národopis was a closely monitored subject under communism, useful and therefore prone to abuse: 'it is a discipline with a very political character, because it studies the historical development of the way of life and culture of the most numerous part of the ethnic community, which includes in its comprehensive field of study the ethnic specificity of models and forms of behaviour, action and thought, and also the communication avenues, contacts and channels through which national identity and the historical consciousness of the nation are strengthened' (Jiřikovská and Mišurec 1991: 9). Here I think the task force pinpointed what národopis really was, or at least where the národopisci saw their strategic importance.

The authors criticised Nahodil and Robek. The latter was forced to resign in 1990 from his post as director of the Institute of Ethnography and Folklore. Nahodil returned to Prague shortly before the end of 1989, but his plea for rehabilitation was unanimously rejected. Instead he was repeatedly blamed for the imposition of Soviet Marxism on Czech národopis and for promoting methods which had worked deleteriously on the legacy of the founder generation of professional národopisci—that is, scholars such as Chotek, Stránská, and Pražák (Jiřikovská and Mišurec 1991; Jeřábek 1992, 1998). When he failed to secure an official hearing, Nahodil resorted to *samizdat* and published a small pamhlet entitled *A Totalitarian Evaluation of Totalitarianism* (Nahodil 1995), by which he meant the report compiled by Jiřikovská and Mišurec. Nahodil argued that he had always been devoted to scientific method:

Etnografie was for me no mere profession but a vocation which I practised with enthusiasm. It is not by chance that I was the first *etnograf* who defended his CSc (1957) and DrSc (1962). I do not need to apologise or defend myself, because a rather voluminous work, with all its positives and negatives, speaks for me and will one day be judged by history. I was never a mere ideologist' (Nahodil 1995: 11).

He also denied any participation in the demotion of Josef Voráček and explained that his high standing in Czechoslovak etnografie had been entirely undermined from 1962 onwards (cf. Mácha 1983; Jeřábek 1998).

Another evaluation of the communist period in Czech národopis was prepared by Richard Jeřábek (born 1931), a národopisec based at the Purkyně/Masaryk University in Brno. A devoted pupil of Václavík's, whose self-critique of the early 1950s (discussed earlier) he explained in terms of political pressure and blackmail (Jeřábek 1967, 1991), Jeřábek assumed a leading role in discussions over the future of národopis and folklore (Jeřábek et al. 1991). Other participants included Ladislav Holý, Josef Kandert, and Mirjam Moravcová. Jeřábek identified himself with národopis but argued that both národopis and etnografie were misleading terms. *Lidopis, lidověda,* and *lidozpyt* were better terms, because they made clear that the discipline dealt not with nation and national culture but with folk and folk culture. Jeřábek was prepared to accept the term ethnology (etnologie), and he admitted that národopis had been a stagnant science. Even when Marxists had demanded the study of 'revolutionary changes', the 'socialist village', 'socialist life-style', 'socialist public ritual', and the 'incorporation of progressive traditions of folk culture into the culture of the socialist society', none of this had actually been implemented. (Characteristically, he did not mention the study of workers or cities.)

Jeřábek condemned all those who had previously pretended that their národopis research had a Marxist content and who were now suddenly trying to pass off the same works as cultural or social anthropology. He concluded that 'Czech science is not prepared for an immediate transition to a universal focus on the study of man and culture, and any superficial coquetterie is bound to end in a total fiasco'. Národopis was 'totally different' from Western anthropology, and Jeřábek suggested that the two should be allowed to coexist and mutually influence each other (Jeřábek et al. 1991: 8–9). In another article, in English, Jeřábek lamented the lack of a thorough critique of the communist period: 'the Czech community of ethnographers did not find enough courage and strength to touch this sore spot and make the decision which was so important for the future of the science' (1992: 45).

David Scheffel and Josef Kandert (1994) attempted a different kind of evaluation, a 'post-mortem of the "people's ethnography" that came into being after Czechoslovakia's adoption of Soviet-style socialism in 1948'.[13] They assigned responsibility for the implementation of Marxism to four 'young Marxists': Nahodil, Kramařík, Hannah Rejchrtová (later publishing as Laudová), and Skalníková (the last of these was described as 'eventually the most influential Marxist transformer'). Scheffel and Kandert admitted 'a gradual opening up to the world' in the 1960s; but then in the post-1968 'normalisation' period, Antonín Robek and his followers 'repeated the steps pioneered by their Stalinist predecessors. *Český lid* once again spoke with a single voice, and the well-established double thrust of the discipline—the culture of socialist farmers and workers—regained its former prominence'. Scheffel and Kandert concluded their critical overview with the admission that 'the subjugation of academic to political interests in Czech ethnography cannot be blamed exclusively on communism'. It was due in part to the difference in the degree of autonomy granted to scholars in Eastern and Western Europe, and partly to the 'limits imposed on memory in a post-totalitarian society' (Scheffel and Kandert 1994: 16, 21, 22).

This contribution, like Jeřábek's 1992 article, was published in English and therefore was inaccessible to most Czech and Slovak researchers. When my Czech translation of Scheffel and Kandert's article appeared in 2002, it caused an avalanche of criticism, sometimes harsh, accusing the authors of factual inaccuracies and distortions. In my commentary, I stressed that the authors failed to distinguish between *národopis* and *etnografie* and that the transition to the latter, heralded by the Marxist generation, never really succeeded. In fact pre-revolutionary Russian and Soviet *etnografiya* *did* study the societies of the world comparatively and thus emphasised theoretical questions. This never happened in communist Czechoslovakia (Skalník 2002).

To close this extended discussion of the pros and cons of socialist era anthropology, I think it appropriate to mention the MA thesis of Jan Grill (2004), a young man with no stake in the past oppositions. He concentrated on a critical analysis of the 1950s in the development of Czech conceptions of 'folk' in order to question the view that assumes a radical disjuncture between pre-1948 *národopis* and the 'new progressive' Marxist-Leninist *etnografie*. Grill demonstrated the falsity of the 'essentialist logic implicitly assuming the existence of real authentic folk culture'. The 'real authentic' alternative vision of *lid* coined by the Marxist-Leninist scholars was just as

---

[13] Scheffel was born in Prague of Czech parents in 1955. He was socialised in Czechoslovakia and the Netherlands before making his home and career in Canada. After 1990 he spent six months in Brno and later embarked upon fieldwork among the Roma of eastern Slovakia.

false as the rejected bourgeois conceptualisation. It was always misleading to assume a 'correct version' of folk culture and national identity, one independent of political influences. The concept of folk 'has always been [a] politicised category serving to legitimise certain ideological ends. Thus, the category of folk remained continuously *essentialist* in form although the ideological messages it carried changed' (Grill 2004: 85).

References

Abramzon, S. M. 1952. O národopisném studiu kolchozního rolnictva. Translated from Russian by H. Hynková. *Český lid* 39 (11–12): 275–77.

Asad, T. (ed.). 1973. *Anthropology and the Colonial Encounter*. London: Ithaca Press.

Bausinger, H. 1961. *Volkskultur in der technischen Welt*. Stuttgart: Kohlhammer.

Beneš, B. 1972. P. G. Bogatyrev a národopis Čechů a Slováků. *Národopisný věstník československý* 7 (1–2): 231–48.

Bogoraz-Tan, V. G. (ed.) 1924. *Staryy i novyy byt*. Leningrad: Gosizdat.

Bromlej, J. V. 1980. *Etnos a etnografia*. Bratislava: Veda.

Brouček, S., Cvekl, J., Hubinger, V., Grulich, T., Kořalka, J., Uherek, Z. and Vasiljev, I. 1991. Základní pojmy etnické teorie. *Český lid* 78 (4): 237-60.

Chotek, K. 1937. *Lidová kultura a kroje v Československu*. Praha: Novina.

———. 1949. Otázka periodisace československé lidové kultury. *Český lid* 4 (1–2): 19–25.

Claessen, H. J. M., and P. Skalník (eds.). 1978. *The Early State*. The Hague: Mouton.

Copans, J. 1970-71. Anthropologie et impérialisme. *LesTemps modernes* 27 (293-294): 1121-93.

Gluckman, M. 1965. *Government, Law and Ritual in Tribal Societies*. Oxford: Basil Blackwell.

Grill, J. 2004. Re-conceptualizing the Folk: Politics of Culture in Czech and Slovak Ethnography. Unpublished MA thesis, Central European University, Budapest.

Holý, L. 1963. *Rozpad rodového zřízení ve východoafrickém Mezijezeří*. With English summary. Praha: Academia.

———. (ed.). 1968. *Social Stratification in Tribal Africa*. Prague: Academia.

———. 1974. *Neighbours and Kinsmen: A Study of the Berti People of Darfur*. London: Hurst.

——, and M. Stuchlík. 1964. Co je a co není etnografie. *Český lid* 51 (4): 228-33.

Hubinger, V. 1990. K vymezení a užití termínu lid v etnografii. *Český lid* 77 (1): 40–46.

Jeřábek, R. 1967. La théorie de l'art populaire dans l'oeuvre d'Antonín Václavík. *Národopisný věstník československý* 35: 3–20.

——. 1991. Antonín Václavík a sebekritika. *Český lid* 78 (3): 216–21.

——. 1992. Czech Studies of Folk Life from Ethnography to European Ethnology. *Anthropological Journal of European Cultures* 1 (2): 37–51.

——. 1998. Z Šavla Pavlem? *Národopisná revue* 8: 52–55.

——, et al. 1991. Etnografie bez ideologie (a co dál?). *Umění a řemesla* 1-2: 1–9.

Jiřikovská, V., and Z. Mišurec. 1991. Příspěvek k vývoji české etnografie a folkloristiky a Národopisné společnosti československé při ČSAV po únoru 1948. *Národopisný věstník československý* 8: 5–35.

Kandert, J. 2001. Ethnographic Research on Religion during the Socialist Era: The Czech Case. In I. Doležalová, L. H. Martin, and D. Papoušek (eds.), *The Academic Study of Religion during the Cold War*, pp. 95–104. New York: Peter Lang.

Kisljakov, N. A. 1952. K otázce o ethnografickém studiu kolchozů. Translated from Russian by K. Fojtík. *Český lid* 39 (1–2): 32–33.

Kosven, M. O. 1952. *Matriarchát: Dějiny problému.* Translated from Russian by L. Kotačka. Praha: Melantrich.

Kušner (Knyšev), P. I. 1952. O ethnografickém studiu kolchozního rolnictva. Translated from Russian by H. Hynková. *Český lid* 39 (5–6): 117–20.

Kramařík, J. 1952a. K některým otázkám národopisného výzkumu družstevní vesnice. *Český lid* 39 (1–2): 3–5.

Kramařík, J. 1952b. Sedmdesát let profesora Dr Karla Chotka. *Český lid* 6 (5–6): 131–32.

——, and O. Nahodil (eds.). 1953. *Anglo-americká etnografie ve službách imperialismu.* Translated from Russian by K. Fojtík, I. Heroldová, J. Chlíbec, and M. Thérová. Praha: Nakladatelství Československosovětského institutu.

Lips, J. 1960. O původu věcí. Praha: Orbis. (translated from the German original *Vom Ursprung der Dinge: Eine Kulturgeschichte des Menschen*). Leipzig: Brockhaus.

Mácha, K. (ed.). 1983. *Kultur und Tradition: Festschrift für Prof. Dr. Dr.Sc. Otakar Nahodil.* Integrale Anthropologie 4. Munich: Minerva Publikation.

Melicherčík, A. 1945. *Teória národopisu.* Liptovský sv. Mikuláš: Tranoscius.

———. 1946. Etnografia ako veda. *Národopisný sborník* 6 (1): 1-13.

———. 1950. Československá etnografia a niektoré jej úlohy pri výstavbe socializmu. *Národopisný sborník SAVU* 9: 25–36.

———. 1952. Sovietska etnografia: Náš vzor. *Národopisný sborník SAVU* 10: 5–23.

———. (ed.). 1954. *Rodová spoločnosť: Národopisné materiály a výskumy.* Foreword by A. Melicherčík. Translated from Russian by J. Pagáč. Bratislava: Vydavateľstvo SAV.

Mjartan, J. 1952. Niektoré otázky národopisného výskumu družstevnej dediny. *Národopisný sborník SAVU* 11: 5–17.

Moravcová, M. 1986. *Národní oděv roku 1848: Ke vzniku národně politického symbolu.* Praha: Academia.

———. 2003. Univ. Prof. PhDr. Antonín Robek, DrSc. 31.8.1931 v Zeměchách. *Lidé města* 9: 147–50.

Morgan, L. H. 1954. *Pravěká společnost.* Translated from English by J. Hornát and V. Šolc. Foreword by O. Nahodil. Praha: NČSAV.

Nahodil, O. 1949. Foreword. In *Sovětská škola v národopise,* by S. P. Tolstov. Translated from Russian by O. Nahodil. Praha: Umění lidu péčí ministerstva informací a osvěty u příležitosti I. národopisné konference.

———. 1950. *Sovětský národopis a jeho pokroková úloha.* Praha: Svět sovětů.

———. 1954a. *O původu náboženství.* Praha: Orbis.

———. 1954b. *Jak vznikly náboženské pověry.* Praha: Mladá fronta.

———. 1956. *Vznik náboženství.* Praha: Orbis.

———. 1957. *O kultuře prvobytné společnosti.* Praha: Státní nakladatelství politické literatury.

———. 1959–60. Mateřské kulty. *Československá etnografie* 7 (1): 3–12, (3): 233–43, (4): 348–65; 8 (1): 3–20, (2): 119–38.

———. 1995. *Totalitní hodnocení totality.* Praha: The Author.

———, and J. Kramařík. 1951. Práce J. V. Stalina o marxismu v jazykovědě a některé otázky současné ethnografie. *Český lid* 6 (1–2): 6–17.

———, ———. 1952. *J. V. Stalin a národopisná věda.* Praha: Nakladatelství Československo-sovětského institutu.

———, and A. Robek. 1959. *České lidové pověry.* Praha: Orbis.

———, ———. 1961. *Původ náboženství.* Praha: Orbis.

Niederle, L. 1909. *Slovanský svět. Zeměpisný a statistický obraz současného Slovanstva.* Praha: Laichter.

———. 1953. *Rukověť slovanských starožitností.* Praha: Nakladatelství Československé akademie věd.

Ol'derogge, D. A., and I. I. Potekhin (eds.). 1953. *Anglo-americká etnografie ve službách imperialismu*. Praha: Nakladatelství československo-sovětského institutu.

Pertold. 1956. *Co je náboženství*. Praha: Naše vojsko.

Petráňová, L., and F. Bahenský. 2002. Institucionální základna českého národopisu v letech tzv. budování socialismu a profilace hlavních periodik. In M. Holubová, L. Petráňová, and J. Woitsch (eds.), *Česká etnologie 2000*, pp. 185–209. Praha: Etnologický ústav Akademie věd České republiky.

Peuckert, W.-E. 1931. *Volkskunde des Proletariats. Aufgang der proletarischen Kultur (Teil 1)*. Frankfurt am Main: Neuer Frankfurter Verlag.

Podolák, J. 1991. Jubileum národopisu na Univerzitě Komenského v Bratislavě. *Český lid* 78 (3): 222–26 [For a much longer English version, see author's Seventy years of ethnology at Comenius University in Bratislava (1921-1991). *Ethnologia Slavica* 23: 221-41].

———. 2003. Etnológia na Slovensku v 20. storočí: Etapy jej vývoja. *Ethnologia Actualis Slovaca* 3: 9–58.

Potekhin, I. I. 1948. Funktsional'naya shkola etnografii na sluzhbe britanskogo imperializma. *Sovetskaya etnografiya* 3: 33-49.

Pražák, V. 1947. Úkoly a organisace slovenského národopisu v přítomné době. *Národopisný sborník SAVU* 8 (1): 1–21.

Robek, A., M. Moravcová, and J. Šťastná (eds.). 1981. *Stará dělnická Praha*. Praha: Academia.

Robakidze, A. I. 1952. K některým sporným otázkám ethnografického studia nového způsobu života. Translated from Russian by O. Nahodil. *Český lid* 39 (7–8): 171–75.

Šalanda, B. 1986. Prof. Dr. Antonín Robek, DrSc—55 let. *Český lid* 73: 182.

Scheffel, D., and J. Kandert. 1994. Politics and Culture in Czech Ethnography. *Anthropological Quarterly* 67 (1): 15–23.

Skalník, P. 1973a. Dynamics of Early State Development in the Voltaic Area (West Africa). Unpublished Candidate of Science thesis. Prague: Charles University.

———. 1973b. Engels über die vorkapitalistischen Gesellschaften und die Ergebnisse der modernen Ethnologie [summaries in Russian and German]. *Philosophica* 12–13: 405–14.

———. 1976. Translation of 'Výpisky K. Marxa o fetišizme' [K. Marx's excerpts on fetishism] from German into Slovak. In K. Marx and F. Engels, *O ateizme, náboženstve a cirkvi*, pp. 394–413. Bratislava: Pravda.

———. 2002. Komentář k článku Davida Scheffela a Josefa Kanderta 'Politika a Kultura v české etnografii'. In M. Holubová, L. Petráňová, and J. Woitsch (eds.), *Česká Etnologie 2000*, pp. 231–34. Praha: Etnologický ústav Akademie věd České republiky.

Skalníková, O. 1951a. Za nový Český lid. *Český lid* 38 (1–2): 1.

———. 1951b. Budování socialismu na vesnici a několik národopisných poznámek. *Český lid* 38 (1–2): 23–24.

———. 1952. K otázce národopisného výzkumu života dělnické třídy. *Český lid* 39 (7–8): 147–51.

———. (ed.). 1959. *Kladensko: Život lidu v průmyslové oblasti*. Praha: Nakladatelství ČSAV.

———, and K. Fojtík. 1971. *K teorii etnografie současnosti*. Praha: Academia.

Stuchlík, M. 1962. Batak Social and Political Organisation. *Annals of the Náprstek Museum* 1: 101–22, 2: 69-139.

Tolstov, S. P. 1949. Sovětská škola v národopise. Translated from Russian by O. Nahodil. Praha: Umění lidu péčí ministerstva informací a osvěty u příležitosti I. národopisné konference.

Toman, J. 1995. *The Magic of a Common Language: Mathesius, Jakobson, Trubetzkoy, and the Prague Circle*. Cambridge, Mass.: MIT Press.

Václavík, A. 1952. Příspěvek k diskusi o některých otázkách naší etnografie. *Český lid* 39 (5–6): 137–43.

Vařeka, J. 1970. K šedesátinám univ. doc. dr. Josefa Voráčka. *Český lid* 57 (1): 1–4.

Voráček, J. 1934. Příspěvek k sociologii německého hnutí národně-socialistického. *Sociální problémy* III: 96-101.

———. 1936. *Počátky vlastnictví a práva ve světle ethnologie a sociologie*. Praha: Melantrich.

———. 1940. *Úvod do studia člověka, společnosti a civilisace: Člověk a společnost na nižších stupních vývoje a kultury*. Praha: Česká grafická unie.

———. 1941. *Primitivní rodina: Rozprava o theoriích a methodách ethnologické sociologie*. Praha: Česká akademie věd a umění.

Vorobjev, N. I. 1952. K otázce o ethnografickém studiu kolchozního rolnictva. Translated from Russian by O. Nahodil. *Český lid* 39 (5–6): 120–22.

Vorobjov, N. J. 1952. Program pre sbieranie materiálu na skúmanie súčasného spôsobu života kolchoznej dediny a dejín jej formovania u národností stredného Povolžia. *Národopisný sborník SAVU* 11: 11-58.

Vozdviženskaja, O. N., and L. P. Lašuk. 1952. O některých otázkách ethnografického studia kolchozního rolnictva. Translated from Russian by K. Fojtík. *Český lid* 39 (1–2): 33–35.

Wolf, J. 1969. Kulturní a sociální antropologie, její historické a metodologické předpoklady v ČSSR. *Sociologický časopis* 5 (4): 361–68.

———. (ed.). 1971. *Kulturní a sociální antropologie*. Sociologická knižnice. Praha: Svoboda.

———. (ed.). 2002. *Integrální antropologie na prahu 21. století*. Praha: Karolinum.

Chapter 4
Hungarian Anthropology in the Socialist Era: Theories, Methodologies, and Undercurrents

Mihály Sárkány

In 1949 Gyula Ortutay, Hungary's minister of education and religion, delivered a lecture to the Hungarian Ethnographical Society (Magyar Néprajzi Társaság) entitled 'Questions of Principles in Hungarian Néprajz'. The word *néprajz* in Hungarian covers all those fields known as ethnography, ethnology, and folklore in other Continental European languages and as social or cultural anthropology in the English-speaking world. This speech can be read today as a kind of manifesto—an attempt at radical reorientation, a signal of a new paradigm—and so it is worth considering it closely.

Nineteen forty-nine was the year when the communist takeover of power was institutionalised in the European countries that remained under Soviet control after the Second World War. The consolidation of political power was followed by a reform of intellectual life, including that of the academic community. The social sciences and humanities were subjected to especially close scrutiny as possible sources of opinions that might call into question socialist attitudes towards social order, democracy, state loyalty, and the nation. As a result of this concern, sociology was soon condemned as a bourgeois science and banned. Gyula Ortutay's speech should be considered in this context.

In addition to his political position, Ortutay was a professor of folklore at the University of Budapest and a corresponding member of the Hungarian Academy of Sciences. Since 1934 he had published a considerable body of work, and he was undoubtedly the most representative figure of the discipline to express a critical stance towards the scholarly output of the previous generation. From the very beginning of his career Ortutay had advocated a different approach to the study of folk culture and rural society (Ortutay 1935, 1937; the latter in English as Ortutay 1972: 15–63.). This approach was based upon an innovative combination of structural-functionalist principles and a dynamic view of socio-cultural change (Sárkány 1972: 527; Bodrogi 1983: 15–16).

The first part of Ortutay's lecture was devoted to a critique, and it began with a repetition of his earlier attacks on traditional Hungarian néprajz. The gist of the criticism was that Hungarian anthropologists had not paid proper attention to social stratification, tensions, and historical changes in rural society. According to Ortutay the neglect was ongoing: 'Our scholars are still degrading the peasant, romanticising and mystifying him, just as they did in the past' (1949: 11). A new research philosophy was needed to make the discipline of néprajz socially relevant. The necessary theoretical and methodological tools were to be created on the basis of Marxism and Leninism, with due regard for historicism and application of the dialectical method. It was time to reconsider the category *nép* (folk, people) and to extend research to the socialist transformation of rural life and to the culture of the working classes. The only Hungarian authors mentioned in the lecture were himself, the object of modest self-criticism, and Edit Fél, the object of a justified but unacceptably harsh critique because she had allegedly neglected the socio-economic conditions of the rural population in her recently published guidelines to the study of Hungarian folk society (Fél 1948). Ortutay warned against adopting the research strategies of Western anthropology and suggested instead following the trends of Soviet scholarship.

The second part of his lecture consisted of a series of propositions concerning research topics and methodology. The main focus was Hungarian folk culture, but Ortutay also took the opportunity to advise scholars of non-European regions that they should study the consequences of colonialism and struggle to overcome racism and various other ideological shortcomings.

This seemingly revolutionary lecture was not discussed in the néprajz community in the years that followed. This was not unusual in Hungarian anthropology. For example, Lajos Katona's conceptual elaboration of ethnographia, ethnologia, and folklore as a complex, multi-level, triangular research field had gone unchallenged since its publication in 1890. Katona's sophisticated abstractions were replaced in practice by a commonsense understanding which, within néprajz, separated the study of material culture from the study of mental phenomena and designated etnológia as the branch investigating non-European cultures and societies, ideally in their pre-colonial conditions, which could be assumed to represent an earlier stage of a common human evolution (Solymossy 1926).[1] Ortutay criticised this way of dividing up the study of culture, yet he introduced the same classifications when, in 1951, néprajz was split into separate departments of material cul-

---

[1] The term *etnológia* has recently begun a new career in Hungary and in some other countries of Central and Eastern Europe. It has been incorporated into the names of several institutions to indicate an expanded, or at any rate more modern, range of research interests, moving beyond the dominant national paradigm of néprajz and its equivalents (Godina 2002).

ture and folklore at the University of Budapest. Throughout the decades in which this division has been maintained, leading scholars have lamented the lack of interest in theory and methodology (Niedermüller 1989; Kósa 2001: 203).

The lack of discussion did not mean that the lecture had no effect. It was taken for granted that Marxism-Leninism, particularly the simplified Marxist schema of human evolution, in which there was no room for the 'Asiatic mode of production', was the only possible theoretical starting point. The works of Marx, Engels, Lenin, and Stalin were published, read, and often quoted, but their theoretical contributions to anthropology were not analysed at the time. The voluminous works of Marx and Engels offered no distinctive theories concerning popular culture and rural society in Europe. With Lenin and Stalin the situation was different, thanks in particular to their interest in national questions. Until 1955 it was common to praise Stalin for his insistence that, although national forms might persist, they must acquire new socialist cultural contents (e.g. Kardos 1954: 437).

The concept of the nép was redefined by Ortutay himself. In Hungarian the word has both an ethnic meaning (as in the German *Volk*) and a sociological meaning (in the sense of the French *peuple*). Ortutay called on anthropologists to restrict its usage to the working people (*dolgozó nép*)— those who were serfs under feudalism and were now the exploited social classes under capitalism, who would 'represent something new, a qualitative change both in content and in form' under socialism (Ortutay 1955: 37). This simplistic solution did little to enrich earlier discussions, but it did express the new policy of extending the scope of anthropology to include the urban working class.

A five-year plan was elaborated and working groups were formed to investigate various topics and subfields. The main authors of the plan were Linda Dégh, a lecturer in the Department of Folklore (later a professor of folklore in Bloomington, Indiana), László Vajda, an etnológia specialist who also lectured in the Department of Folklore (later a professor of Völkerkunde in Munich), and István Tálasi, a professor in the Department of Material Culture at the University of Budapest from 1951 to 1980 (see Kuti, this volume). This attempt to systematise research was supplemented by the establishment of a new control organ, an Anthropological Committee (Néprajzi Bizottság) affiliated with the Hungarian Academy of Sciences.

Anthropologists with non-European interests in the small group centred on László Vajda digested Ortutay's message promptly and began to address the consequences of colonialism. An early brilliant result was Tibor

Bodrogi's study of cargo cults in Melanesia, published in 1951, which launched his career as a specialist in Oceania.[2]

To promote the Soviet example, translations were published from the journal *Sovetskaya etnografiya* in a series called Szovjet néprajztudomány, published by the Museum of Ethnography (Néprajzi Múzeum) between 1950 and 1954. Long articles in the leading journal *Ethnographia* also propagated the main goals and problems of the Soviet discipline (Tolsztov 1949; Tokarjev 1950). Ideologically important issues such as that of the matriarchate as a stage in social evolution (Koszven 1950) and the links between Anglo-American anthropological research and imperialism (Potehin 1953) were addressed in separate publications. Soviet research into ethnogenesis and ethnic specificities attracted the attention of several scholars, among them Vilmos Diószegi, who tried to draw out ethnogenetic consequences from his investigations of Siberian shamanism (Diószegi 1954). This idea reappeared in his interpretation of the distribution of a folk-belief phenomenon which he connected to an internal migration within Hungary (Diószegi 1968). Because both his research strategy and his topic connected him to Soviet scholarship, Diószegi was denounced by the Hungarian émigré Paul Vezényi (1960: 97) as a 'typical representative of communist anthropology in Hungary'. His achievements in Siberia were, however, highly valued in international scholarship. One indication of the recognition of his expertise was the invitation he received to contribute an entry on shamanism to the *Encyclopedia Britannica* (Diószegi 1974).

László Vajda (1954) emphasised the search for ethnic specificities as anthropology's key contribution to the study of universal history. In addition to Soviet publications he relied heavily on the epistemological guidelines offered by Wilhelm Mühlmann in his *Methodik der Völkerkunde*, though he was careful to keep his distance from Mühlmann's theory of the Volk and criticised his racism (see Mühlmann 1938: 227–36). Vajda's paper triggered an exchange of opinions that amounted to perhaps the best debate of the period (see Kuti, this volume), but it had one unforeseen consequence. Because anthropologists had long documented their materials according to ethnic classifications, the new interest in ethnic specificities gave additional succour to those who were determined to explain cultural differences in terms of ethnic differences rather than seeking explanations in social praxis or in other cultural forms.

Some effort was also made to stimulate research into changes in rural society and into the culture of the working classes. It brought limited results, for it was impossible to analyse phenomena of the socialist period in a credible way (Sozan 1977: 313–15). Papers devoted to those features of

---

[2] Cf. Worsley 1957; Lawrence 1964.

material culture studied traditionally were generally more reliable (e.g. K. Csilléry 1952; Bakó 1953; for discussion see Sárkány 2000: 55–56). The study of workers was organised by the Workers' Folklore group, headed by Ortutay himself. Linda Dégh (1953) published a guide for investigating workers ethnographically, but the yield was small. The only major work was a monograph on the *kubikos* ('navvy') construction workers, but even this monograph appeared only in an abridged form (Katona 1957). It dealt with material objects but also with work processes and the general organisation and conditions of the way of life of this very large group of workers.

The collection of data in a campaign-like manner was justified in terms of consolidating a 'progressive tradition'. Amateur enthusiasts were encouraged to collect materials which would forge 'new weapons ... for the construction of socialism, in the fight for peace' (*Az Országos* 1953: 1–2.). A short questionnaire was published for this purpose. Nationwide interest in popular traditions could be traced back into the 1930s, but it received new impetus in the People's Republic. The result was a huge accumulation of data and the formation of folk-dance groups and many other associations devoted to the preservation of folk traditions. Unfortunately, quantity did not translate into quality in terms of scientific output.

The Research Strategies of a Generation

The continuity to be observed in Hungarian néprajz research in the first decades of socialism derived to a large extent from three professors who were close contemporaries. I have already mentioned Gyula Ortutay and István Tálasi, both born in 1910. The third key figure was Béla Gunda, born in 1911 and a lecturer (later professor) in the Department of Néprajz at the University of Debrecen.

Ortutay promoted the study of folktales with the approach he had in-troduced in the 1930s, which involved a concentration on the re-creation of tales by their tellers. The role of the individual and his or her position in the social context was more important than attempting to reconstruct a historical geography revealing how the tale in question had spread. This approach owed something to the experiments of the psychologist Frederic Bartlett and also to the Russian folkloristics of the 1930s (Lindgren 1939: 348–51, 359–63). Ortutay and his students provided full documentation of the social background and personality traits of storytellers and of the occasions when folktales were narrated; they also published volumes containing the full folktale knowledge of some outstanding storytellers, including the same tales in several variants. A theoretical paper Ortutay wrote in 1958, discussing both the principles of oral transmission and the principles which determine the patterning of variants, remains even today a valuable contribution to the field (Ortutay 1972: 132–74). The results of the folktale research undertaken in the early years of socialism were summarised in German by Linda Dégh (1962). Shortly afterwards, however, the Budapest school of folkloristics adopted quite new research goals and methods.

The results of the historical study of material culture were even more notable. István Tálasi was the great initiator, but in a sense this was a collective programme (see Kuti, this volume). Tálasi proposed new answers to old problems, including the Schlegelian question of Hungary's interstitial location between East and West. Since the nineteenth century Hungarian scholars, anthropologists prominent among them, had classified the country in terms of a dual heritage: the nomadic eastern traditions, derived from ancient times, and the western elements, which had penetrated deeply into Hungarian popular culture over the centuries. Tálasi and some of his students drew on written historical sources as well as archaeological findings and linguistic studies to argue that the most conspicuous 'nomadic', or 'eastern', cultural traits—Hungarian animal husbandry and the settlement patterns of the Great Plain—were actually formed in the Middle Ages or even later. He explained their evolution with reference to agro-economic and social factors and to international trading networks. The familiar dichotomy between 'eastern' and 'western' was reinterpreted in many cases with a time dimension replacing the spatial reference. Sometimes the 'eastern' cultural option was selected because it was more conducive to higher productivity than were established 'western' traits. For example, harvesting with a scythe rather than a sickle and utilising cereals as hay were both practices that increased the efficiency of labour under the conditions which prevailed in many parts of the Carpathian basin.

In addition to focusing on well-known cultural traits, from their genesis through the phases of institutionalisation, routinisation, and eventual erosion, Tálasi and his students investigated new elements in agriculture, such as the production of maize, potatoes, tobacco, and paprika, and new tools. These studies demystified traditions and contributed to a much better understanding of the economic and social history of the agrarian population. From the 1960s onwards, enquiries into material culture were supplemented by detailed analyses of property relations and social stratification (e.g. Hoffmann 1963; Takács 1964, 1976, 1987; Kósa 1980; Tálasi 1981).[3]

From his formative years in the 1930s, Béla Gunda maintained a life-long interest in cultural historical and 'cultural morphological' issues in the German and Scandinavian traditions, though his view of anthropology was

---

[3] Tálasi's efforts to explain cultural forms by reference to social context had parallels in research into the origins of ballads (Vargyas 1983) and in the study of calendrical customs and folk beliefs (Dömötör 1964).

by no means confined to these approaches and he encouraged his students to tackle many other kinds of issues. The search for archaic cultural forms and the attempt to map the diffusion of cultural traits and cultural layers made much use of archaeological and linguistic evidence and relied only minimally on written historical sources (e.g. Gunda 1966, 1984). One significant outcome of these efforts was the publication of ethnographic atlases. Gunda had proposed to make such an atlas in Hungary in 1939 and work began on it within the framework of the first five-year plan in the 1950s; but the first results were published only at the very end of the socialist period, under the title *Magyar néprajzi atlasz* (Atlas of Hungarian Folk Culture; Barabás 1987–92). The most elaborate discussion of the cartographic method in anthropology was published by Jenő Barabás, editor of the atlas. He had earlier defined anthropology as 'a science of culture that aims at the discovery of laws governing the formation of culture' in time and space (Barabás 1963: 8). The published atlas, by definition, demonstrates an atomistic view of culture. With more than 900 maps and accompanying photos from around the turn of the twentieth century, it forms an enormous storehouse of peasant cultural forms. It satisfies the demand of Fritz Graebner (1911: 7) that 'the precondition of every scientific work is reliable research material'.

All three professors shared an interest, a heritage of the 1930s, in elaborating the ethnic and cultural divisions of the Hungarian language area and the role of internal migrations. Károly Viski, one of the authors of the massive encyclopaedia *Magyarság néprajza* (Czakó 1933–37), was the pioneer in this field. His regional classifications drew on the work of his anthropological predecessors in the nineteenth and early twentieth centuries and also relied heavily on linguistic studies (Viski 1938). László Kósa, a leading historian of Hungarian anthropology, has emphasised the lack of proper data and the methodological weakness of this kind of research, but also the continuity and caution characteristic of Viski's work (see e.g. Kósa 2001: 128–29). Yet it seems to me that Viski's caution in defining regional groupings allows for another interpretation, too. Viski can be interpreted as having reacted critically to a concept of history that was fashionable in this period, namely, the concept of *Volksgeschichte*, which presupposed a people that remained unitary over the centuries. Viski sought to demonstrate that the Hungarian people consisted of socially and culturally different components. It remained for subsequent researchers to clarify the factors behind these divisions, which according to Viski included not only differences in legal status (which had implications for identity consciousness) and geographical factors (which tended to promote regional identities) but also differences in ethnicity. Later research revealed further cultural differences deriving from economic and social relations and from the experience of different communication fields.

This agglomeration of problems gave rise to two distinct modes of research, one particularistic and the other more comprehensive. The particularists relied more on anthropological findings and local history in defining ethnic, regional, or 'ethnographical' groups. The *Magyar néprajzi atlasz* has become an important tool for checking established assumptions and clarifying questions concerning uncertain boundaries and unexpected phenomena; it has not yet been exploited by researchers as much as it deserves to be. István Tálasi, however, favored the comprehensive approach, which meant focusing on major waves of social and cultural development as manifested in the centre of the Hungarian language area (more or less close to the Danube) and then following their distribution to more remote places, the so-called archaic regions. This procedure was most fully implemented by László Kósa, a student of Tálasi's, who elaborated a comprehensive account of the regional differences within Hungarian folk culture in the era when the peasantry had begun to experience embourgeoisement (Kósa 1990).

If one asks how these research strategies were related to the imperative to apply a Marxist-Leninist orientation in anthropological research, the answer is that they were not. Although anthropologists cited Marx, Engels, Lenin, and Stalin, their actual research goals and methodologies derived from various intellectual strands in anthropology and history and not from the principles of historical materialism. On the other hand, Marxism-Leninism was of real help in explaining evolution, particularly the modification of cultural phenomena in changing social contexts. In this respect socialist ideology complemented 'bourgeois' historicist schools and supplemented them by adding materialist concerns which, though well developed in Western Europe, were either missing or only weakly developed in Hungarian anthropology before 1949.

The ideological need to develop the knowledge base appropriate for a modern socialist society brought some institutional enrichment to anthropology. It meant that the Néprajzi Múzeum grew into a research centre with a huge staff of museologists, although, because it was temporarily housed in one part of a former secondary school, it was unsuited to hosting major exhibitions. Many anthropologists found employment in regional and local museums all over the country as well. The situation was less favourable in the universities. Chairs were consolidated in Budapest and Debrecen after 1949, but Sándor Bálint, the professor of néprajz at Szeged University, was banned from teaching between 1951 and 1956. An important research institute of the pre-socialist period, the Néptudományi Intézet, was dissolved (Barna 2004: 217; Voigt 2004: 197–99).

These circumstances helped strengthen the historical orientation of Hungarian néprajz in the 1950s, but they were not the decisive factor. Not only was the historical orientation in keeping with disciplinary traditions, but it was also the only option available in an era when there was no possibility of preparing honest, unbiased analyses of contemporary social transformations. The embracing of this orientation in the 1950s had long-lasting consequences, because some of the projects established in the early phase of planning took several decades to complete. This hindered the diversification of anthropology to include the study of contemporary society, even when there were no longer any great political obstacles to such an agenda.

Proper Peasants and Openings to Social Anthropology

Although Gyula Ortutay criticised Edit Fél for not appreciating the relevance to anthropology of the studies carried out in the 1930s by rural sociologists and 'sociographers' (*szociográfusok*), she was in fact well trained in sociology. In 1941 she had published a pioneering monograph on the society of Kocs, a trans-Danubian village, in which she described the 'traditional' way of life and how it had changed in the course of the twentieth century. She showed herself sensitive to variations in this way of life according to generation and social stratum, and she argued that a process of organic embourgeoisement (*polgárosodás*) had been disrupted by excessively rapid social transformation.

In another study (1944), Fél gave the first detailed account of a joint family system. It was based on only three cases, and she did not claim that they were typical in a statistical sense, but these families were said to represent an image of the good life still widely held in the Hungarian countryside. Fél's description followed functionalist principles, but she also opened up a comparative perspective by discussing the history of the joint family as a cultural form. Whereas the latter perspective was typical of culture history approaches in European anthropology at this time, her sociological framework for the study of rural society followed the tradition of Ferdinand Tönnies. She adopted his distinction between Gemeinschaft (organic community) and Gesellschaft (the more organised structures characteristic of modern societies) and pinpointed those institutions and social relations which could legitimately be studied as survivals of the traditional 'folk culture'. Fél's work on the joint family was continued by Judit Morvay, who contributed an even more detailed and beautifully written example from the village of Bodony. There, too, the institution was no longer functioning in the present, but it had persisted until the early twentieth century, and Morvay was able to construct an analytical description of the relations within and between the generations and between genders.

In 1951 Edit Fél launched the celebrated field study of the Great Plain village of Átány. Tamás Hofer joined the project in 1954, and fieldwork continued until 1966. Fél and Hofer were heavily influenced by American cultural anthropological studies of the peasantry, notably those of Robert Redfield. Like him, they sought to subordinate an atomistic approach—that is, the detailed study of cultural items separately, for their own sake—to the need to render a comprehensive view of the entire way of life of the 'proper peasant'. In doing so they retained the meticulous techniques and long-term historical perspective characteristic of Hungarian anthropology.

The results were published in three monographs, each dealing with a different dimension of this way of life. The first volume, *Proper Peasants* (Fél and Hofer 1969), was published in English. It analysed social relations in this stratified community with an emphasis on the well-to-do, the minority which was able to realise the ideal model. The second volume (Fél and Hofer 1972) was published in German and focused more on peasants' 'ways of thinking' and decision-taking with regard to their environment, work, and other situations in life. The third volume (Fél and Hofer 1974) dealt with the material environment and people's relations to their tools.

This remarkable trilogy has become a classic not just of Hungarian anthropology. The villagers of Átány are archetypal representatives of the proper peasant, a type which was on the point of disappearing in most of Eastern Europe as a result of the forced collectivisation of agriculture. In this sense the Átány volumes, in which the looming socialist transformation of rural society is barely mentioned, are oriented towards the past. Nevertheless, publication in Hungary was not authorised at the time the books were written (see Hofer, this volume), and they were not made fully available in Hungarian until after 1990. Although they found no direct imitators, interest in the expanding field of peasant studies continued to grow, as we shall see later.

The Átány project and other work by Edit Fél prove that the roots of a more sociologically oriented approach in Hungarian anthropology can be traced back to before the revolution of 1956. However, social anthropological interests expanded significantly only with the publication of a path-breaking paper by Tibor Bodrogi in the journal *Ethnographia* in 1957. Although the study carried the modest title 'On the Question of Anthropological Terminology', Bodrogi offered not only a systematic vocabulary for the description and analysis of kinship and the family but also a survey of the achievements of British and American anthropology in this field and an indication of unsolved problems. He was not a devotee of any 'school' in anthropology, accepting the statements of Marx and Engels on the early condition of mankind only to the extent that these were supported by later research. At the same time, he never questioned the relevance of a Marxist interpretation of history and social phenomena. In this 'terminological' paper he relied heavily on George Peter Murdock's *Social Structure* (1949) in clarifying concepts of social organisation, but he drew also on notions of Lewis Henry Morgan's and Alfred R. Radcliffe-Brown's. Bodrogi also published his ideas about tribal societies in a small book for the wider public (Bodrogi 1962a). Both this and his more specialised works became important components in the training of anthropologists in Hungary and contributed to its modernisation.

For Hungarian research, his paper exploring Hungarian kinship terminology had a more direct impact (in English, Bodrogi 1962b). His model was based on data from various sources and distinguished a 'rural' from an 'urban' type of terminology. Bodrogi carried out a structural-functional analysis of both, demonstrating their continuity but also pinpointing changes. He came to the conclusion that the 'rural' variant displayed features similar to the Ostyak terminology published by Wolfgang Steinitz (1957), whereas the 'urban' variant reflected a different stage of social development, namely, a kinship organisation composed of economically independent nuclear families. Bodrogi's presentation became a model for further descriptions, and his suggestions enlivened the study of Hungarian kinship in the following decades. A profound study of changes in kinship terminology was published by the linguist Réka J. Lőrinczi (1980), and anthropologists collaborated with historians in studying the connections between economic organisation and family patterns. One historian built a bridge between anthropological scholarship on the Hungarian case and historical demography (Faragó 1983).

Bodrogi himself pursued another topic inherited from Morgan, that of an 'Uralic system' of kinship. Comparing the kinship terminologies of Finno-Ugric peoples, he surpassed his predecessor in reconstructing the main features of such a system with the help of Ob-Ugrian kinship terms, explaining their absence in the languages of other Finno-Ugric groups with reference to the dissolution of the clan system (Bodrogi 1975). These hypotheses, however, were not accepted unanimously (Sárkány 1998). Bodrogi's interest in Morgan's work and in evolutionism was not restricted to kinship studies; it was central to his life's work. He helped publish *Ancient Society* in Hungarian (Morgan 1961) and completed a voluminous monograph on Morgan in 1984, which unfortunately remains unpublished to this day.

Bodrogi's last contribution to kinship studies was a brilliant paper on the alleged matriarchy of the ancient Hungarians, a notion that had survived in the anthropological and historical literature despite his earlier efforts to eliminate unfounded concepts. By surveying the tool kit of anthropological concepts and drawing on a large body of comparative materials from Eurasia, he proved that the idea of the matriarchy could not be sustained (Bodrogi 1990).

Fieldwork on Other Continents

Bodrogi's Eurasian kinship studies were of great significance, but his main ethnographic activity was the study of the Oceanian collection in the Néprajzi Múzeum in Budapest (Vargyas 1998). He established an international reputation as a specialist in tribal art, and his books enabled Hungarian readers to appreciate the art of other continents. The last of them, in particular, was a great synthesis, which demonstrated his ability to mobilise regional specialists with diverse backgrounds and interests (Bodrogi 1982).

Although he travelled extensively, Bodrogi had no inclination to carry out long-term fieldwork. This possibility opened up in the milder political climate that developed after 1956, and several anthropologists took advantage of the opportunity. Vilmos Diószegi visited Siberia in 1957, 1958, and 1964 to study shamanism (Sántha 2003). Luiz (Lajos) Boglár worked with the Nambikuara in Brazil in 1959–60, with the Piaroa in Venezuela in 1967–68, 1974, and 1977, and with the Guarani in Brazil intermittently from 1979 onwards (he also worked in French Guyana right up to the time of his death in 2004; see Boglár 2000). Csaba Ecsedy spent six months in Sudan among the Hill Burun in 1972. Gábor Vargyas was able to carry out two years of fieldwork with the Bru of Vietnam in the 1980s. A few scholars studied the Hungarian diaspora in the United States (Fejős 1993; Hoppál 1989). All these field trips enriched anthropology in Hungary, but they were not connected by any unifying theory or thematic interest. The mobilizing theories continued to derive from armchair anthropologists.

Marxist Anthropology from the 1960s

The armchair theorists commonly had a profound knowledge of Marxism, some knowledge of which was obligatory for every university student after 1949, though few engaged with Marxism seriously to address research problems and methodology in anthropology. None was wedded to Stalinist dogmatism. From the point of view of non-European research, the most important theoretical works were those of Ferenc Tőkei, a Sinologist and philosopher who had also studied with László Vajda before the latter's departure to West Germany in 1956. Tőkei was one of those who tried to reinsert the concept of 'Asiatic mode of production' into the Marxist theory of history (see also Noack and Krause, this volume, pp. 37-40). He interpreted it as a socio-economic formation that was transitional between the 'ancient community' (primitive communism) and other formations (antique and feudal). But it was a deviation from the general road of social evolution and not a necessary stage in social evolution, even though it could be detected on many continents (Tőkei 1969).

Tőkei's main study of the Asiatic mode was ready for publication in 1960. He had the opportunity to deliver his main theses as a lecture in Paris in 1964, but he was not allowed to publish a book on the topic until 1965. Even then the publisher emphasised (in an unusual statement on an extra, unnumbered page at the beginning of the volume) that the work was a significant contribution to the exploration of 'this' problem (Tőkei 1965: n.p.). In a more general work on socio-economic formations (1968), Tőkei elaborated his critique of Stalin, whose inadequate concept of dialectic had hindered understanding of the Asiatic mode. In later years Tőkei was able to encourage archaeologists, orientalists, and historians as well as anthropologists to demonstrate the relevance of this concept in the study of societies in many parts of the world (Tőkei 1982, 1983, 1989). Between 1976 and Tőkei's retirement in 1990, this research was integrated in an Orientalists' Working Group (*Orientalisztikai Munkaközösség*) of the Hungarian Academy of Sciences.

Surprisingly, proposals to scrutinize Hungarian rural society and culture through the lens of Marxism had substantially less impact than Tőkei's contribution, although the efforts of one remarkable scholar must be considered an exception. Tamás Hoffmann was a student of István Tálasi's who tried to redefine the object of néprajz and the concept of the nép (people) in the light of the Marxist theory of socio-economic formations. He presupposed a connection between the ethnic meaning of the word *nép* and the concept of nép as deployed in the discipline of néprajz. This connection had been created in a particular moment of social evolution—that is, in the period when a capitalist society was emerging—when romantic anticapitalism and the imperative to construct nations shaped the formation of the new discipline. Consequently, the object of néprajz was to be the history of the way of life and cultural creativity of pre-capitalist populations. In Hoffmann's system, ethnology (etnológia) was the science of tribal societies, and sociology was the science of capitalist and subsequent societies. Each might masquerade as a comprehensive science of human society, but as long as problems and illusions inherited from earlier (feudal) formations survived, néprajz would still have a role to play in the study of both capitalist and socialist societies.

Hoffmann argued that to grasp the history of ways of life (*életmódok*) in all these formations and to render intelligible the various manifestations of the modern nép, it was necessary to lay out new theoretical and methodological principles on a Marxist foundation (Hoffmann 1975: 14–58). His efforts to promote a historical approach to rural culture and society met with wide acceptance, since they were in general accord with Hungarian research traditions. At the same time, Hoffmann's critical analyses of certain phenomena, and especially his demonstration that some cultural features should be viewed as misguided efforts, the results of historical constraints rather than magnificent creations, were rejected or neglected by the mainstream.

Although Hoffmann's approach was deeply rooted in historical materialism, he also drew on the work of British archaeologists and cultural geographers and of French historians of the Annales school. He explained the emergence or decline of cultural phenomena with reference to socio-economic constraints which operated according to regional divisions of labour and not ethnic or national frameworks. The best demonstrations of his ideas came in monographs which appeared after the collapse of socialism, after his retirement as director of the Néprajzi Múzeum (Hoffmann 1997–2001, 2004).

A third effort directly influenced by Marxism was that of Vilmos Voigt in folkloristics. It consisted in relating the aesthetic characteristics of folklore to the social-historical context and the elaboration of a methodology appropriate to this task (Voigt 1972a, 1972b). Voigt drew heavily on the Hegelian strands in Marxist aesthetics, on the philosophical work of Georg Lukács, and on his own exceptionally wide reading in practically every European language. His books remain to the present day standard works in the training of anthropologists in Hungary, but none of his students developed this work significantly. In time even their author moved on, and from 1968 onwards Voigt engaged ever more intensively with communication theory and semiotics (Voigt and Hoppál 2003: i) as well as contributing to many other themes in folkloristics.

Towards Western Anthropology

In a recent retrospective, Voigt reviewed the situation after 1965 as follows (2004: 200):

> When, beginning at the universities, ... from the second half of the 1960s the modernization of folklore, ethnology, and, but only to a limited extent, néprajz in Hungary finally happened, it took place not along Marxist (or even neo-Marxist) lines, but rather followed the paradigms of structuralism, communication theory, semiotics, symbolic anthropology, etc.; it also absorbed the new Soviet trends, such as 'typological conservativism' in folklore, Lotman's semiotics of culture, etc.

This list encapsulates Voigt's own interests and his role in mediating modern folkloristics and anthropology. It needs to be supplemented. About this time numerous researchers began to study contemporary social processes and to do so with reference to similar research elsewhere in Europe and on other continents. Economic anthropology, notably the ideas of Karl Polanyi, and the political analyses of British social anthropologists were introduced, not only as subjects of theoretical critiques but also by being put to work in applied studies (Ecsedy 1970, 1973; Sárkány 1970a, 1970b, 1973). Fieldwork was carried out on new topics such as contemporary religious life (Kardos 1969) and the communication system of a Hungarian village (Hoppál 1970).

The most significant initiative was a teamwork investigation of Varsány, a village in northern Hungary, carried out by the Institute of Ethnography of the Hungarian Academy of Sciences, which resulted in a volume on changing economic conditions, generational relations, morality, and related topics (Bodrogi 1978). A neighbouring village of Varsány, Nógrádsipek, was the subject of a similarly comprehensive study by folklorists in the 1970s (Szemerkényi 1980). These works on the contemporary village stimulated renewed interest among sociologists and political scientists in the socialist transformation of rural society. The results of the Varsány project were also disseminated internationally through the works of British and American anthropologists who worked in Hungary in the 1970s and 1980s and through a collective volume which brought the native and foreign scholars together (Hollos and Maday 1983).

Consolidation of Hungarian Anthropology: Institutions and Collective Works

The new directions I have noted remained marginal to Hungarian néprajz in the 1960s and 1970s, which witnessed an efflorescence of the dominant traditions of the discipline. Many well-trained scholars had graduated from the universities of Budapest and Debrecen in the 1950s and 1960s. Though they bore the stamps of their professors' diverse research interests, they found sufficient overlap to enable collaborative work that led to productive synergies and important contributions to international scholarship (e.g. Belényesy, Földes, and Gunda 1961; Földes 1969; Ortutay and Bodrogi 1965). It was a golden age for the realisation of old plans to prepare major syntheses of Hungarian folk culture.

The coordination of this research was undertaken by a newly established institute of the Hungarian Academy of Sciences (Paládi-Kovács 2001:

199).[4] Its first director was Gyula Ortutay, a member of the academy and still a high-ranking politician in those years. With this step anthropology gained the same status as other disciplines that had had such institutes since 1949, when scientific life was reorganised according to the Soviet example. The majority of the staff of the new institute continued the research interests of its three professors, but representatives of the new directions were also appointed. The fieldwork for the projects already mentioned—Hoppál's and those of the Varsány and Nógrádsipek teams—was carried out by young members of the institute. The blend of established tradition and innovation was well reflected in the first major common venture, the *Hungarian Anthropological Encyclopaedia* (*Magyar néprajzi lexikon*; Ortutay 1977–82), which, in addition to supplying an inventory of Hungarian folk culture, included entries on general anthropological concepts. Many of these concepts were defined and explained in Hungarian for the first time, and in this way the *Lexikon*, to which scholars from many other institutions also contributed, helped promote a far-reaching terminological reform of the discipline.

The foundation of the open-air museum (*skansen*) at Szentendre in 1967 was another important step in the consolidation of the discipline. Its staff carried out many important investigations of 'folk architecture' in the succeeding decades.

In 1975 the Néprajzi Múzeum completed its move into a splendid palace opposite Parliament. It was now able to mount large exhibitions, among them a standing exhibition which represented the peoples of the world arranged according to a principle of social evolution. However, at the very moment when it began to function as a real museum, its research staff was diminished (Fejős 2001: 23–24). Even so, and despite a small expansion in the number of university staff, the proportion of anthropologists working in museums remained high.[5] This helps explain the continuity of cultural morphological and historical research interests in this period, much of the work focusing on museum artifacts and archive materials.

This was the intellectual context in which it was decided in 1975 to prepare a new *Magyar néprajz*, a successor to the four-volume *Magyarság néprajza* of the 1930s (Czakó 1933–37). The main principle was that this compendium should represent a different attitude towards folk culture from

---

[4] Established in 1967, it was called the Néprajzi Kutatócsoport (since 1991, Néprajzi Intézet; the official English translation is now Institute of Ethnology; previously it was Institute of Ethnography).
[5] The staff expansion was especially visible at Szeged, where the department was reorganised in 1961. The proportion of anthropologists working in museums was 67 per cent in 1977 (Paládi-Kovács 1990: 37).

that of its predecessor: it was to demonstrate the results of historically oriented research and pay attention to numerous topics neglected in the *Magyarság néprajza* (see also Kuti, this volume). It soon became evident that many themes demanded a more profound historical investigation, and several significant monographs were born from this perception (e.g. Paládi-Kovács 1979, 1993a, b ; Kisbán 1989). It also became clear that the treatment of geographical and cultural differences deserved closer scrutiny than had been assumed (Kósa and Filep 1978; Paládi-Kovács 1980). Preparing the volume *Society* (the eighth to appear, in 2000, although much of the work was undertaken in the 1980s) was an inspiring task, particularly because it afforded an opportunity to extend the anthropological gaze to the way of life of bearers of traditional culture outside the countryside, including workers and even the nobility.

Overall it may be said that this period was fruitful, in the sense that a great deal of knowledge was accumulated and published to a high standard. Yet it must also be said that this knowledge was produced along traditional lines, only occasionally and cautiously transgressed; indeed, the modernizing efforts of the late 1960s and 1970s lost impetus in the last decade of socialism.

Following the free elections of 1990, the minister of education and culture in Hungary's first postsocialist government was again a néprajzos. Bertalan Andrásfalvy, a student of István Tálasi's with interests in historical ecology, the history of farming, folk dance, and ethnic traditions, was the recently appointed professor of anthropology in the new department established at the University of Pécs in 1989. He also became president of the Magyar Néprajzi Társaság, but unlike his predecessor, Gyula Ortutay, in 1949, he never addressed the society with a new strategy to transform the discpline.

This time the challenge came from a relatively young lecturer in the Department of Communication of the University of Pécs (Niedermüller 1989), who criticised the lack of theory in Hungarian anthropology and suggested that new theoretical and methodological foundations should be adapted from Western interpretive and symbolic anthropology. This paper triggered important theoretical discussions just as the socialist era drew to a close (Barabás 1990; Sárkány 1990). Its consequences, however, which included the formation of new departments of cultural anthropology, belong to another epoch and cannot be discussed here.

References

Az Országos társadalmi néprajzi gyűjtés tájékoztatója. 1953. Szerkesztette az Országos Néprajzi Múzeum Adattára és a Népművészeti Intézet Néprajzi Osztálya. Budapest: Művelt Nép Könyvkiadó.

Bakó, F. 1953. Adatok a szocializmus faluépítkezéseinek történetéhez. (A görgytarlói tanyaközpont kialakulása.) *Ethnographia* 64: 24–86.

Barabás, J. 1963. *Kartográfiai módszer a néprajzban.* Budapest: Akadémiai Kiadó.

—— (ed.). 1987–92. *Magyar néprajzi atlasz.* Budapest: Akadémiai Kiadó.

——. 1990. Válaszút vagy útvesztő? *BUKSZ* 2: 3–5.

Barna, G. 2004. The Szeged School of Ethnology. *Acta Ethnographica Hungarica* 49: 211–27.

Belényesy, M., L. Földes, and B. Gunda (eds.). 1961. *Viehzucht und Hirtenleben in Ostmitteleuropa.* Budapest: Akadémiai Kiadó.

Bodrogi, T. 1951. Colonization and Religious Movements in Melanesia. *Acta Ethnographica* 2: 159–292.

——. 1957. A néprajzi terminológia kérdéséhez. *Ethnographia* 68: 1–55.

——. 1962a. *Társadalmak születése.* Budapest: Gondolat.

——. 1962b. Some Problems Regarding Investigations into Hungarian Kinship Terminology. *Acta Ethnographica* 11: 273–91.

——. 1975. Die Gesellschaftsorganisation der Finnisch-Ugrischen Völker. *Congressus Quartus Internationalis Fenno-Ugristarum* 1: 103–20. Budapest: Akadémiai Kiadó.

——. (ed.). 1978. *Varsány: Tanulmányok egy észak-magyarországi falu társadalomnéprajzához.* Budapest: Akadémiai Kiadó.

—— (ed.). 1982. *Stammeskunst,* vols. 1–2. Budapest: Corvina.

——. 1983. A magyar társadalomnéprajz Ortutay Gyula korai műveiben. *Népi Kultúra—Népi Társadalom* 13: 11–37.

——. 1990. Hungarian Matriarchy? *Acta Ethnographica* 36: 3–40.

Boglár, L. 2000. *Pau brasil.* Budapest: Masszi Kiadó.

Czakó, E. (ed.). 1933–37. *Magyarság néprajza.* Budapest: Királyi Magyar Egyetemi Nyomda.

Dégh, L. 1953. *Útmutató a munkásosztály néprajzi vizsgálatához.* Budapest: Művelt Nép Könyvkiadó.

——. 1962. *Märchen, Erzähler und Erzählgemeinschaft.* Berlin: Akademie-Verlag.

Diószegi, V. 1954. A honfoglaló magyar nép hitvilága ('ősvallásunk') kutatásának módszertani kérdései. *Ethnographia* 65: 20–68.

——. 1968. A palóc etnokulturális csoport határa és kirajzásai. (Az égitestet evő mitikus lény, a markoláb elterjedésének tanulságai.) *Népi Kultúra—Népi Társadalom* 1: 217–51.

———. 1974. Shamanism. *Encyclopaedia Britannica*, 15th ed.

Dömötör, T. 1964. *Naptári ünnepek—népi színjátszás*. Budapest: Akadémiai Kiadó.

Ecsedy, Cs. 1970. A társadalmi struktúra kutatása a mai angol szociálantropológiában. *Népi Kultúra—Népi Társadalom* 4: 357–65.

———. 1973. Termelési viszonyok és tradicionális állam Fekete-Afrikában. *Dissertationes Ethnographicae* 1: 57–111.

Faragó, T. 1983. Háztartás, család, rokonság. *Ethnographia* 94: 216–54.

Fejős, Z. 1993. *A chicagoi magyarok két nemzedéke (1890-1940)*. Budapest: Közép-Európa Intézet.

———. 2001. The Museum of Ethnography. In M. Hoppál and E. Csonka-Takács, *Ethnology in Hungary: Institutional Background*, pp. 21–33. Budapest: European Folklore Institute.

Fél, E. 1941. *Kocs 1936-ban*. Budapest: Pázmány Péter Tudományegyetem Magyarságtudományi Intézet.

———. 1944. *A nagycsalád és jogszokásai a Komárom megyei Martoson*. Budapest: A Kisalföldi Kutató Intézet Kiadványai.

———. 1948. *A magyar népi társadalom életének kutatása*. Budapest: Néptudományi Intézet.

———, and T. Hofer. 1969. *Proper Peasants: Traditional Life in a Hungarian Village*. Chicago: Aldine.

———, ———. 1972. *Bäuerliche Denkweise in Wirtschaft und Haushalt*. Göttingen: Verlag Otto Schwartz.

———, ———. 1974. *Geräte der Átányer Bauern*. Kopenhagen and Budapest: Gyldendal and Akadémiai Kiadó.

Földes, L. (ed.). 1969. *Viehwirtschaft und Hirtenkultur*. Budapest: Akadémiai Kiadó.

Godina, V. 2002. From Ethnology to Anthropology and Back Again. In P. Skalník (ed.), *A Post-Communist Millennium: The Struggles for Sociocultural Anthropology in Central and Eastern Europe*, pp. 1–22. Praha: Set Out.

Graebner, F. 1911. *Methode der Ethnologie*. Heidelberg: Carl Winter's Universitätsbuchhandlung.

Gunda, B. 1966. *Ethnographica Carpathica*. Budapest: Akadémiai Kiadó.

——— (ed.). 1984. *The Fishing Culture of the World*, vols. 1–2. Budapest: Akadémiai Kiadó.

Hoffmann, T. 1963. *A gabonaneműek nyomtatása a magyar parasztok gazdálkodásában*. Budapest: Akadémiai Kiadó.

———. 1975. *Néprajz és feudalizmus*. Budapest: Gondolat.

———. 1997–2001. *Európai parasztok*, vols. 1–2. Budapest: Osiris.

——. 2004. *Mindennapi történelem az ütközőzónában.* Miskolc: Borsod-Abaúj-Zemplén Megyei Múzeumi Igazgatóság.

Hollos, M., and B. C. Maday (eds.). 1983. *New Hungarian Peasants.* New York: Brooklyn College Press.

Hoppál, M. 1970. *Egy falu kommunikációs rendszere.* Budapest: MRT Tömegkommunikációs Központ.

——. (ed.). 1989. *Tanulmányok az amerikai magyar etnikus hagyományokról.* Folklór Archívum 18. Budapest: MTA Néprajzi Kutatóintézet.

J. Lőrinczi, R. 1980. *A magyar rokonsági elnevezések rendszerének változásai.* Bucharest: Kriterion.

Kardos, L. 1954. A Magyar falu szocialista fejlődésének néprajzi kérdései. *MTA II. Társadalmi-Történeti Tudományok Osztályának Közleményei* 5: 409–42.

——. 1969. *Egyház és vallásos élet a mai faluban.* Budapest: Kossuth.

Katona, I. 1957. *A magyar kubikusok élete.* Budapest: Hazafias Népfront.

Katona, L. 1890. Ethnographia, ethnologia, folklore. *Ethnographia* 1: 69–87.

K. Csilléry, K. 1952. Vázlatok a tiszaigari népi lakáskultúrából. *Ethnographia* 63: 83–111.

Kisbán, E. 1989. *Népi kultúra, közkultúra, jelkép: A gulyás, pörkölt, paprikás.* Budapest: MTA Néprajzi Kutatócsoport.

Kósa, L. 1980. *A burgonya Magyarországon.* Budapest: Akadémiai Kiadó.

——. 1990. *Paraszti polgárosulás és a népi kultúra táji megoszlása Magyarországon.* Debrecen: Kossuth Lajos Tudományegyetem Néprajzi Intézete.

——. 2001. *A magyar néprajz tudománytörténete.* Budapest: Osiris.

——, and A. Filep. 1978. *A magyar nép táji-történeti tagolódása.* Budapest: Akadémiai Kiadó.

Koszven, M. O. 1950. *Matriarchátus.* Budapest: Hungária nyomda.

Lawrence, P. 1964. *Road belong Cargo.* Manchester: Manchester University Press.

Lindgren, E. J. 1939. The Collection and Analysis of Folk-lore. In F. Bartlett, M. Ginsberg, E. J. Lindgren, and R. H. Thouless (eds.), *The Study of Society*, pp. 328–78. London: Routledge and Kegan Paul.

Morgan, L. H. 1961. *Az ősi társadalom.* Budapest: Gondolat.

Murdock, G. P. 1949. *Social Structure.* New York: Macmillan.

Mühlmann, W. 1938. *Methodik der Völkerkunde.* Stuttgart: Ferdinand Enke Verlag.

Niedermüller, P. 1989. A néprajztudomány választújai avagy a kultúrakutatás elméleti dilemmái. *BUKSZ* 1: 79–84.

Ortutay, Gy. 1935. A magyar falukutatás új útjai. *Vigilia* 1–2: 109–25.

——. 1937. *Magyar népismeret.* Budapest: Magyar Szemle Társaság.

———. 1949. A magyar néprajztudomány elvi kérdései. *Ethnographia* 60: 1–24.

———. 1955. Bevezetés. In Gy. Ortutay (ed.), *Magyar népköltészet*, vol. 1, pp. 7–79. Budapest: Szépirodalmi Könyvkiadó.

———. 1972. *Hungarian Folklore: Essays*. Budapest: Akadémiai Kiadó.

——— (ed). 1977–82. *Magyar néprajzi lexikon*, 4 vols. Budapest: Akadémiai Kiadó.

———, and T. Bodrogi. (eds.). 1965. *Europa et Hungaria. Congressus Ethnographicus in Hungaria*. Budapest: Akadémiai Kiadó.

Paládi-Kovács, A. 1979. *A Magyar parasztság rétgazdálkodása*. Budapest: Akadémiai Kiadó.

——— (ed.). 1980. *Néprajzi csoportok kutatási módszerei*. Budapest: MTA Néprajzi Kutatócsoport.

——— (ed.). 1988-2001. *Magyar néprajz 2-8*. Budapest: Akadémiai Kiadó.

———. 1993a. *Néprajzi kutatás Magyarországon az 1970-80-as években*. Budapest: MTA Néprajzi Kutatócsoport.

———. 1993b. *A magyarországi állattartó kultúra korszakai*. Budapest: MTA Néprajzi Kutatóintézet.

———. 2001. Néprajzi feladatok, vállalkozások és az Akadémia (1929–1967). *Ethnographia* 112: 191–201.

Potehin, I. I. (ed.). 1953. *Az angol-amerikai etnográfia az imperializmus szolgálatában*. Budapest: Művelt Nép.

Sántha, I. 2003. The Siberian Journeys and Legacy of Vilmos Diószegi. *Acta Ethnographica Hungarica* 48: 313–25.

Sárkány, M. 1970a. Megjegyzések komplex társadalmak szociálantropológiai vizsgálatához. *Népi Kultúra—Népi Társadalom* 4: 243–57.

———. 1970b. Gazdasági antropológiai irányzatok. *Népi Kultúra—Népi Társadalom* 4: 347–56.

———. 1972. A társadalomnéprajzi jelenkutatások. *Magyar Filozófiai Szemle* 16: 526–30, 539–41.

———. 1973. A közösségek közötti csere: Északkelet Arnhelmföld lakói. *Dissertationes Ethnographicae* 1: 27–55.

———. 1990. Vágyak és választások. *BUKSZ* 2: 288–94.

———. 1998. Bodrogi Tibor, a rokonság kutatója. *Ethnographia* 109: 345–52.

———. 2000. A társadalomnéprajzi kutatás hazai története. In A. Paládi-Kovács (ed.), *Magyar néprajz*, vol. 8., *Társadalom*, pp. 29–66. Budapest: Akadémiai Kiadó.

Solymossy, S. 1926. Az ethnológia tárgyköre és módszerei. *Ethnographia* 37: 1–19.

Sozan, M. 1977. *The History of Hungarian Ethnography*. Washington, DC: University Press of America.

Steinitz, W. 1957. A finnugor rokonsági elnevezések rendszere. *MTA Nyelv- és Irodalomtudományok Osztályának Közleményei* 10: 321–34.

Szemerkényi, Á. (ed.). 1980. *Nógrádsipek: Tanulmányok egy észak-magyarországi falu mai folklórjáról.* Budapest: Akadémiai Kiadó.

Takács, L. 1964. *A dohánytermesztés Magyarországon.* Budapest: Akadémiai Kiadó.

———. 1976. *Egy irtásfalu földművelése.* Budapest: Akadémiai Kiadó.

———. 1987. *Határjelek, határjárás a feudális kor végén Magyarországon.* Budapest: Akadémiai Kiadó.

Tálasi, I. 1981. Die wichtigsten Ergebnisse ethnographischer Forschungen über Erntemethoden in Europa. *Acta Ethnographica* 30: 241–94.

Tokarjev, Sz. A. 1950. Az etnogenezis problémája. *Ethnographia* 61: 1–28.

Tőkei, F. 1965. *Az 'ázsiai termelési mód' kérdéséhez.* Budapest: Kossuth.

———. 1968. *A társadalmi formák elméletéhez.* Budapest: Kossuth.

———. 1969. *Zur Frage der Asiatischen Produktionsweise.* Neuwied: Luchterhand.

——— (ed.). 1982. *Őstársadalom és ázsiai termelési mód.* Budapest: Magvető.

———. 1983. *Nomád társadalmak és államalakulatok.* Budapest: Akadémiai Kiadó.

——— (ed.). 1989. *Primitive Society and Asiatic mode of production.* Budapest: MTA Orientalisztikai Munkaközösség.

Tolsztov, S. P. 1949. A szovjet etnográfiai iskola. *Ethnographia* 60: 24–45.

Vajda, L. 1954. A néprajzi adatgyűjtés módszere és jelentősége. *Ethnographia* 65: 1–19.

Vargyas, G. 1998. Bodrogi Tibor, az Óceánia-kutató. *Ethnographia* 109: 353–78.

Vargyas, L. 1983. *Hungarian Ballads and the European Ballad Tradition,* vols. 1–2. Budapest: Akadémiai Kiadó.

Vezényi, P. 1960. *Die Geschichte der ungarischen Märchen- und Aberglaubenforschung im XX. Jahrhundert.* Fribourg: Paulusdruckerei.

Viski, K. 1938. *Etnikai csoportok, vidékek.* Budapest: Akadémia.

Voigt, V. 1972a. *A folklór esztétikájához.* Budapest: Kossuth.

———. 1972b. *A folklór alkotások elemzése.* Budapest: Akadémiai Kiadó.

———. 2004. A Brief Account of More than Two Hundred Years of Teaching Folklore and Ethnography (including Cultural Anthropology) at Hungarian Universities. *Acta Ethnographica Hungaria* 49: 181–210.

———, and M. Hoppál. 2003. *Ethnosemiotic © Hungary.* Budapest: European Folklore Institute.

Worsley, P. 1957. *The Trumpet Shall Sound. A Study of "Cargo" Cults in Melanesia.* London: MacGibbon and Kee.

Chapter 5
Polish Anthropology under Socialism: Intellectual Traditions, the Limits of Freedom, and New Departures

Aleksander Posern-Zieliński

This chapter is based mainly on my personal experiences, observations, and participation in Polish anthropology (known generally during the socialist period as etnografia) from my early student years (beginning in 1960) until the fall of communism in 1989.[1] There is no doubt that my formative years as an anthropologist and the following stages of my professional career in teaching and research assistant positions up to and including my habilitation degree were strongly influenced by the political and social climate of the socialist state, with its one-party regime. I have supplemented my evaluation and interpretation of the conditions prevalent in the discipline in the 1960s, 1970s, and 1980s by drawing on a selection of books and articles published by other Polish scholars during that period. Finally, I have taken account of some recent reports, commentaries, and reviews on the state of the field, both critical and self-glorifying. In other words, I attempt to combine two perspectives, subjective and personal, on the one hand, and analytical and historical, on the other. This chapter may be usefully read alongside an earlier study surveying ethnic studies in Polish anthropology (Posern-Zieliński 1995d). It deals mainly with how ethnicity, ethnic relationships, minority groups, and migration movements were treated by anthropologists before the Second World War, under communism, and in the transition

---

[1] I have been continually involved in projects concerning the history of Polish anthropology since early in my career (Posern-Zieliński 1973). I have written entries for the Polish ethnological dictionary (Staszczak 1987), contributed to sociological and general encyclopaedias (Posern-Zieliński 1995a, 2004), and prepared reports on the situation of Polish ethnography for the Polish Academy of Sciences (Jasiewicz and Posern-Zieliński 1996). I organised a conference devoted to an evaluation of the shift from traditional ethnography (ludoznawstwo) to cultural-social anthropology (Posern-Zieliński 1995c). Finally, I gathered a lot of information as a member of a special governmental commission formed to review all Polish anthropology departments (Mucha 2002; Jasiewicz and Posern-Zieliński 2003a, 2003b). All these activities have given me a broad perspective and the detailed knowledge which qualifies me to write about the history of anthropology in the Polish People's Republic.

years, but it also includes reflections on the general situation of Polish anthropology in the post-war period.[2]

Major Theses

Let me begin with some general theses, which can also serve as working
hypotheses to be tested in the discussion which follows.

Lack of Ideological Influence

Polish anthropology, in sharp contrast to other social sciences and humanities disciplines, was not strongly influenced by Marxism-Leninism or Soviet
anthropological models. The discipline did not come under strong ideological pressure from institutions such as committees of the Communist Party,
the Ministry of Higher Education, or the university administration. We
experienced no strong pressures to incorporate basic principles of historical
materialism into our methodology and discourses. Instead, Polish anthropology drifted between the intellectual traditions of the pre-war period, super-
vised by the generation of older professors, and a minimal adaptation to the
new politics of science and education. The result was a discipline characterised by methodological eclecticism, including only minor influences from
officially sanctioned Marxist philosophy.

Continued Western Orientation

The lack of serious interest in Soviet Marxist concepts and methodology
derived from the general tendency of Polish intellectuals to identify with the
cultural traditions and values of Western civilisation. The incorporation of
Poland into the Soviet political and military bloc was treated simply as a
tragic political fact; it did not cause scholars to change their intellectual
orientation. Relationships between Soviet and Polish anthropologists were
very limited and superficial; few Poles had the opportunity to make even
short visits to the Soviet Union as guest researchers, and in consequence
Soviet anthropological ideas had almost no effect on Polish anthropologists.
New strategies were developed to enable the ties with Western traditions to
be sustained and to ensure flexibility and at least limited opportunities for

---

[2] I shall deliberately refrain from discussing the situation under Stalinism (until 1956), both
because it is out of the range of my personal experience and because my colleague Zbigniew
Jasiewicz has devoted his own chapter in this volume to characterising this period, during
which Polish social sciences and humanities were forced to adapt to the new ideological and
political conditions. Similarly, because Zofia Sokolewicz has chosen to focus on the work of
Polish anthropologists abroad, both in neighbouring socialist countries and elsewhere, I shall
not address this theme in any depth.

innovative intellectual development. Especially from the 1970s onwards, attempts were made to incorporate into Polish anthropology a variety of Western anthropological approaches: from Germany, notions of folklorism (*Folklorismus*); from France, studies of everyday culture, the impetus of the Annales school, and structuralism; from Great Britain, functionalism; and from the United States, ethnohistory, studies of cultural change, and neo-evolutionism.

Marginal Position

Polish anthropology, when compared with sociology, history, and even archaeology, was pushed into a marginal position largely because it was perceived as a discipline that could in no way lend itself to the task of justifying the new social and political order. No leading Polish anthropologist ever assumed prominence in the Communist Party. No one tried to argue that a discipline dedicated almost entirely to the study of peasant culture should be taken seriously and supported by a state founded on the concept of the hegemony of the rural and urban working classes. Anthropology (etnografia) continued to be identified as the study of traditional village life, its focus extended only by the necessity to show how the old folk culture (*kultura ludowa*) was gradually being replaced by new patterns of rural life. But in this latter field, rural sociology occupied a more privileged position, thanks to its more direct focus on socialist transformation of the rural environment, including urban migration, life on state and cooperative farms, and the modernisation of rural society.

'Exotic' and Non-Political Research Focus

Not only did Polish anthropologists concentrate on 'exotic' themes such as traditional folk culture and the cultures of more distant countries, but there was also a tendency within these fields to focus on politically and ideologically neutral topics. When contemporary changes in rural Poland were examined, it was done mostly in a descriptive manner, without serious interpretation of causes and consequences, in order to avoid any risk of official critique and accusations of spreading anti-socialist propaganda. A tendency towards self-censorship developed, along with a preference for themes as far away as possible from the political. This explains why the majority of studies were concentrated on traditional folk culture, folklorism, folk art, folklore, and national cultural history. Those who studied traditional African, Asian, Oceanic, and Native American peoples, in many cases from a distance, on the basis of the literature, shared the same bias. The discipline came to function as a kind of isolated island, free of direct ideological pressure and political manipulation. This made it attractive to young people looking to escape from 'actually existing socialism' and disciplines associated in one way or another with its legitimation.

Modernisation Trends

The relative isolation of Polish anthropology from the mainstream of 'socialist-oriented' social sciences, which deprived the discipline of any contemporary cultural influence and hampered its institutional development, nonetheless facilitated to some degree its modernisation. This manifested itself in a serious interest in different Western anthropological schools, in the rediscovery and reinterpretation of ethnological concepts developed by leading Polish scholars before the Second World War, and last but not least in a gradual shift of interest away from traditional culture towards studies of contemporary urban settings, popular culture, and ethnic relations, all of which were associated with current social changes. This development led in the 1980s to the replacement of the name etnografia by the principal name used for the discipline before socialism, etnologia. It now denoted basically the same intellectual field as socio-cultural anthropology.[3]

Polish Scientific Politics and the Position of Anthropology

With the end of Stalinism, marked in Poland by the Poznań uprising in 1956, the political situation in the country and within academia improved considerably. University departments of Marxism-Leninism were closed, and departments of philosophy and sociology, the so-called bourgeois sciences, were reopened after years of prohibition. Chairs of etnografia, which under Stalinism had been incorporated into 'Studies of the History of Material Culture', could once again initiate their own teaching and research activities.

Post-war Polish anthropology was relaunched in three separate institutional realms. The universities focused on education, the Polish Academy of Sciences (Polska Akademia Nauk, hereafter PAN) focused on research, and museums devoted themselves to the collection, preservation, and documentation of folk and 'exotic' culture. At the leading universities (Warsaw, Poznań, Łódź, Cracow, Wrocław, and Toruń), chairs of etnografia were (re-) established in close proximity to departments of history and archaeology, which reflected the official perception of anthropology not as a social science but as a historical discipline. Despite the reorientation which took place

---

[3] Another popular name for the field was *ludoznawstwo*, a term which corresponds to the German *Volkskunde*, the Czech *národopis*, etc. However, in Poland *ludoznawstwo* was not taken up in academia but remained associated with amateur work (local and region history analogous to German *Heimatforschung*).

in the 1980s and 1990s, this structural location of anthropology has not been altered, and it continues to negatively affect interdisciplinary cooperation with other social sciences.

The centre of gravity for academic anthropology was formed within the institutional structure of the PAN. In 1953 the Institute of the History of Material Culture was founded as the leading research centre for archaeological, anthropological, and material culture studies. Basic units for anthropological research were established in Warsaw, Cracow, Poznań, and Wrocław. The institute continues to exist, but now under the more appropriate name Instytut Archeologii i Etnologii. Some other, more specialised ethnographic research units were founded as sections of the Institute of Art (studies of folk art and ethnomusicology) and the Institute of Literary Research (studies of folklore).The third area of anthropological work was in museums. In addition to departments of the leading national and regional museums, new museums specialising in anthropology were founded, including open-air museums, or 'ethnographic parks' (*skansen*).

In spite of institutional divisions, cooperation was generally quite good, mostly thanks to strong personal ties established at the level of directors and chairpersons. Some professors combined university teaching with research projects carried out at the institutes of the PAN, additional curatorial activities in the museums, or both. This was necessitated by the small number of professors available to take responsibility for this disciplinary expansion. They were also involved in the activities of the Polish Ethnological Society (its official name in English; in Polish it is called the Polskie Towarzystwo Ludoznawcze) and in providing advisory services to folk artisans' associations (Posern-Zieliński 1995c).

State control over science and education was theoretically complete. In reality, from the 1960s onwards there existed limited freedom for lecturers, in particular in the teaching of fieldwork methodology and of foreign schools of thought. The financing of research, including conferences, publications, and travel costs, was monopolised by the state. The Communist Party monitored all scholars to ensure that their activity did not challenge the 'basis for socialist order in Poland' and would have no negative effects on 'eternal friendship' with the Soviet Union. Censorship played an important role, but the decisive factor in marking the limits of scientific expression was rather self-censorship. Everybody knew perfectly well what could not be said out loud, what should be omitted, and what might be presented subtly, so that one could speak the truth without the risk of being submitted to ideological critique and even persecution.

One of the characteristic features of anthropology during the early decades of socialism in Poland was its political and ideological neutrality vis-à-vis 'real socialism'. Anthropologists, although they knew quite well how critical the rural situation was, neither eagerly criticised state policies towards the peasants nor participated in propaganda activities to legitimate socialist transformation. Instead they continued to concentrate on 'safe' areas of traditional folk culture, as well as analysing changes taking place under the pressure of industrialisation. They described modernisation processes without going into details of their causes and consequences. This abstention can be understood as a defensive response to the official ideology, which viewed peasants as living relics of the epochs of feudalism and capitalism and as obstacles to rapid socialist transformation. The state promoted various forms of collective organisation (state farms, cooperative farms, farmers' associations, etc.) to undermine the old-fashioned peasantry. Unfortunately, rather than study these processes, most Polish anthropologists chose to sustain the illusion of traditional peasant villages, abandoning research into new socialist rural relations to rural sociologists.

This combination of subjective (internal) and objective (external) determinants is the key to understanding the weak position of anthropology within the Polish social sciences and humanities. For many years it was treated as a dependent discipline of minor importance, as a kind of cultural history of the passing folk world. Anthropology was a subsidiary discipline which might provide useful data and expertise to assist archaeologists, historians, and sociologists in reconstructing the past. Although there was always some opposition to the discipline's formal association with the historical sciences (Kutrzeba-Pojnarowa 1956), and although by the 1980s anthropologists did begin to reorient themselves towards the study of contemporary social phenomena, the subject remains everywhere in Poland part of the faculty of history, separated from the social sciences.

Anthropology's weak position in Poland was also manifested in its failure to establish its own specialised institute within the PAN. All initiatives to detach anthropology from the Institute for the History of Material Culture and to found an autonomous institute, similar to that in Moscow, were blocked by the academy's administration. The establishment of such an institute remained the dream of many leading anthropologists, who believed it could be the catalyst for overcoming marginality and securing the discipline's future in the Polish academic landscape.

Polish anthropology also remained marginal in the universities. Enrolment quotas were strictly limited at a very low level, starting with 6–7 students per year per department in the 1960s and increasing only to 10–15 in the following decades. It was argued that the number of graduating students should be determined by demand—in other words, by the number of positions available in specialised institutions such as museums, regional culture centres, and folk art cooperatives. The educational profile of the graduating students was shaped strictly by this same logic, in order to prepare them for work in these kinds of institutions. There is no doubt that the small number of students hampered the development of the departments. Many excellent graduates with great academic potential were unable to find assistant positions and instead switched to scientific careers in fields outside of their original specialisation—as sociologists, philosophers, or geographers. This low-level recruitment of students and staff resulted in a serious generation gap which still affects Polish anthropology today.[4]

The perception of anthropology as a minor branch of history dedicated to studies of traditional folk culture was not restricted to academics and administrative authorities. It also remains the dominant public perception of the discipline. Therefore, one of the major goals since the late 1980s has been to challenge this stereotype and build up a new image of the discipline as an original and stimulating way to understand culture and society, both in the past and in the present.

One side effect of the marginal character of anthropology was the difficulty it created for retaining contact with the Western anthropological tradition. It fell to Polish sociologists in the 1970s and 1980s to discover the work of French, American, and British anthropologists, appropriating them as a sociological heritage necessary for the modernisation of their own discipline. Many Polish sociologists were discouraged by the dogmatism of Marxist approaches and found Western anthropological concepts a stimulating addition to their own methodological toolbox. They did not associate cultural and social anthropology with Polish etnografia, even though the latter was also in the process of rebuilding bridges with the Western tradition. This rediscovery of Western anthropology by sociologists was dangerous for the discipline of anthropology, for it was thereby divested of its own exclusive heritage. This has impeded the transformation of the Polish discipline into one which would combine general anthropological orientations with specifically national approaches developed by Polish scholars since the nineteenth century.

The hypothesis that after 1956 the repercussions of Marxist ideology on anthropological research remained very limited can certainly be confirmed. The new climate of 'real socialism' was based on loyalty to the

---

[4] A rapid increase in the number of students studying anthropology in Poland since the early 1990s reflects the general expansionary trend in higher education. Whereas in the 1980s the total number of students registered for anthropology courses approximated 500, by 2001 the discipline could boast 2,372 students in five universities. In the course of 29 years, between 1946 and 1974, only 539 students graduated with a master's degree in etnografia; between 1989 and 2002, the number of graduates in etnologia was 1,143 (Jasiewicz and Posern-Zieliński 2003a and 2003b).

party's politics rather than on ideological orthodoxy. Anthropologists did not participate in any serious discussion concerning the theory and methods of historical materialism. They accepted some basic principles of Marxist interpretation, of course, such as the significance of economic factors in shaping social life, but alien theoretical concepts provided no inspiration for ethnographic analysis and functioned mostly as a superficial epistemological framework.

The weakness of Marxism in Polish etnografia cannot be explained only in terms of a lack of external pressure; it was also the result of strong resistance by the pre-war intellectual generation of professors. It is a paradox that before the Second World War, the Polish anthropologist and sociologist Ludwik Krzywicki played a most important role in adapting Marxist principles to anthropological purposes (Lange 1938; Hołda-Róziewicz 1976). In socialist Poland such agendas remained just as exceptional. The leading figure here was Kazimierz Dobrowolski, a distinguished ethnohistorian and ethnosociologist from Cracow, who in his later years tried to combine his 'integral' approach with a Marxist perspective (Dobrowolski 1973; see also Kutrzeba-Pojnarowa 1977). In general, Marxism was but one influence among many. Polish anthropologists tended to practice pluralism in both theory and methodology. Some followed pre-war orientations, sometimes with minor adjustments, while others developed new approaches, mostly of an eclectic character. One group of young scholars was explicitly interested in adopting Western anthropological ideas and using them in the interpretation of domestic culture.

Areas of Studies and Limits of Freedom

Let us now look more closely at the major areas of study and their relationship to communist politics of science. The study of traditional material culture dominated in the initial post-war period. It included topics such as rural architecture, traditional techniques of farming, animal husbandry, and fishing, and folk artisan production. In the 1960s new fields of interest developed, including social organisation, family life, the local community, regional cultural history, folk religiosity, and folklore. These areas covered both documentation of rapidly vanishing folk culture and the observation of current changes in the culture and day-to-day lives of village inhabitants under the pressure of socialist transformation (Burszta and Kopczyńska-Jaworska 1982; Jasiewicz and Slattery 1995). However, enthusiasm for studying people living on state farms or in agricultural cooperatives was rather weak. The same can be said concerning studies of urban 'worker culture' (*kultura robotnicza*). A few researchers from Cracow and Łódź joined forces in a pilot project on this new topic in order to demonstrate that ethnography was also able to contribute to the interpretation of the everyday life of the new proletarian class, considered in propaganda to be the 'most progressive social stratum' (Pietraszek 1964; Stawarz 2001).

Among the most interesting studies of new, state-driven transformations were investigations of the 'integration and adaptation' processes of both new and old inhabitants of the western and northern territories that were incorporated into the Polish state after 1945 as a result of the Potsdam Treaty. These studies were conducted in collaboration with sociologists, and the latter played the leading role, because they possessed more adequate tools for analysing social and cultural changes than did the anthropologists of that period (Prawda 2002). Not surprisingly, the reports of anthropologists from research centres in Poznań, Wrocław, Olsztyn, and Koszalin who did fieldwork on this topic demonstrate considerable sociological influence. The final results were stimulating and included valuable accounts of the consequences of culture clash, the social and cultural effects of migration, the adaptation of newcomers resettled from the 'Kresy' (former Polish territories to the east that were incorporated into the Soviet Union after the war) to a new ethnogeographical environment, the formation of new, heterogeneous local and regional communities based on different cultural groups, and, finally, the adaptation processes of Polish migrants returning after 1945 from the Balkan Peninsula and from Western Europe (Frankowska 1973).

The authorities of the time supported such studies but expected interpretations of the new culture and society of the western territories (*ziemie odzyskane*) to remain consistent with the official political propaganda. Monographs and reports were thus supposed to create a new image of the ex-German zone as populated by communities living in harmony, well adapted to their 'regained' homeland and integrated into the mainstream of socialist Poland. This requirement certainly constrained the freedom of the investigators and made their work somewhat one-dimensional. However, it would be unfair to say that the results were tailored only to suit official suggestions. In fact, they often revealed a dramatic situation, including conflicts between different groups of settlers, but these phenomena were usually kept in the background and the positive, optimistic aspects of integration processes were highlighted.

The political sensitivity of this research meant that it had to be performed discreetly, avoiding potentially controversial issues. As a result, many important problems remained untouched, despite intensive fieldwork carried out in the western territories. The historical role of Germans in shaping the culture of the area was largely neglected (Simonides 1995; Barska and Michalczyk 1997). So, too, was the destruction (both spontaneous and provoked) of their cultural heritage (Mazur 1997, 2000). The continuing presence of a German minority after the forced resettlement of the greater part of the German population was not merely neglected until the 1990s; it was actually denied by some anthropologists and folklorists, who, if they recognised this ethnic category at all, saw its members as an autochthonous or regional group with an indefinite, amorphous identity. Nobody paid any attention to the 'bicultural' orientation of native (Slavic) inhabitants in the western territories (Silesians, Masurians, Kashubians). In the majority of publications they were presented as typically Polish regional groups which had, despite centuries of separation from their motherland, preserved their Polish culture, language (in the form of a dialect), and identity.

Unfortunately, this official interpretation did not correspond to the actual policies implemented by the state, which tended to view these peoples (because of many German traits in their culture and their German citizenship before 1945) as 'not purely Polish' and thus as untrustworthy. Their treatment as second-class citizens hampered their integration and intensified their readiness to leave their homeland for (West) Germany. Conflicts between different groups, which also hampered the process of integration, were studied only superficially. Anthropologists almost completely avoided research on the consequences of the forced resettlement and dispersion of Ukrainians and Lemkos from their Carpathian homelands to the northern and western territories, though sociologists undertook some important work on that subject (Posern-Zieliński 1995d).

All topics to do with ethnicity, including any discussion of the situation of minority groups, interethnic conflict, post-war ethnic cleansing, continuing ethnic prejudice, and ethnic patterns of emigration, were precarious in the extreme. The Poland that emerged after 1945 was for the first time in the country's history a very homogeneous country, in which ethnic minority groups were statistically inconsequential. The issue of minorities was initially absent from the research agenda, and no serious investigations took place until the 1960s. The reasons for this neglect were strictly political, and three factors deserve to be highlighted. First, the Communist Party had the utopian idea of building a new and uniform socialist society, free of any substantial internal divisions along regional or ethnic as well as ideological and class lines. Second, recent memories of violent interethnic conflict and fear of critical reaction from Moscow combined to silence controversial questions such as anti-Semitism and Polish-Jewish relations in general, Ukrainian resettlement, German expulsion, and the continuing presence of a Polish diaspora in the USSR. Third, the development of a new 'socialist' nationalism at high levels of the Communist Party in the 1960s mitigated against any recognition of 'alien' ethnic or cultural elements.

Thus, when studies of minority and ethnoregional groups were first undertaken in the 1960s, scholars focused on very marginal and 'exotic' groups, because these were considered unlikely to provoke trouble in terms of ideology or international politics. This was a blatant instance of the way the political situation distorted the social sciences. The 'safe' ethnic minority and ethnoregional groups studied were the Gypsies (Roma), Polish Tartars, Belorussians of the Podlasie region, Russian Old-Believers, post-civil-war Greek refugees, Kashubians in Pommerania, Bambers (the polonised descendants of nineteenth-century migrants from south Germany) in Poznań, Masurians, Warmians, and Mountaineers of the Tatra Highlands (Górale) (Posern-Zieliński 1995d). Most publications dealing with minority issues focused on description of the ethnic culture and avoided any discussion of the ethnopolitical situation or indeed the interethnic context and identity formation. New approaches to the analysis of ethnic consciousness and the power of existing stereotypes began to appear, but the general level was still superficial. There was little discussion of the needs and aims of the groups as formulated by their members, and state policy towards minorities was a topic to be avoided. Attention focused instead on the ethnocultural character of minority communities, along with the function of ethnic tradition and ethnic history.

In the 1970s, when Edward Gierek was first secretary, a new, very specific area of ethnic studies came into being, namely, the interdisciplinary study of the Polish diaspora. This project was considered to be important for state propaganda and international politics. It was vital to end the isolation of the country from the Western world and to establish new and friendlier relationships with Polish communities and organisations abroad. An important factor facilitating the consolidation of this field was the biography of the first secretary, who himself had spent many years as an emigrant in France and Belgium. Although historians and sociologists were the most prominent in this work, anthropologists also made a contribution. Thanks to this project and to a special agreement between the Polish government and the Polish-American Kościuszko Foundation in New York City, I was sent to the United States in 1974 to study the transformation of the culture and ethnicity of Americans of Polish descent (Posern-Zieliński 1982).

Like my own work, other studies were oriented mostly towards communities of Polish descent in Western countries (although West Germany was always a significant exception). Only a few scholars investigated Polish communities living in neighbouring socialist countries such as Hungary, Czechoslovakia, or Romania (Kantor 1995). The political situation of the time allowed no scope for studies of Polish communities in the Soviet Union, regardless of whether they were in regions close to Poland or in remote

Kazakhstan. This would have broken the conspiracy of silence veiling the tragic fate of many of these communities. Another important ethnic process not scientifically monitored was the new wave of emigration resulting from the Polish–West German agreement on the recognition of the Oder-Neisse border. This included a clause allowing former (pre-war) German citizens (regardless of ethnicity) living in Poland to emigrate to the Federal Republic. As a result, thousands of Silesians, Masurians, and Kashubians decided to leave their homeland in the 1970s and 1980s. Owing to the sensitive nature of this movement, conditioned not only by economic factors but also by ethnopsychological deprivation and an ambiguous identity as native (Slavic) peoples inhabiting the western and northern territories, it was impossible for scholars to analyse this migration and its socio-cultural consequences (Posern-Zieliński 2000a).

The 1970s also opened new possibilities for undertaking fieldwork abroad. Polish anthropology had always aspired to combine studies of folk culture (ludoznawstwo) with research into the cultures of non-European peoples (this was termed *etnografia powszechna*, literally, general ethnography, analogous to Völkerkunde). This tendency had been present from the very beginnings of Polish anthropology in the second half of the nineteenth century, when folklore studies inspired by Herderian ideas, which fed into emerging nationalism, were pursued simultaneously with a comparative anthropology that was strongly influenced by evolutionist theories. In addition to 'armchair' research activities and the documentation of folk traditions by amateur enthusiasts, numerous scholars undertook field research, both among regional groups in various parts of partitioned Poland and among native peoples elsewhere, such as in Siberia, Central Asia, Africa, Latin America, and Oceania (Posern-Zieliński 1973, 1995a, 2004; Staszczak 1987). This double profile weakened during the inter-war years, when anthropology came to focus almost exclusively on the folk culture of Poles and minority groups inhabiting Poland. This was partially a consequence of new institutional structures and the cultural policy of the re-established Polish state: although fully one-third of the population was not ethnically Polish, or perhaps precisely because of this fact, the state emphasised only Polishness. A more international perspective was not rediscovered and reimplemented until the middle of the socialist period, when the relaxation of state control and new policies towards Third World countries facilitated the organisation of different kinds of scientific travels and 'expeditions'. While most were interdisciplinary, some had a strictly anthropological character, the aim being to study non-European cultures and to gather artefacts for Polish museum collections, which had been heavily damaged during the war (see Sokolewicz, this volume).

One of the most important initiatives in terms of its long-term consequences was the Mongolian expedition organised by a Warsaw team headed
by Professor Witold Dynowski within the framework of an official agreement between the respective Academies of Sciences. Over many years,
Polish anthropologists carried out intensive studies of both traditional culture
and contemporary changes in the lives of Mongolian nomads (Kabzińska
2000). Another major project was a combined expedition of anthropologists
and archaeologists to the Peruvian Andes with the aim of exploring pre-
Columbian settlements, indigenous peasant communities, and, in particular,
people's everyday lives and adaptations to the high mountain environment
(Posern-Zieliński 1981, 2000b). These expeditions were very important for
the development of Asian and Latin American studies in Poland. Many
participants who thus completed their first fieldwork in a 'distant culture'
went on not only to become distinguished representatives of area studies but
also to gain influential positions in contemporary Polish anthropology.

Between East and West: An End to Isolation

The isolation of Polish anthropology diminished in the 1970s thanks to the
domestic and international policies of Gierek's regime. However, this should
not be interpreted as a radical shift towards a Western style of socio-cultural
anthropology. First, as already mentioned, the impact of Soviet anthropology
had never been great. Exchange programmes with Soviet institutions were
limited, and there had been no pressure to adopt their concepts. We monitored, sometimes with curiosity, the achievements of our colleagues in
Moscow and Leningrad, whose access to Western journals and books was
more limited than ours; but their approaches, with the exception of that of
the famous Moscow-Tartu school of semiotics, were seldom adopted.

Second, Polish anthropology had its own intellectual tradition, one
which was conducive to a specific pluralism of approaches and concepts. In
other words, it was more a question of strengthening a long history of disciplinary promiscuity than of discovering Western influences for the first time.
We thus find the simultaneous existence of a cultural-historical school in the
German sense, ethnogeographical and ethnosociological orientations, a
modified critical evolutionism, and an ethnohistorical approach mixed with
ideas taken directly from historical materialism (Damrosz 1996). Among the
younger cohorts of anthropologists, some were attracted to French anthropology and history while others preferred British social anthropology or
American cultural anthropology (in particular, theories of acculturation,
culture change, and ethnicity). Given this wide range of theoretical ideas and
methodological approaches in a relatively small ethnographic community, it
is impossible to speak of any unified school or paradigm in Polish anthro-

pology. It is true that some identified and labelled the mainstream as the 'Polish ethnographic school', but this statement reflects more an ambitious attempt to claim a special position on the map of European anthropologies than an objective diagnosis. Polish anthropology certainly has its own distinctive history in the socialist period, but it hardly adds up to a 'national school'.

As we have seen, in the early years of socialism the ambiguous situation of Polish anthropology did not facilitate the modernisation of the discipline, which remained strongly attached to pre-war traditions, separated from the Western centres of the discipline and largely immunised against Marxist and Soviet influences. Close international ties were confined to other Eastern European socialist countries (notably Czechoslovakia, Bulgaria, Yugoslavia, and Hungary). This intellectual isolation resulted in a predominance of descriptive ethnography and a weak level of theoretical debate. The first substantial changes occurred in the 1970s; when isolation ended, it was thanks to international projects carried out mainly in collaboration with other socialist countries, to fieldwork conducted in distant places (Dzięgiel 1987), and to new programmes for scientific exchange, which allowed anthropologists to visit and study in Germany, France, the United States, Spain, and the United Kingdom. Participation in international conferences increased, and the foreign language journal *Ethnologia Polona* was founded in 1975. It supplemented the journals *Etnografia Polska* and *Lud*, both published in Polish. The latter, an annual published by the Polish Ethnological Society, represented a more traditional orientation, whereas the former, a quarterly issued by the PAN, was intended to be a platform for innovative approaches.

These changes coincided with a significant re-evaluation of intellectual paradigms in Polish anthropology. Lively discussions over the appropriate subject matter for contemporary ethnographic research induced a shift from traditional folk culture to multidimensional studies of cultural and social reality. This reorientation can be viewed as a strategy of adaptation on the part of the discipline, and it was partially inspired by many direct and indirect influences coming from the West. Scholars returning home from their research visits, conferences, and fieldwork brought back new ideas and experiences. Improved access to foreign literature facilitated the spread of modern anthropological concepts, and the first Polish translations of many classic anthropological works, such as those of Bronislaw Malinowski, Ralph Linton, Margaret Mead, Claude Lévi-Strauss, Alfred Kroeber, Ruth Benedict, and Mircea Eliade, contributed to much better knowledge of the principles of modern anthropology.

The growing force of Western anthropological ideas provoked a discussion of how best to incorporate different approaches into Polish anthropology. Structural, functional, semiotic, and even phenomenological ideas were applied. At the same time, works by classical Polish authors from the pre-war period (Jan Stanisław Bystroń, Stefan Czarnowski, Ludwik Krzywicki, Florian Znaniecki, and Józef Obrębski) were rediscovered. The works of these scholars were re-edited, and their most seminal ideas were debated, modified, and finally applied in contemporary research (Olszewska-Dyoniziak 2000).

All these transformations led eventually to the abandonment of old-fashioned etnografia and the enthusiastic embracing of a more modern variant of anthropology. In the Polish context this meant readopting the term etnologia, a process which continued piecemeal from the second half of the 1970s until it was completed in the 1990s. At the Universities of Warsaw and Poznań a more complex administrative name was chosen—in literal translation, 'Department of Ethnology and Cultural Anthropology'. This was intended to manifest the union of European (and national) traditions with Anglo-American patterns of research. A new Committee of Ethnological Sciences (Komitet Nauk Etnologicznych PAN) was founded in 1975 as a branch of the PAN; it was intended to represent and serve as an open forum for a full range of subdisciplines from folklore and ethnomusicological studies to social and cultural anthropology (Jasiewicz 1995; Jasiewicz and Posern-Zieliński 1996). Paradoxically, the switch back to the older name, incorporating etnologia, was carried through by the leading professors of the time as a symbolic expression of the discipline's modernisation. Today the situation is even more complex, because although etnologia is the official name for most educational purposes, etnografia still occurs in the names of many museums, and ludoznawstwo has been preserved in the name of the leading professional association (Polskie Towarzystwo Ludoznawcze). Last but not least, socio-cultural anthropology has gained greatly in popularity, though it still has no official recognition outside the above-mentioned universities.

Concluding Remarks

A full examination of the conditions in Poland during the socialist period is necessary in order to understand and overcome the burden of the past, which continues to affect Polish anthropology and its gradual shift towards more Western, socio-cultural orientations (Kaniowska 1995). I hope I have said enough in this overview to verify the preliminary theses. In summary, three points can be made about Polish anthropology during this period:

First, in socialist Poland the discipline known as etnografia developed gradually but continuously, despite its marginal position and relative isolation. Its traditional orientation was discredited and almost abandoned, but new approaches were adopted step by step. Anthropology did not function as a useful tool in supporting communist or nationalist state and party propaganda. Compared with scholars in archaeology (Rączkowski 1996; Kurnatowska and Kurnatowski 2002; Rutkowska 2004), history (Piskorski 1996; Jaworski 2002), and the applied social sciences, who were expected to engage in the consolidation of socialism (Waśkiewicz 1996), anthropologists were able to maintain a greater distance from politics and ideology.

Second, the ideological impact of Marxism was, like that of Communist Party directives, weak and superficial. Official pressure led to certain research topics being neglected or omitted, but it did not affect the way anthropological works were written. However, only the end of censorship in 1989 freed the discipline from political interference entirely, leaving financial resources as the remaining constraint.

Third, the developmental trajectory of Polish anthropology under socialism can be divided into three stages. Post-war reconstruction and Stalinist marginalisation characterised the first stage, which lasted until the end of the 1950s. In the course of the 1960s the discipline experienced institutional stabilisation, but it continued to be marked by its weak position and traditional orientation. From the 1970s onwards the situation improved gradually, anthropology underwent internal modernisation, participants in national conferences debated new profiles in both education and research, new fields of study were identified, and isolation was broken. This positive tendency, in spite of the political and economic crisis caused by the imposition of a state of emergency in 1981 and the years of stagnation which ensued, was sustained until the end of the socialist period in 1989–90. Thanks to these trends, the passage to postsocialist reconstruction was a relatively smooth one for anthropology (as indeed it was for the Polish social sciences and humanities as a whole). After 1989 Polish anthropology experienced no sudden change in its institutional structure or any general replacement of academic staff, nor has any major shift taken place in its methodological approaches or research foci.

With the end of socialism, there is no doubt that the discipline now known officially as etnologia has moved much closer to socio-cultural anthropology and is in a stronger position as a result. The growing number of students and research centres, a new generation of ambitious scholars, greater flexibility in acquiring financial aid for projects, thorough reform of curricula, increased international exchange at both student and staff levels, more interdisciplinary cooperation, new research and editorial initiatives, and above all stronger interest in the study of contemporary cultural and social phenomena are all positive reflections of the current situation.

The general climate for anthropological research has become very favourable and the subject is even becoming fashionable, especially among sociologists, historians, philologists, political scientists, and educational specialists. This anthropologisation of the humanities and social sciences, a positive reaction to the scientific dogmatism which characterised the socialist period, has created a new situation for the discipline. Professional anthropologists once again must meet the challenge of demonstrating their intellectual and practical usefulness within academia and society. The way to do so appears to me quite simple, although psychologically it may prove far from easy to implement. We need, first, to overcome that element of the socialist legacy which led us to concentrate on topics considered politically and socially neutral, and second, we need to step up efforts to consolidate the discipline's position at the heart of the social sciences.

References

Barska, A., and T. Michalczyk. 1997. German Minority in Opole Silesia: Relations between Minority and Majority. In M. S. Szczepański (ed.), *Ethnic Minorities and Ethnic Majority: Sociological Studies of Ethnic Relations in Poland*, pp. 162–80. Katowice: Wydawnictwo Uniwersytetu Śląskiego.

Burszta, J., and B. Kopczyńska-Jaworska. 1982. Polish Ethnography after World War II. *Ethnos* 47 (1–2): 50–63.

Damrosz, J. 1996. *Myśl teoretyczna w polskiej etnografii i etnologii w okresie powojennym: 1945–1989*. Warsaw: Instytut Kultury-WSRP.

Dobrowolski, K. 1973. *Teoria procesów żywiołowych w zarysie*. Wrocław: Ossolineum.

Dzięgiel, L. (ed.). 1987. *Na egzotycznych szlakach: O polskich badaniach etnograficznych w Afryce, Ameryce i Azji w dobie powojennej*. Wrocław: PTL.

Frankowska, M. 1973. Etnografia polska po II wojnie światowej (1945–1970). In M. Terlecka (ed.), *Historia etnografii polskiej*, pp. 193–270, 338–41. Wrocław: Ossolineum.

Hołda-Róziewicz, H. 1976. *Ludwik Krzywicki jako teoretyk społeczeństw pierwotnych*. Wrocław: Ossolineum.

Jasiewicz, Z. 1995. A Few Remarks on the Past and Present of Polish Ethnology. *Lud* 79: 27–34.

———, and A. Posern-Zieliński. 1996. Stan i potrzeby nauk etnologicznych w Polsce. *Nauka w Polsce w ocenie komitetów naukowych PAN* 4: 39–52.

———, and A. Posern-Zieliński. 2003a. Ethnology Studies at Polish Universities after 1989. In L. Mróz and Z. Sokolewicz (eds.), *Between Tradition and Postmodernity: Polish Ethnography at the Turn of the Millennium*, pp. 269–80. Warsaw: DiG.

———, and A. Posern-Zieliński. 2003b. Studia etnologiczne na uniwersytetach polskich po roku 1989. *Lud* 87: 13–44.

———, and D. Slattery. 1995. Ethnography and Anthropology: The Case of Polish Ethnology. In H. V. Vermeulen and A. A. Roldan (eds.), *Fieldwork and Footnotes: Studies in the History of European Anthropology*, pp. 184-201. London: Routledge.

Jaworski, R. 2002. Deutsche Ostforschung und polnische Westforschung in ihren historisch-politischen Beziehungen. In J. M. Piskorski, J. Hackmann, and R. Jaworski (eds.), *Deutsche Ostforschung und polnische Westforschung im Spannungsfeld vom Wissenschaft und Politik: Disziplinen im Vergleich*, pp. 11–24. Osnabrück: fibre-Verlag.

Kabzińska, I. 2000. W kierunku zrozumienia i interpretacji: Polska ekspedycja etnograficzna w Mongolii. In A. Kuczyński (ed.), *Polskie opisywanie świata: Od fascynacji egzotyką do badań antropologicznych*, pp. 233–50. Wrocław: Wydawnictwo Uniwersytetu Wrocławskiego.

Kaniowska, K. 1995. Inspiracje i konsekwencje antropologizacji etnologii polskiej. In A. Posern-Zieliński (ed.), *Etnologia polska między ludoznawstwem a antropologią*, pp. 61–68. Poznań: Prace Komitetu Nauk Etnologicznych PAN.

Kantor, R. 1995. The Achievements of Polish Ethnology in the Study of Polish Communities Abroad. *Lud* 79: 265–76.

Kurnatowska, Z., and St. Kurnatowski. 2002. Der Einfluss nationalistischer Ideen auf die mitteleuropäische Urgeschichtsforschung. In J. M. Piskorski, J. Hackmann, and R. Jaworski (eds.), *Deutsche Ostforschung und polnische Westforschung im Spannungsfeld von Wissenschaft und Politik: Disziplinen im Vergleich*, pp. 93–104. Osnabrück: fibre-Verlag.

Kutrzeba-Pojanrowa, A. 1956. Aktualna pozycja etnografii w obrębie nauk historycznych. *Kwartalnik Historyczny* 6: 184–90.

———. 1977. *Kultura ludowa i jej badacze*. Warsaw: LSW.

Lange, O. 1938. Ludwik Krzywicki jako teoretyk materializmu historycznego. In L. Krzywickis, *Ludwik Krzywicki: Praca zbiorowa poświęcona jego życiu i twórczości*, pp. 89–113. Warsaw: Instytut Gospodarstwa Społecznego.

Mazur, Z. (ed.). 1997. *Wokół niemieckiego dziedzictwa kulturowego na Ziemiach Zachodnich i Północnych*. Poznań: Wydawnictwo Instytutu Zachodniego.

——. 2000. *Wspólne dziedzictwo? Ze studiów nad stosunkiem do spuścizny kulturowej na Ziemiach Zachodnich i Północnych*. Poznań: Wydawnictwo Instytutu Zachodniego.

Mucha, J. 2002. Post-socialist Institutionalization of Socio-cultural Anthropology (Ethnography, Ethnology) as a University Subject in Poland. In P. Skalnik (ed.), *A Post-Communist Millennium: The Struggles for Sociocultural Anthropology in Central and Eastern Europe*, pp. 87–97. Praha: Set Out.

Olszewska-Dyoniziak, B. 2000. *Zarys antropologii kulturowej*. Zielona Góra: Zachodnie Centrum Organizacji.

Pietraszek, E. 1964. Problematyka kultury robotniczej a etnografia. *Lud* 50 (2): 585–600.

Piskorski, J. M. 1996. 'Deutsche Ostforschung' und 'polnische Westforschung'. *Berliner Jahrbuch für Osteuropäische Geschichte* 1: 379–89.

Posern-Zieliński, A. 1973. Kształtowanie się etnografii polskiej jako samodzielnej dyscypliny naukowej (do 1939 r.). In M. Terlecka (ed.), *Historia etnografii polskiej*, pp. 29–114, 326–32. Wrocław: Ossolineum.

——. 1981. Polish Ethnological Fieldwork in the Peruvian Andes. *Ethnologia Polona* 7: 186–90.

——. 1982. *Tradycja a etniczność: Przemiany kultury Polonii amerykańskiej*. Wrocław: Ossolineum.

——. 1995a. Etnologia. *Nowa Encyklopedia Powszechna* 2: 277–78.

—— (ed.) 1995b. *Etnologia polska między ludoznawstwem a antropologią. Prace Komitetu Nauk Etnologicznych PAN* 6.

——. 1995c. Etnologia i antropologia kulturowa w formalnej i rzeczywistej strukturze nauki. In A. Posern-Zieliński (ed.), *Etnologia polska między ludoznawstwem a antropologią: Prace Komitetu Nauk Etnologicznych PAN* 6: 21–36.

——. 1995d. Ethnic Studies in Polish Ethnology: Their Condition, Contexts and Trends. *Lud* 79: 199–216.

——. 2000a. Zwischen Assimilation und Bewahrung der Identität. In A. Wolff-Powęska, and E. Schultz (eds.), *Polen in Deutschland: Integration oder Separation?*, pp. 41–66. Düsseldorf: Droste Verlag.

——. 2000b. Polskie badania etnologiczne w Ameryce Łacińskiej po 1945 roku. In A. Kuczyński (ed.), *Polskie opisywanie świata: Od fascyna-*

cji egzotyką do badań antropologicznych, pp. 219–32. Wrocław: Wydawnictwo Uniwersytetu Wrocławskiego.

——. 2004. Etnologia. *Encyklopedia Socjologii* 5: 46–50.

Prawda, M. 2002. Der Polnische Westgedanke und die Soziologie. In J. M. Piskorski, J. Hackmann, and R. Jaworski (eds.), *Deutsche Ostforschung und polnische Westforschung im Spannungsfeld von Wissenschaft und Politik: Disziplinen im Vergleich*, pp. 205–22. Osnabrück: fibre-Verlag.

Rączkowski, W. 1996. 'Drang nach Westen'? Polish Archaeology and National Identity. In M. Diaz-Andreu, and T. Champion (eds.), *Nationalism and Archaeology in Europe*, pp. 189–217. London: Routledge.

Rutkowska, G. 2004. Czy archeologia służyła ideologii PRL? Tematyka archeologiczna na łamach 'Trybuny Ludu' w latach 1948–1970. In Z. Kobyliński (ed.), *Hereditaten Cognoscere: Szkice dedykowane profesor Marii Miśkiewicz*, pp. 308–33. Warsaw: Wydawnictwo Uniwersytetu im. Kardynała Stefana Wyszyńskiego.

Simonides, D. 1995. Upper Silesians: A Regional or Ethnic Group? *Lud* 79: 217–29.

Staszczak, Z. (ed.). 1987. *Słownik etnologiczny: Terminy ogólne*. Warsaw: PWN.

Stawarz, A. 2001. Tradycje badań i perspektywy etnologii miasta w Polsce. In Przyszłość etnologii polskiej w jej teraźniejszości. *Prace Komitetu Nauk Etnologicznych PAN* 10: 117–34.

Waśkiewicz, A. 1996. Stan obecny socjologii polskiej. In E. Hałoń (ed.), *Nauka w Polsce w ocenie komitetów naukowych PAN*, pp. 199–208. Warszawa: Polska Akademia Nauk. Komitet Badań Naukowych, CUN PAN.

PART TWO

THE EARLY PHASE

The political fate of East-Central Europe was sealed by 1948. The following years witnessed radical upheaval in all spheres of society. Universities were renamed after Karl Marx; anthropology in its various branches was commonly classified as an 'ideologically retarded discipline', and it, too, was renamed. Bourgeois research traditions were denounced, and Soviet works with titles such as *The Functionalist School in Anthropology [Etnografiya] in the Service of British Imperialism* were translated into local languages. Political criteria influenced academic appointments, many topics were taboo, and contacts with Western scholars were greatly restricted. Yet the papers in this section reveal all this to have been only one side of the coin. Anthropologists succeeded not just in carving out specific 'niches' (the term used by Dietrich Treide with reference to Völkerkunde in Leipzig between 1955 and 1958) but in renewing, consolidating, and professionalising their subject. Censorship was always imperfect, very few anthropologists lost their posts for political reasons, and contacts with Western as well as Eastern anthropologists expanded rapidly from the early 1960s onwards. 'Socialist scientific management' did not, in reality, mean draconian centralisation.

The institution-building which took place in the early years of socialist rule left its mark on all later developments, even when ideological frenzy was relaxed and it became possible to criticize Stalinist excesses. One key development was the establishment of Academies of Sciences along Soviet lines, outlined here by Zbigniew Jasiewicz for Poland and Olga Skalníková for Czechoslovakia. In the other papers in this section Dietrich Treide outlines the early socialist consolidation of Völkerkunde in Leipzig and Wolfgang Jacobeit does the same for Volkskunde in Berlin. Even in the case of the German Democratic Republic, where the discipline was most vulnerable following the catastrophe of National Socialism and where the regime never lost its basically repressive character, anthropologists were able to create room to manoeuvre. Indeed, some succeeded in launching their subject into productive new directions. Jacobeit describes how Volkskundler henceforth devoted themselves to studies of the everyday culture of working people

throughout history, including the present day. This shift of emphasis pres-
aged similar developments in other parts of the German-speaking world,
where scholars were generally slower to come to terms with the Nazi past.
Similarly, Skalníková recalls the innovative enthusiasm shown by a new
generation of Czechoslovak anthropologists, for whom the popular culture of
mining communities was now a legitimate field of enquiry for the first time.

Zbigniew Jasiewicz casts his chapter as a Hegelian encounter between
the discipline of anthropology in Poland, representing an internally diverse
'society', and an oppressive external state authority. The surprising result of
this 'awkward dialogue' was that Polish anthropologists were not significantly influenced by Soviet models, and little effort was expended to make
them conform. Here, as in East Berlin Volkskunde, anthropologists were, by
choice, affiliated with history. This in itself was nothing new for anthropology. The main difference was that their historicism was now expected to
display rigorous materialist underpinnings in the form of Marxist-Leninist
dialectical materialism. More attention was paid to material culture than
previously, as can also be seen in numerous works of the Völkerkundler in
Leipzig, yet their economic anthropology had its own trajectory and relied
only rarely on the Soviet notion of 'economic-cultural types'.

Jasiewicz makes it clear that many scholars did little more than pay lip
service to the new slogans. They could continue to investigate familiar fields
of 'folk culture' because, surprising though it might seem, this was not
merely tolerated but encouraged by the authorities. However, a price was
paid in terms of intellectual vitality. Many contemporary Western trends
were taboo, and local theoretical traditions, including even home-grown
variants of Marxism such as that associated with Ludwik Krzywicki in
Poland, were also neglected. Treide shows that the niche of the 1950s, to
which members of the Leipzig institute were so loyal, came under serious
pressure once again in the late 1960s. Just when ideological danger was
receding elsewhere, plans to integrate anthropology into 'universal history'
foundered, and the upshot was that the very identity of Völkerkunde as an
independent discipline was called into question.

The Hegelian interaction was everywhere shaped by the vagaries of
local as well as national political conditions, and also by the energy and
charisma of particular personalities. Whereas in the Czechoslovak case the
key figure was the 'young Turk' Otakar Nahodil, in the German Democratic
Republic it was the returning exiles of an older generation who played the
leading roles. Jacobeit pays tribute to the democratic vision of Wolfgang
Steinitz in Volkskunde, while Dietrich Treide outlines the extraordinary
impact of Julius and Eva Lips on Völkerkunde in Leipzig. The former died
shortly after taking up his appointment (the archives are silent on why the

post was apparently turned down by Paul Kirchhoff, to whom it was initially offered; one can only speculate on what might have happened if he, rather than Lips, had been appointed to head the discipline's oldest institute in Germany). Eva Lips then took over as administrator and proved adept in cultivating her husband's scholarly legacy (such as his concept of the 'harvesting peoples'). Moreover, she evidently conducted the affairs of the institute with a flexibility which indicated that her first loyalty was to the survival of her adopted discipline rather than to any political ideology.

In summary, the disciplinary field of anthropology in East-Central Europe was transformed in the early decades of socialism, but the effects of new political conditions and institutional changes 'from above' were modified by many local factors and decisively shaped by a few outstanding personalities. The usual outcome was a complex mixture of innovations and strong continuities with pre-socialist research traditions. In the German Democratic Republic, however, the rupture with the past was much more radical, both in Volkskunde and in Völkerkunde.

CH

Chapter 6
Onwards, But in Which Direction? Anthropology at the University of Leipzig between 1950 and 1968

Dietrich Treide

Leipzig holds a special position in the German anthropological landscape, because it was there that the country's very first Institut für Ethnologie was established in 1914. Before the University of Leipzig reopened officially after the Second World War, on 5 February 1946, quite a few members of the teaching staff had already left. Some departed at the end of the war. Others followed when the American forces withdrew in June 1945. Still more had left by February 1946, because they did not approve of the objectives of the Soviet military administration. Yet many academic staff were able to continue their work, and sound scholarship, free of political interference, was not abandoned in the humanities and social sciences. The 'anti-fascist democratic' reorganisation of the university after 1945 met with resistance not only from some of the teaching staff but also from much of the student body. As in other universities, students from non-bourgeois backgrounds were systematically recruited via preparatory institutes (*Vorstudien-anstalten*) and so-called Workers' and Peasants' Faculties (*Arbeiter- und Bauernfakultäten*). Such institutes certainly smoothed the path for women and men who otherwise would have had little chance of receiving higher education. They also enabled a relatively large number of older people to gain or regain a foothold after years of war.

In 1947 the Faculty of Social Sciences was created at the University of Leipzig (renamed after Karl Marx in 1953) with the explicit goal of disseminating Marxism-Leninism and training communist cadres, but the effort met with considerable resistance. The second university reform in 1951 made the study of Marxism-Leninism obligatory in all degree programmes. At the same time, the ten-month academic year and one-subject degree programmes were introduced. This 'streamlining' reduced the duration of undergraduate study, but the action to enforce specialisation—to prevent 'bourgeois academic roaming'—amounted to a narrowing of academic education. The problem was accentuated by the shortage of teaching staff, a result of many departures or politically motivated redundancies. These gaps were filled by academics coming from concentration camps or from western Germany and by returnees from the Soviet Union, the United States, and Great Britain.

The Institut für Ethnologie: A Laborious Start

The staffing situation at the Institut für Ethnologie was unstable until the arrival of Julius Lips from the United States in 1948. Otto Reche, the long-time director of the Institute for Race Studies and Ethnology (Institut für Rassen- und Völkerkunde), had bid farewell to Leipzig academic life in a letter to the university rector on 29 May 1945, in which he complained that an unknown American had removed books from the library of the renamed 'Institute for Ethnologie and Antropologie'.[1] From the autumn of 1945 the physical anthropologist Baron von Eickstedt, previously professor at the University of Breslau, was employed at the institute. However, an application from the rector to appoint him to the vacant chair apparently went unanswered by the state officials for almost a year.[2] In the meantime, on 1 December 1945, Gerhard Sander, who had held no academic post since acquiring his doctorate in 1921, was appointed curator of the Museum für Völkerkunde. On 1 April 1947 he was promoted to acting director; previously, in 1946, he had been appointed to a teaching position at the university. This can be attributed to the influence of the sinologist Eduard Erkes. Erkes was a long-standing member of the Social Democratic Party who had lost his university post under the Nazis. Reinstated in 1945, he was reappointed extraordinary professor for Chinese as well as acting director of the Museum für Völkerkunde and, in 1946, as acting director of the Institut für Ethnologie. The latter appointment followed a communication from the Saxon State Administration to the rector informing him that 'the Department of Science and Research has notified Prof. Dr. Baron von Eickstedt that it sees no possibility for the time being of appointing him to represent anthropology and anatomy at the University of Leipzig'.[3]

Gerhard Sander lectured at the institute on the peoples and cultures of South and Central America until, on 12 August 1950, he was informed by the pro-rector that 'in the course of the restructuring of the assistant positions at the University of Leipzig' his contract would be terminated as of 30 September.[4] His principal colleague in these years was Walter Eisen, who

---

[1] Universitätsarchiv Leipzig (UAL), Phil. Fak. B 1/14:11, Bd. 1, Julius Lips-Institut 1945–1965, Blätter 1–3.
[2] Ibid., Blatt. 11.
[3] UAL, Phil. Fak. B 1/14:11, Bd. 1, Bl. 10.
[4] UAL, Personalakte 2545, Bl. 21; see also Bl. 31, 32.

taught the introductory course 'Principles of General Ethnologie' in the winter semester of 1946–47 and also gave lectures on Oceania. It appears that Eisen managed the administration of the institute until November 1948, when his lectures were cancelled, apparently for reasons of his health. The files of the University Archives give no indication of when and under what circumstances Eisen left the institute. He continued to work for a number of years at the university library, where he often spoke to anthropology students and teaching assistants about his life, including his time as an emigrant in England. At any rate, whatever further data about the years 1945–48 may come to light in the future, it is certainly untrue that Julius Lips took over an 'abandoned and desolate institute', as his widow later alleged (E. Lips 1965b: 280–81).

The files of the University Archives are silent about when the idea of offering the chair to Julius Lips first began to develop. We know that Erkes was decidedly against the proposal, as a letter to the rector dated 12 February 1947 bears witness:

> Lips has, at least for as long as he worked in Germany, largely iden-
> tified himself with the *Kulturkreislehre,* a clerical-reactionary and
> anti-revolutionary doctrine that is rejected by all serious anthropolo-
> gists as well as by Russian specialists. This shows that, despite his
> confession to socialism, he cannot be considered a Marxist. For an
> anthropology [Ethnologie] understood as the basis of all social sci-
> ences, only a Marxist-oriented representative can in my opinion be
> considered.[5]

Erkes emphatically supported the candidacy of Paul Kirchhoff. In the same letter to the rector, Erkes advised:

> For the chair in Ethnologie, the only serious candidate is in my opin-
> ion Prof. Kirchhoff, who has been characterised by both the above-
> mentioned Americans and by all German anthropologists as the most
> outstanding German representative of the discipline, who has
> achieved a great deal scientifically and is known to me as both an
> excellent scholar and a scientifically qualified Marxist.[6]

In his comments on Paul Kirchhoff at the commission meeting held on 12 March 1947 to revive the chair in Ethnologie (successor to Reche), Erkes highlighted the facts that Kirchhoff had been active in the German Commu-nist Party as a student, that he had not found a position in England or the

---

[5] UAL, Personalakte 205, Bl. 1.

[6] Ibid. The American colleagues in question were Robert Lowie and Alfred L. Kroeber, who had indeed made positive remarks about Paul Kirchhoff in letters to Erkes dated 27 November 1946 and 5 December 1946, respectively.

United States and indeed had been expelled from the British Empire, and that Nazi Germany had stripped him of his German citizenship.[7]

The commission comprised the rector, Hans-Georg Gadamer; the dean of humanities, Walter Baetke; the dean of education, Maximilian Lambertz; and four other professors, including Erkes. The proposal to appoint Kirchhoff was taken seriously, even though the commission was by no means left-leaning. An appraisal of the only publication by him available in Leipzig—his dissertation—came to positive conclusions. The Faculty of the Humanities forwarded a recommendation to appoint Kirchhoff to the Saxon State Government, which then formally offered him the chair (on 12 May 1947 and 11 September 1947). No answer was received, whereupon the rector asked the dean of the faculty to submit proposals for other candidates.[8] Consideration was next given to two more emigrants, Wolfram Eberhard and Herbert Baldus, probably at the instigation of Erkes, who in a letter to the dean stressed again that only an exiled scholar could fill the chair for ethnology.[9] Eberhard turned down a possible nomination, and Baldus seems never to have responded.

A way out of this impasse was found by Erkes, who revealed to the commission in April 1948 that he had learned from his colleague Albert Schreiner 'that Prof. Lips throughout his stay in America and especially in the last few years has been hard at work on his anthropological studies and published a whole series of monographs.' On this basis, Erkes suggested nominating Julius Lips for the chair, and a recommendation went forward to the Saxon State Government on 16 April 1948.[10] In fact, the Faculty of Social Sciences had wanted to nominate Lips to a chair in 1947 but had refrained because the chairs for politics and sociology had already been filled. The dean of this faculty had then proposed to offer Lips the chair for comparative sociology of law (*Vergleichende Rechtssoziologie*), with an explicit signal that 'he may also lecture on Ethnologie'.[11] Julius Lips started in the fall semester, giving lectures at the Institut für Ethnologie. In July 1949 he was elected to the office of rector, but he died on 21 January 1950.

---

[7] UAL, Phil. Fak. B 2/22, 35, Bl. 8.

[8] Ibid., Bl. 13, 15, 16. The letters sent to Kirchhoff were returned to the Saxon State Administration unopened on 24 July 1948 (ibid., Bl. 19, 20, 30).

[9] Ibid., Bl. 21.

[10] Ibid., Bl. 26; Bl. 22. Albert Schreiner taught in the Faculty of Social Sciences from 1947 to 1949 and served briefly as its dean. He had lived in the United States since 1941 and was among the founding members of the Council for a Democratic Germany in 1944. A number of members of this council returned to the Soviet zone after the war, including Hermann Budzislawski, Maximilian Scheer, Walter Victor, and Julius Lips. Scheer (alias Walter Schlieper) had minored under Lips in Cologne (see Pützstück 1995: 229, cf. 270).

[11] UAL, Personalakte 205, Bl. 15; see also Bl. 6, Bl. 9.

It is as difficult to say anything concrete about his plans as rector as it is to specify his scientific goals. His inaugural speech as rector indicated only that he intended to continue his previous investigations into early systems of justice and especially the study of 'harvesting peoples' (*Erntevölker*). He also declared his intention to revive his 20-year-old thesis concerning the origins and spread of totemism, a thesis inspired by the Kulturkreislehre.[12]

Probably the last words that Lips wrote concerning a current theme in his discipline can be found in his foreword to the volume *Forschungsreise in die Dämmerung* (Field trip to dusk), about his work at Howard University in Washington, DC. He wrote, in January 1950:

> There is a lot of discussion, in the United States as well, among both whites and Negroes, about the problem of coloured and white. ... American anthropologists avoid this problem by asserting that the American Negro will disappear, and in two hundred years the question of coloured people on the American continent will no longer be an issue. I do not share this opinion. Anyone familiar with the structure of the American economy and society knows that, especially in times of crisis, the Negro problem is and will remain one of the country's most urgent problems, the solution of which in my opinion cannot be found in a capitalist state, given its typical social and economic structure; even attempts to find a superficial solution are doomed to failure. Only the overcoming of class and race differences in the United States, the overcoming of capitalism as such, can lead to a solution to the Negro problem. But this can occur only in a socialist society. (J. Lips 1950: 13)

Today we can say that the idea of the United States as a 'melting pot' of differing cultures has not—at any rate in unrestricted, idealised form—been realised. On the other hand, who today holds out any prospect for a socialist reshaping of social conditions in the United States? Whether such statements adequately represent Julius Lips's political position is a question that must remain unanswered in view of his sudden death.

What Next?

Julius Lips's successor was his wife, Eva, whose return to Leipzig in 1948 was a homecoming in a very comprehensive sense. Her father, Ernst Wiegandt, had worked there as a publisher. She had grown up in a world of books, and her lifelong fascination with words, whether in speech or on paper, had its roots there. Eva Lips had never studied anthropology and

---

[12] See J. Lips 1953 for the text delivered as his *Rektoratsrede* on 31 October 1949. On the link between totemism and the 'harvesting peoples' see J. Lips 1930: 47.

indeed had married before even considering going to university. But her marriage to Julius Lips had brought her in constant contact with the discipline, and she worked with eagerness and dedication as his personal assistant.

The state administration had not, as far as I can judge on the basis of the archival sources, tried to influence the selection procedure that led eventually to the appointment of Julius Lips, but this time it did not show the same restraint. Three days after Lips's death Eduard Erkes wrote to Adolf Jensen—professor of Ethnologie in Frankfurt am Main, director of the Frobenius Institute, and a distinguished scholar who had maintained his distance from National Socialism—asking his advice about possible candidates to succeed Lips. Jensen replied giving the names of numerous eligible colleagues: Hermann Trimborn, Wilhelm Mühlmann, Günther Wagner, Helmut Petri, Rudolf Lehmann, Günter Spannaus, Josef Haekel, and Hermann Baumann. This list was based simply on the fact that these colleagues either did not currently hold a chair or were not actively exercising a position as holder of a chair or as director of an institute. (Jensen's mentioning of Günther Wagner and Wilhelm Mühlmann is remarkable in view of their Nazi history, as is his positive recommendation of Baumann, who had replaced Pater Wilhelm Koppers in Vienna during the Nazi period before being dismissed in 1945. Baumann's accomplishments in the cultural-historical analysis of Africa were nonetheless widely recognised.)

In the same month, however, the Ministry of Education of the Saxon state government took the initiative and proposed Ferdinand Hestermann, from Jena, as the new director of the Institut für Ethnologie. It also recommended that Eva Lips be appointed as the institute administrator (*Geschäftsführer*) and, further, that she might deliver a public lecture based on a manuscript left by Julius Lips. Finally, the ministry recommended to the dean of humanities that Eva Lips be given a research contract to work up her husband's papers.[13] It is not unlikely that these detailed recommendations were the result of suggestions issuing from the University of Leipzig, but this cannot be known for certain. At any rate, the faculty followed the recommendations of the state administration.[14]

Ferdinand Hestermann was one of the founders of the journal *Anthropos* in 1904 and was involved in its publication for 12 years. He received his

---

[13] UAL, Phil. Fak. B 2/22, 35, Bl. 36; see also Bl. 32; Bl. 33.

[14] In the minutes of the meeting of the Faculty of Humanities on 21 March 1950 it is stated that Professor Hestermann was to become director of the Institut für Ethnologie, following Richard Thurnwald's departure from the Humboldt University to become head of the Free University of Berlin. Whether Thurnwald was really being considered for appointment in Leipzig is not revealed clearly (see ibid., Bl. 38).

doctorate in 1916, and his habilitation was completed in 1929. He then lectured in Münster in 1929–30, becoming professor there in 1946. He claimed to be one of the founders of the *Kulturbund zur demokratischen Erneuerung Deutschlands* (Cultural Union for the Democratic Renewal of Germany) in Münster. He moved to the Soviet sector at the end of 1948 and was employed from February 1949 in Jena, where he was appointed to a chair in general philology and cultural studies. Hestermann was a founding member of the Provisional People's Chamber (*Provisorische Volkskammer*), representing the Kulturbund. This political engagement was nevertheless insufficient to strengthen his position in Leipzig. On 2 March 1951, Eduard Erkes informed Eva Lips, in his function as vice-dean of the Faculty of Humanities, that Hestermann had been commissioned to administer the Hilprecht Collection in Jena and that all his lectures and seminars were to be cancelled at the behest of the state government. Hestermann protested, but he was unsuccessful in reversing the decision, at least as far as his lectures in Leipzig were concerned. His relationship with Eva Lips was not free from tension, as is shown by a letter that Lips wrote to Vice-Dean Erkes on 28 May 1950. She was decidedly opposed to Hestermann's plans to raise the profile of anthropology in Jena. She argued that Leipzig should remain the prime 'centre of anthropological research' ('Zentrum für ethnologische Forschung') in the newly established GDR.[15]

In April 1951 Erkes informed Eva Lips that she was to become acting director of the institute, following instructions from the new rector. The support Eva Lips unquestionably received from 'above' could not have failed to astonish her colleagues, Erkes among them. The evaluations of Eva Lips's *Habilitationsschrift* (postdoctoral thesis) were no less astonishing. The faculty in May 1954 appointed Erkes and Georg Mayer, rector and professor of economics with special respect to world economics and agricultural history, to examine this work, which was titled 'The Rice Harvest of the Ojibwa Indians.' The Egyptologist Siegfried Morenz asked whether it would not be appropriate to involve a senior anthropologist, and in November 1954 Bernhard Struck, of Jena, submitted a 'third (short) evaluation', in which he stated that the work was a 'good postdoctoral thesis'.[16] The remainder of the evaluation was briskly completed. Eva Lips was awarded her *venia legendi* for Ethnologie and comparative sociology of law and was appointed university lecturer (*Dozent*) on 1 March 1955.

Eva Lips had already written a number of books before coming to Leipzig, not least of a political nature, such as *Savage Symphony* (1938) and

---

[15] UAL, Phil. Fak., B1/14:11, Bd. 1, Bl. 57, 72, 73, 77; see also UAL, Personalakte 142, Bl. 11; idem 1107, Bl. 3.

[16] UAL, Personalakte 1107, Bl. 53; see also Bl. 31, Bl. 38.

Rebirth in Liberty (1942). However, she was not assessed primarily on this basis in 1951 and 1952. Her episodic reports on life in Roosevelt's United States were viewed with interest but were hardly sufficient to meet the needs of anthropology students, many of them mature students who had been directly involved in the war. They were almost exclusively anthropology majors (students of other disciplines rarely attended anthropology classes after the death of Julius Lips), and they demanded above all a broader thematic as well as regional focus in their education. Following a resolution to this effect, in December 1952 the Office of the State Secretary for Higher Education suggested that the dean incorporate Paul Nedo, Hans Damm, and Fritz Krause into the teaching programme. The specification of these particular names suggests that the students' protest had found an echo. In her reply to the dean, Eva Lips hastened to welcome the proposal relating to Nedo and Damm.[17] Both lectured at the institute (from 1950 known as the Julius Lips-Institut für Ethnologie und vergleichende Rechtssoziologie) in the academic year 1953–54.

On the other hand, Eva Lips vigorously opposed Fritz Krause's taking on a teaching position. Krause had been director of the Museum für Völkerkunde until 1945, although he had not been allowed to exercise this office in the last year of the war after being accused of insubordination by the Nazi city administration. Lips argued that he had written a memorandum titled 'The Significance of Ethnology for the New Germany' in 1934. As chair of the German Anthropological Association (Deutsche Gesellschaft für Völkerkunde), at the time based in Leipzig, Krause had also publicly embraced this new Germany a year earlier, with the endorsing signatures of many leading anthropologists, among them Bernhard Ankermann, Georg Thilenius, Eugen Fischer, Hans Naumann, and Otto Reche.[18] A benevolent reading of this letter might allow the interpretation that Krause was trying to emphasise the category of 'Volk' alongside the new leading category of 'race', with the aim of securing a place for anthropology in the face of the anticipated expansion of racial studies (*Rassenkunde*).

However that may be, as a former exile Eva Lips could not have been expected to sympathise with Krause's political stance, but she seems also to have had other reasons for keeping her distance. According to the widow of

[17] UAL, Phil. Fak. B 1/14: 11, Bd. 1, Bl. 80; Bl. 82. Nedo was one of the folklorists not compromised by any involvement in Nazi politics. Eva Lips never, as far as I recall, discussed such matters. She did sometimes speak condescendingly about 'peasant folklore', but her main concern was probably to ensure that she would not have to share authority with any folklorist. In the case of Damm, who had been dismissed from his curatorship at the Völkerkunde museum in 1945 because of his membership in the Nazi Party, he owed his reinstatement in 1952 and later promotion to director at least in part to Eva Lips.
[18] UAL, Phil Fak. B 1/14: 11, Bd. 1, Bl. 16–18.

Karl Weule, Krause's predecessor as museum director, the relationship between Fritz Krause and Julius Lips had been difficult in the 1920s.[19] Weule had valued Lips's organisational talent and his appeal among students and the public but disapproved of his 'leftist' politics. Lips had been active in the democratic student movement since 1919 and claimed that he had joined the Social Democratic Party (SPD) in that same year. Krause's teaching skills, though excellent according to Mrs. Weule, were less well received, perhaps because of his dry lecturing style. There existed in all likelihood a certain academic rivalry between the two men dating back to 1919–20: the people considered by Krause to be 'advanced gatherers' (*höhere Sammler*) were identified by Lips as 'harvesting peoples'. Finally, it should not be forgotten that Krause had been chair of the German Anthropological Association when accusations of plagiarism were made against Julius Lips in 1930–32. It is no longer possible to reconstruct to what degree students were aware of these particulars in 1952. Most likely they were simply interested in acquiring as broad an education as possible under the prevailing circumstances, and the state bodies acquiesced, apparently without considering the political angles.

That it was no longer possible to study minors or second majors after the second university reform in 1951 did not prevent the great majority of anthropology students from attending courses in prehistory and physical anthropology. There was evidently a strong desire to maintain the traditional triad of physical anthropology, socio-cultural anthropology, and prehistory (archaeology). These courses were supplemented by lectures in geography, introductory philology, and, from the end of the 1950s, non-European religions.

As for Eva Lips, she wrote and translated books and papers intended for a broad readership. Her main academic subject was North American Indians, always popular with the German public. She also devoted considerable time and energy to maintaining the house and property she had inherited in Leipzig. As a 'late starter' in the academic world, she was well aware that she could not always fulfil the expectations of her students and assistants. She was tolerant of her students' interests and allowed them considerable freedom in chasing the topics of their theses. She allowed her staff considerable latitude and was supportive of a great variety of activities.[20]

---

[19] Mrs. Weule, personal communication, 1959.

[20] This can be seen in the publication accompanying the Mozambique exhibit in the Julius Lips Institute in 1953. This exhibit, organised in cooperation with the ethnographic museum, featured materials gathered by the Leipzig Research Institute for Ethnology's expedition to Portuguese East Africa in 1931, headed by Günther Spannaus and Kurt Stülpner.

Teaching Anthropology: 1950–1955

That anthropology had a long history in Leipzig was significant in strengthening its position in the 1950s after the death of Julius Lips. However, local
disciplinary ancestors played only a relatively minor role in teaching in the
1950s. For example, Eva Lips rarely mentioned the work of Friedrich Ratzel,
the teacher of Karl Weule and many other distinguished scholars. In the
years following the Second World War, Ratzel was seen primarily as a
trailblazer of Nazi geopolitics. Certainly some of the protagonists of this
geopolitical agenda did draw on Ratzel's work (Haushofer 1940). It can be
assumed that Eva Lips avoided any detailed reference to Ratzel for this
reason.

On the other hand, she held a very favourable opinion of Karl Weule,
undoubtedly motivated by his role in the early establishment of Ethnologie
as an independent discipline in Leipzig in 1914 (E. Lips 1965a). His actual
work met with little interest in the 1950s, and he was best known for his
efforts to disseminate anthropological information to a broad readership
through his popular *Kosmos* volumes. Little attention was paid to Heinrich
Schurtz, a pupil of Ratzel's, during the 1950s and 1960s. His influence in
establishing a social or political anthropology, which extended far beyond
Leipzig and even beyond the borders of Germany, was barely acknowledged.

Although the work done at the Institute for Race Studies and Ethnology between 1933 and 1945 was of course condemned in principle, National
Socialism and its race ideology were rarely discussed in any detail.[21]

In the case of her late husband, from the onset Eva Lips made every
effort to pay exaggerated homage. She tried to continue his studies in legal
anthropology for some years in the form of a seminar, but the fact that
neither she nor her students had any legal background led to the gradual
phasing out of this project. She emphasised the 'harvesting peoples' concept
as Lips's major academic legacy. Her postdoctoral thesis (published in 1956)
was reviewed in *American Anthropologist* a year later (Landes 1957). Eva
Lips responded to criticism of its evolutionary perspective and the assumption that the development of agriculture could progress only through the

---

[21] For an exception see the lecture given by two *Assistenten* in 1963 in which they drew
attention to a certain reorientation on the part of Otto Reche in 1944, namely, his partial
dissociation from the ideology of the supremacy of a Nordic race allegedly concentrated in
the German people and his emphasis on Atlantic community ties in the decisive battle against
Bolshevism. See 'Die völkerkundliche Lehre und Forschung im Griff der faschistischen
Rassendoktrin: Geist und Tätigkeit Otto Reches 1927–1945', Vortrag am Julius Lips-Institut,
gehalten von Helmut Reim und Dietrich Treide aus Anlaß des 10. Jahrestages der Namenge-
bung der Karl Marx-Universität, Mai 1963 (manuscript in possession of the author).

harvesting peoples by emphasising that a harvesting-based economy constituted *one* route to agriculture, not necessarily the only one (E. Lips 1964).

Other aspects of the legacy of Julius Lips were similarly controversial.
That he attributed individual land rights to 'early' sub-Arctic hunters (J. Lips
1939, 1947a, 1947b) was questioned by those who argued that these individual rights had come into existence only with the advent of the fur trade in the
seventeenth century. (It is all the more surprising that Julius Lips maintained
this opinion in view of the fact that he had completed research on the fur
trade between the Hudson's Bay Company and the Naskapi Indians of the
Labrador Peninsula.) Eva Lips also adopted the notion of 'culture change' as
it had been used by her husband in the United States. She used it and the
term *acculturation* in discussing changes in the lives of Indian peoples
during the colonial period (E. Lips 1962a, 1962b). In the 1950s, however,
analyses of colonially induced cultural change appeared only sporadically at
the Julius Lips Institute. One concept not followed up by Eva Lips was that
of 'ethnopolitics', a research theme initiated by Julius Lips towards the end
of the 1920s and intended by him to subsume the concept of culture
change.[22]

Eva Lips's teaching was not focused exclusively on traditions local to
Leipzig and material left by her deceased husband. The latter's move to
Columbia University in New York in 1938 had been arranged by Franz
Boas. Eva Lips acknowledged this and various features of Boas's personality
in her lectures, without engaging seriously with his work. His student Margaret Mead also received little attention: Mead addressed issues of gender
and generation, but these topics were of little relevance in public debates in
the GDR in these years. Eva Lips devoted more attention to Ruth Benedict
and her insistence on viewing a culture as a whole, which went against what
Lips's students were being taught elsewhere about the need to study interaction between different fields of culture—above all relations between economic and social conditions. Sadly, these students were taught almost nothing about internationally relevant concepts of cultural relativism.[23] As for
British scholars, Tylor, Frazer, Marrett, and others all figured in Eva Lips's
lectures on 'Magic, Myth and Religion', but students learned little about the
post-Malinowski generation of British anthropologists. Only in the 1960s,
when the focus of studies in Leipzig shifted primarily to sub-Saharan Africa,

---

[22] Julius Lips saw a distinct relationship between ethnopolitics and colonial politics; see
Pützstück 1995: 184–86, cf. 268. The term *Ethnopolitik* was first coined by Rudolf Kjellén, a
student of Ratzel's.
[23] Only after the publication of Wolfgang Rudolph's work on cultural relativism (1968) did
teaching in Leipzig begin to consider the debates in this field.

were some of the works of this school read and discussed, with the substantial aid of colleagues in Prague.[24]

If their knowledge of Western anthropology was patchy, students' knowledge of Soviet etnografiya was almost non-existent until 1951. It remains a mystery why the first Soviet guest professor at the University of Leipzig was the ethnographer Sergey Aleksandrovich Tokarev, from the Lomonosov University in Moscow. In 1951–52 he taught for two semesters in Berlin at the Humboldt University and in Leipzig. His very good knowledge of German and French was certainly one reason for sending him; his expertise in the fields of German and French anthropology was another. Tokarev's work in Leipzig was focused less on issues of periodisation in human evolution and more on ethnogenesis, on ethnic and cultural history. This was no doubt due partly to the publication of Stalin's *Concerning Marxism and Linguistics* (Marxismus und die Frage der Sprachwissenschaften, 1950), with its 'historical approach'. This reorientation, however, met with relatively little resonance in Leipzig. Questions of periodisation also remained more or less on the sidelines during the 1950s and early 1960s (see König 1962; Treide 1965). It is no accident that in the sixties and seventies Leipzig anthropologists did not participate in the periodisation discussions launched in the *Ethnographisch-Archäologische Zeitschrift* in 1968, which were primarily an interest of Berlin scholars.[25]

In addition to his own particular field of study in ethnogenesis, Tokarev's lectures on the classification of economic forms (and social phenomena linked to them) were based on the then current studies of Maksim Grigoryevich Levin and Nikolai Nikolayevich Cheboksarov on economic-cultural types (*wirtschaftlich-kulturelle Typen; khozyaystvenno-kul'turnye tipy*) in northern Eurasia. These efforts to classify primarily economic phenomena met with a greater response in Leipzig. Nevertheless, the concept of economic-cultural types was applied only sporadically, though it was based on sound research (Treide 1982). Classification schemes put forward by North American ethnologists such as Kroeber and Clark Wissler were just as important in shaping this work.

Seen as a whole, Tokarev's work at the Julius Lips Institute was hardly more than an interlude. It did not lead to any significant orientation

---

[24] See Holý 1968. I participated in a lively exchange of ideas with Ladislav Holý, Milan Stuchlík, and J. Svobodová in the course of preparatory work for this anthology.

[25] The first work on the periodisation of stateless societies and early states written in the GDR (for some time the only work of significant length) was the dissertation completed by Irmgard Sellnow at the Humboldt University in Berlin in 1956 (Sellnow 1961). Tokarev is mentioned only incidentally in this work, which drew mainly on the Soviet Marxist anthropologists Sergey Pavlovich Tolstov, Mark Osipovich Kosven, and Nataliya Borisovna Gorbacheva. See Noack and Krause, this volume.

towards etnografiya. Closer relations between anthropologists in Leipzig and Moscow did not develop until the 1970s. Only Wolfgang König's work on the peoples of Central Asia and the historical relation between pastoralists and agriculturists, initiated in the late 1950s, derived primarily from collaboration arranged by Tokarev (with Gennadiy Evge'nevich Markov, who was associated with the same chair at the Lomonosov University).

Political Influences

In considering the degree to which Marxism-Leninism affected anthropology at the University of Leipzig, the timing of this influence, and its causes, it is important to note that by 1955 the great majority of SED (Communist Party) members had left the institute. Some moved on to academic institutions in Berlin, and others to the museums for Völkerkunde in Leipzig and Dresden, both of which were staffed largely by graduates of the Julius Lips Institute (including some who were not party members). There was no exchange of staff between the university institutes in Leipzig and Berlin: frequent contacts between the two did not develop until the 1970s, and even then they were not free of tension. This was partly due to the positions the two institutes held within their respective universities, that in Berlin being associated with history and that in Leipzig being integrated into African and Middle Eastern Studies.

The departure of most party members by 1955 meant fewer opportunities for external authorities to exercise political influence. One result of the fact that there were too few members to form a party cell in the institute (three was the minimum) was that discussions of topical political issues had little effect on anthropological work. This was the era in which revolutions in Hungary and Poland shook the 'socialist camp' and put an end to the relaxation of Soviet control that followed Stalin's death. The GDR also experienced demands for a more humane socialism, and Walter Ulbricht's authoritarian leadership style was unpopular with many intellectuals. But their protests were unsuccessful, and in Leipzig Fritz Behrens, the first dean of the Faculty of Social Sciences, was accused of revisionism and eventually forced to take early retirement. The Institut für Ethnologie, however, remained more or less insulated from this backlash. In the years between 1955 and 1958, at least, the Julius Lips Institute existed in a 'niche', although great care had to be taken to protect anthropology students from the sorts of political reprisals suffered by many students in other disciplines.

The staff at the institute discussed many issues openly, including explosive ones, without feeling that their opinions might be reported. During the second half of the 1950s and the 1960s, however, staff numbers were so reduced that colleagues were too busy with everyday academic work to find

the time to communicate in any depth on non-academic matters. Nevertheless, even if contacts became less frequent in these years, the essential feeling remained unchanged. When you arrived at the institute and shut the door
behind you, you felt at home. The small number of staff meant that rivalries
were also limited; there was no forum for forming factions. It was of course
important to secure a certain amount of goodwill from the top—from the
leading organs of the university and the SED. The main concern was to
remain inconspicuous, to give no grounds for reproach, to protect the institute and oneself from sudden and time-consuming wrangling, which could so
easily be triggered by a single act of thoughtlessness. There was no question
of currying favour with the authorities in the hope of advancing one's career:
the curriculum vitae of the Leipzig anthropologists bear witness to this fact.

This temporary niche was inseparable from the fact that anthropology
was seen as relatively insignificant—indeed, it was more or less ridiculed by
representatives of other disciplines, if only in a whisper. Until the early
1960s, at least, the anthropologists themselves fostered this attitude by side-
stepping every possible complication and steering clear of some of the
current trends at the university. This was due in large measure to Eva Lips,
who spread her protective wings over the institute and everyone in it (she
was renowned for saying, 'We are all one big family!'). She created a certain
security which—and this must be said, too—did not directly obstruct the
formation of productive unrest but did not promote it either.

This niche also enabled students to select subjects for degree theses
without external interference. Work on economic issues was prominent, and
it did, of course, follow many of the interests of Julius and Eva Lips. But this
emulation was by no means slavish. Leipzig anthropologists were enthusiastic about the acquisition and analysis of 'hard' quantitative data, about
applying terms such as *means of production* and *division of labour* meaning-
fully, and about being able to utilise analytical methods originating in business management (Liedtke 1964; Schinkel 1964; Treide 1964). The regional
foci were also to a certain extent pre-determined—North (and to a degree
South) America, due to the work of Julius and Eva Lips, but also Oceania-
Australia, a region for which there had been a long-standing interest at the
institute, thanks in part to the teaching of Hans Damm. Both work on North
America and studies of Australian Aborigines treated issues of nutrition
physiology, ecology, and demography. They explored the relationship between kinship and territorial organisation and dealt with issues of social
organisation in less differentiated communities. Publications such as Reim
1962 and Treide 1965 received no acknowledgement from the senior bodies
at the university, but they did gain international recognition, which led to
their authors being invited to participate in fieldwork. In my own work on

western North America I found the works of Julian Steward essential, particularly his concept of multilinear evolution. I later came back to this concept in dealing with Karl Marx's *Excerpts on Ethnology* after these were published by Lawrence Krader (1972) and Hans-Peter Harstick (1974) (see also Treide 1980 and 1990).

Africa and the Demand for Modernisation

Africa, or, to be more exact, sub-Saharan Africa, began to assume prominence in teaching and research at the Julius Lips Institute with the lectures of Ernst Dammann in 1957 (Dammann 1999: 150–51, 170, 294) and with the involvement of Wolfgang Liedtke and numerous students in the cartographic documentation of social development across the continent. This focus was intensified when African students arrived to study in Leipzig in the 1960s. It was also due in part to the move of the America specialist Rolf Kruschke to the Völkerkunde museum in 1967 and to an involuntary shift in my own interests upon the integration of the institute into the Department of African and Middle Eastern Studies in 1969. My *Habilitationsschrift* on the Indians of western North America was almost complete when, in accordance with the new orientation, I had to change the entire focus of my scientific work. With the hiring of Reinhard Escher, Ulrich Bürkmann, and Roma Mildner-Spindler, all Africa specialists, in 1978–82, the new domination of Africa was secured.

André Gingrich (2005) has described 'the return of the old schools' in West Germany after 1945, giving the examples of cultural morphology, historic diffusionism, and functionalism. This tendency was also evident in Leipzig, but to a lesser degree. Eva Lips renewed her pre-1933 contacts with Martin Gusinde and strove to resolve tensions generated during the Nazi era in her relations with Hermann Trimborn and Hans Plischke. This helped young research staff at the Julius Lips Institute to establish contacts with their equivalents in the Federal Republic, but the influence of these contacts on theoretical and methodological orientations in Leipzig was always limited. Works by American and British anthropologists seemed often more attractive to us.

Towards the end of the 1950s a cry to modernise the discipline was first heard in West Germany. When Eva Lips returned from a meeting of the German Anthropological Association in Stuttgart in the autumn of 1959, she recounted repeatedly, with great emphasis, a remark she had made there (unofficially, of course): 'Trappe—shut your trap'. The young sociologist Paul Trappe, who later earned recognition as a development sociologist and expert on cooperatives in sub-Saharan Africa and on the formation of African self-help organisations, had clearly touched a sore spot: relatively few anthropologists had paid any close attention to contemporary social change in the so-called developing countries.[26] Following a pattern set by conferences in Abidjan (1954) and Kampala (1959) organised by British social anthropologists, not to mention the influence of Melville Herskovits and numerous articles in the journals *Africa*, *African Affairs*, and *Human Organization*, all devoted to issues of social change in Africa, Hermann Baumann took up the subject in a paper presented at the German Anthropological Association meeting in Freiburg im Breisgau in 1961. In 1962, a meeting of the German Africa Society (Deutsche Afrika-Gesellschaft) in Cologne was devoted to 'Africa and Its Changing Social Systems'.

During these years the younger anthropologists in Leipzig, not least the students, were developing reservations about the traditional content of their discipline. When I began lecturing on the ethnography of Africa in 1956–57, at the age of 23, I followed a basically cultural-historical approach. I drew heavily on the comprehensive works of Hermann Baumann and Walter Hirschberg, and although I recognised the conceptual and methodological issues in these publications, I did not deal with them explicitly. The extensive work of Diedrich Westermann on the history of Africa seemed to me an instructive example of an attempt to release Africa from its state of being without history.[27]

In a seminar accompanying my lectures on Africa in the autumn of 1958 the idea was born of preparing maps to document both the historic and present-day development of the peoples of Uganda. The subjects treated included economic changes in the colonial period, the development of wage labour after the Second World War, questions of migration and urbanisation, the ethnic makeup of the population in Jinja and Kampala, and the educational situation in the country (Kollektiv des Julius Lips-Instituts 1960). We made use of the work of Diedrich Westermann, Richard Thurnwald, and Günther Wagner without critical reflection, and the fact that the study was published in the scientific journal of the Karl Marx University in 1960 without any objections being raised throws light on the imperfections of censorship in those days. This was possibly a case in which anthropology was lucky, because we happened to find an independent-minded and tolerant editor. The monitoring of publications by the Museum für Völkerkunde in

---

[26] See Trappe 1960. It is no longer possible to ascertain whether the comment of Eva Lips might also have been connected to references made by Trappe to Richard Thurnwald, Diedrich Westermann, Wilhelm Mühlmann and others. Younger GDR anthropologists took a somewhat different view of Trappe's arguments (Reim and König 1960).

[27] Westermann's 'contradictory' personality and his work were later given more intensive treatment in the GDR: see Brauner, Herms, and Legère 1975; Rusch and Sellnow 1976; cf. Mischek 2000.

Leipzig, where we published most of our work, was largely the responsibility of the museum itself.

A little earlier, in 1957, the Julius Lips Institute had experienced a shock when, for the first time, several graduates had been unable to find positions in anthropological institutions. As the number of students was never high (between four and eight new students annually), the matter was taken very seriously, especially because job prospects could not be expected to improve in the future. The 1957 graduates did eventually find suitable professional employment, but it had to be recognised that a degree in anthropology was no longer a guarantee of a career in academia. This accelerated discussion of the contents of what was being taught in the discipline, and there was increasing criticism, especially among the younger colleagues at the institute, of 'so-called hobby anthropology' (*so genannte Hobby-Ethnologie*)—that is, the concentration on themes that were of purely personal interest to the scholars concerned.

It was exceptional in these years for students of anthropology to leave for the Federal Republic, and very few students left the GDR for political reasons. In any case the decision to emigrate was not rooted in the structures of the Julius Lips Institute, and those who did leave frequently returned to visit the institute later (e.g. one graduate who had in the meantime become a French citizen). Those graduates who stayed, and certainly those who formed the core of the staff at the Julius Lips Institute, were driven, indeed obsessed, by the idée fixe of preserving the discipline of anthropology at the University of Leipzig. This motivation had something to do with the distinguished local tradition, but it was also generated to a certain extent by political, and perhaps also youthful, defiance. It was an expression of our resistance to the many incomprehensible and damaging administrative changes that were implemented in these years. This loyalty endured, however imperfect our efforts to take up the intellectual heritage of our celebrated predecessors.

Independent Anthropology at Risk

Beginning in 1959, anthropology's position at the University of Leipzig changed dramatically: it was drawn out of its 'niche'. The temporary head of the Department of African and Middle Eastern Studies held a seminar at the Julius Lips Institute at his own request, not least in order to announce that anthropology had no future. The argument was based largely on the discipline's colonial past, and the activities and publications of Diedrich Westermann drew particularly severe criticism. We need to remember that the discipline's colonial entanglement had not yet been seriously investigated in any Western country. The major role in the development of African studies in the GDR was played by historians who had worked on colonialism, some of them making use of primary source material while others analysed the publications of German historians, geographers, and social scientists. In view of the low level of staffing, ongoing teaching assignments, and time spent supervising theses at the Julius Lips Institute at the end of the 1950s, there was little time for a thorough discussion of the extent to which anthropology had served colonialism, or of colonialism in general. No one at the institute tried to defend colonialism, and everyone included some discussion of the specific colonial situation when evaluating field materials.[28] Yet a simplistic and indiscriminate condemnation of colonialism and of anthropologists' complicity in it would have been inappropriate to the institute's style of work. We had a feeling of unease, of being drawn involuntarily into debates and activities outside the proper scope of the discipline. These misgivings turned out to be justified.

Some years later, in 1974, Jürgen Franke submitted his dissertation, 'The Chagga in Contemporary Reports, 1885–1916: A Contribution to the History of the Chagga in the German Colonial Period'. This was a remarkably meticulous evaluation of the files of the Imperial Colonial Office and also of the materials held by the archives of the 'Leipziger Mission'.[29] As Franke's supervisor, I was asked by the head of African and Middle Eastern Studies whether such a dissertation could possibly be accepted at all.

Attempts to drag ethnology out of its 'niche' in one way or another were pursued vigorously from the end of the 1950s onwards. In April 1958 Walter Markov wrote to Eva Lips in his capacity as managing chair of the Academic Council of Historical Institutes as follows:

> The SED Central Party Administration at the Karl Marx University has ... issued a programme dealing in detail with all issues relating to the transformation of our university into a socialist educational establishment. In this programme it has been suggested that in the course of the socialist development of the Humanities Faculty, a principle of strengthened unity among the historical sciences be realised in a single department incorporating the Institutes for Prehistory and Early History, Art History, Musicology, Classical Philology, the Julius Lips Institute and others into a single Academic Council of

---

[28] It is to be hoped that Bernhard Streck will present evidence to support his statement that the Leipzig institute remained 'a stronghold of colonial nostalgia until well beyond the end of the Second World War' (Streck 1997: 57, 66).

[29] Work on preparing annotated bibliographies on former German colonies was begun at the Julius Lips Institute at the end of the 1960s. It was carried out in a very thorough and objective way, at both undergraduate and graduate levels.

Historical Institutes. I herewith beg your cooperation in achieving this goal.[30]

Eva Lips was the central figure in what followed. In January 1959 she informed the State Secretary's Office for Higher Education that she was not currently in a position, for health reasons, to organise a conference on the topic of 'Ethnologie and History' at the Julius Lips Institute, as had been requested of her. In October 1960 the Egyptologist Siegfried Morenz submitted a motion that Lips, having been promoted to a full lectureship (*Professor mit vollem Lehrauftrag*) on 1 January 1960, now be appointed to the vacant chair of the institute. Apparently in response to a letter from the dean of the faculty in September 1961, Paul Nedo suggested four possible experts to review this proposal: Hans Damm (Leipzig), Karl-Heinz Otto (Berlin), Walter Ruben (Berlin), and Irmgard Sellnow (Berlin).[31] Why the dean addressed the folklorist Nedo rather than the two *Ethnologen* at the Humboldt University in Berlin is unclear. In any case, since Eva Lips was not appointed chair until 1966, this particular procedure clearly ended inconclusively. Nevertheless, these events were not without importance. It is likely that one of the reasons Morenz proposed Lips for the chair was to forestall the unmistakable attempts of the historians, primarily specialists in modern history, to extend their influence over the Julius Lips Institute.

An event in 1961 is widely assumed to have had a serious effect on anthropology in Leipzig. Eva Lips had made several attempts since the end of Second World War to clear up the misunderstandings which had arisen between colleagues during the Nazi era. She had re-established contact with Hermann Trimborn in Bonn, among others, and invited him to give a public lecture in Leipzig. The lecture was accompanied by a seminar, during which Eva Lips asked a student what he understood by the term *higher civilisation* (*Hochkultur*). The reply satisfied Lips fully but led to a great deal of headshaking from two modern historians who took part in the seminar as guests. At this time, historians of Latin America were particularly interested in contacts with anthropologists (as demonstrated by their participation in the Thirty-fourth International Congress of Americanists in Vienna in 1960). This seminar was 'evaluated' without consultation with any of the staff at the Julius Lips Institute. It is probably correct to assume that the resulting report contributed to an interruption in enrolment for the anthropology major for some years in Leipzig as of 1962. Eva Lips was officially informed that only four students would be enrolled in the academic year 1962–63, of whom two would be Volkskundler. For practical reasons, all four students would be registered at the Humboldt University in Berlin. The reason given

---

[30] UAL, Personalakte 1107, Bl. 115.
[31] Ibid., Bl. 139; see also Bl. 135; Bl. 117, 144.

was a general cutback in the quotas for social sciences, and the state official pointed out that some graduates in anthropology had been assigned to positions not associated with that subject.[32]

The anthropologists in Leipzig had, independently of this development, been considering for some time how their teaching could be made more relevant in terms of subsequent professional praxis. There were different interpretations of the expression 'positions not associated with subjects studied' (berufsfremd). In any case, after the elimination of the quota of students for 1962 no new students for anthropology were enrolled again in Leipzig until 1968—and then only after lengthy negotiations. This abrupt suspension caused great dismay among the staff of the institute, who feared that it could easily become prey to tactical and strategic decisions—for example, concerning the modification or discontinuation of research projects. (This was not possible when students were in the middle of their courses, since long-term projects always had student participation and the students had a right to complete their courses.)

Necessity Is the Mother of Invention

The shortage of students majoring in anthropology presented the staff of the Julius Lips Institute with a challenge to which they reacted as follows. First, special courses were laid on whenever there was demand, such as from other institutions or from individuals who somehow succeeded in forcing their enrolment. Some teaching in sociology was also integrated into these courses for the first time. Second, classes were held for people already in full-time employment, among them librarians, doctors, and specialists in tropical and subtropical agriculture. The Leipzig public showed significant interest in this new opportunity for postgraduate education. Third, anthropology continued to be taught as a major to foreign students, particularly those sent by the governments of Ghana, Mali, Niger, Somalia, Sudan, Syria, Lebanon, Peru, Guatemala, and Bolivia and also by social organisations in Norway. Most of these students also took courses in sociology.

The ad hoc teaching projects were very labour intensive, and responsibility fell almost always to the same three or four people. Each project had also to be 'pushed through' the relevant university bodies or the ministry, leaving little time for other work. Particular mention must be made of Wolfgang Liedtke's contributions concerning foreign students undertaking fieldwork in their home countries. He was an outstanding, attentive supervisor in all phases of their projects, as numerous publications testify (e.g. Asamoa 1971; Mirreh 1978).

---

[32] UAL, Phil. Fak. B 1/14:11, Bd. 1, Bl. 158–59.

Looking back on those years in the GDR, it is impossible to ignore the scarcity of opportunities for doing field research. The great majority of anthropologists continued to see fieldwork as fundamental to the discipline, yet the GDR had no institution comparable to, for example, the West German Research Council to finance such research. Charitable or non-profit foundations did not exist either. To obtain approval for travel abroad (even just to attend conferences) was significantly more difficult for university anthropologists than for those based in museums, which reported directly to the administrative authorities. The prospects of being allowed an extended sojourn in a non-European country were reasonably good only if that country was a political ally of the GDR (e.g. the study of Arabic was relatively well cultivated, because numerous Arab states were friendly towards the GDR). Occasionally, personal academic contacts reaching beyond the frontiers of the GDR could enable authorisation of a research visit to a non-socialist country. This was how I and Helmut Reim were able to visit Finland and Australia in 1965 and 1968–69, respectively. But the third university reform in 1968 imposed new constraints which made the continuation of these projects impossible.

The fiftieth anniversary of the establishment of anthropology in Leipzig, in 1964, presented an ideal opportunity to highlight its relatively long tradition and to reflect on the current state of the discipline. The anniversary conference was unmistakably biased toward themes of economic anthropology (see Liedtke 1964; E. Lips 1964; Schinkel 1964; Treide 1964). The actual contents of the papers were, however, only vaguely related. The main concern was to demonstrate the range of international academic relations maintained by Leipzig anthropologists. Speakers included two colleagues from the Federal Republic, one from Austria, three from Czechoslovakia, one from Poland, a British citizen resident in the GDR, and just one citizen of the GDR itself. No colleagues from the USSR attended the anniversary. Although Eva Lips and several staff members of the Julius Lips Institute had participated in the Seventh World Congress of Anthropological and Ethnological Sciences in Moscow earlier in 1964, those first encounters with scientists from the USSR since Tokarev's stay in Leipzig had not yet blossomed. The contribution of the West German Rüdiger Schott, entitled 'Principles of the Analysis of the Economy of African Hunting and Gathering', led to a scandal, because some other participants objected to its contents and asked how it could have been put on the agenda. Schott's invitation was based on a publication in which he had applied the terms *private economy* and *planned economy*. The Communist Party members in attendance met to discuss this 'case', but at the time there was still no separate party cell at the institute.

Between 1964 and 1966 a great deal of effort was invested in the preparation of a popularising volume, *Völkerkunde für jedermann* (Everyman's anthropology). It was published in 125,000 copies in 1967. The opportunity to produce such a 'map book' (*Kartenbuch*), as it was also called, resulted from the fact that an institute graduate, Willi Stegner, was employed at Hermann Haack, the famous cartographic publishing house in Gotha. The publisher specified the design and length of the book, in which it was possible to avoid repeating simplistic ideological dogmas. The bibliography shows that the authors succeeded in maintaining a good scientific standard: among the major scholars to whom reference was made were Walter Hirschberg, Wolfram Eberhard, Robert Heine-Geldern, George Peter Murdock, Felix Speiser, Erhard Schlesier, A. P. Elkin, A. R. Radcliffe-Brown, John Swanton, Dmitriy Alekseevich Ol'derogge, and Sergey Aleksandrovich Tokarev. The resonance enjoyed by this publication encouraged the authors to revise and expand the work, but this, too, was obstructed by the third university reform in 1968. The drastic deterioration of opportunities for purchasing so-called Western literature, or 'specialist literature from non-socialist countries', in the 1970s and 1980s, due partly to the lack of foreign currency, also affected our work. The funds allocated to the institute were continually being reduced. In this respect the Museum für Völkerkunde was an enormous help. It obtained a considerable number of new publications through its world-wide exchange agreements, and at least until the mid-1970s it was able to maintain the core of its subscriptions to journals.

An Uncertain Future

Once the Julius Lips Institute had weathered its first crisis, around 1960, its situation by 1964–65 was relatively stabilised. But the question in everyone's mind concerned what would happen after 1966, the year in which Eva Lips was due to retire. How were things to continue without her unassailable persona? On the day on which she acquired emeritus status, 6 February 1966, Lips was finally appointed professor of anthropology. Did this imply official recognition of the chair for Ethnologie in an institutional sense? Experience was to show that, after Eva Lips left the university in 1968, the structural persistence of the chair would be repeatedly called into question.

When the third university reform took effect, the author, then a senior lecturer (*wissenschaftlicher Oberassistent*), was appointed acting director of the Julius Lips-Institut für Ethnologie und vergleichende Rechtssoziologie, effective 1 March 1968. During discussions later that summer it was decided that anthropology should be located in the new *Sektion* for universal history. Walter Markov, the nominated director of this section, believed that this would produce fruitful synergies for the entire field. This plan could be traced back to the foundation in Leipzig of the Research Institute for Cultural and Universal History under Karl Lamprecht in 1914.

Markov's hopes that the upheavals triggered by the university reform could be channelled to yield positive scientific effects were dashed when it was decided in Berlin that, instead of universal history, the Karl Marx University in Leipzig would be concerned primarily with the history of the GDR and its Communist Party. The anthropologists were allocated instead to the Section for African and Middle Eastern Studies, without being consulted. They were expected to lose their independence and constitute only a so-called disciplinary group (*Fachgruppe*), and degrees were to be in African Studies–Ethnographie or in Arab Studies–Ethnographie (see Noack and Krause, this volume). This would have meant that after half a century, anthropology would have ceased to exist at the university as an independent major.

Following lengthy and trying negotiations and the enrolment of four majors in 1968—the first since 1960—we succeeded in maintaining anthropology as a major. The Julius Lips Institute became the anthropological unit of the Section for African and Middle Eastern Studies. Under its new name, Lehr- und Forschungsbereich für Ethnographie 'Julius Lips', the department enjoyed at least formal parity with the units for Africa and the Middle East, and that is how things stayed until 1989–90.

References

Asamoa, A. 1971. *Die gesellschaftlichen Verhältnisse der Ewe-Bevölkerung in Südost-Ghana*. Veröffentlichungen des Museums für Völkerkunde zu Leipzig 22. Berlin: Akademie-Verlag.

Brauner, S., I. Herms, and K. Legère. 1975. Diedrich Westermann (1875–1956): Werdegang, Leistungen, Widersprüche und Irrwege eines bürgerlichen Afrikanisten. *Asien-Afrika-Lateinamerika* 3: 504ff.

Dammann, E. 1999. *70 Jahre erlebte Afrikanistik*. Marburger Studien zur Afrika- und Asienkunde 32. Berlin: Reimer.

Gingrich, A. 2005 Manuskript eines Beitrags zur Ethnologie in den deutschsprachigen Ländern in der Zeit von etwa 1780 bis in die 80er Jahre des 20. Jahrhunderts.

Harstick, H.-P. 1974. *Vergleichende Studien zur Geschichte des Grundeigentums im Nachlaß von Karl Marx: Exzerpte aus M. M. Kovalevskij: Obščinnoe zemlevladenje (1879)*. Thesis. Münster: Univ. Phil. Fak.

Haushofer, K. (ed.). 1940. *Friedrich Ratzel, Erdenmacht und Völkerschicksal*. Stuttgart: Alfred Kröner Verlag.

Holý, L. (ed.). 1968. *Social Stratification in Tribal Africa*. Prague: Academia Publishing House of the Czechoslovak Academy of Science.

König, W. 1962. *Die Achal-Teke, zur Wirtschaft und Gesellschaft einer Turkmenen-Gruppe im XIX. Jahrhundert*. Veröffentlichungen des Museums für Völkerkunde zu Leipzig 12. Berlin: Akademie-Verlag.

Kollektiv des Julius Lips-Instituts. 1960. Kartographische Darstellungen zur Wirtschaft, Gesellschaft und Geschichte der Bevölkerung von U-ganda. *Wissenschaftliche Zeitschrift der Karl-Marx-Universität Leipzig, Gesellschafts- und Sprachwissenschaftliche Reihe* 9 (5): 775–808.

Krader, L. (ed.). 1972. *The Ethnological Notebooks of Karl Marx: Studies of Morgan, Phear, Maine, Lubbock*. Assen: Van Gorcum.

Landes, R. 1957. Review of *Die Reisernte der Ojibwa-Indianer*, by Eva Lips. *American Anthropologist* 59 (6): 1097–98.

Liedtke, W. 1964. Prinzipien einer Analyse der Ökonomie des tropischen Feldbaus. Beiträge zur Wirtschaftsethnographie. Zum 50 jährigen Jubiläum des Julius Lips-Instituts für Ethnologie und vergleichende Rechtssoziologie. *Wissenschaftliche Zeitschrift der Karl-Marx-Universität, Gesellschafts- und Sprachwissenschaftliche Reihe* 13 (2): 271–75.

Lips, E. 1938. *Savage Symphony*. New York: Random House.

———. 1942. *Rebirth in Liberty*. New York: Flamingo Publishing.

———. 1956. *Die Reisernte der Ojibwa-Indianer: Wirtschaft und Recht eines Erntevolkes*. Deutsche Akademie der Wissenschaften zu Berlin, Völkerkundliche Forschungen der Sektion für Völkerkunde und Deutsche Volkskunde 1. Berlin: Akademie-Verlag.

———. 1962a. Die gegenwärtige Akkulturationssituation der Montagnais-Naskapi-Indianer von Lake St. John, Kanada. *Proceedings of the Thirty-fourth Congress of Americanists*, pp. 514–21. Wien: Verlag Ferdinand Berger.

———. 1962b. Zum Wirtschaftswandel der Montagnais-Naskapi-Indianer am Lake St. John, Kanada. *Abhandlungen und Berichte des Staatlichen Museums für Völkerkunde Dresden* 21: 41–56.

———. 1964. Prinzipien einer Analyse der Ökonomie der Erntevölker. Beiträge zur Wirtschaftsethnographie. Zum 50jährigen Jubiläum des Julius Lips-Instituts für Ethnologie und vergleichende Rechtssoziologie. *Wissenschaftliche Zeitschrift der Karl-Marx-Universität, Gesellschafts- und Sprachwissenschaftliche Reihe* 13 (2): 258–63.

———. 1965a. Karl Weule. In M. Steinmetz (ed.), *Bedeutende Gelehrte in Leipzig*, vol. 1, pp. 149–57. Leipzig: Universitätsverlag.

———. 1965b. Julius Lips. In M. Steinmetz (ed.), *Bedeutende Gelehrte in Leipzig*, vol. 1, pp. 275–82. Leipzig: Universitätsverlag.

Lips, J. 1930. *Einleitung in die Vergleichende Völkerkunde.* Leipzig: Verlag Ernst Wiegandt.

———. 1939. Naskapi Trade: A Study in Legal Acculturation. *Journal de la Société des Americanistes*, n.s., 31: 130–95.

———. 1947a. Notes on Montagnais-Naskapi Economy (Lake St. John and Lake Mistassini Band). *Ethnos* 1–2. Stockholm: Ethnographical Museum of Sweden.

———. 1947b. Naskapi Law: Law and Order in a Hunting Society. *Transactions of the American Philosophical Society*, n.s., 37 (4): 379–492.

———. 1950. *Forschungsreise in die Dämmerung.* Weimar: Kiepenheuer Verlag.

———. 1953. Die Erntevölker, eine wichtige Phase in der Entwicklung der menschlichen Wirtschaft. Rektoratsrede, gehalten am 31. Oktober 1949 in der Kongresshalle zu Leipzig. *Berichte über die Verhandlungen der Sächsischen Akademie der Wissenschaften zu Leipzig, Phil.-Hist. Klasse* 101 (1): 1–18.

Mirreh, G. A. 1978. *Die sozialökonomischen Verhältnisse der nomadischen Bevölkerung im Norden der Demokratischen Republik Somalia.* Veröffentlichungen des Museums für Völkerkunde zu Leipzig 31. Berlin: Akademie-Verlag.

Mischek, U. 2000. Autorität außerhalb des Fachs: Diedrich Westermann und Eugen Fischer. In B. Streck (ed.), *Ethnologie und Nationalsozialismus.* Veröffentlichungen des Instituts für Ethnologie der Universität Leipzig 1, pp. 69–81. Gehren: Escher-Verlag.

Pützstück, L. 1995. *Symphonie in Moll: Julius Lips und die Kölner Völkerkunde.* Pfaffenweiler: Centaurus-Verlags-Gesellschaft.

Reim, H. 1962. *Die Insektennahrung der australischen Ureinwohner.* Veröffentlichungen des Museums für Völkerkunde zu Leipzig 13. Berlin: Akademie-Verlag.

———, and W. König. 1960. Tagung der Deutschen Gesellschaft für Völkerkunde in Stuttgart 1959. *Ethnographisch-Archäologische Zeitschrift* 1: 67-68.

Rudolph, W. 1968. *Der kulturelle Relativismus: Kritische Analyse einer Grundsatzfragen-Diskussion in der amerikanischen Ethnologie.* Berlin: Duncker und Humblot.

Rusch, W., and I. Sellnow. 1976. Diedrich Westermann und die Ethnographie. *Wissenschaftliche Zeitschrift der Humboldt-Universität zu Ber-

lin, Gesellschafts- und Sprachwissenschaftliche Reihe 25 (2): 191–95.

Schinkel, H.-G. 1964. Prinzipien einer Analyse der Ökonomie des afrikanischen Großviehnomadismus. Beiträge zur Wirtschaftsethnographie. Zum 50 jährigen Jubiläum des Julius Lips-Instituts für Ethnologie und vergleichende Rechtssoziologie. *Wissenschaftliche Zeitschrift der Karl-Marx-Universität, Gesellschafts- und Sprachwissenschaftliche Reihe* 13 (2): 275–80.

Schott, R. 1955. *Anfänge der Privat- und Planwirtschaft: Wirtschaftsordnung und Nahrungsverteilung bei Wildbeutervölkern*. Braunschweig: Limbach.

Sellnow, I. 1961. *Grundprinzipien einer Periodisierung der Urgeschichte*. Deutsche Akademie der Wissenschaften zu Berlin: Völkerkundliche Forschungen der Sektion für Völkerkunde und Deutsche Volkskunde 4. Berlin: Akademie-Verlag.

Streck, B. 1997. *Fröhliche Wissenschaft Ethnologie*. Wuppertal: Edition Trickster im Peter Hammer Verlag.

Trappe, P. 1960. Zur ethnologischen Problematik der Entwicklungsländer. *Tribus. Veröffentlichungen des Linden-Museum Stuttgart* 9: 16-36.

Treide, D. 1964. Prinzipien einer Analyse der Ökonomie der kombinierten Fischerei-, Jagd- und Sammelwirtschaft in der gemäßigten und subarktischen Zone. Beiträge zur Wirtschaftsethnographie. Zum 50 jährigen Jubiläum des Julius Lips-Instituts für Ethnologie und vergleichende Rechtssoziologie. *Wissenschaftliche Zeitschrift der Karl-Marx-Universität, Gesellschafts- und Sprachwissenschaftliche Reihe* 13 (2): 263–71.

——. 1965. *Die Organisierung des indianischen Lachsfangs im westlichen Nordamerika*. Veröffentlichungen des Museums für Völkerkunde zu Leipzig 14. Berlin: Akademie-Verlag.

——. 1980. Bemerkungen zur Stellung des Kovalevskij- und des Morgan-Konspekts in der Entwicklung der Marxschen Auffassungen über die Urgesellschaft, ihre Auflösung und den Übergang zur Klassengesellschaft. *Ethnographisch-Archäologische Zeitschrift* 21 (4): 399–416.

——. 1982. Zur wirtschaftlichen Klassifizierung und Typisierung in der Ethnographie. *Ethnographisch-Archäologische Zeitschrift* 23 (4): 570–600.

——. 1990. Karl Marx' Kowalewski- und Phear-Exzerpte und die koloniale Frage. *Marx-Engels-Forschungsberichte der Karl-Marx-Universität Leipzig* 6: 5–36.

Chapter 7
The Adaptation of Soviet Models in Polish Anthropology before 1956

Zbigniew Jasiewicz

In this chapter, after outlining the situation in Poland and in its anthropological community during and after the Second World War, I examine Soviet models and the conditions, mechanisms, and consequences of their introduction and adaptation by Polish anthropologists.[1] In the Polish case it is important to go back before 1944–45, when the Red Army occupied the country and paved the way for the establishment of the Polish People's Republic. The Soviet army had already occupied the eastern parts of the Polish state in 1939–41. During these years attempts were made at the University of Lwów to persuade eminent Polish scholars, including anthropologists, to work for the benefit of Soviet science and the Soviet state. This development in Lwów, although very specific, can be regarded as the first stage of the introduction of Soviet models to Polish science (Jasiewicz and Rieszetow 2003: 37).

In the first post-war years, Polish universities received significant donations of books, including the works of Bronisław Malinowski, from Western states. At this point the future system of the 'people's democracy' had not yet been defined. The autonomy of university education was formally restricted in 1947 and abolished entirely in 1951. However, I am not concerned here primarily with reconstructing the chronology of events or documenting fine differences from one year to the next. Rather, I aim at a general analysis of the dissemination and adaptation of Soviet models in Poland

---

[1] By Soviet models I mean the ways in which the discipline of anthropology was defined, institutionalised, and practised by Soviet researchers. In Polish universities the comparative discipline was generally known as etnologia. The first department with this name was established at the University of Lwów in 1910. In the following decades etnologia and etnografia were pursued together: the difference was that the latter implied a lower level of generalisation, e.g. *etnografia Polski* (Warsaw) or *etnografia Slowian* ('the ethnography of the Slavs', Cracow). They were sometimes combined with *antropologia* (physical anthropology). Etnologia was combined with *socjologia* at the Jagiellonian University in Cracow when the chair of Jan Stanisław Bystroń was renamed in 1930.

down to 1956. Drawing on Hegel's distinction between state and society, I treat the Polish anthropological community as an object of state influence while recognising that there existed differences of opinion within this community and that some scholars and scholarly institutions had particularly close connections to the state. On the other hand, I treat the dominant Soviet state and its associated science as a monolithic entity, irrespective of the differences among Soviet ethnographers.

The situation of the Polish anthropological community was shaped not only by the tragic years of war and Nazi occupation but also by the development of the state and of the discipline in the preceding decades. I shall attempt to give an idea of ingrained ways of thinking and informal views, in addition to official behaviour in the public sphere. I am interested not so much in the models introduced to the Soviet satellite state but in how they were introduced and how members of the scholarly community adapted to them, given their own experiences and personal goals. My account makes use of both Polish and Soviet sources but draws also on recollections of my own education in the history of material culture in Cracow and Poznań in the period under review and on personal communications with a number of senior colleagues.[2]

The Politics of an Awkward Dialogue

Let us begin our account in Lwów, where the leading scholars in 1939 were Jan Czekanowski, who had worked for the Museum of Anthropology and Ethnography in St. Petersburg in pre-revolutionary Russia and the Museum für Völkerkunde in Berlin and had taken part in the German expedition to Africa in 1907–9, and Adam Fischer, one of the most active Polish scholars of the inter-war period. Both men continued their work at the university after the Soviet invasion. Fischer corresponded with Dmitriy Konstantinovich Zelenin of Leningrad, from whom he received a letter of reference that helped him to pass the screening procedure, the so-called 'pre-attestation' (*weryfikacja*), without which he could not have been employed at a Soviet university. The contacts between Zelenin, who was the object of ideological attacks from his own colleagues in the 1930s, and Fischer were doubtless observed by the Soviet political authorities. Their treatment of Fischer and Czekanowski suggests that they were keen to secure the cooperation of eminent Polish scholars, irrespective of their previous activity. Polish public opinion was ready to accept a scholar's working at a Soviet-controlled

---

[2] See also the published interviews: Kutrzeba-Pojnarowa 1995; Armon 2001.

university if this was the only way to survive and preserve scholarly traditions (Jasiewicz and Rieszetow 2003: 35).[3]

After the establishment of the Polish People's Republic in 1944–45, the situation in the scholarly community was determined, on the one hand, by the policy of the state, which sought to re-establish university education and other scholarly institutions while subordinating them to political controls, and, on the other, by the actions of the academics themselves. The latter, though burdened with the experiences of the war, tried initially to resume their scholarly work. Despite losses due to death, severe illness, and emigration, chairs of anthropology (now called etnografia) were re-established at the universities of Warsaw, Cracow, and Poznań, and it was also possible to fill the new chairs that were founded in 1945 and 1946 at the universities of Lublin, Łódź, Toruń, and Wrocław. Some professors, those who had stood for socialist or at least democratic politics in the pre-war period, were attracted by the prospect of addressing important social problems. Others, with a more nationalist orientation, were excited by the prospect of studying the western and northern territories newly acquired from Germany, which in their eyes marked a return to the ancient boundaries of the Polish state. All understood the impossibility of changing the political situation in a Poland exhausted by war and obliged, as a result of international treaties, to remain under the influence of the Soviet Union.

No professors of anthropology were arrested or removed from their posts. Some, however, were sanctioned in other ways. Jan Stanisław Bystroń, both anthropologist and sociologist, was harshly criticised by some students and journalists (Bieńkowski 2002: 31). He was also an object of manipulation by the authorities and by colleagues seeking to improve their own positions, but even he was not removed from his chair at Warsaw University. Andrzej Waligórski, a student of Bronisław Malinowski's who returned to Poland from England in 1948, was subjected to administrative persecution, and his legitimate professional expectations were for a long time ignored (Dzięgiel 2002: 299). Kazimiera Zawistowicz-Adamska was accused in 1950 by a sociology professor of yielding to the influences of functionalism: her punishment was to be deprived of her right to teach in her department at the University of Łódź (Kutrzeba-Pojnarowa 1995: 411; Kopczyńska-Jaworska 2002: 316). No professors of anthropology assumed significant political roles in their scholarly communities, although some did

---

[3] Fischer died in Lwów (L'viv) during the German occupation in 1943. Czekanowski managed to return to Poland in 1944 and, after a brief period in Lublin, headed the department of physical anthropology in Poznań until his retirement in 1960.

attempt to improve their own positions by explicitly signalling their acceptance of the new ideology.[4]

Overall one can say that the community of professors responded to the post-war situation with a strategy of collective consolidation, irrespective of pre-war animosities and post-war differences. Among the acknowledged leaders were Józef Gajek (supported above all by Czekanowski) and later Witold Dynovskiy. The traditional authority of Kazimierz Moszyński, a Slavist known throughout the Soviet Union and Europe, was strengthened. On the initiative of the professors an important memorandum was prepared in 1951 for the First Congress of Polish Science, the purpose of which was to lay the foundations for a Polish Academy of Sciences.[5] This document included the usual obligatory self-criticism, but excessive assertions of Marxist ideology were subjected to informal criticism and even mockery. For example, after Kazimierz Dobrowolski had presented such a paper at the conference of the Polish Ethnological Society (Polskie Towarzystwo Ludoznawcze) in Toruń in 1949, Eugeniusz Frankowski remarked to Czekanowski that the talk resembled 'old ravioli freshly stuffed with *diamat* [dialectical materialism]' (Armon 2001: 326).

As far as I know, no Soviet anthropologists visited Poland before 1956. Polish scholars did not go to the Soviet Union, either, although Moszyński did prepare a paper for the Congress of Slavists in Moscow in 1948 (Moszyński 1948: 210). There is no doubt, however, that some Poles corresponded with Soviet colleagues. In Moszyński's diary from the 1950s I found the addresses of Petr Grigorievitch Bogatyrev, Petr Semenovich Kuznetsov, Sergey Aleksandrovich Tokarev, and Sergey Pavlovich Tolstov (Rieszetow and Jasiewicz 2001: 281). The Soviet scholarly community was informed about Polish anthropology in the journal *Sovetskaya etnografiya* by Irina Kaloeva, a specialist in Slavic intellectual history (Kaloeva 1951, 1953). The latter of these articles was translated into Polish (Kałojewa 1954). Without naming names, she called upon Polish anthropologists to overcome their bourgeois past and join in the building of socialism. This

---

[4] As in other countries, socialist scientific management not only involved the organisation of Communist Party groups within the scholarly community but also involved the appointment of ideologically and politically engaged informal 'commissioners' (*komisarze*) whose task was to promote the views of the party and Marxism-Leninism generally. In the field of etnografia such fervour was found not among the professors but among outsiders, specifically a historian of antiquity and an administrative employee of the Polish Ethnological Society (Polskie Towarzystwo Ludoznawcze).
[5] 'Ocena dorobku polskiej etnografii i etnologii z punktu widzenia postępowej myśli społecznej' (An evaluation of the achievements of Polish ethnography and ethnology from the point of view of progressive social thought). These materials were published in *Lud*, the discipline's leading journal, in 1952 (vol. 39: 626–29).

criticism was really directed at a number of well-known sociologists, among them Florian Znaniecki, who had long been based in the United States, Józef Chałasiński, Tadeusz Szczurkiewicz, and Jan Szczepański (Kałojewa 1954: 14).[6] Information about developments in Poland was also disseminated by Witold Dynowski, who sent a paper to the aforementioned Congress of Slavists; it was published as an article in *Sovetskaya etnografiya* (Dynovskiy 1948).

Turning to the other side of the coin, a few articles about Soviet ethnography were published in Polish periodicals. For example, Jan Lutyński contributed a very informative article, by no means a mere apologetic, which treated Soviet etnografiya simply as one anthropological school among others (see Kłoskowska and Lutyński 1950). This article was later expanded and in 1956 published as a monograph (Lutyński 1956). Numerous translations of Soviet articles and books on religion and folklore appeared—for example, in the 1953 anthology *Nowe drogi etnografii radzieckiej* (New roads of Soviet anthropology). Some of these translations, such as Ivan Izosimovich Potekhin's *Funkcjonalna szkoła w etnografii w służbie brytyjskiego imperializmu* (The functional school in anthropology in the service of British imperialism; Potiechin 1949) and the 1951 anthology *Angloamerykańska etnografia w służbie imperializmu* (Anglo-American anthropology in the service of imperialism) were sophisticated but clearly propagandistic. The latter, although recommended to anthropology students by its Polish reviewers (Kulczycki 1952: 133; Stęślicka 1954: 686), never became obligatory reading for students of the history of material culture. Soviet scientific publications were broadly accessible in their original versions and extremely inexpensive in Poland during these years.

No joint Soviet–Polish research projects were initiated during the period under consideration. Moszyński (1948: 228) issued an appeal to establish contacts with 'colleagues—Slavic ethnographers', but it seems to have gone unheard.

Reorganisation and Resistance

The Soviet models introduced into Poland had far-reaching effects on the organisational structure of science and university education, on the name of the discipline, its object, and its methods of research, on the stance taken towards the same discipline in Western countries, and on the functions of the discipline, both inside and outside academia.

As regards organisational structures, the most important innovation was the establishment of the Polish Academy of Sciences in 1952. The

---

[6] These distinguished sociologists were specifically contrasted with the anthropologists.

scholarly community, anthropologists included, reacted positively to this idea, believing that the new academy would enable an intensification of research and improve funding. A conference of anthropologists in Cracow in February 1951 therefore proposed, following the Soviet model, that the new Polish Academy of Sciences have an Institute of Anthropology (Etnografia) (Gajkowa 1952: 625). Such an institute, unfortunately, was never established. Instead, the Institute of the History of Material Culture was established in 1953 with a section called Etnografia modelled on an institute in the USSR which carried the same name (in the USSR it was renamed the Institute of Archaeology in 1958).

In the academic year 1950–51 the study of anthropology at the universities was radically reshaped, for reasons of ideology rather than intellectual coherence.[7] From now on the Departments of the History of Material Culture were to subsume the anthropology (etnografia) and archaeology of Poland as well as classical archaeology (Frankowska 1973: 198; Burszta and Kopczyńska-Jaworska 1982: 52; Jasiewicz and Slattery 1995: 193). In this context it is worth mentioning that, as early as 1940, when etnografia at the University of Lwów was closed, Adam Fischer had expressed in a letter to Zelenin his surprise at the failure of Soviet universities to separate this discipline from folklore studies (Jasiewicz and Rieszetow 2003: 40). Kazimierz Majewski, the most politically influential archaeologist of the time, argued that as a result of the introduction of the history of material culture, 'such separate and ideologically retarded disciplines as the archaeology of Poland, Mediterranean archaeology, and etnografia can be given a more scholarly status from the position of historical materialism' (Majewski 1953: 24).

In their research programmes and curricula, Polish *etnografowie* never in practice restricted themselves to problems of material culture. However, given the character of the Academy of Sciences institute, branches concerned with folk literature and artistic creativity moved to other institutes (Frankowska 1973: 199). Studies of the history of material culture at universities were continued until the end of the 1950s, and the academy institute did not change its name until 1992. Within the institute, the etnografia section played an important role, and it facilitated the implementation of research programmes initiated by the Polish Ethnological Society. However, what really differentiated research in Poland from anthropological research in the Soviet Union was the much more important role of the universities in Poland.

---

[7] The dissolution of sociology departments in 1951 resulted from the same developments (Szacki 1995: 112). This had implications for anthropology, because some of the sociologists were re-employed in anthropological institutions.

The term *etnologia* was considered by Soviet anthropologists to be 'bourgeois' and therefore banned. Terms related to social anthropology and cultural anthropology were similarly unacceptable. Instead, following the Soviet model, etnografia was elevated to the status of an historical science, or at any rate an 'auxiliary discipline' to history. It is significant that those now classified as etnografowie themselves demanded that their subject be included not in the division of philosophy and social sciences of the new academy but in the division of history (Gajkowa 1952: 624). This was probably motivated by fear of exceptionally strong ideological pressure and internal controversies in the social sciences. The professors acquiesced in the new delimitation of their subject matter: the history of culture, from the most remote to the most recent times. This was to be studied using the so-called concrete-historical method and from the point of view of the need to consolidate socialism.

In practice, work of an historical character pertaining to material culture, such as investigations of rural buildings and rural social relations, was pursued by anthropologically oriented historians (Józef Burszta, Bohdan Baranowski). Considerable attention was paid to folk culture, which was presented both as the product of historical processes and as a valuable resource for modern culture, important for the building of socialist society. In the field of folk culture, research into popular art forms, sometimes conducted jointly with art historians, tended to dominate. It intensified as a result of the establishment in 1946 of a new State Institute for Research into Folk Art, which launched its own periodical, *Polska Sztuka Ludowa* (Polish folk art) in 1947 (Jackowski, Jot-Drużycki, and Benedyktowicz 2000: 165).

Research into rural attitudes towards labour and cooperation was initiated by Zawistowicz-Adamska (1950–51) and presented at the conference in Cracow in 1951 as being highly relevant to the establishment of new production cooperatives (*kolkhozy*) in the villages (Ocena... 1952: 628). However, investigations of workers' culture did not prosper in Poland as they did in other socialist countries in this period.

A lot of effort was put into the preparation of the *Polish Ethnographic Atlas,* the principal research project of this period (Kłodnicki 2001: 237). Studies of non-European societies, referred to as 'primitive societies', continued within the framework of etnografia, but in a limited way (Burszta and Kopczyńska-Jaworska 1982: 52). Field studies of these societies were, with only a few exceptions, impossible.

The need to be familiar with the principles of historical materialism was often asserted during this period, both in Soviet publications and in declarations made by Polish scholars. However, it tended to mean little more than giving priority to certain research topics (notably material culture, class relations, and the creativity of the working people) and the ritual citing of Marxist-Leninist works and of a few Soviet scholars such as Nikolay Jakov-levich Marr, Mark Osipovich Kosven, Dmitriy Alekseevich Ol'derogge, and Sergey Pavlovich Tolstov. This is not to argue that no Polish anthropologists were sympathetic to the Marxist method. Yet the lack of viable models for the application of Marxism in anthropology and the fact that it was imposed dogmatically, in an authoritarian way, acted as deterrents.

Scholars needed to pay close attention to the political implications of the recommended Soviet models, the interpretation of which could change unpredictably. This is well illustrated by the case of Eugeniusz Frankowski, who in 1950, after the publication of Stalin's work *W sprawie marksizmu w językoznawstwie* (On Marxism in linguistics), felt obliged to withdraw his article 'Nicolai Marr and His Scientific Theories' from *Slavia Antiqua* (Armon 2001: 327). When Moszyński wrote, 'They [Polish anthropologists] expect a lot from the nine-volume Russian publication entitled *The Peoples of the World*, which, I think, will demonstrate the specific results that can be achieved from applying the materialist direction to ethnographic research' (Moszyński 1948: 228), he was probably expressing in a subtle way the scepticism of Polish etnografowie towards Marxism-Leninism.

A critical attitude towards Western science was an important element of the Soviet model. In addition to the anti-imperialist publications already noted, functionalism, particularly that of Malinowski—'a cosmopolitan of Polish origin', as he was called—was attacked with special vigour.[8] The aggressive, overtly propagandistic language of such publications ensured that, although they might receive good reviews from Polish scholars in the official journals, they were not in fact read, at any rate not without a sharply critical perspective. Antonina Kłoskowska, a sociologist, published an important study of American ethnosociology (see Kłoskowska and Lutyński 1951), which impressed Kaloeva, the Soviet scholar responsible for monitoring the discipline in Poland at the time. The Russian did have reservations about the fact that Kłoskowska failed to discuss explicitly the class ideology of American scholars and their role as servants of imperialism (Kałojewa 1954: 9). But she concealed, fortunately for Kłoskowska, the latter's basically positive opinion of Malinowski. Polish anthropologists in this period, including the sociologists in their ranks, generally refrained from criticising Western trends, partly because they did not believe such criticism to be

---

[8] This description of Malinowski belongs to Wanda Stęślicka (1954: 687). The Soviet authors of the book under review described him as 'the English-Austrian-Polish anthropologist Bronisław Malinowski, a reactionary representative of the British colonial-anthropological service' (Potiechin 1951: 12).

warranted but also because they hardly had sufficient knowledge of what was going on internationally.

The Soviet insistence on analysing practical problems in social life was attractive to most Poles and corresponded to beliefs dominant in Polish science. On the other hand, the belief that scientific research should reflect the ideology of the ruling party (*partyjność nauki*)—that it should be subordinate to the party, since this was a guarantee of improved scientific results—was not accepted. While the influence of communist ideology in science was discussed in Polish reviews of Soviet etnografiya, I know of no work by a Polish anthropologist endorsing this ideology.

Conclusion

Some scholars nowadays describe the entire period of the Polish People's Republic as the 'freezer of history', but I favour a dynamic approach. Attempts by the political establishment to subjugate Polish science, to isolate it from global trends, and, in general, to impoverish the scholarly community were most intense between 1945 and 1956. Yet scientific institutions were expanded, some important research projects were started, and many anthropologists were educated during those years. Attempts to impose Marxism-Leninism led to a shift from theoretical studies and research on culture as a whole to 'niche studies' of folk culture examined historically or morphologically. Such spaces opened up because 'folk studies', the main components of these niches, were attractive not only to the party and state authorities but also to scholars and to society. The pre-war traditions of anthropology, whether based on the cultural-historical school (Stanisław Poniatowski), phenomenology (Cezaria Baudoin de Courtenay Ehrenkreutz Jędrzejewiczowa), functionalism (Józef Obrębski), or Marxism (Ludwik Krzywicki), were all interrupted. Certain benefits of the turn towards historicism appeared after 1956, when numerous regional monographs and a comprehensive historical survey of Polish etnografia were published. In other words, the discipline was not frozen but rather redirected onto a path from which it has been it difficult to return to mainstream anthropology.

References

Armon, W. 2001. Czytać samodzielnie i krytycznie dawne teksty: Odpowiedzi na pytania Zbigniewa Jasiewicza. *Lud* 85: 323–34.
Bieńkowski, W. 2002. Jan Stanisław Bystroń (1892–1964). In E. Fryś-Pietraszkowa, A. Kowalska-Lewicka, and A. Spiss (eds.), *Etnogra-*

fowie i ludoznawcy polscy, vol. 1, pp. 29–35. Kraków: Wydawnictwo Naukowe DWN.

Burszta, J., and B. Kopczyńska-Jaworska. 1982. Polish Ethnography after World War II. *Ethnos* 47 (1–2): 50–63.

Dynovskiy, W. 1948. Nauchnye raboty po etnografii i folkloru v Polshe. *Sovetskaya etnografiya* 3: 168–73.

Dzięgiel, L. 2002. Andrzej Waligórski (1908–1974). In E. Fryś-Pietraszkowa, A. Kowalska-Lewicka, and A. Spiss (eds.), *Etnografowie i ludoznawcy polscy*, vol. 1, pp. 298–302. Kraków: Wydawnictwo Naukowe DWN.

Frankowska, M. 1973. Etnografia polska po II wojnie światowej. In M. Terlecka (ed.), *Historia etnografii polskiej*, pp. 193–270. Wrocław: Zakład Narodowy im. Ossolińskich.

Gajkowa, O. 1952. Konferencja etnografów w Krakowie, 17–19.02.1951. *Lud* 39: 624–25.

Jackowski, A., J. Jot-Drużycki, and Z. Benedyktowicz. 2000. Konteksty: Polska Sztuka Ludowa. In E. Krasiński (ed.), *Instytut Sztuki Polskiej Akademii Nauk*, pp. 165–71. Warszawa: Wydawnictwo Polskiego Instytutu Sztuki PAN.

Jasiewicz, Z., and M. Rieszetow. 2003. Korespondencja między Adamem Fischerem a Dymitrem Konstantynowiczem Zieleninem: Z materiałów Archiwum Naukowego Polskiego Towarzystwa Ludoznawczego i Archiwum Rosyjskiej Akademii Nauk w Sankt Petersburgu. *Etnografia Polska* 47 (1–2): 31–47.

——, and D. Slattery. 1995. Ethnography and Anthropology: The Case of Polish Ethnology. In H. F. Vermeulen and A. A. Roldan (eds.), *Fieldwork and Footnotes: Studies in the History of European Anthropology*, pp. 184–201. London: Routledge.

Kaloeva, I. A. 1951. Etnograficheskaya rabota v narodno-demokraticheskoy Polshe v 1945–1950 godakh. *Sovetskaya etnografiya* 3: 185–91.

——. 1953. Pervyi kongress polskoy nauki i polskaya etnografiya. *Sovetskaya etnografiya* 4: 137–45.

Kałojewa, I. 1954. *Pierwszy Kongres Nauki Polskiej i polska etnografia.* Special supplement to *Archiwum Etnograficzne* 6. Poznań: PTL.

Kłodnicki, Z. 2001. Polski Atlas Etnograficzny: Historia, stan obecny i perspektywy. *Lud* 85: 237–75.

Kłoskowska, A., and J. Lutyński. 1951. Z zagadnień teorii i metodologii współczesnych badań nad społeczeństwami pierwotnymi. *Przegląd Nauk Historycznych i Społecznych* 1: 263–327.

Kopczyńska-Jaworska, B. 2002. Kazimiera Zawistowicz (1897–1984). In E. Fryś-Pietraszkowa, A. Kowalska-Lewicka, and A. Spiss (eds.), *Et-*

nografowie i ludoznawcy polscy, vol. 1, pp. 314–19. Kraków: Wydawnictwo Naukowe DWN.

Kulczycki, J. 1952. Review of 'Anglo-amerykańska etnografia w służbie imperializmu'. *Życie Nauki* 7 (5): 133–53.

Kutrzeba-Pojnarowa, A. 1995. 'Etnologia jest zawsze jakby in statu nascendi ...': Odpowiedzi na pytania Zbigniewa Jasiewicza. *Lud* 78: 396–427.

Lutyński, J. 1956. *Ewolucjonizm w etnologii anglosaskiej a etnografia radziecka*. Łódź: Zakład im. Ossolińskich we Wrocławiu.

Majewski, K. 1953. Historia kultury materialnej. *Kwartalnik Historii Kultury Materialnej* 1 (1–2): 3–24.

Moszyński, K. 1948. Stan i zadania etnografii polskiej. *Lud* 38: 210–28.

Nowe drogi ... . 1953. *Nowe drogi etnografii radzieckiej Archiwum Etnograficzne* 6. Poznań: Polskie Towarzystwo Ludoznawcze.

Ocena ... . 1952. Ocena dorobku polskiej etnografii i etnologii z punktu widzenia postępowej myśli społecznej. *Lud* 39: 626–29.

Potiechin, I. I. 1949. *Funkcjonalna szkoła etnografii w służbie brytyjskiego imperializmu*. Biblioteka Naukowa Po Prostu 14. Warszawa: Czytelnik.

———. (ed.). 1951. *Angloamerykańska etnografia w służbie imperializmu*. Warszawa: Państwowe Wydawnictwo Naukowe.

Rieszetow, A. M., and Z. Jasiewicz. 2001. Korespondencja Kazimierza Moszyńskiego z Dymitrem Konstantynowiczem Zieleninem: Z materiałów Archiwum Rosyjskiej Akademii Nauk w Sankt Petersburgu. *Lud* 85: 277–88.

Stęślicka, W. 1954. Review of *Anglo-amerykańska etnografia w służbie imperializmu*. *Przegląd Antropologiczny* 20: 686–89.

Szacki, J. 1995. Wstęp: Krótka historia socjologii polskiej. In J. Szacki (ed.), *Sto lat socjologii polskiej*, pp. 11–119. Warszawa: Wydawnictwo Naukowe PWN.

Zawistowicz-Adamska, K. 1950–51. Pomoc wzajemna i współdziałanie w kulturach ludowych. *Prace i Materiały Etnograficzne* 8–9: 1–151.

Chapter 8
The Foundation of the Czechoslovak Academy of Sciences in 1952 and Its Importance for Czech Národopis

Olga Skalníková

The Czechs can boast a very old tradition of scientific societies. The Royal Learned Society (Královská česká společnost nauk) was founded in 1770, and the Academy for Czech Science, Literature, and Arts (Akademie pro českou vědu, literaturu a umění), in 1888. The Masaryk Labour Academy (Masarykova akademie práce) was added in the twentieth century. All of these societies were basically associations of outstanding individual scholars, rather than institutions equipped and staffed to implement research programmes. Until the foundation of the Czechoslovak Academy of Sciences (Československá akademie věd), the best research conditions were to be found in the universities. Czechoslovakia's first department of anthropology (národopis; see Skalník, this volume) was created in the 1920s at Comenius University in Bratislava. Following Karel Chotek's move to Prague, a národopis seminar (Národopisný seminář) was established at the Charles University, and in the same period Antonín Václavík represented the discipline at the Masaryk University in Brno.

The idea of founding a Czechoslovak Academy of Sciences had its roots in the political changes of 1948. It was established at the initiative of Professor Zdeněk Nejedlý, then a high-ranking politician, and was to be organised according to the Soviet prototype and based on Marxism-Leninism. The governmental commission responsible for making recommendations proposed including a národopis section (Národopisný kabinet) in the framework of the new academy. It also proposed incorporating an existing institution, the State Institute for Folk Song (Státní ústav pro lidovou píseň), which dated back to 1919.

The possibility of creating a new forum for the discipline of národopis led to a challenge to the authority of the major národopis institution, the Czecho-Slav Society for Národopis (Národopisná společnost československanská), founded in 1893 and headed in the late 1940s by Karel Chotek, Drahomíra Stránská, and Vilém Pražák. The young Turks were a post-war

generation of graduates in národopis, represented in Prague by Otakar Nahodil, who had studied ethnography in the USSR, and his colleague and
friend Jaroslav Kramařík.[1] In Brno their leading representative was Karel
Fojtík, a pupil of Václavík's.[2] These men and their colleagues, most of
whom worked in the Ministry of Information, had the necessary political
backing and convened the two state-wide národopis conferences of 1949 and
1952. These meetings attracted not only graduates in národopis from universities and museums but also amateur enthusiasts from folk ensembles and
other institutions of applied národopis. In other words, there was a certain
retreat from academic exclusivity.

The first state-wide národopis conference (*První celostátní národopisná konference*), in 1949, put forward demands to learn from the experiences of Soviet science, to place národopis on the secure footing of Marxism-Leninism, to study new forms of popular creativity, and in general to
investigate and support the creativity of members of the working class. All
this was expressed in Nahodil's keynote address, 'Ethnography in Socialist
Society and Our Tasks in the Construction of Socialism'.[3] The aim of the
conference was to define the further direction of work in národopis, even
though there was no institution to ensure the fulfilment of these tasks.[4]

---

[1] Otakar Nahodil (1923–95) was the son of a Czechoslovak army officer who had served in
Russia during the First World War and married there. According to Ludvík Baran (personal
communication), it was Chotek who sent Nahodil to study in the Soviet Union. He also
studied for one semester in Bulgaria. For further detail on his career see Jeřábek 1998.
Nahodil founded a so-called Marxist Circle, which in his absence was led by Kramařík and
other Marxist-Leninist enthusiasts such as Hannah Rejchrtová, Dagmar Palátová, and Hana
Dymerová. The circle was to be a platform for Communist Party members, to promote new
methods in the národopis seminar. Instead of an ideological offensive, however, it busied
itself primarily with the self-education of its members by analysing basic works, especially
those by Engels and Morgan. Nahodil's analysis and application of Engels's *Origin of the
Family, Private Property and the State* won a prize in the faculty competition for youth
creativity, but it had no effect on the majority of the teaching members of the seminar. The
rigor of some members of the circle discouraged non-members of the party from participating,
even as observers. The circle soon exhausted itself and faded into obscurity.
[2] Karel Fojtík (1918–99) studied history, languages, and národopis. He was interested in
historical ethnography and the ethnography of workers. With me he developed a theoretical
interest in the ethnography of contemporary life (Skalníková and Fojtík 1971).
[3] One of the main arguments of this talk was that many hidden talents were waiting to be
discovered among the workers and peasants, talents which under the former regime could not
be realised but which now in the new era could enrich Czech and Slovak culture.
[4] Participants presenting papers included university lecturers such as Drahomira Stránská,
Karel Plicka, Antonín Václavík, Jaroslav Kramařík, Andrej Melicherčík, and Soňa Kovačevičová, from Bratislava (Chotek's paper was read by Ludvík Baran). Papers were also given by
workers from the Ministry of Information and some leading functionaries of educational
organisations. The participants resolved to establish a 'Czechoslovak Národopis Union', but
this never materialised.

The second such conference gathered in Prague in April 1952 at the initiative of the Department of Národopis and Prehistory (Katedra národopisu a pravěku) of the Faculty of Philosophy at Charles University and under the auspices of the government commission for the establishment of the Czechoslovak Academy of Sciences. Confirmation that národopis would receive a place in the future academy came in the speech of the vice-president of the government commission, the archaeologist Jaroslav Böhm, who urged the conference delegates to set up their own commission to plan exactly how národopis would figure within the future academy. His call was answered in papers by Nahodil, Melicherčík, Kramařík, and Stránská, who outlined programmes for the institutes in Prague, Brno, and Bratislava. The papers were discussed thoroughly, and there were clashes of opinion, but in the end the conference unanimously passed a resolution which stipulated that the národopis research centre would be divided into four sections: theory, history, and general národopis; Czech and Slavic ethnography; folkloristics; and documentation and bibliography. It was recommended that the centre should have a minimum staff of ten researchers, three of them at the Brno branch. Other recommendations touched upon publications, the acquisition of further archival materials, and relations with existing institutions such as the Czechoslovak Národopis Society and the State Conservation Institute, with its photographic collections.

The resolution adopted by the conference was published in *Český lid* (Čl), a popular-scientific journal published at that time by the agricultural publishing house Brázda.[5] It was anticipated that this would be the outlet for publications based on new research into cooperative villages and the life of the working class. Čl also published a report on research sponsored by the government commission and carried out even before the foundation of the new academy. The report confirmed that the money allocated had been spent correctly and that the future centre had excellent prospects.

Jaroslav Kramařík, the designated head of the centre, was one of the first graduates in the discipline after 1945. He hailed from Chodsko, a region well-known in the národopis literature, from which he drew data for his doctoral dissertation. He studied with both Chotek and the archaeologist Jan Eisner (the combination of národopis and archaeology was very popular at the time) and selected his future academy colleagues from among his current university colleagues and his most talented students. For example, Emanuel Baláš was an expert in folk architecture,[6] Vladimír Scheufler specialised in

---

[5] The other significant journal at the time was *Národopisný věstník českoslovanský*, published by the Czechoslovak Národopis Society.
[6] Emanuel Baláš (1914–66) came from the Valašsko region in north-eastern Moravia, a district particularly noted for its rich folk culture. Besides národopis he also took courses in

ceramics,[7] and Hana Hynková stood out in Slavic národopis.[8] Kramařík was a close friend of Nahodil's, and they planned the future activities of the centre together. As early as 1951 they took control of *Český lid*, until then edited by Chotek and the archivist Václav Černý. I replaced Lubomír Soukup as editor-in-chief after Soukup resigned due to other commitments (he was employed at the radio).[9]

Otakar Nahodil was also the main representative and champion of Marxist etnografie in Czechoslovakia in these years.[10] Why did this dominant figure not take up a leading position in the Czechoslovak Academy of Sciences? At that time he was deputy secretary general (the secretary general was never appointed) of the Czechoslovak-Soviet Institute, a prestigious position because several ministers were members of its governing body. This institute was the political and scientific fulcrum for the implementation of Soviet science, and it possessed its own publishing house and a number of periodicals. Only after the establishment of the academy did its role gradually decline. Nahodil demanded his own journal from the academy, and he got it: in 1953, *Československá etnografie* began to appear four times a year under his editorship, with Emanuel Baláš as the executive editor and Ludvík Baran the pictures editor.[11] This journal existed for ten years.

Activities

The Centre for Národopis (Kabinet pro národopis) was established on 1 October 1952. The State Institute for Folk Song, led by Jiří Horák, was merged into the academy, initially as the Centre for Folk Song (Kabinet pro

---

religious studies with Professor Otakar Pertold. He was also an excellent administrator with an interest in legal science.

[7] Vladimír Scheufler (1922-1995) studied at the archbishop's gymnasium in Prague. After earning his doctorate he worked for a while at the Ostrava museum. Besides národopis he studied musical science.

[8] Hana Hynková (1921–2004) came from the Eagle Mountains region in eastern Bohemia. Her studies focused on Bulgarian národopis and Slavic themes.

[9] I was born in 1922, the daughter of an accountant in the ČKD concern. I developed an interest in the history of mining while still a student (I attended the seminars of Professor Václav Husa, a Marxist historian). Owing to my family ties to the Příbram region, where silver was mined, I chose to focus on mining there.

[10] The term *etnografie* was taken over from the Soviet Union and used by Nahodil from 1949 onwards. However, it never fully penetrated into local usage in Czechoslovakia. See Skalník, this volume.

[11] Ludvík Baran (b. 1920) also came from the Valašsko region. He studied with Chotek and accompanied him during some fieldwork trips. He also worked as a voluntary assistant to Karel Plicka, a famous photographer and film-maker, because he wanted to work in photography. Later he became a professor at the film faculty of the Academy of Musical Arts in Prague.

lidovou píseň). In 1954 the two centres merged to form the Institute for Ethnography and Folklore (Ústav pro etnografii a folkloristiku). Its first director was Kramařík, who was followed briefly by Ján Stanislav, a composer and professor at the Academy of Musical Arts. Jiří Horák took over as director in 1956, the same year he was elected an academician.[12]

From 1953 onwards the Prague centres jointly planned and executed fieldwork in the mining area of Kladensko, while the Brno ethnographers and folklorists worked in the Rosice-Oslavany mining zone. Both research projects were crowned with collective monographs (Skalníková 1959; Fojtík and Sirovátka 1961), which provided tangible evidence of the importance of the institute in the academy.[13] The first impetus for the národopis study of miners was the celebration of 700 years of Czech mining in 1949, with the participation of many národopis students. The songs collected in several mining areas provided material for a slim volume, *Lidová poesie hornická* (Folk poetry of miners), which was read not only among the miners but also by academic specialists. When it came to the preparation of working plans for the Centre for Národopis, it was natural to include research into mining life as part of a contemporary research strategy.

The first fieldwork in the mining areas, especially in Kladensko and Rosicko-Oslavansko, was made easier by the attitude of the miners and their families, who very much welcomed our interest in their lives and problems. We were overwhelmed by the wealth of song, narration, and musical creativity we found there. Especially interesting were the life histories and humorous stories we were able to collect, which we utilised in preparing our later monographs. We focused on men and women who had worked in this sector for generations. Politically they were oriented towards workers' parties, in particular the Social Democratic Party (which in 1948 was incorporated into the Communist Party), but also the Communist Party and the National Socialist Party. Our research was not, however, directed towards political

---

[12] Jiří Horák (1884–1975) was trained as a Slavist and became a professor at Charles University. He was responsible for the State Institute for Folk Song during the period of its independent existence. The State Institute succeeded the Working Committee for Czech National Song in Moravia and Silesia, founded in Brno in 1905.

[13] Other publications completed by members of the institute during the first decade of its existence were *Folk Songs and Dances in the Valašsko-Kloboucko*, volumes 1 and 2 (Vetterl 1955; Vetterl and Jelínková 1960), and other dance literature. Meanwhile, Kramařík edited the monograph *Chodsko* (Jindřich 1956). The publishing house of the academy also published a voluminous work by Václavík (1959), with many colour illustrations. This publication, which had been prepared by the author in the pre-socialist era, provoked a major discussion, initiated by critical remarks by Kramařík and Fojtík, who contributed an introduction to the volume. The author defended himself but also engaged in self-criticism. The discussion was finally ended with an article by Václavík's pupil Richard Jeřábek giving an objective evaluation of Václavík's life work as a whole (Jeřábek 1991).

questions. Rather, we were interested in the miners' way of life, family and
social relations, literary and musical culture, and so forth (see Vařeka and
Plessingerová 2002: 249). Some practitioners took the view at the time that
such subjects had no place in the discipline of národopis. Even today some
anthropologists, such as Josef Kandert (this volume), are unwilling to recognise that research on the 'proletariat' made an original contribution to the
theory of the discipline. Yet this has long been recognised by Scandinavian
and German colleagues, who have established new institutes to specialise in
such topics.[14]

The establishment of the independent Centre for Národopis and the
consolidation of the Institute for Ethnography and Folklore in 1954 were
very important for international cooperation. At the first gathering to mark
the launch of the academy, contacts and discussions took place between
Kramařík, the head of the centre, and foreign guests. Wolfgang Steinitz, the
representative of the GDR Academy of Sciences, showed the most active
interest in cooperation. The institute soon established cooperation in the
research on mining communities with Friedrich Sieber, Helmut Wilsdorf,
Karl-Ewald Fritzsche, and Siegfried Kube at the institute in Dresden. Czech
specialists in the anthropology of mining participated at a major conference
in Dresden in 1958. Kramařík, a specialist in folk agriculture, had good links
with Wolfgang Jacobeit, and the Czech folklorists with Gisela Schneide-
wind, the ethnomusicologist Erich Stockmann, and others. Cooperation with
Sorbian colleagues, especially Paul Nedo, was particularly close. The first
contact with Soviet scholars came with the participation of Pavel Ivanovich
Kushner at the third state-wide conference, held at Liblice in 1953.[15] In the
following years we were invited to contribute to the volume on western
Slavs as part of the *Narody mira* (Peoples of the world) series. Leonid Pavlovich Potapov, who was the editor of the volume,[16] visited Prague several
times, as did Nataliya Nikolaevna Gratsianskaya, who specialised in the

---

[14] Another new topic was research into collectivised (cooperativised) villages. This was
generally extremely difficult due to the unstable political situation, and we therefore decided
to concentrate on research in border areas, in the resettlement villages where collectivisation
was proceeding fairly well.
[15] This conference was designated etnografie and not národopis. Kushner gave a paper on
Soviet rural research and criticised the plans of Czech and Slovak researchers, which in his
view were altogether too ambitious (megalomaniac) in terms of the large numbers of research
staff projected and the tasks expected of them. He pointed out the opportunity for Czechoslovak researchers to follow from its beginning the path of socialist transformation, an opportunity which Soviet researchers had been denied. Kushner's speech was diplomatic: contrary to
the assertion of some later critics, he did not come as a missionary or attempt to impose a
Soviet line on a reluctant scholarly community.
[16] Fojtík was the editor on the Czech side.

anthropology of Czechs and Slovaks at the Moscow Academy. The manuscript was written but never published.[17]

Over the first decade of the institute, many fruitful contacts were established with Polish, Romanian, and Hungarian colleagues and with specialists from countries outside the Soviet bloc. In 1960 Czech and Slovak anthropologists were accepted as members of the International Union of Anthropological and Ethnological Sciences (IUAES) and the folklorist organisations IFMC and ISFNR. In 1962 the Czechoslovak Academy of Sciences hosted a meeting of the Permanent Council of the IUAES, which cemented relations with the global scholarly community. Among the participants were renowned scholars such as Melville Herskovits from the United States, Antonio Jorge Dias from Portugal, Daryll Forde from Great Britain, Vinigi Grottanelli from Italy, Johan Huizinga from the Netherlands, Sergey Tolstov from the USSR, Mihai Pop from Romania, and Gyula Ortutay from Hungary. The entire group visited Brno and Slovakia, where the guests were treated to live folklore performances in Slovak villages.[18]

Soon afterwards our links were also extended to include the Federal Republic of Germany: Gerhard Heilfurth invited Karel Fojtík and Oldřich Sirovátka, from Brno, for a stipend sojourn in Marburg. I myself had contacts with Heinrich Winkelmann, director of the Mining Museum in Bochum. Ingeborg Weber-Kellermann arranged gifts of books for us from the German Cultural Fund. From the mid-1960s onwards we were invited to participate in conferences of both the Deutsche Gesellschaft für Volkskunde and the Deutsche Gesellschaft für Völkerkunde. In 1966 it was again the Institute for Ethnography and Folklore in Prague which hosted the first postwar meeting of the Société Internationale d'Ethnologie et Folklore. During these years we were also in the forefront of European research in the field of ethnographic atlases.

Conclusion

Recently the Research Centre for the History of Science in Prague, jointly established by the Archives of the Czechoslovak Academy of Sciences and the Archives of the Charles University, organised a number of conferences concerning Czech science in the twentieth century. Lydia Petráňová, vice-president of the Academy of Sciences of the Czech Republic and a senior

---

[17] Only recently have I learnt that the volume was not published as planned, because of disagreements between Soviet and Polish authors.
[18] There were 53 participants in all. This meeting of the Permanent Council took place in the building of the academy on the Národní třída; a formal reception was held at the ethnographic collections of the Náprstek Museum.

member of the institute that was renamed in 1998 as the Ethnological Institute (Etnologický ústav), delivered a paper which concluded as follows:

The period 1953–1963 can be understood as a period of ideological pressure on democratic institutions. It eliminated a certain section of the graduates of the discipline, but it also brought a generational change, with the gradual ripening of a new generation of Marxist ethnographers, and with a gradual softening of extreme positions. For those given the opportunity to study národopis and work in the discipline, it was at the same time a period of unusual effervescence, of an expansion of research and publication possibilities, of which they took systematic advantage. (Petráňová 2000: 320)[19]

This positive trend continued in the 1960s, but unfortunately it was reversed by the so-called normalisation which followed the Warsaw Pact invasion of Czechoslovakia in 1968.

Let me return now to the title of this chapter. What was the significance of the inclusion of národopis in the Czechoslovak Academy of Sciences? Above all, it gave the discipline a professional base and the financial backing to ensure field research and to guarantee that the results would be published by the Czechoslovak Academy of Sciences and other publishers. Commissions, on which all disciplines were represented, evaluated staff according to a finely graded hierarchy which ranged from technical worker (*technický pracovník*) to leading scientist (*vedoucí vědecký pracovník*). The rules of the academy provided for the training of aspirants (i.e. doctorands) and the defence of theses to attain scientific degrees. Here, too, the model distinguishing the Candidate of Sciences (CSc) from the Doctor of Sciences (DrSc) was inspired by the Soviet example. Academicians (i.e. full members of the academy) and corresponding members were formally elected by the members, but their nominations were ultimately subject to approval by the Communist Party organs. The university titles of 'docent' and 'professor' could be attained by academy staff through the process of habilitation, but they had to be approved by the Communist Party, and an 'invitation' from a university was also necessary.

The academy had international contacts, mainly with academies and other institutes in the countries of the so-called socialist camp. This enabled staff to participate in international conferences, with the eventual possibility

---

[19] It should be added that the existence of the academy and the jobs it created for anthropologists in Prague and Brno, as well as at the Národopis Institute of the Slovak Academy of Sciences in Bratislava, enabled extended fieldwork which was not limited to the boundaries of Czechoslovakia. The research programme of the Prague Institute included field research in Africa and the Americas, as well as among the Czech minorities in Poland, Romania, and Yugoslavia and among Slovak minorities in Hungary and Ukraine (see Skalník, this volume).

of publishing abroad (again with the approval of party organs). In some divisions of národopis it was possible to participate in international projects. For example, Josef Vařeka, Vladimír Scheufler, and others participated in an ethnographic atlas project coordinated by Professor Matthias Zender in Bonn, work on which still continues.

Now under its new name, the Ethnological Institute of the Academy of Sciences of the Czech Republic celebrated its first five decades in 2004. In spite of political convulsions in 1968 and 1989, it has continued to produce high-quality scholarship. As elsewhere, it was easier to change the discipline's name (from národopis to etnologie) than to conduct a thorough critical evaluation of the past (for an early attempt see Mišurec and Jiříkovská 1991). After Czech historians had paved the way, however, anthropologists eventually followed suit in carrying out such an evaluation. Lydia Petráňová, vice-president of the Academy of Sciences of the Czech Republic and head of the division of historical ethnology in the Ethnological Institute, opened the discussion with an important conference paper in 1999, from which I quoted earlier (Petráňová 2000; Skalníková and Petráňová 2002; cf. Petráňová and Bahenský 2002). The conference 'Česká etnologie 2000' (Czech ethnology 2000), organised by the Ethnological Institute just one year later, deepened this critical reappraisal. A lively discussion took place around the Czech version of a paper by David Scheffel and Josef Kandert (2002); the English version, 'Politics and Culture in Czech Ethnography', had been published in 1994 in *Anthropological Quarterly*. Some of us old enough to recall the establishment of the Academy of Sciences in 1952 feel that this account distorts the development of Czech národopis as we recall it from that era (see, for example, Baran 2002; Petráňová 2002; Skalník 2002; Skalníková 2002; Vařeka and Plessingerová 2002).

References

Baran, L. 2002. K boji paměti proti zapomnění. In M. Holubová, L. Petráňová, and J. Woitsch (eds.), *Česká etnologie 2000*, pp. 241–45. Prague: Etnologický ústav Akademie věd České republiky.

Fojtík, K., and O. Sirovátka. 1961. *Rosicko-Oslavansko: Život a kultura v kamenouhelném revíru*. Praha: Nakladatelství ČSAV.

Jeřábek, R. 1991. Antonín Václavík a (sebe)kritika: K stému výročí narození. *Český lid* 78 (3): 216–21.

———. 1998. Z Šavla Pavel? (Komentář redakce k nekrologu 'Osud ateisty' z pera K. Máchy.) *Národopisná revue* 1: 53-55.

Jindřich, J. 1956. *Chodsko*. Praha: Nakladatelství ČSAV.

Mišurec, Z., and V. Jiříkovská. 1991. Příspěvek k vývoji české etnografie a folkloristiky a Národopisná společnost československá při ČSAV po únoru 1948: Zpráva pracovní skupiny NSČ pro Valné shromáždění NSČ v Boskovicích v říjnu 1990. *Národopisný věstník československý* 8 (50): 5–35.

Petráňová, L. 2000. Lid, národ a český národopis v letech 1953–1963. In H. Barvíková (ed.), *Věda v Československu v letech 1953–1963*, pp. 305–22. Praha: Nakladatelství Arenga pro Archiv AV ČR.

——. 2002. Promarněná příležitost. In M. Holubová, L. Petráňová, and J. Woitsch (eds.), *Česká etnologie 2000*, pp. 263–65. Praha: Etnologický ústav Akademie věd České republiky.

——, and F. Bahenský. 2002. Institucionální základna českého národopisu v letech tzv: Budování socialismu a profilace hlavních periodik. In M. Holubová, L. Petráňová, and J. Woitsch (eds.), *Česká etnologie 2000*, pp. 185–206. Praha: Etnologický ústav Akademie věd České republiky.

Scheffel, D., and J. Kandert. 2002. Politika a kultura v české etnografii. In M. Holubová, L. Petráňová, and J. Woitsch (eds.), *Česká etnologie 2000*, pp. 213–29. Praha: Etnologický ústav Akademie věd České republiky.

Skalník, P. 2002. Komentář k článku Davida Scheffela a Josefa Kanderta: 'Politika kultura v české etnografii'. In M. Holubová, L. Petráňová, and J. Woitsch (eds.), *Česká etnologie 2000*, pp. 231–34. Praha: Etnologický ústav Akademie věd České republiky.

Skalníková, O. (ed.). 1959. *Kladensko: Život a kultura v průmyslové oblasti*. Praha: Nakladatelství ČSAV.

——. 1999. Etnografické výzkumy všedního dne i svátečních aktivit českých horníků. *Národopisný věstník* 15 (57)–16 (58): 132–42.

——. 2002. Příspěvek do diskuse. In M. Holubová, L. Petráňová, and J. Woitsch (eds.), *Česká etnologie 2000*, pp. 235–40. Praha: Etnologický ústav Akademie věd České republiky.

——, and K. Fojtík. 1971. *K teorii etnografie současnosti*. Praha: Academia.

——, and L. Petráňová. 2002. Etnografické studium v letech 1964–1975. In A Kostlán (ed.), *Věda v Československu v období normalizace [1964–1969: Skalníková, 1970–1975: Petráňová]*, pp. 287–304. Praha: Výzkumné centrum pro dějiny vědy.

Václavík, A. 1959. *Výroční obyčeje a lidové umění*. Praha: Nakladatelství ČSAV.

Vařeka, J., and A. Plessingerová. 2002. Diskusní příspěvek k článku D. Scheffela a J. Kanderta 'Politika a kultura v české etnografii'. In M. Holubová, L. Petráňová, and J. Woitsch (eds.), *Česká etnologie*

2000, pp. 247–49. Praha: Etnologický ústav Akademie věd České republiky.

Vetterl, K. 1955. *Lidové písně a tance z Valašskokloboucka I*. Praha: Nakladatelství ČSAV.

———, and Z. Jelínková. 1960. *Lidové písně a tance z Valašskokloboucka II*. Praha: Nakladatelství ČSAV.

Chapter 9
The Genesis of Volkskunde in the German Democratic Republic

Wolfgang Jacobeit

I taught Ethnographie at the Institut für Völkerkunde und deutsche Volks-kunde at the Humboldt University in Berlin for more than 30 years, towards the end as a full professor. In addition, I was active in the Institut für deutsche Volkskunde of the GDR Academy of Sciences for 15 years, and I served as director of the Museum für Volkskunde for nearly 10 years. On the basis of this academic experience, I feel well qualified to comment on the development of Volkskunde, bearing in mind how it was shaped by condi-tions in the GDR but also acknowledging that it was able to mature into an historically sound, scientific discipline with a firm interdisciplinary founda-tion. Like most of my colleagues, I was interested primarily in developing a new profile for the subject as a whole, and only secondarily in some of the discrete research fields of the traditional disciplinary canon. I shall demon-strate that the Institut für Europäische Ethnologie that flourishes at the Humboldt University today, together with Berlin's Museum for European Cultures, represents a large measure of continuity with the disciplinary vision we developed during the socialist era.

When speaking of the conditions which prevailed in the GDR, I do not mean the often unspeakable treatment of social scientists by the Communist Party (SED) regime. This has been discussed often enough since 1989 and need not be reiterated here. My intention is rather to trace the formative period of GDR Volkskunde. To do this one must begin by acknowledging the political element—that is, the post-war emergence of two German states.

German Volkskunde—this cannot be denied—was one of the disci-plines closest to National Socialism and its ideology. After 1945 a coming to terms with this fact and an analysis of the reasons for it should have been

Note: This is an amended version of the paper Professor Jacobeit prepared for the workshop on which this volume is based. He was prevented by illness from attending. The editors are grateful to Dagmar Neuland-Kitzerow, who read the original text at our meeting and helped to facilitate this revised version.

viewed as urgent tasks. This appraisal was, in fact, gradually undertaken in
succeeding years, but the initial developments in the two German states were
completely disparate. Most older representatives of the discipline found
themselves in West Germany, where they took pains to exonerate one another of all responsibility. Hardly anyone was willing to face up to the self-
inflicted misappropriation of their discipline. The philippic of the sociologist
Heinz Maus (1946), with its harsh critique of Volkskunde, either went
unnoticed or was repudiated. The main object of study remained the intellectual or mental components (*geistig-seelische Komponente*) of folk culture
(*Volkskultur*) in the present day. New research interests focused above all on
refugee populations from the former German east. The revanchist tendencies
implicit in some of this work were a constant obstacle to occasional attempts
to promote cooperation between the disciplines in the two Germanies. No
'refugee Volkskunde' ever existed in the GDR.[1]

In East Germany the situation was completely different. Adolf Spamer
was appointed to the Academy of Sciences and in 1952 was charged with
establishing a Volkskunde commission that would bring together all significant representatives of the discipline still resident in the country (Jacobeit
and Mohrmann 1982). Spamer had in mind the realisation of plans, initiated
by him during the Nazi period as part of the 'Atlas of German Volkskunde'
project, to create a central Volkskunde institute (Jacobeit, Lixfeld, and
Bockhorn 1994; see also Spamer 1935, 1936). His appointment as an academician was political to the extent that an earlier nomination had been
revoked by the Nazis, and this reappointment could be seen as a rehabilitation of an internationally recognised scholar, of whom it could hardly be said
that he was a communist sympathiser, much less a member of the SED.

His leading advocate was Wolfgang Steinitz, born in 1905 into an intellectual upper-middle-class Jewish family, who had been a proponent of
Marxism in the 1920s. After sojourns in the Soviet Union and Sweden,
Steinitz returned to the Soviet sector of Berlin in order to participate in the
democratic restoration of the university system and in research (see Noack
and Krause, this volume). Since Spamer was already very ill and in no
position to meet his obligations towards the academy, Steinitz, at the time
vice-president of the academy, acted in his stead, taking over the direction of
the Volkskunde commission from Spamer shortly before the latter's death.
The commission, with its initially small staff, including Spamer's student
Ingeborg Weber-Kellermann, who acted as vice-director, soon expanded into
a full-fledged institute, and this metamorphosis marked the birth of GDR

[1] In February 1962 the Institutes for Volkskunde at the Academy of Sciences and the Humboldt University jointly organised a conference in West Germany with the title 'East German
Volkskunde'.

Volkskunde. Steinitz was much more than its institutional initiator. He was also the inspiration for a completely new scholarly approach based in historical materialism, which, by explicitly disavowing nationalism in favour of a new, democratic politics, delineated the consequences of the discipline's horrendous recent past (Steinitz 1955).

As a Marxist, Steinitz had long been a member of the Communist Party, and he even sat on its Central Committee from 1954 to 1958. But he was neither a functionary nor a propagandist, always preferring to seek scholarly excellence in his own work and in the work of his institute. He demonstrated his abilities in his masterpiece (which was also his debut in the discipline), *Deutsche Volkslieder demokratischen Charakters aus sechs Jahrhunderten* (Steinitz [1954] 1962). This was an absolute novelty in the study of folklore, which had previously overlooked the genre of protest—songs as found in mass struggles against both feudal oppression and capitalist exploitation, together with antiwar and resistance songs—which Steinitz traced into the Nazi period. This lyric tradition was for him an unmistakable marker of the attitudes of the working classes towards the mechanisms of authority controlled by the upper classes. It was thus historically determined.

Steinitz also postulated, in accordance with his Marxist concept of a new, democratic Volkskunde, that the main carrier of culture was the working population: the peasants and other social groups in the villages, the petty bourgeoisie in the cities, among them tradesmen, and, since the industrial revolution, factory workers and their kin in the service sector. He initiated numerous publications covering legends, folktales, and proverbs of a democratic character—that is, folklore in the traditional sense of the term (Burde-Schneidewind 1977; Woeller 1979). He demonstrated their complexity while at the same time shifting away from dominant sentimentalised perceptions. He did not deny the latter, but his portrayal of the working population as a carrier of culture was his most significant innovation, and it exerted great influence on Volkskunde research outside the GDR as well as within it. Suffice it to note that more than 50 volumes were published in the new institute's book series, all of them bearing testimony to Steinitz's democratic vision. In 1959 he was also one of the founders of the '*Arbeiterliedarchiv*' at the Academy of Arts in East Berlin, under the leadership of Inge Lammel.

Steinitz made a third contribution to GDR Volkskunde, beyond his institutional and intellectual inputs. Just as the folklore of subordinate groups had previously been a stepchild of Volkskunde (despite Johann Gottfried Herder's comments on the necessity of including accusations and protest songs to achieve genuine insight into the mentality [*Mentalität*] of ethno-regional groups), so, too, had the material foundations of popular culture, namely, the sphere of 'work and economy', been largely excluded from

Volkskunde. True, there were many studies of archaic agricultural machinery as a supposed relict of 'ancient' times, but the heuristic value of such studies was minimal. The general research concept Steinitz developed for his institute in the mid-1950s included the establishment of a section on 'work and economy'. The scholars of this section quickly acquired international recognition.

It is worth asking why this essential sphere of study had hardly been examined previously. The question was indeed posed, and the answer I gave to it in my 1965 book was one of the first studies in disciplinary history to be published since the war. It attracted a great deal of attention from representatives of the discipline all over Europe. It had already been demonstrated, in studies pointing to the birth of the discipline in the romantic period, that the authors of the 'classics' in Volkskunde had been interested in so-called material folk culture and had made useful observations on the subject. This tradition was continued in a diluted manner by Wilhelm Heinrich Riehl and, in particular, by the philologist Karl Weinhold, who towards the end of the nineteenth century took a critical stance against the *Herren Folkloristen*, with their narrow view of the primacy of the ideo-mental nature of the common man (*Primat des Geistig-Seelischen, der sog. Volksmenschen*) (see his programmatic essay, Weinhold 1890). What united all protagonists, including Weinhold, in their protracted discussions of the appropriate object of study for Volkskunde was a concentration on the rural and the technical. It was precisely there that one could observe the fundamental transformation of socio-economic and socio-cultural ways of life in the nineteenth century under the sway of capitalism. But these scholars did not examine this process and its effects, preferring to limit their investigations to the pre-industrial period.

This position did not change in the twentieth century, despite the pervasive ideological crisis which set in during and following the First World War. Volkskunde remained associated with the traditional and the pre-industrial, and this tendency was strengthened by citizens' movements and by the continuing legacy of German historicism (see Petzold 1978). This profile found an apologist in Hans Naumann, who confined folk culture to the 'degenerate cultural values' (*gesunkenes Kulturgut*) of intellectual elites (Naumann 1921). This fundamentally ahistorical thesis found an energetic opponent in Wilhelm Fraenger, who challenged Naumann by insisting that the relationship between popular culture and the culture of the upper classes was complementary, based on give and take.

Fraenger was hired by Wolfgang Steinitz at the new institute of the Academy of Sciences (Weckel 2001). There, on the basis of his *Historische Jahrbücher*, which had been banned by the Nazis, he built the *Deutsches*

Jahrbuch für Volkskunde into one of the most respected publications in the German-speaking world. Only a few years before the end of socialism, it was renamed *Jahrbuch für Kulturgeschichte und Volkskunde*, a visible sign of the change of paradigm which had taken place in GDR Volkskunde. This development was accompanied by a series of dissertations on Hans Naumann, Eugen Mogk, and others, discussing, among other things, Naumann's stance vis-à-vis National Socialism (as rector of the university in Frankfurt am Main and initiator of the book burnings there in May 1933, his sympathies were clear) (Schmook 1993). In this reappraisal of the past, an important—albeit unofficial—link developed to West German Volkskunde, and especially with the institute in Tübingen under Hermann Bausinger. These parallel discussions of Volkskunde under the Nazis found their visible consummation in an inter-German conference in Munich in 1988 (Gerndt 1987) and also in a voluminous compendium in which East German, West German, and Austrian scholars were represented (Jacobeit, Lixfeld, and Bockhorn 1994).

Another important personality in Steinitz's inner circle was the Sorbian Paul Nedo (1908–84; see Bresan 2002), who saw an historically oriented Volkskunde, as represented by Steinitz, as the basis for reviving a Sorbian ethnic identity after years of its suppression in imperial Germany and, even more so, under the Nazis. This was also the goal of the interdisciplinary Institute for Sorbian Studies established in Bautzen in 1951 under the directorship of Paul Nowotny. Although initially Paul Nedo began to examine 'democratic' elements in the folklore of his nation as these had developed through history, he was equally interested in the study of contemporary Sorbian culture. This was novel at the time and resulted in more than one dispute with more traditionally oriented representatives of the discipline. This did not deter Nedo from arguing that contemporary culture was an absolutely essential field of study. He maintained this position consistently in his research and his teaching when he assumed the chair for German Volkskunde at the Humboldt University in 1966. The distance education teaching in Volkskunde which he founded reflected his approach as well. Nedo also initiated an inter-German conference on 'Problems and Methodology in Contemporary Volkskunde Studies', during which the limits and subject matter of Volkskunde in the GDR were defined (Jacobeit and Nedo 1969).

In conclusion, let me underline that the approach initiated by Wolfgang Steinitz, namely, to focus on the working population—Wilhelm Fraenger spoke of 'Homo faber'—as the carrier of national culture, advanced not only the historicity but also the interdisciplinarity of our work in the GDR Academy of Sciences, the university, and the museums, despite the various ideological impediments put in our way by the SED authorities. Long before the *Wende* of 1989–90, we had productive discussions concerning the concepts of culture and way of life and their application to working populations both in the city and on the land under conditions of massive social change. We also adopted the category of everyday life (*Alltag*) as proposed by Jürgen Kuczynski in his five-volume opus *Geschichte des Alltags des deutschen Volkes* (Kuczynski 1980–86), to which my and my wife, Sigrid's, three-volume study *Illustrierte Alltagsgeschichte des deutschen Volkes (1550–1945)* was a supplement (Jacobeit and Jacobeit 1985–87, 1995).

Even if the numerous publications by me and my colleagues are rarely cited any more (with the exception of the compendium addressing the discipline's complicity with the Nazis), I believe we contributed to the development of our discipline, especially by helping to make the category of 'everyday life' into an established subject of investigation by a unified German Volkskunde.

References

Bresan, A. 2002. *Paul Nedo 1908–1984: Ein biographischer Beitrag zur sorbischen Geschichte*. Bautzen: Domowina Verlag.

Burde-Schneidewind, G. 1977. *Historische Volkssagen aus dem 13. bis 19. Jahrhundert*. Berlin: Akademie-Verlag.

Gerndt, H. (ed.). 1987. *Volkskunde und Nationalsozialismus: Referate und Diskussionen einer Tagung der Deutschen Gesellschaft für Volkskunde, München 23. bis 25.10.1986*. München: Münchner Vereinigung für Volkskunde.

Jacobeit, S., and W. Jacobeit. 1985–87. *Illustrierte Alltagsgeschichte des deutschen Volkes*, vol. 1 (1550–1810), vol. 2 (1810–1900). Leipzig: Urania Verlag.

——, ——. 1995. *Illustrierte Alltags- und Sozialgeschichte Deutschlands*, vol. 3 (1900–1945). Münster: Verlag Westfälisches Dampfboot.

Jacobeit, W. 1965. *Bäuerliche Arbeit und Wirtschaft: Ein Beitrag zur Wissenschaftsgeschichte der deutschen Volkskunde*. Berlin: Akademie-Verlag.

——, and U. Mohrmann. 1982. Zur Geschichte der volkskundlichen Lehre unter Adolf Spamer an der Berliner Universität (1933–1945). *Ethnographisch-archäologische Zeitschrift* 23 (2): 283–98.

——, and P. Nedo (eds.). 1969. *Probleme und Methoden volkskundlicher Gegenwartsforschung: Vorträge und Diskussionen einer internationalen Arbeitstagung in Bad Saarow 1967*. Berlin: Akademie-Verlag.

——, H. Lixfeld, and O. Bockhorn. 1994. *Völkische Wissenschaft: Gestalten und Tendenzen der deutschen und österreichischen Volkskunde in der ersten Hälfte des 20. Jahrhunderts*. Wien: Böhlau.

Kuczynski, J. 1980–86. *Geschichte des Alltags des deutschen Volkes: 1600– 1945*. Berlin: Akademie-Verlag.

Maus, H. 1946. Zur Situation der deutschen Volkskunde. *Die Umschau. Internationale Revue* 1: 349–59.

Naumann, H. 1921. *Primitive Gemeinschaftskultur: Beiträge zur Volkskunde und Mythologie*. Jena: Diederichs.

Neumann, S. A. 1980. *Den Spott zum Lachen: Prosasprichwörter aus fünf Jahrhunderten*. Rostock: Hinstorff.

Petzold, J. 1978. *Konservative Theoretiker des deutschen Faschismus: Jungkonservative Ideologen in der Weimarer Republik als geistige Wegbereiter der faschistischen Diktatur*. Berlin: Deutscher Verlag der Wissenschaften.

Schmook, R. 1993. '*Gesunkenes Kulturgut—Primitive Gemeinschaftskultur*': *Der Germanist Hans Naumann (1886–1939) in seiner Bedeutung für die Volkskunde*. Wien: Institut für Volkskunde.

Spamer, A. 1935. Stand und Aufgaben der Deutschen Volksforschung. *Mitteldeutsche Blätter für Volkskunde* 10: 97–105.

——. 1936. Aufgaben und Arbeiten der 'Abteilung Volkskunde' in der 'Reichsgemeinschaft der Deutschen Volksforschung'. *Niederdeutsche Zeitschrift für Volkskunde* 14: 145–54.

Steinitz, W. 1955. *Die volkskundliche Arbeit in der Deutschen Demokratischen Republik*. 2nd ed. Kleine Beiträge zur Volkskunstforschung H. 1. Leipzig: VEB Hofmeister.

——. [1954] 1962. *Deutsche Volkslieder demokratischen Charakters aus sechs Jahrhunderten*. 2 vols. Berlin: Akademie Verlag.

Weckel, P. 2001. *Wilhelm Fraenger (1890–1964): Ein subversiver Kulturwissenschaftler zwischen den Systemen*. Potsdam: Verlag für Berlin-Brandenburg.

Weinhold, K. 1890. Was soll die Volkskunde leisten? *Zeitschrift für Völkerpsychologie und Sprachwissenschaft* 20: 1–15.

Woeller, W. (ed.). 1979. *Deutsche Volksmärchen von arm und reich*. Berlin: Akademie-Verlag.

PART THREE

SOCIALIST ANTHROPOLOGY AT HOME

Under socialism one might have expected a strengthening of those strands in anthropology which address issues of long-term social evolution and analyse the 'global' forces to which Marx and Engels drew attention in their *Communist Manifesto* (1848). Yet the evidence presented in this volume points by and large to a different story in East-Central Europe. More support was directed towards the consolidation of research and teaching in the field of 'anthropology at home'—in other words, to a profile of activities which derived from the discipline's genesis alongside and often in the service of nationalist movements and which had little or nothing in common with the universalist aspirations of 'scientific socialism'. The majority of anthropologists, in the broad definition we have adopted, worked in fields which bore a closer resemblance to those of local historians and traditional folklorists than to those of comparative socio-cultural anthropologists or other social scientists.

Of course there were significant national variations. In the first chapter of this section, Ute Mohrmann (following Wolfgang Jacobeit in the preceding chapter) describes how the old German Volkskunde was transformed by a dynamic rapprochement with history and Kulturwissenschaft. Innovations included the deployment of the concept of 'way of life' and large-scale projects with a regional focus—for example, in Magdeburg and among the Sorbs. When the rapprochement peaked in the 1980s, Volkskundler were extending their interests into quite new fields, such as women's studies. Some topics, however, were neglected to the end, especially religion and other subjects not readily reducible to the theory of historical materialism. The neglect of contemporary urban social life reflected the 'unloved' character of everyday life in the GDR. The Volkskundler of the socialist period, unlike their predecessors, did not romanticise the rural past, and perhaps their most solid achievements were historical studies of peasant modernisation (though they were not supposed to use the term *Modernisierung*). The thorny question of whether or not there existed a separate East

German nation in the sense of Soviet *ethnos* theory was one which scholars tried to avoid, but they could not entirely prevent the political instrumentalisation of their work, as when the authorities sought to appropriate feelings of belonging to one's locality (*Heimat*) or region in order to strengthen feelings of belonging to the socialist state.

Dagmar Neuland-Kitzerow complements Mohrmann's account by describing how the exhibitions mounted at Berlin's Museum für Volkskunde became progressively more imaginative towards the end of the socialist era. Museum staff worked closely with their colleagues at the university and the Academy of Sciences in order to present some of the most creative fruits of the 'history of everyday life' (*Alltagsgeschichte*) approaches. Representations of contemporary life were sometimes oversimplified, and the museum sufferered from a lack of funding as well as from a lack of contact with Western museologists. Despite these deficiencies, the Museum für Volkskunde was highly successful in its outreach to the public, and the GDR museums as a whole were innovators in their support for anti-colonial struggles and in their policies concerning cultural property.

In contrast to these chapters highlighting the innovations introduced in Berlin, the remaining chapters in this section tend to highlight continuities. Petr Lozoviuk and Josef Kandert offer similar diagnoses of the Czech case. The former notes the long-term tendency for národopis, from its nineteenth century origins, to be instrumentalised for political purposes. Socialist ideology did not so much do away with the discourses of nation and ethnicity as graft a few new themes onto the existing discipline. It did not seriously question the foundations of the theory or methodology of národopis. Lozoviuk pays particular attention to the country's 'ambiguous relationship' with Germany. Since the nineteenth century, Czech národopis had developed by replicating the theories and methods of German Volkskunde. But whereas the latter was obliged after 1945 to break with its traditions, the Czech discipline remained preoccupied with the Czech national character and approached ethnicity in terms of essentialist identities, rather than in terms of dynamic processes between different groups sharing a common territory.

The shortcomings of 'real-socialist ethnoscience' (Lozoviuk) are picked up in Josef Kandert's discussion of Czech 'home anthropology'. Kandert is careful to distinguish the work of the národopisci from the much more interesting accomplishments of those Czech anthropologists who worked abroad in this period, about which he has written elsewhere. Some národopisci, especially museum staff, continued to work on the old folk culture as if nothing had changed. Others were determined to break the mould by undertaking investigations in urban, industrial settings. Whereas the discipline had historically privileged rich peasants, the major focus of attention now shifted to the poor, in both countryside and town. However, according to Kandert, the authors of these 'proletarian studies' failed to address contemporary social transformations adequately; and their 'quasi-Marxism' was hardly more sophisticated than the theories of those who preferred to remain in the niche of positivism.

There follow two chapters concerning Slovakia. Juraj Podoba argues that the apparent productivity of Slovak národopisci in the last decades of socialism concealed a rigid conservatism and a reluctance on the part of the mainstream to engage in theoretical reflection or methodological innovation. The causes lay in the late development of the country's national movement and Bratislava's peripheral position in relation to Prague, which was in turn peripheral in relation to Germany. Comparative anthropology outside Europe did not figure on the anthropological agenda in the socialist era, and minority groups within the country were also neglected (as they were by the Czech národopisci). Socialist ideology had minimal impact here, being little more than a 'veil to conceal pragmatism and romantic nostalgia'. The result was even greater continuity with pre-war nation-centred traditions than in Bohemia (Moravia being generally closer to Slovakia). This was partly due to the more rural nature of Slovak society, which led researchers (almost all concentrated in the capital) to concentrate on archaic features and 'salvaging' knowledge of the peasant past for posterity. With few exceptions, the socialist národopisci were sterile positivists. Even a programme devoted to the 'anthropology of the present' brought few results, and when Slovak researchers turned their attention to the town they repeated the bias of their approach to rural folk culture by indulging in 'urban romanticism'.

Gabriela Kiliánová outlines a more positive account of a specific school within Slovak anthropology, namely 'folkloristics', which was separate from etnografia and generally considered to be more scholarly and more rigorous. Here one notes continuities of a different order, since the founding impulses for this school were given by Roman Jakobson and, above all, Petr Bogatyrev in the decades before socialism. Kiliánová draws attention to the dramatic *volte-face* in the Stalinist years of Andrej Melicherčik, the key figure among Bogatyrev's successors. Until the mid-1950s there was strong pressure to conform to Soviet dogmas concerning historical materialism. From this point on, however, the folklorists, including Melicherčik himself, turned their attention to contemporary subjects and also to promoting theory, drawing not only on Soviet schools but also on Western currents, especially French structuralism. Most remarkably, this school was able to continue its development in the 1970s and 1980s. In the period when almost all other anthropological currents in Czechoslovakia experienced repression, Bratislava semioticians were able to refine their analyses of symbols and of culture as a system of communication. The school's success was not simply a function of its scholarly merits, though these were significant. One conducive factor mentioned by Kiliánová was the booming demand for folklorists to staff socialist cultural institutions. Another was the fact that these folklorists, even when they began to address contemporary phenomena, chose not to focus on politically sensitive issues or groups.

In the last chapter of this section Klára Kuti focuses on 'historicity' in Hungarian néprajz. The origins of this discipline in Hungary, as elsewhere in the region, were tied to a nationalist agenda. Kuti shows that the scholars of the pre-socialist period focused on archaic survivals and in effect froze time in order to postulate an 'authentic' national culture in the centuries preceding modernity. From 1949, however, anthropologists were expected to replace this essentialism with a dynamic approach grounded in historical materialism. Kuti outlines the implementation of this materialism in the Budapest department headed from 1951 by István Tálasi. It turns out that Marxism was not significantly integrated, and the classical object of research, Hungarian 'folk culture', did not change. Kuti goes on to outline lively debates over the division of labour between anthropologists and historians. Although some of the former, notably Tibor Bodrogi, Tamás Hofer and Mihály Sárkány, favoured a more expansive focus on social relations, the majority of Hungarian anthropologists proved reluctant to change their notions of history and to adopt new objects and methods in their research. It seems likely that the other major influence from Soviet etnografiya, namely its preoccupation with the theory of ethnos, helped to facilitate this conservatism. Only towards the end of the socialist era did a few Hungarian anthropologists begin to engage significantly with innovative Western schools of historical anthropology.

CH

Chapter 10
Volkskunde in the German Democratic Republic on the Eve of Its Dissolution

Ute Mohrmann

> ... that in the end the Volkskunde/Ethnographie of the German Democratic Republic vanished for the most part without a trace from the scientific map of Europe is a singular occurrence, above all when we consider what happened to Volkskunde in other Eastern and Central European countries.
>
> > Reinhard Johler, 'Wieviel Europa braucht die Europäische Ethnologie?'

As Reinhard Johler observed, the end of the German Democratic Republic spelled the end of East German Volkskunde, but this rupture and its sociopolitical background are not the subject of this chapter. The liquidation of this Volkskunde in the course of German reunification led to upheavals that have not yet been examined. Here, however, I restrict myself to discussing the last decade of the Volkskunde of the GDR. The dissolution of this tradition is to be understood as a symbolic marker, as the 'ordering of our memory' (*Ordnung unserer Erinnerung*), of a chapter of German scientific history that is now closed. Its analysis 'from within' has already begun (Mohrmann 1994, 2001; Jacobeit 2000).[1] 'From without' we have been offered selective readings and have heard denunciatory voices, but also the occasional judicious assessment of disciplinary history and the scientific culture of the GDR. A thesis completed recently by a young historian (Lee 1998) stands out for the density of its sources and its discriminating interpretation.

The appeal to 'discover ... GDR Volkskunde' has nevertheless not found a broad echo (Köstlin 1991). The 'systematic study of what was accomplished in the field during the GDR years and of what was dictated or prevented and by whom' (Kaschuba 1999: 88–89) has yet to be undertaken. This contribution is intended to be one building block in the analysis of the

---

[1] See also Scholze and Scholze-Irrlitz 2001; Krause, Neuland-Kitzerow, and Noack 2003.

different trajectories of the unequal partners in East and West. I was formerly head of the Department of Ethnographie of the Humboldt University in Berlin and was active in the cultural life of the GDR. This needs to be kept in mind. Konrad Köstlin observed in 1991 that 'there are today as many perceptions of East German Volkskunde as there are people trying to sketch it' (Köstlin 1991: 232), and this point remains true today.

Theoretical Positions between Expansion and Persistence

A transformation of Volkskunde occurred in the 1970s with a new rapprochement with history. The adoption of an historical methodology and a focus on the cultural and social history of the modern era prevailed over the 'traditional canon with its narrowly defined historical frame' (Scholze-Irrlitz and Scholze 1991: 36). The controversies of the past were largely set aside, and the foundation was laid for a new form of studying culture and ways of life (*Kultur- und Lebensweiseforschung*), going beyond the parameters of Soviet etnografiya. The concept 'way of life' identified a sphere of tension between living conditions and actual social activities, and it became the essential constituent of a broad concept of culture. The theoretical model developed by the group of GDR cultural scientists (*Kulturwissenschaftler*) around Dietrich Mühlberg was advanced above all by Paul Nedo, Wolfgang Jacobeit, and their students, while the socio-cultural anthropologist Günter Guhr played an important role in emphasising ethnographic research. This model was applied both to cultural traditions of the pre-industrial period and to the study of working-class culture.

The way-of-life approach was interdisciplinary and was widely adopted throughout German-speaking Volkskunde. Progress was hampered in the GDR in the 1980s by a significant shortcoming: ignorance of contemporary international scientific trends. There was no official recognition of Anglo-American cultural and social anthropology. Similarly, the new understandings of the terms *culture* and *class* promoted by scholars such as Raymond Williams and E. P. Thompson were ignored in public debate and in teaching. Pierre Bourdieu's concept of *habitus* was discussed only towards the end of the 1980s. This 'GDR complacency' mirrored a similar introversion in the discipline in West Germany and in Austria, but the GDR's isolation from international scholarship was more enduring. Inter-German recognition was selective; although contacts were intensified in the 1980s, they remained restricted almost exclusively to high-ranking representatives of the discipline. The younger generation was left to cultivate relationships with researchers in other socialist countries.

This ignorance of contemporary 'bourgeois' science was the result of a particular mix of political factors and factors specific to the discipline.

Politically motivated isolationism at the level of the state lay behind the intention to create as much distance as possible from Western discourse. An all-encompassing Marxism-Leninism was officially propagated, and shortage of hard currency limited the acquisition of Western literature. At the same time, the discipline did offer scholars the chance to withdraw to ambiguous positions; it is important to stress that not all scientists were involved politically and motivated ideologically to the same degree.

Thanks especially to cooperation between Volkskundler and Kulturwissenschaftler and a few social and economic historians, the concepts of culture and way of life were deepened in the course of the 1980s in both historically oriented and contemporary Volkskunde. The investigation of human relationships and behaviour was predicated on an understanding of way of life as a collective experience and of everyday life as consisting of regular, subjectively learned practices and socially binding behavioural norms. This approach, in its theoretical essence, enabled scholars to investigate the entire span between the socio-economic structures of societal reproduction processes and the minutiae of individual everyday lives (Dehne 1989: 143). The outcome was a new focus on the history of everyday life and experience, on biography, and on oral history.

This theoretical step forward took place in an environment of GDR historiography that had been slow to recognise the need for a history of everyday life and *Mentalitätsgeschichte* and to open up to women's or gender studies. Western developments such as the work of the French 'Annales' school were either not recognised or actively criticised. Several academics saw themselves pressed to defend such developments at the beginning of the 1980s, among them the economic historian Jürgen Kuczynski and later, above all, Wolfgang Jacobeit and Jan Peters, along with several other historians. It is also worth noting the lack of attention paid to Soviet authors such as Aaron Gur'yevich, whose *Mittelalterliche Volkskunde* was published in German only in 1986 and not debated theoretically until even later (Scholze-Irrlitz 1994). Thus, while always needing to struggle with its own legitimation concerns, the Volkskunde of the GDR was, through its new commitment to the history of everyday life (*Alltagsgeschichte*), nonetheless able to contribute actively to broader understandings of history.

Another valuable component was the addition of a distinct regional dimension to the research agenda. While the range of approaches remained varied, Volkskunde, with its social historical slant, played a central role. There was general agreement that a region should be analysed as a spatial or spatial-temporal organisation of social relations, as a concrete historical habitat for living, acting, and communicating. This conception included the dialectical relationship with the trans-regional, that is, linkages between the

regional, the national, and the international.[2] Implementation of the regionalist orientation was much influenced by contemporary social developments.
The renaissance of 'home[land] and region' (*Heimat und Regionalität*) in
industrialised societies in both East and West Germany from the mid-1970s
onward proved to be an enduring phenomenon.

The politicisation of the 'homeland and region' movement took a particular form in the GDR. The party's model of a new social identity was tied
to forging deeper identifications on the part of the populace with its immediate habitat, city, and village and, finally, with 'the GDR—my home'. In
order to stabilise the system, understandings of history, heritage, and tradition were given new significance (Strobach 1988). Representatives of the
discipline of Volkskunde were initially very sensitive to this instrumentalis-
ing of local identities (*Heimat, Heimatgefühl*), given their awareness of how
this had functioned in the past in national-romantic and nationalist intellectual traditions. But at the same time they saw an opportunity to gain acceptance and backing for their long-marginalised discipline through improved
recognition of regional culture and folklore, as well as through a renewed
appreciation and institutionalisation of history at the sub-national level
(*Landesgeschichte*).

At about the same time, a 'new usage of the old terms' *people, popular culture,* and *ethnos* was under discussion throughout the German-
speaking scientific community (Girtler 1982; Strobach 1983; Köstlin 1984;
Willenberg 1986, 1987). The intentions behind this discussion varied. In the
GDR the general understanding of the term *people* (*Volk*) was summarised
by Hermann Strobach (1983: 163f., 170f.), who described it as both a socio-
logical-historical and an ethnic category (*demos* and *ethnos*, respectively).
He emphasised historicity and the development of the term in both its social
and ethnic meanings. Soviet ethnos theory here became entangled with the
contemporary political position on the German national question. Several
historians and philosophers as well as politicians looked to the Volkskundler
to come up with answers to this challenging question. The majority of GDR
scholars tried to avoid defining the conditions of an 'East German ethnic
identity' or of a 'socialist German nation'.

Along with several others, I was drawn into the professional debate,
which did not produce the hoped-for solutions. This failure was due, among
other reasons, to an excessive 'culturalisation' of the term *ethnic*—that is, a
one-sided stressing of 'ethnic particularities' and their interpretation as
cultural characteristics. No attempt was made to go beyond the theoretical
definition of ethnicity exemplified in the approach of the Soviet scholar

---

[2] Cf. *Probleme regionaler Volkskultur: Internationales Symposium vom 3. bis 5.10.1985 in
Schwerin.* Jahrbuch für Volkskunde und Kulturgeschichte 29 (1986).

Yulian Bromley (Bromlej 1977). The positions of the Soviet etnografiya school prevailed in both Völkerkunde and Volkskunde in the GDR, and critical observations or attempts to expand the scope of the discourse were rare. In any case, the perspective of Volkskunde generally favoured a focus on the 'demos' rather than the 'ethnos'; many scientists therefore perceived these discussions as largely irrelevant. Nevertheless, the dialogue between Volkskundler and Völkerkundler concerning culture, way of life, and ethnos stimulated attempts to form a common discipline of Ethnographie, grounded in a unifying anthropological point of view. This orientation has proved itself tenable and conducive to interdisciplinary research down to the present day (but see also Noack and Krause, this volume).

In comparison with the situation during the 1970s, this empirical and theoretical synthesis was closely tied to an intensified examination of disciplinary history in both Volkskunde and Völkerkunde during the 1980s. It included a critical analysis of the role of Volkskunde in National Socialism as well as an examination of more recent work in the GDR. The entire history of Volkskunde since its emergence as an independent discipline at the turn of the twentieth century was included in this enterprise (Jacobeit and Mohrmann 1982; Jacobeit 1987; Strobach 1987; Mohrmann 1991; Mohrmann and Jacobeit 1991). The principal locations for this and other academic activities during the 1980s were conferences held in the GDR and in other socialist countries, together with institute colloquia and events coordinated by mass organisations. The close association of scientific discourse with the state apparatus and mass organisations was a continuing manifestation of the centrally directed academic system.[3] Nevertheless, the tenor of the 1980s, in comparison with the dirigisme of the 1970s, when it was still *de rigueur* to insist on a critique of 'bourgeois Volkskunde and Völkerkunde' (Weißel 1980), afforded GDR academics more room for manoeuvre. It was possible for a comparatively independent discussion of anthropological work to take place. It is also true, however, that towards the end of the 1980s some researchers were significantly affected by restrictions 'from above'; these

---

[3] The respective bodies included the Subcommittee for Anthropological Problems (*Problemrat für Ethnographie*) of the History Committee in the Scientific Section of the Central Committee of the SED; the Anthropology Work Group (*Arbeitsgemeinschaft Ethnographie*) of the Historical Society of the GDR, the Anthropology Section of the Museum Committee in the Ministry of Culture, the central commission for cultural history–Volkskunde of the GDR Cultural League (*Kulturbund der DDR*), and the Berlin 'anthropologists' assembly' as a forum for communication at the university level. Another important forum was the commission 'Contemporary Anthropological Study of Socialist Countries' (*Ethnographische Gegenwartsforschung sozialistischer Länder*), which was attached to the respective academy institutes and which organised regular conferences.

people tended not to be the Volkskundler themselves but employees of state institutions co-opted into particular research projects.

The Institutional Structures of Research and Teaching

The institutionalisation of Volkskunde in East Germany took place at the beginning of the 1950s and was not modified significantly until 1989–90. This might be taken to imply that no changes took place in the way the discipline was instrumentalised in a politico-ideological sense. The reform of the universities and the Academy of Sciences in 1968–69 and the alignment of Volkskunde with the historical sciences did, however, mark a form of politicisation. Many representatives of the discipline saw these changes as a loss of independence, as acts of coercion. Others saw them as a chance for the discipline to open itself to interdisciplinary research. GDR Volkskunde remained, in contrast to its West German counterpart, a '(small) mass discipline' ([*kleines*] *Massenfach*) (Kaschuba 1999: 94), one of the more esoteric sciences. It comprised two research institutes, one (central) museum for Volkskunde, and one university chair. In the 1980s the research of the cultural history–Volkskunde section of the GDR Academy of Sciences was concentrated in Berlin,[4] with branches in Rostock,[5] Dresden,[6] and Bautzen (the Institute for Sorbian Studies).[7] A total of no more than 25 scientists was employed in these institutions,[8] of whom a sizeable number were hired as researchers immediately after completing their first degree or their PhD. A few were recruited from other disciplines. The second half of the 1980s witnessed a generational change, which also affected the four staff members of the department at the Humboldt University. This caesura, too, was a significant aspect of the situation on the eve of the discipline's dissolution.

As in other socialist countries, most research was carried out in institutes of the Academy of Sciences, on the basis of a system of central planning. Foci of research in the 1980s included the history of everyday life in the nineteenth century and the beginning of the twentieth, contemporary everyday life, the popular culture (*Volkskultur*) of Saxony since the sixteenth century and of Mecklenburg-Vorpommern from the eighteenth to the twentieth century, and the study of contemporary Sorbian culture.[9] The Museum

---

[4] Directors: Hermann Strobach, Evemarie Badstübner-Peters (after 1990).
[5] Directors: Ulrich Bentzien, Siegfried Neumann.
[6] Directors: Rudolf Weinhold, Bernd Schöne.
[7] Director: Frank Förster.
[8] For details concerning individuals, see Martischnig 1990.
[9] The institutes published the *Jahrbuch für Volkskunde und Kulturgeschichte*, the journal *Demos: Internationale ethnographische und folkloristische Informationen (Annotationen zu*

für Volkskunde in Berlin was active in the museological realisation of these projects,[10] as exemplified in the exhibition *Urban Proletariat: On the Way of Life of a Class* (1980–87). To mark its one-hundredth anniversary, the museum stood at the centre of disciplinary debate on one last occasion in 1989 when it organised a colloquium entitled 'History of Everyday Life in Ethnographic Museums: Collecting and Exhibiting in International Comparison'. The museum landscape in East Germany also included about 50 similar institutions devoted either exclusively or primarily to themes of a Volkskunde nature. The staff of these museums were generally well qualified, thanks to a distance education programme for museologists initiated by the Humboldt University in 1966. Approximately 100 museum employees had graduated in Ethnographie by the end of the 1980s. Praxis-oriented training and the integration of students into university research facilitated high-quality museological work.[11]

The Department of Ethnographie of the Humboldt University was the only institution in which both Volkskunde and Völkerkunde could be studied.[12] While the latter was also offered in Leipzig, the study of Volkskunde was limited to Berlin, where it was supplemented by a distance education programme. The universities of Berlin and Leipzig each admitted roughly eight students in alternate years. The programme in Berlin aspired to teach the two specialised disciplines in their unity through an extensive ethnographic introduction focusing on the theory, history, and methodology of both traditions. For students studying Volkskunde, this was followed in the last decade of the GDR by classes intended to communicate the understanding of a Volkskunde based on cultural and social history (including contemporary history), above all the history of everyday life, together with specialist courses on material, intellectual, and social culture. Coverage of the neighbouring disciplines of cultural theory, sociology, demography, agrarian and economic history, and regional history, to name only a few, was also offered. This combination of historical and anthropological elements dated back to the beginning of the 1960s and was considered binding after the university reform in 1968. It lasted until 1992–93. Like the mandatory instruction in Marxism-Leninism, the history courses usually ran parallel to the major courses, and there was little productive integration, despite the historical-materialist focus of the discipline. Cooperative links were espe-

---

Publikationen aus sozialistischen Ländern Ost- und Südosteuropas wie aus der DDR), and the Volkskunde series of the journal *Lětopis*.
[10] Director: Erika Karasek.
[11] For further details see Mohrmann 1998, especially the contribution by Dagmar Neuland-Kitzerow; see also Neuland-Kitzerow, this volume.
[12] The chairs of the department were, successively, Wolfgang Jacobeit and Ute Mohrmann.

cially strong between the Volkskunde institutions of the academy, the museums, and the university; they were essential to the successful realisation of a broad, research-focused, and praxis-oriented teaching programme.

From Way-of-Life Studies to the History of Everyday Life and Experience

The way-of-life concept was applied in the study of working-class culture. Initially, representatives of East German Volkskunde played no small part in the development of theories, practical research, and museological representations of the 'culture and way of life of the proletariat' (Jacobeit and Mohrmann 1973; Jacobeit 1982; Karasek et al. 1983). But the discipline did not keep up with the rapid international development of increasingly interdisciplinary research on the culture of the working class and the labour movement. Unlike the comprehensive descriptions of proletarian culture published by the team centred around the Kulturwissenschaftler Dietrich Mühlberg (Mühlberg 1983, 1986; Neef 1988), the works of GDR Volkskundler were based primarily on individual case studies of working-class life (e.g. the working world of female factory workers or maids), drawing on remembered and oral history.[13]

The interest of the discipline was instead concentrated primarily on the social history of rural, proto-industrial, and regional cultures, including new theoretical approaches and analyses of the scientific canon. Studies of narrative genres, tradition (*Brauchtum*), and folk art gave way to an emphasis on the totality of ways of life and creative endeavours in their historical origins, their internal inconsistencies, and their regional underpinnings. Although the number of researchers was limited, the fields covered a broad range. Only a few research projects can be roughly sketched here. Pride of place must be given to the paradigmatic, long-term project on the Magdeburg Plain completed in the 1980s (Rach and Weißel 1978–79, 1982; Rach, Weißel, and Plaul 1986, 1987). It examined the historical development of this agrarian region from the end of the eighteenth century to the 1960s. The focus was on increasingly varied ways of life among the peasant and proletarian classes of the region in their relationship to, and their distinction from, a growing village bourgeoisie. The series of publications and the numerous graduate theses arising out of this research documented important facets of the everyday life of the village population in this early-industrialised agrarian region.

---

[13] See the bibliography in Strobach 1991.

Peasants and agricultural labourers were also the objects of more specialised research into construction and housing conditions, as well as into work, labour relations, and technology, especially with regard to technical developments in agriculture in Mecklenburg during the transition to capitalism (Bentzien 1983, 1990; Baumgarten 1985). Towards the end of the 1980s, within the framework of international scientific cooperation, studies of the development of the village and the rural population in the nineteenth century contributed to topical discussions of 'embourgeoisement' (Jacobeit, Mooser, and Strath 1990). Although the term *modernisation* (*Modernisierung*) was avoided in GDR Volkskunde, this was nonetheless the process under scrutiny in analyses of the historical transition to capitalism and of the changes which took place in rural life in the nineteenth and twentieth centuries. Plebeianism (*Plebejertum*), trades and manufacture, and the rural classes in the former Electorate of Saxony and the neighbouring Duchy of Altenburg were the objects of similar studies (Weinhold 1982). These studies focused on continuity and change in ways of life and culture, including anti-feudal and democratic attitudes and educational activities. The researchers firmly rejected any romanticising of pre-modern conditions. The regionalist focus can also be seen in projects on Mecklenburg (Bentzien and Neumann 1988) and on the 'Villages of Berlin' (Rach 1988).

The historical-materialist approach proved itself productive for a culturally and social-historically oriented Volkskunde. But the exclusive concentration on this concept resulted in a disregard for the history of mentality, gender-oriented research, and the study of religious life and the church. Despite these limitations, a democratic documentation of cultural history is recognisable in the mere fact that the 'many small people' and their day-to-day lives (*Aller Tage Leben*) were considered worthy of historical study (Dehne 1985). The premise that social groups and individuals could be understood as carriers of objectivised cultural forms based in their existential context was one of the strengths of Marxist-influenced social sciences. This was demonstrated best by the economic historian Jürgen Kuczynski in his *Alltagsgeschichte des deutschen Volkes* (1980–82), through which GDR Volkskunde was drawn into the history of everyday life at the beginning of the 1980s. Sigrid and Wolfgang Jacobeit responded to this challenge in their *Illustrierte Alltagsgeschichte des deutschen Volkes* (Jacobeit and Jacobeit 1985–87, 1995). They adopted Kuczynski's concepts of 'background and "wider world"' (*Hintergrund und 'Große Welt'*) and 'everyday life of the working population' (*Alltag der Werktätigen*) and convincingly extended this point of view thematically to all existential aspects of everyday life—for example, to phenomena such as fear of war, plagues, violence, basic needs, work, sociability, and leisure.

This positive tendency in Volkskunde research did not entirely dispel scientific inflexibility, and there were major gaps, above all in the study of urban and contemporary life (Scholze 1990). The discipline was burdened by the 'unloved [character of GDR] everyday life' (*ungeliebter Alltag*) (Badstübner-Peters 1993: 7) and the lack of any model for cultural analysis focusing on contemporary issues.

Representatives of the discipline at the academy in Berlin were hardly interested in such issues, for the most part for political reasons, but a group of researchers focusing on contemporary issues did develop around Evemarie Badstübner in the mid-1980s, in conjunction with representatives of history, Kulturwissenschaft, and sociology. Their studies focused primarily on the history of the everyday life of workers and women in the post-war period and on their memories.[14] Research into 'culture and way of life after 1945' flourished in higher education, with many student projects, dissertations, and monographs on urban and rural ways of life, foreign workers in the GDR, family and (sub)group cultures, celebrations, festivals, and leisure time.[15] These scholars were obliged to toe the official line in cultural politics, though some maintained that empirical research and personal engagement in the cultural field could lead to policy modifications (Mohrmann 1983). Elements of a 'respectably applied Volkskunde' (*respektable angewandte Volkskunde*) were confirmed 'from outside' after 1989–90 (Köstlin 1991: 235). Sorbian ethnographers stood out, not only for their regional research into Sorbian culture but also for their work on transformation processes in brown coal mining in the Lausitz, where open-pit mining had led to the resettlement of tens of thousands of people (Förster 1990). Careful criticism of the ideological nature of the culture of everyday life and of festival culture was practised only towards the end of the 1980s, when themes of everyday praxis previously considered taboo were slowly prised open for discussion, not least due to insistence on the part of students (Mohrmann 1992).

The Cultural Accord of 1988 between the two Germanies resulted in an increasing number of academic contacts. The project *Blick-Wechsel Ost-West* (View-change east-west), conceived by students in Berlin and Tübingen in 1988–89 and realised during the *Wende* (see Kaschuba and Mohrmann 1992), proved, finally, to be symbolic. Students and scientists doing 'fieldwork' in the 'other' Germany had to undertake a balancing act—and suddenly the project was overwhelmed by history. But this study of German differences based on the life ways and life worlds (*Lebenswege und Lebenswelten*) of the respective cohorts of 30- to 40-year-olds was not rendered

---

[14] See note 13.
[15] See the contributions on contemporary anthropological studies, including an extensive bibliography, in *Ethnographisch-Archäologische Zeitschrift* 1 (1986); Mohrmann 1989.

obsolete. To examine these differences again today, as perceived socially and interpreted culturally long after the end of German division, would be an interesting subject for contemporary Volkskunde.

References

Badstübner-Peters, E. 1993. Der ungeliebte Alltag: Zu den Schwierigkeiten alltagsgeschichtlicher Forschungen in der DDR. *Thüringer Hefte für Volkskunde* 2: 7–25.
Baumgarten, K. 1985. *Das deutsche Bauernhaus: Eine Einführung in seine Geschichte vom 9. bis zum 19. Jahrhundert.* 2nd ed. Berlin: Akademie-Verlag.
Bentzien, U. 1983. *Landbevölkerung und agrartechnischer Fortschritt in Mecklenburg vom Ende des 18. bis zum Anfang des 20. Jahrhunderts: Eine volkskundliche Untersuchung.* Berlin: Zentralinstitut für Geschichte, Akademie der Wissenschaften der DDR.
------. 1990. *Bauernarbeit im Feudalismus: Landwirtschaftliche Arbeitsgeräte und -verfahren in Deutschland von der Mitte des 1. Jahrtausends u.Z. bis um 1800.* 2nd ed. Berlin: Akademie-Verlag.
------, and S. Neumann (eds.). 1988. *Mecklenburgische Volkskunde.* Rostock: Hinstorff.
Bromlej, J. V. 1977. *Ethnos und Ethnographie.* Berlin: Akademie-Verlag.
Dehne, H. 1985. Aller Tage Leben: Zu neuen Forschungsansätzen im Beziehungsfeld von Alltag, Lebensweise und Kultur der Arbeiterklasse. *Jahrbuch für Volkskunde und Kulturgeschichte* 28: 9–48.
------. 1989. Dem Alltag ein Stück näher? In A. Lüdtke (ed.), *Alltagsgeschichte: Zur Rekonstruktion historischer Erfahrungen und Lebensweisen,* pp. 137–68. Frankfurt a M.: Campus Verlag.
Förster, F. 1990. *Um Lausitzer Braunkohle, 1849–1945.* Bautzen: Domowina Verlag.
Girtler, R. 1982. 'Ethnos', 'Volk' und soziale Gruppe: Zum Problem eines zentralen Themas in den anthropologischen Wissenschaften. *Mitteilungen der Anthropologischen Gesellschaft in Wien* 112: 42–57.
Jacobeit, S., and W. Jacobeit. 1985–87. *Illustrierte Alltagsgeschichte des deutschen Volkes,* vol. 1 (1550–1810) and vol. 2 (1810–1900). Leipzig: Urania-Verlag.
------, ------. 1995. *Illustrierte Alltags- und Sozialgeschichte Deutschlands 1900–1945.* Münster: Westfälisches Dampfboot.
Jacobeit, W. 1982. Volkskunde und Arbeiterkultur: Zur Eröffnung. In H. Fielhauer and O. Bockhorn (eds.), *Die andere Kultur: Volkskunde,*

Sozialwissenschaften und Arbeiterkultur. Ein Tagungsbericht, pp. 11–25. Wien: Europaverlag.

——. 1987. Die Auseinandersetzung mit der NS-Zeit in der DDR-Volkskunde. In H. Gerndt (ed.), *Volkskunde und Nationalsozialismus: Referate und Diskussionen einer Tagung der Deutschen Gesellschaft für Volkskunde, München, 23. bis 25.10.1986*, pp. 301–18. München: Münchner Vereinigung für Volkskunde.

——. 2000. *Von West nach Ost und zurück: Autobiographisches eines Grenzgängers zwischen Tradition und Novation*. Münster: Westfälisches Dampfboot.

——, and U. Mohrmann (eds.). 1973. *Kultur und Lebensweise des Proletariats: Kulturhistorisch-volkskundliche Studien und Materialien*. Berlin: Akademie-Verlag.

——, ——. 1982. Zur Geschichte der volkskundlichen Lehre unter Adolf Spamer an der Berliner Universität (1933–1945). *Ethnographisch-Archäologische Zeitschrift* 23: 283–98.

——, J. Mooser, and B. Strath (eds.). 1990. *Idylle oder Aufbruch? Das Dorf im bürgerlichen 19. Jahrhundert. Ein europäischer Vergleich*. Berlin: Akademie-Verlag.

Johler, R. 2002. Wieviel Europa braucht die Europäische Ethnologie? Die Volkskunden in Europa und die 'Wende'. In K. Köstlin, P. Niedermüller, and H. Nikitsch (eds.), *Die Wende als Wende? Orientierungen Europäischer Ethnologien nach 1989*, pp. 150–65. Wien: Verlag des Instituts für Europäische Ethnologie.

Karasek, E., et al. (eds.). 1983. *Großstadtproletariat: Zur Lebensweise einer Klasse*. Berlin: Ausstellungskatalog des Museums für Volkskunde.

Kaschuba, W. 1999. *Einführung in die Europäische Ethnologie*. München: Beck.

——, and U. Mohrmann (eds.). 1992. *Blick-Wechsel Ost-West: Beobachtungen zur Alltagskultur in Ost- und Westdeutschland*. Tübingen: Tübinger Vereinigung für Volkskunde.

Köstlin, K. 1984. Die Wiederkehr der Volkskultur: Der neue Umgang mit einem alten Begriff. *Ethnologia Europaea* 14: 25–31.

——. 1991. Die DDR-Volkskunde: Die Entdeckung einer fernen Welt? *Zeitschrift für Volkskunde* 87: 225–43.

Krause, M., D. Neuland-Kitzerow, and K. Noack (eds.). 2003. *Ethnographisches Arbeiten in Berlin: Wissenschaftsgeschichtliche Annäherungen*. Berliner Blätter: Ethnographische und ethnologische Beiträge 31. Münster: LIT Verlag.

Kuczynski, J. 1980–82. *Geschichte des Alltags des deutschen Volkes*. Studien 1–5. Berlin: Akademie-Verlag.

Lee, Y. J. 1998. *Volkskunde in der DDR zwischen innovativen Methoden und politischer Einbindung 1963–1973*. Diploma thesis, Freie Universität, Berlin.

Martischnig, M. 1990. *Volkskundler in der Deutschen Demokratischen Republik heute: Nach Unterlagen des bibliographischen Lexikons der Volkskundler im deutschsprachigen Raum des Instituts für Gegenwartsvolkskunde der Österreichischen Akademie der Wissenschaften*. Mitteilungen des Instituts für Gegenwartsvolkskunde, Sonderband 4. Wien: Im Selbstverlag des Österreichischen Museums für Volkskunde.

Mohrmann, U. 1983. *Engagierte Freizeitkunst: Werdegang und Entwicklungsprobleme des bildnerischen Volksschaffens in der DDR*. Berlin: Verlag Tribüne.

——. 1989. DDR-Alltag als volkskundliches Forschungsfeld? Eine Frage im wissenschaftsgeschichtlichen Kontext. *Wissenschaftliche Zeitschrift der Humboldt-Universität zu Berlin* 38 (10): 1059–66.

—— (ed.). 1991. *Geschichte der Völkerkunde und Volkskunde an der Berliner Universität: Zur Aufarbeitung des Wissenschaftserbes*. Beiträge zur Geschichte der Humboldt-Universität zu Berlin 28. Berlin: Humboldt-Universität.

——. 1992. Wegmüssen: Entsiedlung im Kohlerevier. Versuch einer Wahrnehmung laufender Ereignisse. *Österreichische Zeitschrift für Volkskunde* 95: 355–67.

——. 1994. Volkskunde in der DDR während der fünfziger und sechziger Jahre. In W. Jacobeit, H. Lixfeld, O. Bockhorn, and J. R. Dow (eds.), *Völkische Wissenschaft: Gestalten und Tendenzen der deutschen und österreichischen Volkskunde in der ersten Hälfte des 20. Jahrhunderts*, pp. 375–94. Wien: Böhlau.

——. 1998. Museen und Volkskunde in der DDR. 'Gab es eine Museumskultur in der DDR?' *Arbeitshefte der Landesstelle für Berlin-Brandenburgische Volkskunde am Institut für Europäische Ethnologie der Humboldt-Universität zu Berlin* 6: 12–21.

——. 2001. 'Roundabout 68': Zur DDR-Volkskunde Ende der sechziger und während der siebziger Jahre. In S. Becker and A. C. Bimmer [et al.] (eds.), *Volkskundliche Tableaus: Eine Festschrift für Martin Scharfe zum 65. Geburtstag von Weggefährten, Freunden und Schülern*, pp. 375–85. Münster: Waxmann Verlag.

——, and W. Jacobeit (eds.). 1991. *Beiträge zur Geschichte der Volkskunde: Eine Wissenschaft im Widerspruch zwischen Leistung und Versagen*. Wissenschaftliche Zeitschrift der Humboldt-Universität zu Berlin 11. Berlin: Humboldt-Universität.

Mühlberg, D. [et al.]. 1983. *Arbeiterleben um 1900*. Berlin: Dietz.

——. 1986. *Proletariat: Kultur und Lebensweise im 19. Jahrhundert*. Leipzig: Ed. Leipzig.

Neef, A. 1988. *Mühsal ein Leben lang: Zur Situation der Arbeiterfrauen um 1900*. Köln: Pahl-Rugenstein.

Rach, H.-J. 1988. *Die Dörfer in Berlin: Ein Handbuch der ehemaligen Landgemeinden im Stadtgebiet von Berlin*. Berlin: Zentralinstitut für Geschichte, Akademie der Wissenschaften der DDR.

——, and B. Weißel (eds.). 1978–79. *Landwirtschaft und Kapitalismus: Zur Entwicklung der ökonomischen und sozialen Verhältnisse in der Magdeburger Börde vom Ausgang des 18. Jahrhunderts bis zum Ende des Ersten Weltkrieges*. 2 vols. Berlin: Akademie-Verlag.

——, —— (eds.). 1982. *Bauer und Landarbeiter im Kapitalismus der Magdeburger Börde: Zur Geschichte des dörflichen Alltags vom Ausgang des 18. Jahrhunderts bis zum Beginn des 20. Jahrhunderts*. Berlin: Akademie-Verlag.

——, ——, and H. Plaul (eds.). 1986. *Die werktätige Dorfbevölkerung in der Magdeburger Börde: Studien zum dörflichen Alltag vom Beginn des 20. Jahrhunderts bis zum Anfang der 60er Jahre*. Berlin: Akademie-Verlag.

——, ——, —— (eds.). 1987. *Das Leben der Werktätigen in der Magdeburger Börde: Studien zum dörflichen Alltag vom Beginn des 20. Jahrhunderts bis zum Anfang der sechziger Jahre*. Berlin: Akademie-Verlag.

Scholze, T. 1990. *Im Lichte der Großstadt: Volkskundliche Erforschung metropolitaner Lebensformen*. Wien: Österreicher Kunst- und Kulturverlag.

——, and L. Scholze-Irrlitz (eds.). 2001. *Zehn Jahre Gesellschaft für Ethnographie: Europäische Ethnologie in Berlin. Wolfgang Jacobeit zum 80. Geburtstag*. Münster: LIT Verlag.

Scholze-Irrlitz, L. 1994. *Moderne Konturen historischer Anthropologie: Eine vergleichende Studie zu den Arbeiten von Jacques Le Goff und Aaron J. Gurjewitsch*. Frankfurt a. M.: Lang.

——, and T. Scholze. 1991. Vom wissenschaftlichen Alltag des Wolfgang Jacobeit: Ein Gespräch nach der 'Wende'. *Info-Blatt der Gesellschaft für Ethnographie e.V.* 2: 17–39.

Strobach, H. 1983. Zum Volksbegriff bei Marx und Engels. In W. Küttler (ed.), *Das geschichtswissenschaftliche Erbe von Karl Marx*, pp. 153–83. Berlin: Zentralinstitut für Geschichte, Akademie der Wissenschaften der DDR.

———. 1987. '... aber wann beginnt der Vorkrieg?' Anmerkungen zum Thema Volkskunde und Faschismus (vor und um 1933). In H. Gerndt (ed.), *Volkskunde und Nationalsozialismus: Referate und Diskussionen einer Tagung der Deutschen Gesellschaft für Volkskunde, München, 23. bis 25.10.1986*, pp. 23–38. München: Münchner Vereinigung für Volkskunde.

———. 1988. Einige volkskundliche Probleme des historischen Erbes. In H. Meier and W. Schmidt (eds.), *Erbe und Tradition in der DDR: Die Diskussion der Historiker*, pp. 160–70. Berlin: Akademie-Verlag.

———. 1991. Forschungen in den achtziger Jahren zur Geschichte von Kultur und Lebensweise des deutschen Volkes. *Zeitschrift für Geschichtswissenschaft* 39 (5): 467–79.

Weinhold, R. (ed.). 1982. *Volksleben zwischen Zunft und Fabrik: Studien zu Kultur und Lebensweise werktätiger Klassen und Schichten während des Übergangs vom Feudalismus zum Kapitalismus*. Berlin: Akademie-Verlag.

Weißel, B. (ed.). 1980. *Kultur und Ethnos: Zur Kritik der bürgerlichen Auffassungen über die Rolle der Kultur in Geschichte und Gesellschaft*. Berlin: Akademie-Verlag.

Willenberg, U. 1986. Ethnische Kulturen, regionale Volkskulturen, Klassenkulturen und das Problem der Ethnogenese: Bemerkungen zur historischen Stellung regionaler Volkskulturen im Ethnogeneseprozeß. *Ethnographisch-Archäologische Zeitschrift* 27: 96–124.

———. 1987. 'Ethnos'—'Ethnogenese'—'Nationsbildung' und das Problem der Staatsentwicklung: Zum Denken über Geschichte als Ethnogeneseprozeß. *Ethnographisch-Archäologische Zeitschrift* 28: 272–87.

Chapter 11
Culture, Lifestyle, and Everyday Life: The Museum für Volkskunde in Berlin under Socialism

Dagmar Neuland-Kitzerow

The Berlin Wall had only just fallen when representatives of Volkskunde from eight European countries met at a conference at the Museum für Volkskunde (MfV) on Museum Island in East Berlin.[1] This unique backdrop left its mark on the conference proceedings (Korff 1990; Böth 1991: 26; Mohrmann 1991: 15, this volume). This international conference had been planned to celebrate the centenary of the MfV.[2] Central to the discussions between colleagues from Eastern and Western Europe were questions concerning 'everyday life', a concept already prominent in both scientific research and museology (Jacobeit and Mohrmann 1973; Jacobeit 1982; Jacobeit and Jacobeit 1985–87; Karasek 1991c). The term 'history of everyday life' (*Alltagsgeschichte*) seemed useful in opening complex interpretations of culture and lifestyle as they evolved through time. The contributions touched upon educational structures, recent research in Volkskunde, and the possibilities for implementing this knowledge in museum work. A few papers focused on conceptual frameworks, their implementation in museums, and future strategies for the MfV itself (Ganslmayr 1991: 50–4; Korff 1991: 87–92).

---

[1] The conference, which took place between 13 and 16 November 1989, was titled 'Alltagsgeschichte in ethnographischen Museen: Möglichkeiten der Sammlung und Darstellung im internationalen Vergleich'. The papers were published in Karasek 1991a. See also Neuland-Kitzerow 2001.

[2] With the division of Germany and Berlin after the Second World War, two separate museums developed in east and west. Each made its preparations for the 1989 anniversary independently. Thus, on 25 October 1989 the Museum für deutsche Volkskunde (MDV) in West Berlin opened an exhibition, *Aufs Ohr geschaut: Ohrringe aus Stadt und Land vom Klassizismus bis zur neuen Jugendkultur* (exhibition catalogue by Karin Göbel, Theodor Kohlmann, Heidi Müller, and Konrad Vanja, Berlin, 1989). The exhibition included a small section on the history of science. Two days later, the Museum für Volkskunde on Museum Island opened the exhibition *Kleidung zwischen Tracht und Mode: Aus der Geschichte des Museums 1889–1989* (catalogue with the same title by Erika Karasek, Berlin, 1989b).

212   DAGMAR NEULAND-KITZEROW

The conference turned out to be of much greater importance than anybody could have imagined when it was planned (Karasek and Tietmeyer 1994; Karasek 1995; Böth 2001). Rapid political changes were felt at all levels of the museums—institutionally, intellectually, and in terms of personnel. Rather than examine these changes in detail, I focus on the situation in 1989–90 as a vantage point from which to look back at the concepts and research initiatives of Volkskunde in the German Democratic Republic in the 1970s and 1980s and some of the people who contributed to it, with special reference to the MfV in Berlin, which was by far the most significant museum in the country. My perspective is that of an 'insider' and is necessarily retrospective, but it is also motivated by the wish to salvage from the legacy of socialist museology whatever might be worthy of salvaging.

As Erika Karasek observed (1991b: 4), the dissolution of the GDR involved the incorporation of some 700 museums and collections into the Federal Republic.[3] These included art collections of international repute as well as scientific, natural history, agricultural, and local history museums. Approximately 50 institutions specialised in anthropology, including both Volkskunde and Völkerkunde traditions. In addition to the well-known and long-established museums in Berlin, Erfurt, and Schwerin and the Dresden museum of folk art, newer open-air museums had also been established in the GDR in the 1950s and 1960s, particularly in the northern parts of the country, where they were intended to supplement historical collections in the various regions (Raschke 1995: 331–32; Köpp 2003: 97–107). A political consensus on the general need to promote folklore and museology in order to preserve the national heritage had existed since the 1950s, uniting both conservative educationists and intellectuals of a more radical persuasion (Guhr and Weinhold 1989; Jacobeit 1997: 23–29; Köpp 2003).

The museums of Völkerkunde in Dresden and Leipzig, together with their branches, could look back at a long history of research and collection.[4] They found a new niche as anti-colonial movements gathered strength, and they were active in supporting the new independent national states that emerged in the 1960s and in reappraising the work of museum collectors (Arnold 1989; Tiesler 1989). GDR specialists were ahead of their time in discussing what measures were needed to protect traditional cultural property in a time of great cultural change and in recognising both the strength of new cultural identities and the dangers of homogenisation due to the influ-

---

[3] Erika Karasek was employed at the MfV from 1962 until 1999 and served as its director from 1980 to 1992 and again from 1995 to 1999. See Neuland-Kitzerow 2001: 47–52.
[4] Despite suffering serious damage to their collections during the war, the museums resumed a full range of activities in the 1950s. See Guhr and Neumann 1982: n. 10; see also Treide, this volume.

ence of modernity. These debates had a significant effect on GDR Völkerkunde in general (see van der Heyden, this volume). The positions taken by GDR specialists were directly determined by Cold War political rivalries on the world stage. In terms of theory, too, Soviet influences were important; for example, the contributions of Bernd Arnold and Frank Tiesler, both of the Völkerkunde museum in Dresden, were based on declarations by Yulian Bromley to the effect that anthropology should concern itself not only with archaic or primitive societies but should extend its research 'to include the present time' (Bromlej 1977: 242–44).

Volkskunde in Berlin

By the end of the 1970s the anthropological museums of the GDR, especially those specialised in Volkskunde, were actively expanding their collections or creating new ones and mounting high-quality exhibitions covering a vast range of themes. Nonetheless, in comparison with the importance of the historical museums, the cultural and political significance of Volkskunde remained small (Karasek 1989b; Mohrmann 1998: 12–21, this volume; Scholze and Scholze-Irrlitz 2001: 33–36). The rhetoric of a GDR 'socialist national culture' and the rejection of the unity of German culture, as dictated in the 1950s by ideologists, privileged the newly established disciplines of Marxist-Leninist sociology and cultural sciences (*Kulturwissenschaft*) as well as history. The reasons for this were manifold. Unlike its new rivals, Volkskunde was strongly identified with pre-industrial culture and lifestyles. The belief that Kulturwissenschaft would guarantee more 'contemporary relevance' and a 'pro-socialist approach', and thereby political legitimacy, was confirmed by the choice of research and exhibition themes.[5] Only after the mid-1960s did more modern ideas and discourses enter GDR Volkskunde, and until then the museums associated with the discipline received little attention from the public (Hofmann 1989; Kreschel 1989, 2003; Jacobeit 2000, 2001).

Given this unpromising background, how did the MfV succeed in introducing new initiatives in all aspects of its work in the 1970s and 1980s?

The museum was re-established in 1953, after the difficult post-war years, as the Museum of Folk Art (*Volkskunst*) and was housed temporarily in the north wing of the Pergamon Museum (Karasek 1989b: 5–48). It acquired the name Museum für Volkskunde in 1957 (replacing 'Staatliches

---

[5] The traditional canon of Volkskunde, with themes such as folk art, domestic crafts, toys, and handicrafts, dominated in the exhibitions of the early socialist period. This was to some extent dictated by the collections themselves, but the homeland (*Heimat*) focus was also emphatically expected by the public.

Museum für Deutsche Volkskunde' in a deliberate shift away from the ethnic denomination) and reached a degree of institutional stability by the mid-1960s. This was the result of good management, a focused collection policy, and intensive exhibition work, even if only a single, 300-square-metre room was available for exhibitions at the time. Despite inadequate working conditions, the museum was able to present to the public exhibitions covering not only traditional themes such as crafts, toys, and annual festivals but also new topics concerning agriculture and the economy.[6]

Wolfgang Jacobeit, who had acquired extensive research experience with the Academy of Sciences, took over as director of the MfV in 1972.[7] Under his leadership, priority was given to the presentation of more contemporary themes. Unequivocal signs of the reorientation of Volkskunde as a historical discipline were three major exhibitions: *The Sorbs in the GDR: About the Life of the Smallest Slavonic People. An Historical Outline of the Social and Cultural Development of the Sorbs from the Nineteenth Century until Their Thriving as a People in the GDR* (1973–74); *Folk Music and Folk Musicians: From Minstrels to Singeklub. Traditions and Present Day in the Field of Folk Music* (1978–79); and *Farming in the Past and in the Present* (1979–80). Such topics both allowed the use of artefacts already held by the museum and justified the acquisition of new objects in the course of documenting cultural and lifestyle processes. They also reflected the theoretical debates over concepts of culture and lifestyle, initiated in the mid-1960s, which now encompassed all working classes (Jacobeit and Mohrmann 1968–69: 98–101; Weißel, Strobach, and Jacobeit 1972). Other exhibition projects represented folk art in terms of modern anthropological perspectives.[8] Yet others served to promote contacts with anthropologists outside Germany.[9] Joint exhibition projects with Völkerkundler helped to strengthen the unity of the profession.[10]

Jacobeit's extensive experience and close contacts with related disciplines provided a good basis for interdisciplinary cooperation and network-

---

[6] Between 1961 and 1968 the following exhibitions, among many others, were mounted: *Animal Representations in Folk Art* (1961), *Toys in the Past and Present Time* (1962), *Christmas Is All Around Us* (1965–66), *Pottery: From Medieval Times to Modern Times* (1965–68), and *Agricultural Tools* (1967). See also Karasek 1991b: 5–48, 171–74.
[7] Of the seven staff members at this time, only three were academics.
[8] For example, *Our World: Artistic Folk Productions of the GDR* (1974) and *Folk Artists in the Museum* (1976).
[9] For example, *Aspects of Ordinary Life in the GDR: Love and Weddings* (1975–76) was mounted in Hungary; *Nikolaus Copernicus in Polish Artistic Folk Productions* (1976–77) and *Christmas Folk Art* (1971–72) were staged in Brno, Czechoslovakia.
[10] For example, *Women in Africa* (1975).

ing.[11] In 1966 the consortium Anthropological Museums was founded by the Ministry of Culture, and in 1972 Jacobeit took over its administration.[12] In his role as museum director, Jacobeit also taught Ethnographie at the Humboldt University and held various other scientific posts. Yet in spite of Jacobeit's energy and innovations, the MfV continued to be treated as a poor relation by the State Museums of Berlin. Activities were hindered by insufficient exhibition space, understaffing, and the scarcity of financial resources (Karasek and Tietmeyer 1995: 15–22; Roth 1995: 23–26). In 1980 Jacobeit was appointed to the chair for Ethnographie at the Humboldt University, and he came to develop a rather critical opinion of his years as a museum director, preferring not to see himself as an expert in this field (Scholze and Scholze-Irrlitz 2001; Jacobeit 2000).

The discrepancy between aspirations and the limited possibilities to hand could not be ironed out in the following years under the administration of Erika Karasek. Research, collection, and exhibitions (such as *Metropolitan Proletariat*, mounted in 1980–87) were of high quality and international relevance, but this did not lead to a substantial improvement in funding or to a gain in prestige. Still, the MfV was increasingly perceived as open to new topics and interested in new exhibition ideas.[13] Karasek became chair of the Anthropological Museums network in 1984 and was able in promoting contacts with other museums throughout the GDR. It was clear to all that new academic ideas could be put into practice in the museums, especially the larger ones, only if staff themselves, especially the directors, were fully committed. Enthusiasm was particularly evident for agricultural spheres and for economic life in general (Jacobeit 1965; Jacobeit and Quietzsch 1965; Jacobeit and Plaul 1969; Jacobeit 1975).

---

[11] Wolfgang Jacobeit was also very active in the GDR Culture Association (*Kulturbund*) and drew on his own field experience as well as the commitment of local historians to promote regional research on culture and lifestyle. He also worked in history research. For further information see Zentral Archiv der Staatlichen Museen zu Berlin, VA 5569, 1973.

[12] This organisation was founded to provide ethnographic museums with research support and a common infrastructure. It had two subsections, Völkerkunde and Volkskunde. For further information see Zentral Archiv der Staatlichen Museen zu Berlin, VA 5568, April 1987.

[13] One of the most innovative was the 1987 exhibition *Signs–Images–Street Ballads* (*Schilder–Bilder–Moritaten*), which presented the media around 1900.

Figure 1. The exhibition *Signs—Images—Street Ballads* (*Schilder—Bilder—Moritaten*) 1987–1989.

The Academy of Sciences had its own Volkskunde Institute, and in the 1960s it cooperated with the MfV and with other museums in building up regional collections. The expanding discussions about culture and lifestyles functioned as a catalyst for new approaches to collecting, research, and exhibiting. From the 1970s onwards, history was viewed increasingly positively (Kreschel 1989, 2003: 117–31; Jacobeit 2001: 14–17; Kaschuba 2003: 15–25). However, assigning Volkskunde to history institutionally, as was the case at the Academy of Sciences and the Humboldt University from 1968–69 onwards, did not go unchallenged. Many representatives of the discipline considered it a loss of independence (Mohrmann 2001: 378–80, this volume). This discussion continued well into the 1980s.

The Berlin MfV was much more than a gathering point for colleagues from the provinces: it was a fulcrum for cooperation between the leading Volkskunde institutions of the GDR. Many employees of the regional and local history museums completed degrees in Ethnographie at the Humboldt University, and from 1966 forward it was possible to take these courses by correspondence (Mohrmann 1991: 15–18, 2002; Mohrmann and Rusch 1991: 61–72; Ziehe 2003: 143–49). The links in theoretical discourse between the university and the Academy of Sciences, and the practical realisation of theory in collections and exhibitions at museums and other cultural institutions, were exceptionally close in GDR Volkskunde, thanks in particular to the long-distance graduates. This development of internal networks helped to ensure that the discipline maintained at least a limited public profile. Ideas were generously shared in seminars, committee meetings, and informal conversations with colleagues. At the same time, it is clear in retrospect that international anthropological trends were neglected. Contacts with scholars in allied Eastern European countries were cultivated officially, but contacts with Western museologists were highly restricted.

From Culture and Lifestyle to the History of Everyday Life

Beginning in the late 1970s, the history-of-everyday-life approach became central to the scientific work of GDR Volkskunde, including the work of the museums (Kuczynski 1980; Jacobeit and Jacobeit 1985-87; see also Mohrmann, this volume). This shift was increasingly visible in collecting and research activities and, finally, in a number of major exhibitions in Berlin, Brandenburg, and Karl-Marx-Stadt.[14] Preparations for these exhibitions brought the museums into cooperation with specialists in both Volkskunde and Kulturwissenschaft, as well as regional historians. Altogether, they contributed significantly to knowledge of working-class culture. At the MfV this approach was promoted by both Wolfgang Jacobeit and Erika Karasek (see Ziehe 2003: 143–50). The exhibition *Metropolitan Proletariat: About the Life of This Social Class,* devised by Karasek, which opened with much fanfare at the MfV in November 1980, was the fruit of long-standing contacts between Volkskundler (notably Jacobeit and Mohrmann) and the Kulturwissenschaftler at the Humboldt University (particularly Dietrich Mühlberg). This kind of cooperation was especially important in view of the museums' meagre staff resources. It was, however, not without tensions,

---

[14] These exhibitions included *About the Life of a Proletarian Child,* by Ernst Hofmann in Karl-Marx-Stadt, *The Brennabor Proletarian: Working-Class Life in the Town of Brandenburg from 1918 to 1933,* and *Upstream and Downstream: About the History of Shipping on the Havel.* The latter two were realised under the direction of Katharina Kreschel, a correspondence-course graduate in Ethnographie in Brandenburg. Other exhibitions, such as *How Toymakers in the Erzgebirge Mountains Work and Live,* were prepared by Helmut Bilz and Roland Schmidt from Seiffen.

such as those concerning the pertinence of different categories of source materials in research and exhibition-related work.

Conflicts of a different kind arose in the second half of the 1980s over how to use the concept 'everyday life'. Although some exhibitions were well researched and presented concrete new results, quite a few others were superficial and greatly simplified the approach. The monotonous, unimaginative presentation of 'the working-class kitchen' was an example of the latter. Many museums interpreted the increasing international demand for more research into urban life as an invitation to concentrate one-sidedly on 'proletarian life'.[15] As a result, the same simplified kitchen exhibitions were mounted everywhere, without background research into local and regional living conditions or into how kitchen space was actually used.

Museum staff were repeatedly encouraged to cooperate closely with other institutions in order to overcome such distortions and fulfil their educational task.[16] Networks such as Anthropological Museums promoted these discussions, and it was recognised that cooperation was essential in order to maintain a high standard of research in all the sectors of Volkskunde. Museums sometimes bemoaned the inaccessibility of academic research results, while the academic departments reproached the museums for paying insufficient attention to theory. Of course such tensions between different anthropological research institutions were not unique to the GDR; they have characterised the history of anthropology everywhere. Some view museums as merely a 'projection surface' for theoretical ideas developed by the academic strand of the discipline, whereas others hold that museums themselves can and should develop their own independent scientific positions. It is evident that museums have led the way in presenting research results to the public. The debate which preceded the centenary of the MfV in the autumn of 1989 was particularly lively. Some argued that the museum should do more to present the history of anthropology; others rejected this. It was eventually decided that the MfV would devote an exhibition to the history of the subject, as well as to a specific theme. Clothing was chosen as this theme, and the exhibition *Clothing between Folk Costume and Fashion* was mounted in line with the most modern approaches internationally (Ottenjann 1985; Böth 1991: 21–23).

---

[15] This extension to all social classes and to big cities was not a new phenomenon: it had found its way into the museums in the 1970s. See Jacobeit and Mohrmann 1973; Kramer 1981; Badstübner-Peters 1993: 7–9; see also Kohlmann and Bausinger 1985.

[16] See Hofmann 1989: 28–31. On the occasion of the GDR workers' festival (held every four years), parallel regional folklore festivals were organised from the 1970s onwards. Provincial museums and the MfV in Berlin were encouraged to present exhibitions depicting the traditional, regional folk culture of the working classes.

Figure 2 + 3. The exhibition *Clothing between Traditional Costume and Fashion. From the History of the Museum 1889–1989* (*Kleidung zwischen Tracht und Mode. Aus der Geschichte des Museums 1889–1989*) 1989.

Prospects

Like other museums belonging to the State Museums of Berlin (Museum Island), the MfV was embedded in the structures of the cultural politics of the GDR. The 1989 conference, which brought together colleagues from Eastern and Western Europe, was an opportunity to begin exchanges and to discuss problems. Neither the anthropological profession as a whole in the GDR nor the MfV within it ever engaged actively in oppositional politics. Rather, even in 1989 the debates focused on questions specific to the discipline. It was a coincidence that these debates took place just as the Berlin Wall collapsed (a backdrop which is reflected in the conference volume; see Karasek 1991a).

The concepts of culture, lifestyle, and everyday life, all deployed in an historical framework, have remained prominent in the theoretical tool kit of Volkskunde and in museum presentations in the postsocialist years. New discussions have developed concerning *Mentalität*, communication structures, and how people cope with changing living conditions. Anthropology has become broader and ever more complex, with all aspects of contemporary culture, lifestyle, everyday life, and mental processes falling within its remit. For the museums, this means the continuous addition of new types of sources to their established holdings, asking new questions of the old collections, and responding to the challenge to ensure that museum work is always relevant in the present.

References

Arnold, B. 1989. Die afrikanische Touristenkunst und die Frage der Fortsetzung ethnographischen Sammelns. In G. Guhr and R. Weinhold (eds.), *Ethnographie im Museum. II. Tagung der Arbeitsgemeinschaft Ethnographie der Historikergesellschaft der DDR, 17.-19. September 1985 in Dresden*, pp. 98–102. Dresden: Staatliches Museum für Völkerkunde.

Badstübner-Peters, E. 1993. Der ungeliebte Alltag: Zu den Schwierigkeiten alltagsgeschichtlicher Forschungen in der DDR. *Thüringer Hefte für Volkskunde* 2: 7–25.

Böth, G. 1991. Kleidungsforschung und Museum. In E. Karasek (ed.), *Alltagsgeschichte in ethnographischen Museen: Möglichkeiten der Sammlung und Darstellung im internationalen Vergleich. Wissenschaftliches Kolloquium anläßlich des 100jährigen Bestehens des*

Museums für Volkskunde, pp. 21–23. Berlin: Staatliche Museen, Museum für Volkskunde.

———. 2001. Kontaktbörse zwischen Ost und West: Begegnungen im Museum für Volkskunde. In D. Neuland-Kitzerow (ed.), *Objekte im Kontext: Museumsgeschichte(n)—Forschungsgeschichte(n)*, pp. 26–30. Berliner Blätter 22. Berlin: Gesellschaft für Ethnographie.

Bromlej, J. V. 1977. *Ethnos und Ethnographie.* Veröffentlichungen des Museums für Völkerkunde Leipzig 28. Berlin: Akademie-Verlag.

Ganslmayr, H. 1991. Über fremde Alltagsgeschichte in europäischen Museen für Völkerkunde: Solidarität oder Exotismus. In E. Karasek (ed.), *Alltagsgeschichte in ethnographischen Museen: Möglichkeiten der Sammlung und Darstellung im internationalen Vergleich. Wissenschaftliches Kolloquium anläßlich des 100jährigen Bestehens des Museums für Volkskunde*, pp. 50–54. Berlin: Staatliche Museen, Museum für Volkskunde.

Göbel, K., T. Kohlmann, H. Müller, and K. Vanja (eds.). 1989. *Auf's Ohr geschaut. Ohrringe aus Stadt und Land vom Klassizismus bis zur Jugendkultur.* Schriften des Museums für Deutsche Volkskunde 16. Berlin: Staatliche Museen Preußischer Kulturbesitz.

Guhr, G., and P. Neumann (eds.). 1982. *Ethnographisches Mosaik. Aus den Sammlungen des Staatlichen Museums für Völkerkunde Dresden.* Berlin: Deutscher Verlag der Wissenschaften.

———, and R. Weinhold (ed.). 1989. *Ethnographie im Museum. II. Tagung der Arbeitsgemeinschaft Ethnographie der Historiker-Gesellschaft der DDR, 17.-19. September 1985 in Dresden.* Dresden: Staatliches Museum für Völkerkunde.

Hofmann, E. 1989. Alltag gestern—Alltag heute: Vorschlag für ein gemeinsames Ausstellungsprojekt ethnographischer Museen. In G. Guhr and R. Weinhold (eds.), *Ethnographie im Museum. II. Tagung der Arbeitsgemeinschaft Ethnographie der Historikergesellschaft der DDR, 17.-19. September 1985 in Dresden*, pp. 28–31. Dresden: Staatliches Museum für Völkerkunde.

Jacobeit, S., and W. Jacobeit. 1985–87. *Illustrierte Alltagsgeschichte des deutschen Volkes*, vol. 1 (1550–1810), vol. 2 (1810–1900). Leipzig: Urania Verlag.

Jacobeit, W. 1965. *Bäuerliche Arbeit und Wirtschaft: Ein Beitrag zur Wissenschaftsgeschichte der deutschen Volkskunde.* Berlin: Deutsche Akademie der Wissenschaften zu Berlin, Institut für deutsche Volkskunde.

———. 1975. Zu den Aufgaben des Berliner Museums für Volkskunde als zentrale Einrichtung des volkskundlichen Museumswesens in der DDR. *Informationen für die Museen der DDR* 7 (4): 12–14.

———. 1982. Volkskunde und Arbeiterkultur: Zur Eröffnung. In P. Fielhauer, and O. Bockhorn (eds.), *Die andere Kultur: Volkskunde, Sozialwissenschaften und Arbeiterkultur. Ein Tagungsbericht*, pp. 11–25. Wien: Europaverlag.

———. 1997. Marginalien eines nachdenklichen Volkskundlers. *Volkskunde–Europäische Ethnologie–Ethnologie. Berliner Blätter* 13–14: 23–29.

———. 2000. *Von West nach Ost und zurück: Autobiographisches eines Grenzgängers zwischen Tradition und Novation*. Münster: Westfälisches Dampfboot.

———. 2001. Wissenschaftsgeschichtliche Überlegungen zu einem 'Museum Europäischer Kulturen'. In D. Neuland-Kitzerow (ed.), *Objekte im Kontext: Museumsgeschichte(n)—Forschungsgeschichte(n)*, pp. 14–17. Berliner Blätter 22. Berlin: Gesellschaft für Ethnographie.

———, and U. Mohrmann. 1968–69. Zum Gegenstand und zur Aufgabenstellung der Volkskunde in der DDR. *Lětopis*, Reihe C 11–12: 98–101.

———, —————— (eds.). 1973. *Kultur und Lebensweise des Proletariats: Kulturhistorisch-volkskundliche Studien und Materialien*. Berlin: Akademie-Verlag.

———, and H. Plaul. 1969. Untersuchungen zur Entwicklung der Volkskultur in der Magdeburger Börde: Aufgabenstellung, Forschungsmethoden und Forschungsstand. In W. Jacobeit and P. Nedo (eds.), *Probleme und Methoden volkskundlicher Gegenwartsforschung: Vorträge und Diskussionen einer Internationalen Arbeitstagung in Bad Saarow, 1967*, pp. 17–32. Berlin: Akademie-Verlag

———, and R. Quietzsch. 1965. Forschungen zur bäuerlichen Arbeit und Wirtschaft im Institut für deutsche Volkskunde der Akademie der Wissenschaften Berlin. *Deutsches Jahrbuch für Volkskunde* 11: 59–82.

Karasek, E. 1989a. Geschichte und Perspektiven ethnographischer Sammlungen und Ausstellungen am Beispiel des Berliner Volkskundemuseums. In G. Guhr and R. Weinhold (eds.), *Ethnographie im Museum. II. Tagung der Arbeitsgemeinschaft Ethnographie der Historikergesellschaft der DDR, 17.-19. September 1985 in Dresden*, pp. 142–53. Dresden: Staatliches Museum für Völkerkunde.

———. 1989b. Ein Jahrhundert Engagement für die Volkskunde. 1889–1989. In Museum für Volkskunde, *Kleidung zwischen Tracht und Mode: Aus der Geschichte des Museums 1889-1989* (Katalog), pp. 5–48. Berlin: Staatliche Museen.

—— (ed.). 1991a. *Alltagsgeschichte in ethnographischen Museen: Möglichkeiten der Sammlung und Darstellung im internationalen Vergleich. Wissenschaftliches Kolloquium anläßlich des 100 jährigen Bestehens des Museums für Volkskunde.* Berlin: Staatliche Museen, Museum für Volkskunde.

——. 1991b. Die Volkskundemuseen in den neuen Bundesländern. *Mitteilungen der Deutschen Gesellschaft für Volkskunde* 1 (100): 4–5.

——. 1991c. 100 Jahre Museum für Volkskunde: Alltagsgeschichte im Wandel. In E. Karasek (ed.), *Alltagsgeschichte in ethnographischen Museen: Möglichkeiten der Sammlung und Darstellung im internationalen Vergleich. Wissenschaftliches Kolloquium anlässlich des 100 jährigen Bestehens des Museums für Volkskunde*, pp. 9–13. Berlin: Staatliche Museen, Museum für Volkskunde.

——. 1993. Museen für Europäische Ethnologie – eine Perspektive? In G. Korff, and H. U. Roller (ed.), *Alltagskultur passè? Positionen und Perspektiven volkskundlicher Museumsarbeit. Referate und Diskussionen der 10. Arbeitstagung der Arbeitsgruppe 'Kulturhistorisches Museum' in der Deutschen Gesellschaft für Volkskunde*, pp. 188–94. Tübingen: Tübinger Vereinigung für Volkskunde.

——. 1995. Vorwort. In D. Neuland-Kitzerow and I. Ziehe (eds.), *Wege nach Europa: Ansätze und Problemfelder in den Museen. 11. Tagung der Arbeitsgruppe Kulturhistorische Museen in der deutschen Gesellschaft für Volkskunde vom 4.–8. Oktober 1994.* Berlin: Staatliche Museen, Museum für Volkskunde.

——, and E. Tietmeyer. 1994. Das Museum Europäischer Kulturen. In J. Bunkelmann (ed.), *Standorte—Standpunkte. Staatliche Museen zu Berlin*, pp. 32-33. Berlin: Ars Nicolai.

——, ——. 1995. Wege nach Europa: Ein neues Museum entsteht. In D. Neuland and I. Ziehe (eds.), *Wege nach Europa: Ansätze und Problemfelder in den Museen. 11. Tagung der Arbeitsgruppe Kulturhistorische Museen in der Deutschen Gesellschaft für Volkskunde vom 4.-8. Oktober 1994*, pp. 15–22. Berlin: Staatliche Museen, Museum für Volkskunde.

Kaschuba, W. 2003. Splitter, Facetten, Erinnerungen: Versuch einer subjektiven Bestandsaufnahme. In M. Krause (ed.), *Ethnographisches Arbeiten in Berlin. Wissenschaftsgeschichtliche Annäherungen*, pp. 15-25. Berliner Blätter: Ethnographische und ethnologische Beiträge 31. Münster: LIT Verlag.

Köpp, U. 2003. Heimat DDR: Im Kulturbund zur demokratischen Erneuerung Deutschlands. In M. Krause (ed.), *Ethnographisches Arbeiten in Berlin. Wissenschaftsgeschichtliche Annäherungen*, pp. 97-107.

Berliner Blätter: Ethnographische und ethnologische Beiträge 31. Münster: LIT Verlag.

Kohlmann, T., and H. Bausinger (eds.). 1985. *Großstadt. Aspekte empirischer Kulturforschung*. Schriften des Museums für Deutsche Volkskunde 13. Berlin: Staatliche Museen Preußischer Kulturbesitz.

Korff, G. 1990. S-Bahn-Ethnologie. *Österreichische Zeitschrift für Volkskunde* 1: 5–26.

——. 1991. Aporien der Alltagspräsentation im volkskundlich-ethnographischen Museum. In E. Karasek (ed.), *Alltagsgeschichte in ethnographischen Museen: Möglichkeiten der Sammlung und Darstellung im internationalen Vergleich. Wissenschaftliches Kolloquium anläßlich des 100jährigen Bestehens des Museums für Volkskunde Berlin*, pp. 87–92. Berlin: Staatliche Museen, Museum für Volkskunde.

Kramer, D. 1981. Zur Geschichtsschreibung zweiter Kultur. *Gulliver. Deutsch-Englische Jahrbücher* 9: 9-40.

Kreschel, K. 1989. Ethnographische Arbeit im Museum einer mittleren Industriestadt: Brandenburg/Havel. In G. Guhr and R. Weinhold (eds.), *Ethnographie im Museum. II. Tagung der Arbeitsgemeinschaft Ethnographie der Historikergesellschaft der DDR, 17.-19. September 1985 in Dresden*, pp. 41–54. Dresden: Staatliches Museum für Völkerkunde.

——. 2003. Alltagskultur im Museum: Zur ethnografischen Arbeit am Museum Brandenburg von 1970 bis 1997. In M. Krause (ed.), *Ethnographisches Arbeiten in Berlin. Wissenschaftsgeschichtliche Annäherungen*, pp. 117-32. Berliner Blätter: Ethnographische und ethnologische Beiträge 31. Münster: LIT Verlag.

Kuczynski, J. 1980. *Geschichte des Alltags des deutschen Volkes 1600–1650*, vol. 1. Berlin: Akademie-Verlag.

Mohrmann, U. 1991. Volkskundliche Universitätsausbildung für Museumspraktiker der DDR. In E. Karasek (ed.), *Alltagsgeschichte in Ethnographischen Museen: Möglichkeiten der Sammlung und Darstellung im internationalen Vergleich. Wissenschaftliches Kolloquium anläßlich des 100jährigen Bestehens des Museums für Volkskunde Berlin*, pp. 15–18. Berlin: Staatliche Museen, Museum für Volkskunde.

——. 1998. Museen und Volkskunde der DDR im kulturpolitischen Kontext: Gab es eine Museumskultur der DDR? *Arbeitshefte der Landesstelle für Berlin-Brandenburgische Volkskunde: Materialien des 6. Workshops 'Museen und Universität'*, pp. 12–21.

——. 2001. 'Roundabout 68': Zur DDR-Volkskunde Ende der sechziger und während der siebziger Jahre. In S. Becker [et al.] (ed.), *Volkskundli-*

che Tableaus: Eine Festschrift für Martin Scharfe zum 65. Ge-burtstag von Weggefährten, Freunden und Schülern, pp. 375–84. Münster: Waxmann Verlag.

——. 2002. Sächsische Museologen und Berliner Fernstudium: Ein Mosaik-stein der DDR-Volkskunde. In M. Simon (ed.), *Volkskunde in Sachsen 13–14. Zur Geschichte der Volkskunde. Personen–Programme–Positionen*, pp. 347–61. Dresden: Thelem, Universitätsverlag.

——, and W. Rusch. 1991. Vier Jahrzehnte Ethnographie an der Humboldt-Universität zu Berlin. In Der Rektor (ed.), *Geschichte der Völkerkunde und Volkskunde an der Berliner Universität: zur Aufarbeitung des Wissenschaftserbes*, pp. 61–72. Beiträge zur Geschichte der Humboldt-Universität zu Berlin 28. Berlin: Rektor der Humboldt-Universität.

Neuland-Kitzerow, D. (ed.). 2001. *Objekte im Kontext: Museumsgeschichte(n)—Forschungsgeschichte(n)*. Berliner Blätter 22. Berlin: Gesellschaft für Ethnographie.

Ottenjann, H. (ed.). 1985. *Mode, Tracht, regionale Identität: Historische Kleidungsforschung heute*. Cloppenburg: Museumsdorf Cloppenburg.

Raschke, H. 1995. Volkskunde kontra Geschichte: Der mühevolle Weg zu einer volkskundlichen Ausbildung in der DDR. Fachfrauen—Frauen im Fach. *Beiträge zur 6. Arbeitstagung der Kommission Frauenforschung in der Deutschen Gesellschaft für Volkskunde: Schriftenreihe des Instituts für Kulturanthropologie und Europäische Ethnologie der Universität Frankfurt/M.* 52: 325–37.

Roth, M. 1995. Volkskunde-Museum und Europa: Ein Widerspruch? In D. Neuland-Kitzerow and I. Ziehe (eds.), *Wege nach Europa – Ansätze und Problemfelder in den Museen. 11. Tagung der Arbeitsgruppe Kulturhistorische Museen in der Deutschen Gesellschaft für Volkskunde vom 4.-8. Oktober 1994*, pp. 23–27. Berlin: Staatliche Museen, Museum für Volkskunde.

Scholze, T., and L. Scholze-Irrlitz. 2001. Vom wissenschaftlichen Alltag des Wolfgang Jacobeit: Ein Gespräch nach der Wende (September 1990). Zehn Jahre Gesellschaft für Ethnographie: Europäische Ethnologie in Berlin. Wolfgang Jacobeit zum 80. Geburtstag. *Berliner Blätter* 23: 33–39.

Tiesler, F. 1989. Prinzipien des völkerkundlichen Sammelns unter gegenwärtigen Bedingungen. In G. Guhr and R. Weinhold (eds.), *Ethnographie im Museum II. Tagung der Arbeitsgemeinschaft Ethnographie der Historikergesellschaft der DDR, 17.-19. September 1985 in*

Dresden, pp. 126–33. Dresden: Staatliches Museum für Völkerkunde.

Weißel, B., H. Strobach, and W. Jacobeit. 1972. *Zur Geschichte der Kultur und Lebensweise der werktätigen Klassen und Schichten des deutschen Volkes vom 11. Jahrhundert bis 1945: Ein Abriss.* Wissenschaftliche Mitteilungen der Deutschen Historiker-Gesellschaft, 1/3. Berlin: Deutsche Historiker-Gesellschaft.

Ziehe, I. 2003. Zwischen Praxis, Lehre und Forschung: Das Fernstudium Ethnographie an der Humboldt-Universität zu Berlin aus der Perspektive einer ehemaligen Fernstudentin. In M. Krause (ed.), *Ethnographisches Arbeiten in Berlin. Wissenschaftsgeschichtliche Annäherungen*, pp. 143-50. Berliner Blätter: Ethnographische und ethnologische Beiträge 31. Münster: LIT Verlag.

Chapter 12
The Pervasive Continuities of Czech Národopis

Petr Lozoviuk

Czech anthropologists who study their own country have so far been unable to develop a discourse critical of the ideology of their discipline, národopis. Fifteen years after the collapse of the socialist regime, only an insignificant number of reflective or analytical historiographical works have been published, fewer than has been the case for most other 'small anthropologies' in Eastern Europe. This assertion of unreflectivity applies not only to recent developments but also to anthropological practice before the socialist period. The most recent historical outline of Czech anthropology was written by Antonín Robek and published in 1979. It is largely a descriptive work, but at the same time it is ideological, factually unreliable, and well short of contemporary scholarly standards. Other recent works either address particular subfields or discuss the historical development of Czech národopis and folklore studies in a different context.[1]

Only after 1989 did it become possible to discuss how and to what extent the discipline was used for ideological purposes after the communist take-over of Czechoslovakia in 1948. The early 1990s saw a number of attempts to initiate a discussion about the links between folklore studies and state ideology in the recent past (see Jeřábek et al. 1991; Jiříkovská and Mišurec 1991). Sporadic publications since then and the reactions to them show that it is not yet possible to subject the dominant Czech tradition of anthropology, constituted in the nineteenth century as národopis, to sufficient critical scrutiny. There are a number of reasons for this (see Holubová, Petráňová, and Woitsch 2002). The relevant issues for such a reflective analysis have only been touched upon, without being placed into a proper context. Many questions have remained unanswered, the history of the discipline in socialist Czechoslovakia has been addressed only superficially, and no standpoint has been taken on the state of Czech národopis today. The few recent accounts do not look outside the Czech-speaking discipline and

---

[1] See Kudělka, Šimeček, and Večerka 1995; Havránek 1997; Kudělka et al. 1997; Havránek and Pousta 1998.

make no attempt to examine how anthropologists elsewhere have coped with the burden of ideology.

Two serious attempts have been made since 1989, however, to counteract the inertia inherent in the discipline in the Czech Republic. The first might be called, following Josef Wolf, 'the way from folklore studies to anthropology' (Wolf 1997). This label reflects the wave of renaming in the early 1990s, in which almost all Czech anthropological institutions changed their names from národopis to etnologie. This was obviously an attempt to demonstrate a change of paradigm to the outside world, but it did not necessarily mean any change of contents. The second attempt to modernise the Czech discipline consists in the foundation of new institutions and new journals.[2] The names of university institutions founded after 1990 contain the word *antropologie*, prefaced by either *sociální* or *kulturní*, and are clearly oriented toward the Anglo-American anthropological tradition. The complexity of this undertaking in modernisation has been analysed recently by Peter Skalník (2002; see also Brouček 1991; Vařeka 2002) and is not pursued further here.

In sum, there has been no debate on the history of národopis in the Czech Republic that can be compared, for example, to recent reappraisals of German Volkskunde, both in the pre-socialist period and under socialism. This chapter cannot fill the gap; instead, I focus on the degree to which we can identify continuities and discontinuities in Czech národopis before and after the Second World War. It is obvious that major changes in the organisation of scholarly work were imposed in the early socialist period (see Skalníková, this volume). Personal relations were often of vital importance, because they determined whether or not the general strategy of 'restricted conformity' to the regime would succeed in each particular case. The leading positions were at the Academy of Sciences (Ústav pro etnografii a folkloristiku Československé akademie věd, founded in 1954), the chairs at the two major universities (Prague and Brno), the Institute for Folk Art in Strážnice, and the most important museums (Prague, Brno, Plzeň, Olomouc, Opava, Rožnov p.R., Uherské Hradiště, and others).[3] All research projects were carried out within the framework of centrally controlled 'state plans for basic research' (*Státní plán základního výzkumu*). But within this new institutional environment there was, I suggest, strong continuity with what had come before, especially in the ideologisation and ensuing instrumentalisation of anthropological work.

---

[2] Among the new journals are *Cargo* and *Lidé města*.
[3] The Institute for Folk Art (Ústav lidového umění) was founded in 1956 and renamed the Institute of Folk Culture (Ústav lidové kultury) in 1991.

Real-Socialist Ethnoscience

In chapter 3, Peter Skalník outlined the Czech anthropological nomenclature. The most exact expression for what was practised in the Czech Republic between 1945 and 1989 would, in my opinion, be 'real-socialist ethnoscience' rather than, as one might expect, a form of Marxism. By *real-socialist* I mean that, although the word Marxism was often used in the texts produced in this period, it was little more than a stock phrase, an accommodation to the imperatives of the system. By *ethnoscience* I mean that the theory and methods of this discipline derived to a significant degree from the older národopis, with its focus on the nation as an enduring ethnic collectivity. What socialist národopis adopted from other disciplines and what new stimuli it generated have yet to be clarified. To address these questions we must first address a more general one concerning the essential nature of Czech anthropology. To what extent can Czech národopis be seen as a national tradition? Is it rather, as Justin Stagl (1995: 23) has phrased it, a 'small national sub-tradition' of a larger scientific province? What are the specific characteristics of the Czech scientific discourse, if it exists at all? How substantial was the influence of other traditions, above all German Volkskunde and English-language anthropology (see Kandert 2002), on národopis in the period when it was officially imitating Soviet role models? Just how far was the discipline dependent on Soviet etnografiya in the Czechoslovak case?

At first glance, Soviet influence appears to have been considerable. Národopis was divided into ethnografie and folkloristika, as in the USSR. According to Oldřich Sirovátka, one of the most prominent Czech scholars of the 1970s and 1980s, 'folklore studies were [thus] united with ethnographie as a unified národopis' (Sirovátka 1992: 83).[4] The declared goal of anthropological research remained, according to another prominent representative of the discipline, the 'inventorying of the national character' (Jech 1992: 81).[5] This was a self-perception which differed from the new models developing in Germany, both East and West, and was closer to the Soviet model. Some affinities existed, however (possibly unconscious), with German Volkskunde, particularly in the context of linguistic enclave studies (Walther Kuhn [1934], Gustav Jungbauer [1930, 1938]) and the ethnography of the proletariat (Will-Erich Peuckert [1931]). German models were partly

---

[4] 'Folkloristika je spojena s etnografií do dvojjediné disciplíny—do národopisu.'
[5] 'Pravdivé postižení národní specifičnosti.'

concealed and to some extent forgotten under socialism, but the ambiguous relationship with Germany nonetheless persisted.[6]

The manipulation of anthropological knowledge outside academia has been a structural element of the discipline in the Czech case.[7] The profound impact of ideology can be readily demonstrated, for example, by looking carefully at key concepts. The concept of folk culture (*lidová kultura*) was taken over from the old folklore studies and further developed, notably by Olga Skalníková and Karel Fojtík (1971).[8] In Marxist approaches, Czech folk culture was usually considered an 'important element of the emancipatory process' (Robek and Vařeka 1988: 197), referring to the emancipation of the Czech nation.[9] The real-socialist scholars, therefore, like their predecessors, tried to demonstrate 'strong Czech national consciousness' (Robek and Vařeka 1988: 198) among the masses, and they deliberately concentrated their attention on Czech-German relations in Bohemia. A project titled 'The Ethnographie of the National Rebirth' was initiated to prove that Czech folk culture was a full equivalent of the German but needed to be distinguished from it (Robek and Vařeka 1988: 199).[10] In this sense, reference was made to the 'dis-integrating role of Czech ethnographic work' (Robek and Vařeka 1988: 199; cf. Johler 1995; Stagl 1995, 2002) in the nineteenth century. Unlike those Austrian Volkskundler of the later nineteenth century who wanted to develop their discipline as an objective ('value-neutral') science, the Czech scholars devoted themselves exclusively to the Czech national cause.

The ethnic emphasis in Czech anthropology was seen as positive and was highly valued by Marxists in the second half of the twentieth century. Official communist ideology could thus be projected directly into the concept of folk culture as developed by socialist folklorists. According to a report on the current state of research, 'investigations had demonstrated the leading role of the broad folk masses [in Czech national history]' (Robek and Vařeka 1988: 197).[11] Since the working class was able to unite 'interests

---

[6] I am currently investigating this topic in more detail in the project 'Interethnik im Wissenschaftsprozess: Die gesellschaftlichen Auswirkungen volkskundlicher Forschungen in Böhmen von der zweiten Hälfte des 19. Jahrhunderts bis zur Gegenwart' at the Institut für Sächsische Geschichte und Volkskunde in Dresden.

[7] The Czech-Canadian cultural anthropologist David Scheffel and the Prague anthropologist Josef Kandert jointly wrote a pioneering study which points to exactly this conclusion (Scheffel and Kandert 1994); see also Kandert, this volume.

[8] On the concepts of 'folk culture' (*lidová kultura*) and 'the people' (*lid*) in Czech anthropology see also Hubinger 1990.

[9] 'Významnou složkou (českého národního) emancipačního procesu.'

[10] 'Lidová česká kultura je stejně cenná, ale od německé lidové kultury se liší.'

[11] 'Dosavadní výzkumy ... prokázaly, vedoucí úlohu širokých lidových vrstev v procesu národního obrození.'

of class and nation' (Robek and Vařeka 1988: 198),[12] it could be attributed, in complete accordance with communist ideology, a 'prominent role' in national emancipation.

Ethnic Processes

Continuity and the political instrumentalisation of národopis can be seen most clearly in the examination of so-called ethnic processes, both in border regions of the socialist republic and in the 'study of Czechs abroad'.[13] This work was organised by the Czechoslovak Academy of Sciences and was strongly reminiscent of the tradition of German linguistic enclave studies (*Sprachinselvolkskunde*). Research into ethnic enclaves abroad has a long history in Bohemia. Most research focused either on the description of cultural artefacts considered typical of Czech folk culture or on groups abroad that officially declared themselves Czech.[14]

The investigation of ethnic processes in the post-war years concentrated primarily on border territories from which the indigenous German-speaking population had been expelled after 1945 and where several migrant groups from other parts of Czechoslovakia and abroad had been settled. 'Group-specific differences' between Czech and non-Czech immigrants were to be illuminated in this research, which was expected to show how successfully different groups of migrants had been integrated into Czech society (see Heroldová 1998). This was inherently paradoxical, considering that in fact the precise opposite, their ethnic and cultural persistence, was the topic of study. In any case, newcomer groups continued to be seen as enclaves with their distinctive cultural values and were examined individually, just as studies of the Germans had proceeded in the past. Research began with an investigation of the 'newly settled border territory'

---

[12] 'Dělnictvo je totiž schopno spojovat zájmy třídní a národní.'
[13] 'Výzkum Čechů v cizině.' The EU AVČR continues to publish a book series under the title *Češi v cizině* (Czechs Abroad).
[14] Scholars of the Sudeten Germans had also taken great interest in their 'countrymen' living abroad, i.e. the Germans of Bohemia. At the German University in Prague, the three major representatives of Volkskunde were Adolf Hauffen, 'the founder of scientific Volkskunde in German Bohemia' (Jungbauer 1931: 30), Gustav Jungbauer, the long-time director of the Department of German Folklore Studies at the university, and Josef Hanika. Each of these scholars carried out a form of linguistic enclave studies and, beginning with Hauffen's 1895 monograph *Die deutsche Sprachinsel Gottschee* (The German linguistic enclave of Gottschee), a solid body of scholarship was built up. This field of study was strongly ideologised during the Second World War, at which time research was begun on the 'study of lost modern-day [German] settlements on Czech soil' (Beranek 1944). Scholars were expected to explain and justify 'scientifically' the German claim to power in the Bohemian-Moravian region and why 'Czechised Germans should be won back'. Linguistic enclave studies thus shifted in the 1940s into the racist study of 'blood-mingling' (*Blutvermischungsforschung*).

(*novoosídleneckého pohraničí*) in the Horšovskotýnecko region in 1953. It was designed to culminate in the 1980s in a theoretically oriented 'Dictionary of Ethnic Processes', based on the primordialist concept of *ethnos* as developed in the work of the Soviet anthropologist Yulian Bromley (1973). Like many other ambitiously conceived projects, this one was not completed, and the dictionary was never published. After 1989 the work came to a complete standstill, though in the early 1990s some partial results were published as articles.

Politics and Socialist Modernisation

The tight links between národopis and politics can also be seen in the research carried out in industrial areas during the 'era of the building up of socialism', research which remains an interesting model for contemporary applied ethnography. The first investigations of the 'social changes' brought about by socialism were made in the early 1950s by a new generation of Marxist folklorists. Field research carried out in that context was part of the scientific investigation of the 'development of industrial areas in the phase of the consolidation of socialism', one of the central topics of Marxist anthropology from the early 1950s onwards (see Skalníková, this volume). During the 1950s and 1960s the Žďár region, the industrial areas of northern Bohemia, Ostrava, Brno, Zlín, and Kladno were all systematically studied, with particular attention to the origins of their inhabitants, to migrations, and to the 'problem of methodology in the research of industrial development under socialism' (Vytiska 1981: 270). This research was supposed to culminate in a 'summary of the general laws and specific features of the development of industrial areas in the socialist countries' (Vytiska 1981: 271).

Jaroslav Kramařík, one of the leading participants in these projects, argued that národopisci 'should use all scientific means to help accelerate the socialisation of our villages' (Skalníková 1952: 1). The discipline of národopis was expected to become 'a valid force in the realisation of socialism in our country' (Skalníková 1952: 2). In practice, as a first step, information was collected on traditional life in the rural research areas (see Šach 1954). Attention was focused in this phase on conventional folk culture. In the course of time, more emphasis was placed on modern topics such as 'the influence of socialism on the economic and cultural life of the region, on the life of the people' (Skalníková 1956: 5). The goal was to prove that the modernisation process initiated by the regime had been accepted and was even approved of by the people, on the grounds that it would eventually lead to a 'more progressive' social system. Politically engaged anthropologists tried to show that this was all occurring in full conformity with local (folk) and national traditions.

The anthropologists of the 1960s studied 'the influence of economic changes on the emergence of modern ethnographic areas' (see Fojtík and Skalníková 1965; Skalníková 1965, 1967). This trend continued in the 1970s and 1980s in the form of 'ethnographie of the proletariat' studies and in historically oriented research into working-class culture. This component of národopis was genuinely new, but like some other cautious innovations, it led to no invigorating theoretical or methodological discussions.[15]

Conclusion

In summary, the methodology of Czech národopis in the socialist era continued to focus on the collection, description, and classification of traditional ethnographic materials. Thematically, too, with few exceptions, researchers continued to prioritise traditional problems dating back to the nineteenth century. Occasional attempts were made to widen the field of folklore studies, but no new theories were established. The major consequence of socialist rule was therefore that 'the entirety of Czech science and with it ethnografie and folkloristika fell behind theoretically and methodologically, and the reception and adaptation of new trends could proceed only on an individual basis' (Sirovátka 1992: 83). That Czech anthropology 'lost its respected position in the international context' is attributed exclusively to the 'ideological ballast' of the time (Jech 1992: 80).

But postsocialist Czech anthropology needs to move beyond such apologetic positions, as Scheffel and Kandert (1994) have shown. Anthropology, like other social sciences, had always served the ruling ideology, whether its practitioners were aware of this or not. The 'politicisation' of science, far from being a peculiarity of socialism, dates back 'to the very roots of the discipline in the nineteenth-century bourgeois nationalism' (Scheffel and Kandert 1994: 15). Certain characteristics seem to have survived until today, and this helps us to understand why there is no Czech scientific tradition commensurate with Anglo-American socio-cultural anthropology—or even with German Volkskunde.

---

[15] The work of Soňa Švecová on social relations in Central Slovakia (1975, 1984) is the only major exception in this respect.

234   PETR LOZOVIUK

References

Beranek, F. 1944. Neuzeitliche Deutschensiedlungen in Böhmen und Mähren. *Deutsche Volksforschung in Böhmen und Mähren* 3 (1–2): 23–36.

Bromley, Y. 1973. *Etnos i etnografiya*. Moskva: Nauka.

Brouček, S. 1991. Das Institut für Ethnografie und Folkloristik an der Tschechoslowakischen Akademie der Wissenschaften: Aufgaben und Ziele der Institute in Prag und Brünn. *Zeitschrift für Volkskunde* 87 (2): 257–62.

Czakó, E. (ed.). 1933-37. *Magyarság néprajza*. Budapest: Királyi Magyar Egyetemi Nyomda.

Fojtík, K., and O. Skalníková. 1965. Výzkum průmyslových oblastí v československé etnografii. *Český lid* 52: 131–43.

Hauffen, A. 1895. *Die deutsche Sprachinsel Gottschee*. Österreichische Quellen und Forschungen 3. Graz: Styria.

Havránek, J. (ed.). 1997. *Dějiny Univerzity Karlovy III 1802–1918*. Praha: Univ. Karlova.

———, and Z. Pousta (eds.). 1998. *Dějiny Univerzity Karlovy IV 1918–1990*. Praha: Univ. Karlova.

Heroldová, I. 1998. Ethnische Prozesse in den böhmischen Grenzgebieten nach dem Zweiten Weltkrieg. In H. Lemberg, J. Kren, and D. Kovác (eds.), *Im Geteilten Europa: Tschechen, Slowaken und Deutsche und ihre Staaten 1948–1989*, pp. 95–109. Essen: Klartext-Verlag.

Holubová, M., L. Petráňová, and J. Woitsch (eds.). 2002. *Česka etnologie 2000*. Praha: Etnologický ústav, Akademie věd České republiky.

Hubinger, V. 1990. K vymezení a užití termínu lid v etnografii. *Český lid* 77 (1): 40–47.

Jech, J. 1992. Česká a slovenská folkloristika v mezinárodním kontextu. *Český lid* 79 (1): 79–82.

Jeřábek, R., J. Kandert, M. Moravcová, and L. Holý. 1991. Etnografie bez ideologie. *Umění a řemesla* 1–2: 2–4.

Jiříkovská, V., and Z. Mišurec. 1991. Příspěvek k vývoji české etnografie a folkloristiky a Národopisné společnosti československé při ČSAV po únoru 1948. *Národopisný věstník československý* 8 (50): 5–35.

Johler, R. 1995. Das Ethnische als Forschungskonzept: Die österreichische Volkskunde im Europäischen Vergleich. In K. Beitl and O. Bockhorn (eds.), *Ethnologia Europaea, 5: Internationaler Kongreß der Société Internationale d'Ethnologie et de Folklore (SIEF), Wien, 12.-16.9.1994*, pp. 69–101. Wien: Institut für Volkskunde der Universität Wien.

Jungbauer, G. 1930. Sprachinselvolkskunde. *Sudetendeutsche Zeitschrift für Volkskunde* 3: 143–50, 196–204, 244–56.
——. 1931. Einleitung. In A. Hauffen, *Bibliographie der deutschen Volkskunde in Böhmen*, pp. 5–48. Reichenberg: Sudetendeutscher Verlag Franz Kraus.
——. 1938. Die volkskundliche Forschung in der Tschechoslowakei. *Deutsches Archiv für Landes- und Volksforschung* 2: 434–51.
Kandert, J. 2002. The 'Czech School' in Social Anthropology. In P. Skalník (ed.), *A Post-Communist Millennium: The Struggles for Sociocultural Anthropology in Central and Eastern Europe*, pp. 43–48. Prague: Set Out.
Kudělka, M., Z. Šimeček, and R. Večerka. 1995. *Česká slavistika, 1: V prvním období svého vývoje do počátku 60. let 19. století*. Praha: Historický ústav AVCR.
Kudělka, M., Z. Šimeček, V. Šťastný, and R. Večerka. 1997. *Česká slavistika od počátku 60. let 19. století do roku 1918*. Praha: Historický ústav AVCR.
Kuhn, W. 1934. *Deutsche Sprachinsel-Forschung: Geschichte, Aufgaben, Verfahren*. Plauen: Wolff.
Peuckert, W.-E. 1931. *Volkskunde des Proletariats. Aufgang der proletarischen Kultur (Teil 1)*. Frankfurt am Main: Neuer Frankfurter Verlag.
Robek, A. 1979. *Dějiny české etnografie I*. Praha: Universita Karlova.
——, and J. Vařeka. 1988. Dosažené výsledky a současné úkoly základního výzkumu etnografie národního obrození. *Český lid* 75 (4): 197–202.
Šach, F. 1954. Etnografický průzkum žďárského okresu v r. 1954. *Český lid* 41 (6): 287–88.
Scheffel, D. Z., and J. Kandert. 1994. Politics and Culture in Czech Ethnography. *Anthropological Quarterly* 67 (1): 15–23.
Sirovátka, O. 1992. Hledání cest české slovesné folkloristiky. *Český lid* 79 (1): 82–84.
Skalník, P. 2002. Politics of Social Anthropology in Czech Universities after 1989: A Report by an Observing Participant. In P. Skalník (ed.), *A Post-Communist Millennium: The Struggles for Sociocultural Anthropology in Central and Eastern Europe*, pp. 49–66. Prague: Set Out.
Skalníková, O. 1952. II. celostátní národopisná conference. *Český lid* 39 (1–2): 1–2.
——. 1956. Příspěvek k studiu současného způsobu života na Žďársku. *Československá etnografie* 4: 5–24.
——. 1965. Beitrag zum Studium des Einflusses ökonomischer Veränderungen auf die Bildung neuzeitlicher ethnographischer

Gebiete. In Gy. Ortutay and T. Bodrogi (eds.) *Europa et Hungaria. Congressus Ethnographicus in Hungaria*, pp. 217-23. Budapest: Akadémiai Kiadó.

——. 1967. Předpoklady pro vytvoření kulturního typu nové průmyslové oblasti. In *Kolokvium k otázkám vymedzenia východoslovenskej priemyselnej oblasti (1900–1950)*, pp. 68–74. Košice: Vychodoslovenské múzeum.

——, and K. Fojtík. 1971. *K teorii etnografie současnosti*. Praha: Academia, Nakladatelsví Československé akademie věd.

Stagl, J. 1995. Ethnologie und Vielvölkerstaat. In B. Rupp-Eisenreich and J. Stagl (eds.), *Kulturwissenschaften im Vielvölkerstaat: Zur Geschichte der Ethnologie und verwandter Gebiete in Österreich ca. 1780 bis 1918*, pp. 22–27. Wien: Böhlau.

——. 2002. Das 'Kronprinzenwerk': Eine Darstellung des Habsburgerreiches. In A. Ackermann and K. E. Müller (eds.), *Patchwork: Dimensionen multikultureller Gesellschaften. Geschichte, Problematik und Chancen*, pp. 151–72. Bielefeld: transcript.

Švecová, S. 1975. *Kopanicové sídla a dedina: Národopisná štúdia o spoločenských vztahoch medzi obyvateľmi jednej slovenskej obce*. Praha: Universita Karlova.

——. 1984. *Lazy v 19. a 20. storočí: Vývoj rol'nickych chotárnych sídiel v oblasti Krupinskej planiny*. Praha: Universita Karlova.

Vařeka, J. 2002. Die tschechische Ethnologie nach 1989. In B. Emmerich and J. Moser (eds.), *Europäische Ethnologien im neuen Millennium: Osteuropäische Ethnologien auf neuen Wegen—Abschied vom Referatenorgan DEMOS*, pp. 67–77. Dresden: Thelem.

Vytiska, J. 1981. Der Stand und die Perspektiven der Erforschung industrieller Gebiete in der Periode des Sozialismus. In J. Kutnohorská (ed.), *K některým otázkám vývoje průmyslových oblastí v podmínkách výstavby socialismu: Konference o vývoji průmyslových oblastí v podmínkách výstavby socialismu Třinec 16.-18. září 1980*, pp. 268–71. Opava: Slezský ústav ČSAV.

Wolf, J. 1997. Česká cesta od národopisu k etnologii. *Národopisný věstník 8* (55): 5–16.

Chapter 13
The Unchanging Praxis of 'Home Anthropology': Positivists and Marxists in the Czech Case

Josef Kandert

The Czech language draws a distinction similar to the German between anthropologists who practise their discipline at home, the národopisci (Volkskundler) and those who work on non-European societies, the mimoevropští etnografové (Völkerkundler). The task of the former was to study the folk culture of the Czechs, Moravians, Silesians, Slovaks, and various minority groups. The wider Slavic world was largely ignored;[1] the rest of Europe was ignored altogether, since it fitted into neither of the categories available. These two branches of anthropology developed independently, connected by few links of theory or methodology. Between 1962 and 1990 at least 13 anthropologists published the results of fieldwork conducted outside Europe, in either Czech, English, or German, but these studies went unnoticed by their colleagues who worked at home. Some specialists in non-European anthropology tried to keep abreast of developments in 'home anthropology' and did fieldwork in Czechoslovakia,[2] but this interest was not reciprocated.

From the late 1950s národopis and folkloristika were separate strands within a single discipline. The outsider might have been forgiven for failing to notice the separation, since the two sets of scholars were always to be found alongside each other, both in the universities and in the institutes of the Academy of Sciences. However, like their colleagues in Slovakia (see Kiliánová, this volume), the Czech *folkloristé* were influenced by structuralism, semiotics, and other modern social science theories. This was not the case with the národopisci, who throughout the socialist era preferred to

---

[1] Only three Czech researchers managed to combine home anthropology with Slavic anthropology in general: Jaroslav Kramařík, Václav Frolec, and Hana Hynková. The wider Slavic field was better covered in Slovakia, such as in the works of Ján Podolák and Ján Komorovský.

[2] For example, Václav Šolc did fieldwork among rafters of the Vltava River, and Josef Kandert and Peter Skalník both worked in rural Slovakia.

ignore the theories and methods used in adjacent fields, both international anthropology and folklore studies. The explanation for this parochialism lies in the role of národopis in Czech nationalism during the nineteenth century, even if some elements necessarily experienced changes in the Marxist ideological mist (Scheffel and Kandert 1994).

The theoretical background of Czech národopis lay in quasi-evolutionist and quasi-diffusionist doctrines dating back to Habsburg days, before the establishment of any specialist institutions for the discipline. The existence of the Prague Linguistic Circle during the 1930s and 1940s had no effect on these anthropologists, with only one exception. Antonín Václavík, head of the ethnographic department at Brno University (today, Masaryk University), published two monographs between the wars resulting from long-term fieldwork and making use of both functionalist and structuralist methods (1925, 1930). These books, however, had little influence on his colleagues, and in the early 1950s Václavík was criticised as a reactionary.[3]

Apart from the elite academics in the universities and the newly established Academy of Sciences, most národopisci were employed in regional and urban museums. A wave of professionalisation grew as graduates took over from amateur enthusiasts in such positions. In addition to the three main museums (the National Museum in Prague, the Moravian Museum in Brno, and the Silesian Museum in Opava), the country boasted a dense net of smaller, provincial museums. In many counties both the Houses of Culture (*kulturní domy*) and the Historical Monuments Offices (*památkové úřady*) were directed by qualified národopisci. From the point of view of the ruling socialist regime, these anthropologists could be divided into two groups.

First, there were those who found socialism distasteful and were therefore disinclined to serve Marxist ideology. Such scholars retreated into the niche of pure positivism and tended to publish their field data without commentary. This strategy, understandable in personal terms, hindered the intellectual development of the discipline. Such positivism was most common in the museums and in institutes for the preservation of historical monuments.[4] The Communist Party tolerated this strategy and allowed museums to serve as the 'last address workplaces' (in Czech, *koncová pracoviště*) for troublesome academics.[5]

---

[3] A study of customs and folk art by Antonín Václavík was published in 1959. It displays a mixture of the methods of functionalism and historical materialism, and it shows clearly the requirement for anyone with theoretical aspirations to conform to a Marxist paradigm. But few národopisci had such aspirations to begin with.

[4] For example, both leading figures of the Prague Ethnographic Museum, Helena Johnová and Alena Plessingerová, relied heavily on this strategy throughout their professional careers.

[5] Researchers considered politically unsound were often obliged to accept jobs in archives, and these too were popularly referred to as 'last address workplaces'. For example, the

Second, there were those who were ready to serve the new ideology, which proclaimed the pure culture of the working class as the key ingredient in consolidating socialism. In the rest of this chapter I explore how this group of anthropologists was able to influence the lives of ordinary citizens under socialism. It was well represented at the universities in Prague and Brno and also at the Institute of Ethnographie and Folklore Studies of the Academy of Sciences (with branches in Prague and Brno). An analysis of editorials and leading articles in the two most influential ethnographic journals, *Český lid* (hereafter Čl) and *Československá etnografie* (hereafter Če), allows us to identify two main subgroups of ideologists.[6] The first shaped anthropological ideology in the 1950s and most of the 1960s.[7] The second was in control during the last decades of socialism, that is, during the 'normalisation' era which followed the Soviet occupation.[8]

Politics and Ideology

The Communist Party understood folk culture as a means to influence citizens and promote political goals. According to this view, the discipline of národopis was charged with the following goals. First, it was expected to identify progressive phenomena in the pre-socialist folk culture, notably in the culture of the working classes, in both towns and rural areas. Attention was focused on the village poor—the so-called rural proletariat—and on the lower strata of the urban population. Whereas in pre-socialist times anthropologists had paid disproportionate attention to the culture of the rich peasants (*sedláci*), the culture of the workers was similarly privileged under socialism.

Second, the národopisci were expected to describe the new folk culture of the socialist era. Emphasis was placed on the study of newly cooperativised villages (*družstevní vesnice*) and on the study of workers, especially miners.

Third, národopisci were to study the culture of repatriates—native Czechs who returned to their homeland after the Second World War from the Ukraine, Bulgaria, Romania, Yugoslavia, Hungary, and so forth. The

famous historian of French literature Václav Černý was employed in the archive of the Academy of Sciences after having to give up his position at the Faculty of Arts of the Charles University.
[6] *Český lid* (literally, Czech folk) was first published in 1891. In the 1950s it published six issues per year; this was later reduced to four issues per year. *Československá etnografie* appeared quarterly between 1953 and 1963 and specialised in socio-cultural anthropology; its main editor was Otakar Nahodil.
[7] Leading representatives of this subgroup are Karel Fojtík, Jaroslav Kramařík, Otakar Nahodil, and Olga Skalníková.
[8] The two most important figures in this subgroup are Antonín Robek and Hana Hynková.

study of so-called ethnic processes was largely the study of how these groups were assimilated into the local Czech mainstream (see Lozoviuk, this volume). This research has continued down to the present day.

Fourth, special problems existed in connection with the 'fight against Christianity', and národopis research was expected to show folk superstitions and beliefs as obscurantist, old-fashioned, and perhaps funny. They were to be depicted as obstacles to the modern, socialist way of life (Kandert 2001).[9]

Finally, it was expected that anthropological data would help in building up the new socialist folk culture in both towns and villages. The materials gathered were used in the staging of regional and national folk festivals as well as in radio, television, and film. They were also to serve as the inspiration for artists, architects, and craftsmen. Socialist Czechoslovakia had numerous establishments such as ÚLUV (Centre of Folk Art Production) and ÚBOK (Centre of Home and Living Culture), which in a sense continued cooperative traditions which dated back to the early years of the century, when anthropologists and artists came together in cooperatives to record and commoditise Czech folk culture.

Between 1949 and the 1980s, what I would call proletarian studies dominated Czech národopis (see Skalníková, this volume; for a late example see Robek, Moravcová, and Šťastná 1981). The study of life in villages with agricultural cooperatives was effectively launched only in the 1960s, some years after full collectivisation, when the financial and material situation of the cooperatives had begun to change for the better. It continued until the 1980s. The study of repatriates was another long-term project which in the 1970s was expanded to include the entire socialist world. The dominant framework for these investigations was that of Soviet anthropologists and their ideologist Yulian Bromley (1977). The study of superstitions was promoted vigorously in the 1950s and the early 1960s, but thereafter the národopisci rather neglected religion. The utilisation of anthropological materials in constructing a new culture continued throughout the socialist era. Many scholars supplemented their salaries by working as field researchers for ÚLUV or ÚBOK or as advisers to radio and television or to folklore dancing ensembles.[10]

---

[9] The main representatives of religion studies in národopis were Otakar Nahodil and his student Antonín Robek. Together they published the book *O původu náboženství* (On the origin of religion) in 1961 (see also Kandert 2001).

[10] The 1951 film *Zitra se bude tančit všude* (Tomorrow all the people will dance) is the clearest example of ideological collaboration between anthropologists and communist ideologists.

For most národopisci, the political context did not represent a theoretical or methodological problem. They were able to gather their data using theoretical tools which, for the most part, dated back to the turn of the century. The main topics had not changed, either. They consisted of material culture (architecture, tools, crafts, etc.), spiritual culture (ceremonies, customs, superstitions, etc.), and folklore. Why did so many scholars accept this petrified situation? For one thing, the tried methods were safe: there was no danger that they would suddenly be declared to issue from Western imperialist influences.[11] Soviet influence was undoubtedly important: some of the Czechs who could read Soviet articles thought that simply by imitating 'Soviet patterns', they were doing Marxist theoretical work. A further factor is that it was easy to make use of the traditional themes of the discipline in order to contrast the 'old' and the 'new' and thereby demonstrate the superiority of the new and of the 'progressive' in earlier ages. Finally, Czech scholars had always been concerned to distinguish themselves from German Volkskundler carrying out research in Czech lands. The theory, methods, and data of the opposite camp were taboo for 'our camp'.[12] The greatest anthropological exhibition ever mounted in Bohemia, which took place in 1895, presented Czech folk culture only. In the eyes of its organisers, the folk culture of Germans living in the Czech counties did not exist. This insularity persisted after the emergence of Czechoslovakia, and its legacy can still be felt today.

The combination of positivism and quasi-Marxism blocked the road towards theoretical and methodological development of the discipline. In purely descriptive terms, anthropologists were unable to give a satisfactory picture of socialist life. Even today, those who sustain the tradition of národopis prefer, not surprisingly, to concentrate on the past life of the folk. There is little willingness among these scholars to grapple with contemporary culture, and participant observation (i.e. fieldwork in the standard Western sense) remains highly unusual.

Conclusion

I have dealt here with only one dimension of Czech anthropology, the variant which is practised at home. In another paper I have described many aspects of Czech anthropology overseas (Kandert 2002; see also Skalník, this volume). That is a rather more exciting story than that of the náro-

---

[11] This was a serious worry for sociologists and for some of the anthropologists working outside Europe.
[12] These Volkskundler left the scene in 1946–47, but any topic pertaining to the German heritage of the Czech lands remained taboo until the late 1970s.

dopisci. The central actors in what became known as the 'Czech school' in social anthropology were Ladislav Holý, Milan Stuchlík, and their students.[13] The creative talents of that cohort came to long-term fruition elsewhere, notably in Britain. Had the country's political evolution been more favourable, it is possible that the two facets of anthropology might have been brought together fruitfully within Czechoslovakia. A classmate of Holý and Stuchlík's, Soňa Švecová (b. 1929), specialised in the study of kinship and, together with several other Czechs, I among them, did fieldwork in Slovakia (Švecová 1975, 1984). Later she headed the 'sub-commission for the study of social relations' of the International Commission for the Study of Carpathians. This collaborative work, undertaken mainly by graduates in non-European anthropology in Prague and Bratislava in the 1960s and 1970s, resulted in a rich inter-disciplinary harvest, including a monograph on Hont County (Botík 1988).

Only after 1990 could the efforts of this generation, in conjunction with new cohorts of young enthusiasts, lead to a more sustained reappraisal of traditional Czech home anthropology. The support of 'professors from abroad', among them Ernest Gellner, Leopold Pospíšil, Zdeněk Salzmann, Ladislav Holý, and Andrew Lass, was especially helpful—but that is another story.

References

Botík, J. 1988. *Hont: Tradície l'udovej kultúry*. Martin: Vyd. Osveta.

Bromlej, J. V. 1977. *Ethnos und Ethnographie*. Berlin: Akademie-Verlag.

Kandert, J. 2001. Ethnographic Research on Religion during the Socialist Era: The Czech Case. In I. Doležalová, L. H. Martin, and D. Papoušek (eds.), *The Academic Study of Religion during the Cold War: East and West*, pp. 95–104. New York: P. Lang.

———. 2002. The 'Czech School' in Social Anthropology. In P. Skalník (ed.), *A Post-Communist Millennium: The Struggles for Sociocultural Anthropology in Central and Eastern Europe*, pp. 43–48. Prague: Set Out.

Nahodil, O., and A. Robek. 1961. *O původu náboženství*. Praha: Orbis.

Robek, A., M. Moravcová, and J. Šťastná (eds.). 1981. *Stará dělnická Praha: Život a kultura dělnických čtvrtí 1848–1939*. Praha: Academia.

---

[13] The overall history of non-European anthropology in the Czech case resembles the Hungarian case analysed by Mihály Sárkány (this volume).

Scheffel, D., and J. Kandert. 1994. Politics and Culture in Czech Ethnography. *Anthropological Quarterly* 67 (1): 15–23.

Švecová, S. 1975. *Kopanicové sídla a dedina*. Praha: Universita Karlova.

——. 1984. *Lazy v 19. a 20. storočí: Vývoj roľníckych chotárnych sídiel v oblasti Krupinskej planiny*. Praha: Universita Karlova.

Václavík, A. 1925. *Podunajská dědina v Československu*. Bratislava: Vydavateľské družstvo.

——. 1930. *Luhačovické zálesí*. Praha: Národopisná Společnost.

——. 1959. *Výroční obyčeje a lidové umění*. Praha: Nakl. Českoslo. Akad Věd.

Chapter 14
On the Periphery of a Periphery: Slovak Anthropology behind the Ideological Veil

Juraj Podoba

Analysing the pasts of disciplines in the humanities is no easy task, especially when they are deeply embedded in national and regional traditions. This general difficulty is accentuated in the case of Central and Eastern Europe by the continuing effects of political repression. In the case of anthropology even the nomenclature of the field has long been muddled, and it has been rendered still more chaotic by borrowings from English terminology in recent years (for a discussion of the resulting inconsistencies see Podolák 2003). The history of science is always a cultural matter, but this applies with special force to the social sciences and humanities. It goes without saying that state ideology and politics are of fundamental importance.[1] However, it is also necessary to explore local social and cultural contexts.

It is clear that some of the similarities between developments in the countries of Central and Eastern Europe derived not from Marxism but from older intellectual traditions dating back to the nineteenth century. The exact functioning of Marxism-Leninism could vary even within one country, and it changed over time. The ideology might serve as a playground for dogmatists at one moment and as a veil to conceal pragmatism and romantic nostalgia in the next. The latter was the case in Slovakia between 1948 and 1989, when the real character of anthropology (národopis) was by and large disguised rather than impregnated with the political ideology. In the journal *Slovenský národopis* one was required to include ritual citations of Marx, Lenin, and

---

Note: This paper was prepared while I was a member of a Centre of Excellence of the Slovak Academy of Sciences investigating 'Collective Identities in Modern Societies: Central Europe'.

[1] For example, most of the papers presented at the international conference 'Polish Humanities in the Years 1945–1989', held in Warsaw in April 2004, emphasised the role of Marxism-Leninism. But it is easy to exaggerate the extent to which intellectuals fought for freedom and independence and to overlook the fact that working conditions were often rather comfortable and conducive to high-quality research.

even Engels, but there was no serious engagement with the philosophy underpinning the regime. How was it possible that developments in Slovakia showed so much more continuity than was possible in the Czech part of the country? The answer is to be found in the Slovaks' doubly peripheral position: developments here lagged behind developments in Prague, which were in turn followed models that originated in Germany.

The small, relatively isolated national intellectual traditions in this part of Europe make up a colourful mosaic in which highly local pursuits (*vlastiveda, Heimatkunde*, etc) often seem to carry more weight than the kind of anthropology taught nowadays in Western universities. These disciplines are suffused with nostalgic memories and national sentiment. In the German academic environment today, those who have transformed their discipline into *Europäische Ethnologie* refer to the activities which still flourish among their eastern neighbours as 'die gute alte Volkskunde'. As Josef Kandert (2002: 172–73) has shown for the Czech case after the Soviet occupation in 1968, the assumption of leading positions by orthodox communists led to a strengthening not of Marxism but of anthropology's traditional national orientation and to resistance to foreign influences and innovations of any sort. Following Kandert, I argue that Marxism-Leninism, far from transforming a positivist, descriptive discipline into a modern Marxist social science, instead conserved the Slovak variant of the 'gute alte Volkskunde'.

In Slovakia up to the beginning of the 1990s anthropology had a variety of names: národopis, etnografia, etnografia a folkloristika, and *národopisná veda* (ethnographic science).[2] In the Slovak professional discourse (unlike the Czech) these terms were treated largely as synonyms. This terminological idyll was interrupted only sporadically—for example, by those who insisted that folklore studies (folkloristika) was not just a part of etnografia/národopis but an independent discipline (see Kiliánová, this volume). To understand the socio-cultural context it is important to note that anthropological research in Slovakia was concentrated in just one university department and one research institute at the Slovak Academy of Sciences. It was an intimate community (cf. Vidacs, this volume, on the Hungarian case).[3]

---

[2] See Skalník, this volume. The term etnológia was used only in the title of the research institution (Kabinet etnológie) at Comenius University in Bratislava that was devoted to research into ethnic minorities and the relations between Slovak folk culture and the Slavs and other nations of Central and South-Eastern Europe. During the 1990s many other institutions took up the name etnológia, but this did not necessarily indicate any change in their activities (see Skalník 2002: 234; cf. Horváthová 1988, Podolák 2003).

[3] See also Bandić (1990) on his research colleagues in Serbia in the 1980s, whom he described as a primary group displaying highly personal bonds and commitments.

The Historical Background

Previous attempts to outline the history of Slovak národopis between 1948 and 1989 (Kiliánová 1993, Podolák 2003) have proceeded chronologically, listing scientific and cultural organisations, projects, and so forth, but they have neglected the discipline's intellectual and ideological foundations. The formative years of Slovak anthropology were very much shaped by the Czechs. Karel Chotek, a pupil of Lubor Niederle, became the first professor of národopis at the Comenius University in Bratislava in 1921. Other major figures in the inter-war period were Antonín Václavík, Vilém Pražák, and Jozef Vydra. Student interest was strong, but jobs for anthropologists were few (Michálek 1969). Národopis graduates usually ended up as schoolteachers. This was the case with Rudolf Bednárik and Ján Mjartan, who went on to play important roles in the discipline's professionalisation in the 1940s.

Thus, thanks mainly to Karel Chotek and his Slovak students, anthropology in Slovakia was launched in an atmosphere still soaked in the Bohemian nationalism of the 1890s and in an idealised enthusiasm for the common people of the countryside. The more remote antecedents of Slovak národopis are to be found in German historicism. The 'awakeners' (*buditelia*) of the Slovak nation resembled those of other late-developing national movements.[4] As Ernest Gellner has argued, such intellectuals were in reality creating the nations which they claimed to be reviving. One of the means they used was the codification of the folk culture, in order to preserve it for posterity as the essence of the nation. In doing so they necessarily depicted it as a unity and not merely as an accidental cluster of atomistic features (Gellner 1994: 99).

The importance of this legacy for Slovak národopis was summarised by Rudolf Bednárik in the introduction to his 1942 *Handbook*, the first theoretical text written by a Slovak anthropologist (Bednárik 1942: 3–79). Bednárik's theoretical views were deeply rooted in the German intellectual tradition; his most frequently quoted authors were Pater Wilhelm Schmidt, Wilhelm Mühlmann, and Chotek. The book was also intensely patriotic: the 'magnificent task' of Slovak národopis could be undertaken only by a native; the 'Slovak folk culture ... has its own life, its own soul, its own development, its own mission, all comprehensible only to a Slovak' (Bednárik 1942: 4, 8). The discipline of národopis was to concentrate on the lower socio-economic strata because they had conserved old ways of life. There was indeed some truth in this, because large areas of the Slovak countryside still exhibited many elements of a pre-industrial culture when Chotek and his

---

[4] See Breuilly (1993: 54–71) for a discussion of the relationship between national ideology and the state in this period.

students investigated them during the inter-war decades. Field research was oriented not towards the ongoing transformations of this culture but towards archaisms and survivals.[5]

Vilém Pražák's address to the 1946 annual meeting of the národopis group within the patriotic association Matica Slovenská, published in *Národopisný sborník* (Pražák 1947), sketched a more concrete research programme for the emerging discipline. Only four years after the publication of Bednárik's *Handbook*, the emphasis now shifted to 'saving the folk culture'. This was a more realistic appraisal of the modernisation processes which were gathering force in the country as a whole, even before the impact of socialist industrialisation and the collectivisation of agriculture. Pražák also helped to design an institutional base for Slovak národopis, based on Czech prototypes. He assigned priority to the publication of 'monumental works', though in the build-up to such works the Matica Slovenská association would also publish monographs dealing with particular regions or specific branches of folk art (Pražák 1947: 15). This way of thinking can be read as a charter for the Slovak národopis of the following four decades.

The Paradoxes of Socialist-Era Národopis

In line with Pražák's address, Slovak národopis scholars produced plenty of monographs rooted in a 'salvage' approach to what they considered to be 'folk culture'.[6] It was a positivist programme which involved the gathering of material through collective field trips, followed by its classification and typologisation. Yet it also remained a romantic, even an aesthetic project. Gradually, from the 1960s onwards, more attention was paid to everyday culture and to the effects of stratification and social processes. But no significant theoretical or methodological development took place in intellectual thinking within the discipline. Slovak anthropologists had not yet taken on board the basic precept that an ethnographer must approach culture in its wholeness (Malinowski 1922).

The most important legacy from German Volkskunde was the preoccupation with one's own group and with ethnic theory. The latter was introduced into Slovak intellectual discourse by Czech forerunners and teachers who were motivated above all by anti-German sentiments. Later, when

---

[5] I thank Ján Mjartan and Vojtech Budínsky-Krička for sharing their memories of the collective summer fieldwork trips organised by Karel Chotek and later by Ján Mjartan. Budínsky-Krička used the method of participant observation during his study of the village of Liptovské Revúce (central Slovakia). Disillusioned with Chotek's insistence on collective fieldwork, he turned away from anthropology and became the 'founding father' of Slovak archaeology.

[6] New 'ethnocartographic' methods developed from the 1960s onwards did not modify this approach in any fundamental way.

Bruno Schier, a leading representative of German ethnic theory, became professor at the university in Bratislava, this influence became more direct (see Frolec 1976, 1983; Podoba 2000). For Slovak národopis, ethnic origin became the basis for interpretations of folk culture, and indeed of 'everything'. Ethnic theory was not a problem from the perspective of Marxist-Leninist ideology, because it fitted with Stalinist theories of nation, too. As elsewhere in Eastern Europe, in the 1950s Slovak anthropologists were required to follow the example of Soviet etnografiya (see Melicherčík 1951). In 1950 Andrej Melicherčík published a new programme for the discipline, one that conformed to the conditions of socialist society (Melicherčík 1950: 25–36). But národopis in Slovakia (unlike in Prague; see Scheffel and Kandert 2002) was not severely affected by the ideological deformations that were typical of Stalin's last years.

I do not wish to maintain that nothing at all changed or that no critical discussion took place within the Slovak národopis community. Two conferences held in Smolenice in 1964 and 1966, devoted, respectively, to 'the history of folk culture' and 'the influence of industrialism on folk culture', offered new, sometimes original and even inspiring perspectives on the changing object of ethnographic research. East-Central European historicist traditions were radically challenged—for example, by Emília Horváthová, who wanted to expand the focus beyond the established notion of folk culture. Milan Leščák (1966: 369–80) also critiqued theoretical stagnation and called into question the basic concepts of ľud and ľudová kultúra. Yet despite these questioning voices, no alternative conceptions were put forward. The opportunity for a genuine paradigm shift was not taken—because, perhaps, of the conservatism of the Slovak národopis community, the dislocation caused by the Soviet invasion of 1968, or both factors together.

One of the fields in which the discipline was supposed to break new ground in these decades was that of the 'contemporary collectivised village'. This research programme was modelled on Soviet examples (Mjartan 1952). Staff of the newly established institute of the Slovak Academy of Sciences carried out fieldwork in three villages in western, central, and eastern Slovakia. Although the ostensible aim was to study contemporary sociocultural processes during socialist collectivisation, no data on these processes were ever published, and the actual main outcome was a very traditional 'reconstructionist' monograph about the region of Horehronie.

Much the same happened when anthropological investigation into the culture of the industrial working classes was introduced into the discipline as a consequence of the theories of historical materialism. Slovak národopisci were expected to follow the examples provided by their Czech colleagues who produced monographs on mining communities (see Skalníková, this volume). However, as Leščák (1966: 373) pointed out, 'anthropologists (národopisci) in Slovakia have avoided the [urban] industrial zone and instead stayed at home—in the village'.[7]

During the 1970s, many scholars in Moravia espoused the 'ethnography of the present' (*etnografia súčasnosti*). They conducted long-term field research in the countryside, organised symposia in Strážnice, and published a series of volumes under the general title 'Folk Culture and the Present' (*Lidová kultura a současnost*). Slovak národopisci were influenced by this research and applied similar methods in studying the Slovak village of Sebechleby. From 1982 onwards, 'ethnography of the present' featured officially in the project 'Integration of Progressive Traditions of Folk Culture into the System of Socialist Culture and the Lives of Working People' (*Včleňovanie pokrokových tradícii ľudovej kultúry do systému socialistickej kultúry a života pracujúcich*). As the complicated title suggests, investigations of socialist settlements were subject to many limitations. The focus here was once again exclusively rural, and ideological insistence on studying 'progressive traditions of the folk culture' hindered any possible methodological or theoretical innovation. But the more serious problem lay in the ideology of the discipline, with its obsessive romantic pursuit of the traditional in the present. Socialist society was becoming increasingly complex, industrialised, and urbanised, yet in spite of some original empirical contributions giving insights into the reality of socialist rural society, the 'ethnography of the present' brought no substantial theoretical breakthrough.

The 1980s also saw some discussion of a new urban anthropology.[8] Národopis in the city could no longer base itself on the national tradition; it was obliged to accept multiculturalism. Yet Slovak anthropologists were so wedded to the idealism of národopis that they developed a kind 'urban romanticism' (see Salner 1991). They locked themselves into a specific time cage, that of the inter-war Czechoslovak republic. Data collection and analysis drew on published memoirs as well as archival documents and oral history methods. There were some new elements here, but they were hardly enough to amount to methodological innovation or to instigate new theoretical discussions.

---

[7] One village monograph was produced, *The Mining Village of Žakarovce* (Mjartan et al. 1956).

[8] It was not yet named as such. The designation *urbánna etnológia* emerged only in the early 1990s.

Conclusion

I have suggested that the small size of the národopis community in Slovakia, its late development, and its peripheral status vis-à-vis the Czech discipline (itself peripheral in relation to the German, and later in relation to that of the Soviet Union) all help to explain the high degree of continuity we find behind the veil of Marxism-Leninism. Only a few individuals deviated from the mainstream, beginning in the later 1960s. One significant figure is Zora Apáthyová-Rusnáková (1975, 1984a, 1984b, 1999; see Podoba 2002). Emília Horváthová (1973a, 1973b, 1980, 1982), Adam Pranda (1970, 1975, 1978, 1978-79, 1981) and Milan Leščák (1982, 1991a, 1991b) also tried to develop the theory and methodology of the discipline, though the isolation of the periphery and the lack of interest among colleagues made this very difficult. Soňa Švecová studied in Budapest, where she was inspired by the historicism of leading Hungarian néprajz scholars in the 1960s (Švecová 1975, 1984). Combining their approaches with the methods of social anthropology, as these were debated in Prague in the years before 1968, her work offered a significant alternative to mainstream Slovak národopis. Jiří Langer was another original scholar, whose understanding of folk culture and how to study it led to original analyses of the western Carpathian region (Langer 1984, 1987, 1997; see Podoba 1999).

Dušan Kováč has identified three almost self-evident discontinuities in twentieth-century Slovak historiography: after 1919, 1953, and 1989, the priorities for the writing of history were radically redefined (Kováč 2004: 234). Národopis presents us with quite a different case, not only because in 1919 it did not yet exist as a professional discipline but also because anthropologists were never obliged to revise their theories and methods to the extent required of historians. Their marginality was undoubtedly an advantage in this respect. This does not mean that they were free to do what they pleased; censorship was still enforced in the late 1980s. The taboos on particular problems remained clearly defined, and few individuals dared to break them. Like other humanities subjects under socialism, národopis, too, was distorted by the 'community of fear', as it was called by an influential dissident (Šimečka 2003).

Although every discipline has a tendency to mythologise its history, and a certain myth of resistance against the socialist regime has developed in the národopis community, the reality is that anthropologists never experienced a genuine rupture. They were never subjected to pressures to change their methodological foundations and epistemologies or even to adopt a different interpretation of 'folk culture'. No competing schools ever emerged. As Milan Leščák pointed out, 'a boom in the theory from the end of the 1960s was indisputable. There have been many courageous, sometimes original attempts, deriving from related scientific disciplines. However, there are only a few works which follow up on these attempts and stabilise them. Too often we start as if from the beginning' (Leščák 1988: 106–7).

Given this history, it should come as no surprise that the continuity maintained under socialism was able to reproduce itself after the rupture of 1989. Thus the very title of the *Encyclopaedia of Slovak Folk Culture*, published in 1995, shows that the preoccupation with folk culture continues. The methodological trap formed under the influence of German historicism persisted during four long decades.[9] Whereas anthropological institutions in Prague in the 1950s and 1960s were regularly marked by cleavages based on generation or on differences of opinion, the peripheral conditions of Slovakia promoted greater unison. When the Soviet invasion devastated the Czech academic environment (less so in Moravia, which in many respects resembled Slovakia), anthropologists in Bratislava were able to continue business more or less as usual. The signs of intellectual revitalisation of the earlier 1960s were extinguished, and instead Slovak anthropologists were condemned to decades of inertia. During these last years of socialism the main projects at the institute of the Academy of Sciences were a regional monograph on Hont County (Botík 1988) and two large-scale synthetic works, the *Ethnographic Atlas of Slovakia* and the previously mentioned *Encyclopaedia of Slovak Folk Culture*. Individuals who sought to counter the sterility fostered by these genres were unwelcome in the národopis community.[10]

The upshot was that, after 40 years of Marxism, Slovak anthropology at the end of the 1980s was no more Marxist than it had been in the 1930s and 1940s. The basic characteristics had not changed since the discipline's formative years under the influence of the German intellectual tradition, mediated through the Czech academic environment. The socio-cultural context of socialist institutions, characterised by an absence of critical discussion, created ideal conditions for the persistence of the romantic nationalist paradigm based on the concept of 'folk culture'. That socio-cultural context and the staff who fill it have changed only slowly since the political revolution of 1989. Closer attention to this context can help us to understand the ambiguities and controversies which continue to impede progress in the reform of Slovak národopis.

---

[9] There has, however, been a 'quiet transformation' (Bitušíková 2002) which is evident, for example, in the introduction of new terminology from Western anthropology. The drawback of this is the lack of coordination and the continuing failure to debate matters of theory and epistemology.
[10] Such persons were not generally prevented from publishing their work in journals, though in a few cases even this proved impossible and publication had to wait until the 1990s.

References

Apáthyová-Rusnáková, Z. 1975. Metodologická úvaha nad poznávacou situáciou slovenskej etnografie. *Slovenský národopis* 23: 11–114.

——. 1984a. Tradičné a netradičné ako súčasť etnokultúrneho systému (Na príklade javov ľudového obyčajového práva). *Národopisné informácie* 2: 48–54.

——. 1984b. Pokus o riešenie štruktúry hodnôt a meranie hodnotových orientácií (Rodinný stôl—na základe materiálov z prípravy EAS). *Národopisné informácie* 3: 108–35.

——. 1999. Znakový sytém: Sonda o charakteru ľudovej kultúry (Na materiáli kostolného zasadacieho poriadku). *Etnologické rozpravy* 1: 37–76.

Bandić, D. 1990. K výskumu hodnotových orientácií vedeckej ustanovizne ako špecifickej spoločenskej skupiny. *Slovenský národopis* 38: 1–2, 11–116.

Bednárik, R. 1942. *Príručka pre národopisný výskum slovenského ľudu.* Turčiansky Sv. Martin: Matica Slovenská.

Bitušíková, A. 2002. Anthropology as a Taboo: A Few Comments on Anthropology in Slovakia. In P. Skalník (ed.), *A Post-Communist Millennium: The Struggles for Sociocultural Anthropology in Central and Eastern Europe*, pp. 141–46. Prague: Set Out.

Botík, J. 1988. *Hont: Tradície ľudovej kultúry.* Martin: Vyd. Osveta.

Breuilly, J. 1993. *Nationalism and the State.* Manchester: Manchester University Press.

Frolec, V. 1976. Etnická teorie a interetnické vztahy při studiu lidového stavitelství. *Slovenský národopis* 23: 132–48.

——. 1983. Etnická teorie. In V. Frolec and J. Vařeka (eds.), *Lidová architektura: Encyklopedie*, p. 55. Praha: SNTL, Alfa.

Gellner, E. 1994. Čo teraz potrebujeme? Sociálna antropológia a jej nový globálny kontext. *Text* 1: 97–103.

Horváthová, E. 1973a. Hlavné smery a činnosti Národopisného ústavu SAV od založenia Slovenskej akadémie vied. *Slovenský národopis* 21 (1): 169–81.

——. 1973b. Teoretické otázky súčasnej etnografie. *Slovenský národopis* 21 (3): 311–16.

——. 1980. K výskumu národností na Slovensku. *Národopisné informácie* 3: 1–5.

——. 1982. K teoretickým aspektom problematiky tradície. *Slovenský národopis* 30 (1): 45–59.

——. 1988. Tradition as a Complex of Theoretico-Methodological Problems. *Ethnologia Slavica* 20: 15–31.

Kandert, J. 2002. Poznámky k dějinám národopisu/etnografie v českých zemích: Soupeření 'etnografie' s 'etnologií'. In M. Holubová, L. Petráňová, and J. Woitsch (eds.), *Česká etnologie 2000*, pp. 157–78. Praha: Etnologický ústav AV ČR.

Kiliánová, G. 1993. Volkskunde in der Slowakei: Ein Überblick. *Österreichische Zeitschrift für Volkskunde* 47 (96): 1–16.

Kováč, D. 2004. O slovenskej historiografii v Collegium Carolinum. *Historický časopis* 52 (2): 233–37.

Langer, J. 1984. Proletarizace horských agrárních prostředí na východní Moravě. *Český lid* 71: 200–208.

———. 1987. Příspěvek k typologii topenišť. *Archaeologia historica* 12: 233–43.

———. 1997. *Co mohou prozradit lidové stavby: Lidové stavební tradice v severozápadních Karpatech a jejich kulturní funkce*. Rožnov pod Radhoštěm: Ready.

Leščák, M. 1966. Úvahy o predmete národopisného bádania. *Slovenský národopis* 14 (4): 369–80.

———. 1982. Včleňovanie progresívnych tradícií ľudovej kultúry do systému socialistickej kultúry a života pracujúcich. *Slovenský národopis* 30 (1): 6–16.

———. 1988. Úvaha o súčasnom národopise. *Národopisné informácie* 1: 105–10.

———. 1991a. The Beginnings of Functional Structuralism in Slovak Ethnology. *Slovenský národopis* 39 (3–4): 336–47.

———. 1991b. Horizonty súčasného slovenského národopisu (od etnológie cez etnografiu, ľudovedu, národopis k etnológii). *Múzeum* 2: 1–5.

Malinowski, B. 1922. *Argonauts of the Western Pacific*. London: Routledge.

Melicherčík, A. 1950. Československá etnografia a niektoré jej úlohy pri výstavbe socializmu. *Národopisný sborník SAVU* 9: 25–36.

———. 1951. Sovietska etnografia: náš vzor. *Národopisný sborník SAVU* 10: 5–23.

Michálek, J. 1969. Národopis na Univerzite Komenského. *Slovenský národopis* 17: 185–91.

Mjartan, J. 1952. Niektoré otázky národopisného výskumu družstevnej dediny. *Národopisný sborník SAVU* 11: 5–17.

———, et al. 1956. *Banícka dedina Žakarovce*. Bratislava: Vydavateľstvo SAV.

Podoba, J. 1999. Čo prezrádzajú ľudové stavby severozápadných Karpát. *Slovenský národopis* 47 (1): 111–23.

——. 2000. Etnicita v materiálnej kultúre: Realita alebo ideologický koncept? In E. Krekovič (ed.), *Etnos a materiálna kultúra*, pp. 20–39. Bratislava: STIMUL.

——. 2002. Zorka Rusnáková jubiluje. *Slovenský národopis* 50 (2): 228–31.

Podolák, J. 2003. Etnológia na Slovensku v 20. storočí: Etapy jej vývoja. *Ethnologia Actualis Slovaca* 3: 9–58.

Pranda, A. 1970. Niektoré teoretické otázky štúdia ľudovej kultúry v súčasnosti. *Slovenský národopis* 18 (1): 39–57.

——. 1975. K problematike chápania a zamerania národopisného výskumu súčasnosti. *Slovenský národopis* 23 (4): 581–601.

——. 1978. Formovanie nového systému hodnotových orientácií na súčasnej slovenskej dedine. *Slovenský národopis* 26 (2): 235–48.

——. 1978–79. The Process of Building Up Socialism as Reflected in Value Orientations of the Slovak Village. *Ethnologia Slavica* 10–11: 119–31.

——. 1981. Zmeny myslenia a postojov človeka na súčasnej slovenskej dedine. *Národopisné informácie* 3: 39–48.

Pražák, V. 1947. Úkoly a organisace slovenského národopisu v přítomné době. *Národopisný sborník SAVU* 8 (1): 1–21.

Salner, P. (ed.). 1991. *Taká bola Bratislava*. Bratislava: Veda.

Scheffel, D., and J. Kandert. 2002. Politika a kultura v české etnografii. In M. Holubová, L. Petráňová, and J. Woitsch (eds.), *Česká etnologie 2000*, pp. 213–29. Praha: Etnologický ústav AV ČR.

Skalník, P. 2002. Komentář k článku Davida Scheffela a Josefa Kanderta 'Politika a kultura v české etnografii'. In M. Holubová, L. Petráňová, and J. Woitsch (eds.), *Česká etnologie 2000*, pp. 231–34. Praha: Etnologický ústav AV ČR.

Šimečka, M. 2003. *Společenství strachu a jiné eseje*. Bratislava: Nadácia Milana Šimečku.

Švecová, S. 1975. *Kopanicové sídla a dedina*. Praha: Universita Karlova.

——. 1984. *Lazy v 19. a 20. storočí. Vývoj roľníckych chotárnych sídiel v oblasti Krupinskej planiny*. Praha: Universita Karlova.

Chapter 15
Continuity and Discontinuity in an Intellectual Tradition under Socialism: The 'Folkloristic School' in Bratislava

Gabriela Kiliánová

Folklore has long been one of the most important orientations of anthropological research in Slovakia, and the study of storytelling, song, customs, dance, and theatre as living cultural phenomena retained its importance under socialism. Folklore was regarded as a part of current popular or everyday culture, to be investigated in its social context and alongside other cultural phenomena. Folklore research was grounded in fieldwork and employed both qualitative methods (participant observation, interviews, recordings) and quantitative ones (questionnaires, statistical data). Under socialism, Slovak folkloristics (folkloristika) was established on a scientific basis as part of národopis. Institutionally, however, it evolved towards the status of an independent discipline and earned both academic recognition and attention from the wider public. Bratislava's folkloristic school reveals implicit continuity with Slovak (and Czechoslovak) interdisciplinary theoretical traditions of the 1930s, the so-called functional-structural method. Yet the 1950s brought a clear break with previous intellectual traditions. Anthropology (národopis, made up of etnografia and folkloristika) was now understood as an historical science based on dialectical and historical materialism. Members of the folkloristic school in Bratislava played a leading role in this theoretical discourse from the 1950s to the 1980s.

In this chapter I consider the Bratislava school from five points of view:

- As an important current within Slovak anthropology during the socialist period, productive both empirically and in its contributions to theory and methodology

- As an interesting example of continuity and discontinuity in the development of a scientific tradition in a society experiencing radical political and social change

- As a school which, during the socialist period, drew strongly on intellectual influences from Eastern Europe but combined these at times with Western European sources, a combination which generated positive scientific synergies

- As a school which received systematic institutional support due to the political and ideological situation of the time, support that extended to university teaching, research institutes, and special projects

- As a group of talented personages whose creativity rendered the discipline vibrant and attractive and whose lives and research illustrate both the challenges and the restrictions and contradictions of the era

I concentrate on the situation in the central research and educational institutions: the Institute of Anthropology (Národopisný ústav) of the Slovak Academy of Sciences and the Department of Anthropology at the Comenius University in Bratislava. It should be noted that in Slovakia, as elsewhere in the region, the nomenclature of the discipline has changed several times during the twentieth century. Národopis was the usual term in the inter-war period, although the term etnografia was not unknown; in the 1940s, the latter came to be understood primarily as the description of the results of field research (Melicherčík 1945). After 1948, under Soviet influence, the term etnografia was promoted in new ways in Czechoslovakia (see Skalník, this volume). The term národopis nonetheless survived in the scientific vocabulary as an umbrella term uniting etnografia and folkloristika.

Slovak Národopis, 1918–1947

Both before and after the founding of the Czechoslovak Republic in 1918, Slovak society was exposed to far-reaching economic, political, social, and ideological changes in processes of nation-building that were rendered unusually complex by the special relationship with the Czechs. Anthropology was viewed as a component of homeland studies (*Heimatkunde*), its mission being to promote the concept of Slovak folk culture as the basis of national culture and thereby of national identity. The establishment of the Czechoslovak state and the construction of a new state identity complicated the task of constructing a Slovak cultural nation: some saw these processes as entirely compatible, but for others they were contradictory. In any case,

Slovak anthropologists after 1918 oriented their studies almost exclusively towards Slovaks and took virtually no interest in the country's minority groups, such as the Hungarians, Ruthenians, Germans, and Roma. Research was concentrated mainly on material culture and until the mid-1930s it was characterised by a theoretical eclecticism (Melicherčík 1945).

The effects of structuralism on the Czech and Slovak social sciences and humanities were substantial. Structuralism was introduced by members of the Prague Linguistic Circle and the Union for Scientific Synthesis in Bratislava, notably Roman Jakobson (1896–1982) and Pyotr Grigoryevich Bogatyriov (1893–1971; also known Petr Bogatyrev). The latter developed a functional-structural methodology as part of his broader, inter-disciplinary perspective (Bogatyriov 1935). It was derived from the principles of Saussure's synchronic linguistics and from the Russian formalist school. Bogatyriov argued that studying the whole structure of the culture of a society would reveal its origin and social developmental processes. Transformations and changes in culture and society were rigorously explained in terms of relations between structures and functions (Bogatyriov 1935: 558).

Bogatyriov's works (1929, 1935, 1937, 1940) and his teaching at the Comenius University in Bratislava (1936–39) paved the way for the adoption of functional-structural methodology in Slovak anthropology. His pupils in Bratislava, Andrej Melicherčík (1917–66) and Soňa Kovačevičová (b. 1921), were the country's avant-garde anthropologists in the 1940s (Leščák 1991: 343–45). Melicherčík propagated the new methodology in his important work *Teória národopisu* (1945), which was put to use especially in the study of folk art and folklore (see also Melicherčík 1945–46a, 1945–46b, 1947a, 1947b; Kovačevičová-Žuffová 1945–46, 1947). The emphasis given to contemporary cultural phenomena allows us to speak of an 'anthropologisation' of research; similar processes were occurring in neighbouring countries, such as in the study of storytelling in the 1930s in Hungary (Dégh 1962, 1977; Sárkány 1978: 295).

Anthropology's institutional basis was relatively well developed in the pre-socialist period. From 1921 národopis was taught as a subject in its own right at the Comenius University (by Karel Chotek, a Czech). The Folklore Department of Matica Slovenská was also very active in these decades.[1] The Slovak Academy of Sciences and Arts was founded in 1943, and its Institute of Anthropology (Národopisný ústav), in 1946 (Filová 1995: 398; Urbancová 1995: 126; Michálek and Podolák 1995: 232).

---

[1] The cultural and scientific institute Matica Slovenská—literally, 'Slovak Mother'—was founded in 1863 in the central Slovak town of Turčiansky Svätý Martin. It was closed because of Hungarian political pressure in 1875 but was re-established in 1919 in the new Czechoslovak Republic.

From 1948 to the Mid-1950s

After the communist take-over in February 1948, the political and ideological situation changed rapidly, with far-reaching consequences for the humanities and social sciences. Marxism-Leninism was adopted as the leading philosophy, and historical materialism was supposed to dictate methodology. It fell to Andrej Melicherčík to attempt to explain the application of the new methodology in Slovak ethnology. In his article 'Czechoslovak Ethnography and Some of Its Tasks in the Building of Socialism' (1950) he criticised theoretical developments in the discipline before 1948, including formalism, structuralism, idealistic evolutionism, and anti-historicism. As a well-known representative of the functionally-structural method, he practised self-criticism and distanced himself from his earlier works, especially his 1945 book, *A Theory of Ethnography (Národopis)* (Melicherčík 1950: 31).

In the same paper, Melicherčík also outlined the theoretical framework and research aims of etnografia, carefully avoiding the use of the term národopis. He defined the object of ethnographic research as the people (*l'ud*) 'in its historical process of genesis and development. The task of ethnographic research is the study of the life and culture of the people, regardless of its stage of development'. Etnografia was to be understood 'according to the line of dialectical and historical materialism and the resulting general principles of the development of nature and of human society' (Melicherčík 1950: 29–30). The new historicism was to be consistently materialist. 'This means that the study of the material world [*javová skutočnost*] in its origin, development, and decline will proceed in conjunction with analysis of the specific historical conditions which created it, that is, in conjunction with the development of the means of production and of production relations' (Melicherčík 1950: 30). According to Melicherčík, the most important research topics for the new discipline in Czechoslovakia were the ethnogenesis of the Czechs and Slovaks since the earliest settlement of the territory now belonging to Czechoslovakia, the differentiation of the national cultural heritage along the lines of class, and the study of folklore and folk culture as progressive elements in a new future culture. He expected Czechoslovak etnografia to contribute to 'the construction of a consistent class consciousness and Marxist insight into folk culture' (Melicherčík 1950: 35).

In the following year Melicherčík edited a selection of recent Soviet anthropological papers in the Slovak Academy of Sciences journal *Národopisný sborník SAVU*. His programmatic introduction opened with a two-page eulogy of the Soviet Union and the achievements of Soviet science: 'Soviet science is not one among many sciences. To date it is the only science built on a Marxist-Leninist foundation' (Melicherčík 1952: 6). He also used a quotation from Stalin: 'Marxist-Leninist science is materialist not conceptually, but starting from the real reality, and continuing through real reality, it verifies and so finally leads to real knowledge. It is the only possible real science' (Stalin 1950: 78–79).[2] Soviet anthropologists were praised for their consistent historicism, which had led them to study all peoples as dynamic entities in history, thereby overcoming the widespread tendency of bourgeois anthropologists to divide peoples into historical nations, *Kulturvölker* (*kultúrne národy*), on the one hand, and 'natural peoples', *Naturvölker* (*prírodné národy*), on the other.

According to Melicherčík, Soviet colleagues had exposed 'the reactionary foundations of English functionalism and the functional-structural method'. The works of Malinowski, Radcliffe-Brown, and others were founded on 'a reactionary theory which serves the class interests of imperialism' (Melicherčík 1951: 19). The Soviet authors represented in Melicherčík's edited volume covered general questions of anthropology, the history of Russian and Soviet anthropology, questions of ethnogenesis, colonial anthropology, Soviet anthropology under socialism (working-class culture and folk culture on collective farms), and museology (Čeboksarov 1951; Maslovová 1951; Potapov 1951a, 1951b; Potechin 1951a, 1951b; Sergejev 1951; Tokarev 1951a, 1951b, 1951c; Tokarev and Čeboksarov 1951; Tolstov 1951a, 1951b, 1951c).

In his 1950 article, Melicherčík clearly stated the future research themes and methods to be adopted by Slovak researchers in the 1950s. Together with his introduction to the 1951 volume of Soviet works, the paper is a good example of how a political situation can transform a scholar's work. It is not only the contents of the article that surprise the reader (especially one who knows Melicherčík's earlier works); politics also leaves its mark on the vocabulary, structure, and language of the text, which is aggressive in tone and uses emotionally loaded words instead of arguments. The author sometimes employs irony, but his scathing criticism of so-called bourgeois anthropology is sometimes so sweeping that it is hard to know exactly which authors or works are meant (see, for example, Melicherčík 1950: 30). Both the 1950 and 1951 articles were too schematic, normative, and dogmatic to succeed in establishing a new theoretical orientation. They differed markedly from the logical and well-constructed articles that

---

[2] From the 1950s until the 1970s, similar passages punctuate large numbers of works in the humanities and social sciences. Quotations from Stalin were later replaced by citations of leading Czechoslovak politicians and the resolutions of congresses of the Communist Party of Czechoslovakia, the Soviet Union, and others. See, for example, the journal *Slovenský národopis*, vol. 9 (1961), no. 4.

Melicherčík and his colleagues had published before 1948 (e.g. Kovačevi-čová-Žuffová 1945–46, 1947; Kolečányi 1947).

How were the new doctrines applied in research? Melicherčík and his students investigated 'the historical revolutionary traditions of our people'—for example, by researching the tradition of romantic heroes such as Juraj Jánošík (Melicherčík 1952).[3] Here he proceeded from the thesis that 'elements of the revolutionary ideology also appear in the struggle of the downtrodden masses and find their expression in folklore: songs, stories, and proverbs' (1952: 11). From this perspective he analysed a wealth of data concerning the outlaw theme, which he sought to locate in precise historical context.

This work surfed on the folklore wave which, in the early years of socialism, saw the founding of numerous folklore groups and strong support for folk art and folklorism in general. However, Melicherčík's work can also be read as a defence of folkloristics as a scientific endeavour. Paradoxically, in this very period of the folklore boom, národopis came under intense attack in Slovakia. It was declared a bourgeois nationalist science, and the academy institute was dissolved in 1951. Some of its staff were dismissed, and other researchers and facilities were incorporated into the Institute of History. Melicherčík was the head of department at this time. When the institute was dissolved, he returned to the university, where he had been Pyotr Bogatyriov's assistant before the war. The národopis seminar remained part of the Department of Historical Science in the 1950s. (An independent národopis department was not established at the Comenius University until 1969 [Michálek and Podolák 1995: 233]). The Národopisný ústav within the newly established Slovak Academy of Sciences was re-established after a three-year hiatus in 1955, with Ján Mjartan as its director (Filová 1995: 398).

From the Mid-1950s to the End of the 1960s

At the beginning of 1958 the writer Vladimír Mináč published the article 'Tíha folkloru' (The burden of folklore) in the Czech literary weekly *Literární noviny*, in which he sharply criticised the omnipresence of folk music and folklore groups in the media and in cultural life. A lively discussion followed in the journal *Kultúrny život* (Cultural life) and in *Pravda* (the newspaper of the Slovak Communist Party), with contributions from many academics and leading figures in the field of culture (Bžoch 1958; Čečetka 1958; Horanská 1958; Kaliský 1958; Krno 1958; Mrlian 1958; Slivka 1958; Šimút 1958; Števček 1958). Andrej Melicherčík (1958) and his colleagues

---

[3] Jánošík (1688–1713) was a robber and folk hero, commemorated both in the romantic national literary tradition and in popular culture.

and pupils Ján Michálek (1958) and Svetozár Švehlák (1958) were prominent in these exchanges, which show how the term folklore was understood at the time by the wider public: it encompassed folklore groups and festivals and folklore as a national art form, but also folklore as a rural art form, tied to backward groups. The academics attempted more or less successfully to present a broad, colourful picture of folklore as cultural heritage and as a living cultural phenomenon. Despite some ambivalence in the results, this flurry of debate was genuinely open and relatively free, indicating a liberalisation in both politics and the academic atmosphere.

The institutional basis of Slovak anthropology stabilised in the second half of the 1950s, and research activity moved up a gear. The Slovak Národopis Society (Slovenská národopisná spoločnosť pri SAV) was founded in 1958, and a year later Andrej Melicherčík and his colleague Ján Michálek launched a field research project lasting several years, in the course of which they collected stories, songs, and other data concerning the Second World War and the Slovak national uprising. Together with field investigations of the culture and social life of collectivised farmers (begun in the mid-1950s), this project showed how the discipline could address contemporary phenomena and their social functions (Melicherčík 1961; Gašparíková 1963; Burlasová 1964). This research already represented a quiet deviation from officially dominant historical methods.

Discussion of contemporary research came into the open in 1966 with the seminar 'The Effects of Industrialisation on Folk Culture'. Melicherčík (1966) gave the main paper, following which his younger colleagues Ľubica Droppová (1966) and Milan Leščák (1966) opened a debate on field research methods and aims. In a lively discussion, Melicherčík returned to basic questions concerning the objects of etnografia and folkloristika. He reflected on culture as Malinowski used the concept, demanding a broad anthropological view of 'man' as the creator of culture (see Leščák 1969: 377). Melicherčík's participation at this seminar was his last public appearance. He died two months later during field research, at the age of 49. His early death silenced the voice of a sharp intellectual who was fully aware that he had changed his ideological views, theoretical premises, research themes, and teaching activity, and of the grounds for this shift, namely, coercion. He was nevertheless influential in educating and shaping a new generation of scholars, among them Ľubica Droppová, Milan Leščák, Viera Gašparíková, and Soňa Burlasová.

The end of the 1960s saw a more dramatic phase of liberalisation in Czechoslovak society. At the beginning of 1968, Milan Leščák and Viera Nosáľová (1968) organised a general survey of their colleagues concerning topical methodological questions, concepts, and the organisation of research.

The results were published in an issue of the periodical *Slovenský národopis* (1968, no. 4: 519–42). Differences are apparent between the concepts favoured by the more practically oriented field researchers, those adhering to an historical approach, and those calling for a dynamic, processual social science. A conference followed in December 1968 in which the aims, methods, and theory of the discipline were all called into question.

Milan Leščák (1969) reviewed the ways in which the categories of historical materialism had been applied in anthropology and concluded that, especially in the 1950s, scholars had been dealing with a pseudo-scientific 'dogma', even if it was declared to be Marxist. He summarised recent international trends, criticised the isolationism of the Slovak discipline, and called for a cultural anthropological approach. When it came to defining the object of research, Leščák argued initially that it must be the general principles governing the development of human culture. He later modified this and specified folklore research in Slovakia in the 1930s and the legacy of the functional-structural method. In doing so he brought highly topical problems to light in a precise and fruitful way. In addition to openly criticising some pseudo-Marxist works from the 1950s, Leščák formulated convincing arguments for a general reorientation of anthropological research (1969: 372).

The end of the 1960s also brought a discussion of newly translated works by the French structuralists Roland Barthes (1967) and Claude Lévi-Strauss (1966, 1969). Scholars of the inter-war generation such as Mária Koléčanyi-Kosová, who had been dismissed from the Academy of Sciences institute in the 1950s, were now able to submit their dissertations for the degree of candidate of science in the area of folkloristika, and their works were strongly influenced by French structuralist anthropology (Kolečányi-Kosová 1973). In these years folkloristika achieved equal status with etnografia. It was taught separately at the university, and a folkloristic section was established at the academy institute in 1970. Its first head was Milan Leščák.

From 1970 to 1990

The so-called normalisation process in Czechoslovak society opened in 1970 with the political persecution of intellectuals, a new wave of emigration, and a sharpening of the authoritarian character of the regime. Discussion of semiotics and research into sign systems and symbolism continued nevertheless to develop in Slovak anthropology, especially in the branch of folkloristika. In the mid-1970s Leščák launched a series of seminars for young researchers at the academy institute, where old and new ideas were discussed. They included the study of folklore as a special form of cultural communication in small social groups, under the influence of the works of

Václav Lamser (1969) and later Edmund Leach (1983). The principles of fieldwork and research into contemporary 'everyday culture' (*každodenná kultúra*) were also recurrent topics of discussion.[4]

In the late 1970s and throughout the 1980s, three generations of researchers worked alongside each other in the field of folkloristics at the university and at the academy institute. The folkloristic section at the academy had 12 members, 8 of them under 35 years of age. They produced five new doctoral theses based on empirical data from their own fieldwork, which was subject to interpretation using a variety of theoretical models (Krekovičová 1981; Luther 1983; Profantová 1988; Hlôšková 1990; Kiliánová 1989). The middle generation completed monographs on folklore phenomena of a more traditional kind (Gašparíková 1980, 1984–85, 1991–92; Leščák 1981; Burlasová 1982, 1984, 1991; Leščák and Sirovátka 1982). Comparative studies were once again encouraged, although they were restricted mainly to the Slavonic field (Gašparíková and Putilov 2002). In spite of the difficult political situation, some reputable scientific work continued in the 1980s. A long-term project investigating Slovak folk culture resulted in the publication of the *Ethnographic Atlas of Slovakia* in 1990, the *Encyclopaedia of Slovak Folk Culture* in 1995, and several thematic monographs. After 1990 the focus shifted towards contemporary research and the symbolic functions of folklore, but this trend falls outside the period examined in this chapter.

Conclusion

Apart from a brief period in the early 1950s which was dominated by historical research of the type promoted by Soviet anthropologists, the scholars who worked in Slovak folkloristika dealt with folklore primarily in terms of contemporary cultural phenomena. They studied folklore in the context of the local social network, on the basis of the concept of the small social group (*lokálne spoločenstvo*). They viewed folklore as a special form of social and cultural communication and 'as a special form of creative activity' (Jakobson and Bogatyrev 1929) with aesthetic functions. The research retained as its theoretical foundation the functional-structural method of the mid-1930s.

The relatively brief but nonetheless devastating interruption which occurred at the beginning of the 1950s directed attention towards historical studies and propagated historical materialism in simplified and dogmatic forms. Token references to the works of Stalin, Lenin, Marx, and Engels, inspiration drawn from certain works of Soviet colleagues, and a dismissal of Western European anthropology had a negative effect on Slovak anthro-

---

[4] I took part in this seminar from 1974 onwards.

pology in this period. The first half of the 1950s was characterised by insecurity in academic life and anxiety among the population in general. Yet this
difficult period was quickly pushed aside in the memories of most actors,
who learned to read and cite the works of the 1940s and the 1960s and to
neglect or ignore the academic output of the 1950s.

From the later 1950s onwards, Slovak anthropologists gradually returned to ideas and traditions dating back to the pre-socialist period. They
emphasised synchronic analysis of the functions of folklore phenomena and
insisted on high-quality fieldwork with a clear methodology and well-
defined theoretical premises. Of course, this resumption of synchronic
analysis had its limits. Throughout the socialist era researchers avoided
contemporary issues which might be interpreted as politically sensitive. The
discipline's institutional basis was strengthened both at the Academy of
Sciences institute and at the Comenius University. Andrej Melicherčík, a
scholar of acute intelligence who was also an effective debater and a highly
productive author, was both the outstanding founder of the folkloristic
school in Bratislava and for a time its greatest enemy. His pupils, especially
Milan Leščák but also Viera Gašparíková, Soňa Burlasová, and Ľubica
Droppová, ensured the dynamic persistence of the discipline. From the
1960s onwards these scholars took an expansive interest in theoretical and
methodological discussions in general anthropology. Thanks to the rigorous-
ness of its research, the folkloristics they established was increasingly perceived as a more demanding academic discipline than etnografia. This
perception was fostered by the work of several able personalities and, in
particular, by the seminar for young researchers under Leščák's leadership,
which persuaded a new generation to concentrate on folkloristics in the
1970s. There were also pragmatic arguments for such a choice, because
specialists were still required for folklore groups, houses of culture, folklore
festivals, and even to work in the mass media. Folklore in all its forms and
functions played an important role in Slovak mass culture until the end of
socialism in 1989.

The influence of Soviet folkloristics was always strong, but it was received critically. Apart from the well-known historical school of folkloristics, which studied folklore genres in history, the main stimuli came in the
areas of semiotics (Yuriy Lotman, Eleazar Moiseevich Meletinskiy, Grigoriy
L'vovich Permyakov, Yuriy Levin, and others), the study of working-class
and kolkhoz folklore, and the study of contemporary cultural phenomena.

The strongest influences from Western European anthropology came
from the French structuralists, from the works of Hermann Bausinger and his
colleagues in Tübingen, and from the Scandinavian anthropologists who
established the journal Ethnologia Europaea. The influence of American and

British folklore studies could be seen in the reception of the works of Alan Dundes, Linda Dégh, Gillian Bennet, and others. American and British cultural and social anthropology were little known, however, and exerted little influence.

The four decades of Slovak anthropology under socialism were by no means valueless or monotonous. The folkloristics school in Bratislava produced significant results in both theoretical and empirical fields, on the basis of a solid institutional foundation. Academics were obliged to observe constraints, sometimes broader, sometimes narrower, which restricted the open and critical exchange of ideas. Contact with foreign colleagues was limited, as was access to foreign literature. This restricted participation in international debates encouraged tendencies of complacent isolationism and resulted in declining academic quality. Changes due to political pressure hindered research and led in extreme cases to the closing of institutions, interference in the choice of themes, and even the removal of individual staff. If nothing else, the story told here should remind us how fragile and restricted academic freedom was under socialism and how easily it could be jeopardised again.

References

Barthes, R. 1967. *Nulový stupeň rukopisu: Základy semiológie*. Praha: Československý spisovatel.

Bogatyriov, P. G. 1929. *Actes magiques, rites et croyances en Russie Subcarpatique*. Paris: Librairie Ancienne Honoré Champion.

——. 1935. Funkčno-štrukturálna metóda a iné metódy etnografie a folkloristiky. *Slovenské pohľady* 51: 550–58.

——. 1937. *Funkcie kroja na Moravskom Slovensku*. Turčiansky Sv. Martin: Matica slovenská.

——. 1940. *Lidové divadlo české a slovenské*. Praha: F. Borový.

Burlasová, S. 1964. K problémom genézy, funkcie a štýlu ľudovej piesne s družstevnou tematikou. *Slovenský národopis* 12 (1): 3–67.

——. 1982. *V šírom poli rokyta: Balady a iné epické piesne*, vol. 1. Bratislava: Veda.

——. 1984. *V šírom poli rokyta: Balady a iné epické piesne*, vol. 2. Bratislava: Veda.

——. 1991. *Vojenské a regrútske piesne*. Bratislava: Veda.

Bžoch, J. 1958. Utrpenie folklóru a utrpenie z folklóru. *Kultúrny život* 13 (17): 5.

Čeboksarov, N. N. 1951. Etnografické štúdium kultúry a života moskovských robotníkov. *Národopisný sborník SAVU* 10: 295–312.

Čečetka, L. 1958. V úlohe štatistu. *Kultúrny život* 13 (20): 4.

Dégh, L. 1962. *Märchen, Erzähler, Erzählgemeinschaften.* Berlin: Akademie-Verlag.

——. 1977. *Biologie des Erzählguts: Enzyklopädie des Märchens.* Berlin: De Gruyter Verlag.

Droppová, L. 1966. K problematike národopisného výskumu súčasnosti. *Slovenský národopis* 14 (4): 594–600.

Filová, B. 1995. Národopisný ústav Slovenskej akadémie vied. In J. Botík and P. Slavkovský (eds.), *Encyklopédia ľudovej kultúry Slovenska,* p. 398. Bratislava: Veda.

Gašparíková, V. 1963. Príspevok k štúdiu spoločenského dosahu ľudovej rozprávky. *Slovenský národopis* 11 (2–3): 360–78.

——. 1980. *Ostrovtipné príbehy i veliké cigánstva a žarty: Humor a satira v rozprávaniach slovenského ľudu.* Bratislava: Tatran.

——. 1984–85. *Zlatá podkova, zlaté pero, zlatý vlas: Čarovné rozprávky slovenského ľudu.* 2 vols. Bratislava: Tatran.

——. 1991–92. *Katalóg slovenskej ľudovej prózy.* 2 vols. Bratislava: NÚ SAV.

——, and B. Putilov (eds.). 2002. *Geroy ili razboynik.* Budapest: European Folklore Institute.

Hlôšková, A. 1990. *Historické tradície na Slovensku a ich fabulované formy ako etnokultúrny identifikačný faktor.* Bratislava: Národopisný ústav SAV.

Horanská, E. 1958. Ako možno využiť a zneužiť umeleckú tvorbu ľudu. *Kultúrny život* 13 (22): 6–7.

Jakobson, R., and P. G. Bogatyrev. 1929 [1971]. Die Folklore als eine besondere Form des Schaffens [Folklór jako zvláštní forma tvorby]. In P. G. Bogatyrev, *Souvislosti tvorby: Cesty k struktuře lidové kultury a divadla,* pp. 36–47. Praha: Odeon.

Kaliský, R. 1958. Folklór dnes. *Kultúrny život* 13 (19): 4.

Kiliánová, G. 1989. *Ekológia súčasných procesov v ľudovej próze.* Bratislava: Filozofická fakulta Univerzity Komenského.

Kolečányi, M. 1947. Nositelia ústnej slovesnej tradície. *Národopisný sborník Matice slovenskej* 8: 221–31.

Kolečányi-Kosová, M. 1973. *Magické usmrcovanie protivníka na diaľku.* Bratislava: Národopisný ústav SAV.

Kovačevičová-Žuffová, S. 1945–46. Zákonitosť diania a vnútorná podmienenosť zmien jednotlivých javov v krojovej oblasti. *Národopisný sborník Matice slovenskej* 6–7: 74–83.

———. 1947. Semiologické problémy važtianskeho kroja. *Národopisný sborník Matice slovenskej* 8: 81–90.

Krekovičová, E. 1981. *Funkcia a život piesne v súčasnom dedinskom prostredí*. Bratislava: Národopisný ústav SAV.

Krno, M. 1958. Slovo o dialektike vo folklóre. *Kultúrny život* 13 (22): 7.

Lamser, V. 1969. *Komunikace a společnost: Úvod do teorie společenské komunikace*. Praha: Academia.

Leach, E. 1983. *Kultura i komunikacija*. Beograd: Prosveta.

Leščák, M. 1966. Príspevok k metodike výskumu súčasného stavu folklóru. *Slovenský národopis* 14 (4): 570–78.

———. 1969. Úvahy o predmete národopisného bádania. *Slovenský národopis* 17 (3): 369–80.

———. 1981. *Slovenské ľudové hádanky*. Bratislava: Tatran.

———. 1991. The Beginnings of Functional Structuralism in Slovak Ethnology. *Slovenský národopis* 39 (3–4): 336–47.

———, and V. Nosáľová. 1968. Diskusne k súčasnej situácii v slovenskom národopise. *Slovenský národopis* 16: 519–20.

———, and O. Sirovátka. 1982. *Folklór a folkloristika*. Bratislava: Smena.

Lévi-Strauss, C. 1966. *Smutné tropy*. Praha: Odeon.

———. 1969. Štrukturálna antropológia. *Národopisné informácie* 1 (3): 4–43.

Luther, D. 1983. *Dynamika vývoja obyčajovej tradície v období výstavby socializmu*. Bratislava: Národopisný ústav SAV.

Maslovová, G. S. 1951. Kultúra a život na jednom z kolchozov Podmoskovska. *Národopisný sborník SAVU* 10: 313–40.

Melicherčík, A. 1945. *Teória národopisu*. Liptovský sv. Mikuláš: Tranoscius.

———. 1945–46a. Príspevok k skúmaniu ľudovej rozprávky. *Národopisný sborník Matice slovenskej* 6–7: 117–32.

———. 1945–46b. Svadobný obrad ako znak. *Národopisný sborník Matice slovenskej* 6–7: 28–38.

———. 1947a. Funkcie nefolklórnej piesne v dedinskom prostredí. *Národopisný sborník Matice slovenskej* 8: 69–80.

———. 1947b. *Funkčné premeny v dnešnom dedinskom speve*. Thesis, Bratislava.

———. 1950. Československá etnografia a niektoré jej úlohy pri výstavbe socializmu. *Národopisný sborník SAVU* 9: 25–36.

———. 1952. Sovietska etnografia—náš vzor. *Národopisný sborník SAVU* 10: 5–23.

———. 1952. *Jánošíkovská tradícia na Slovensku*. Bratislava: Nakladatelstvo SAVU.

———. 1958. Presýtenosti z folklóru. *Kultúrny život* 13 (16): 3.

——. 1961. Boj proti fašizmu za Slovenského národného povstania v ústnom podaní slovenského ľudu. *Slovenský národopis* 9 (3): 358–407.

——. 1966. Tradičné a netradičné v ľudovej kultúre. *Slovenský národopis* 14 (4): 563–68.

Michálek, J. 1958. Za hlboké poznanie folklórnej tvorby nášho ľudu. *Kultúrny život* 13 (24): 6.

——, and J. Podolák. 1995. Katedra etnografie a folkloristiky Univerzity Komenského v Bratislave. In J. Botík and P. Slavkovský (eds.), *Encyklopédia ľudovej kultúry Slovenska*, pp. 232–33. Bratislava: Veda.

Mináč, V. 1958. Tíha folkloru. *Literární noviny* 12 (22nd March).

Mrlian, R. 1958. K názorom na folklór včerajška a dneška. *Pravda*, 16 November 1958.

Potapov, L. P. 1951a. Výskum socialistickej kultúry a spôsobu života Altajcov. *Národopisný sborník SAVU* 10: 263–94.

——. 1951b. Hlavné otázky etnografickej expozície v sovietskych múzeách. *Národopisný sborník SAVU* 10: 341–50.

Potechin, I. I. 1951a. Úlohy boja s kozmopolitizmom v etnografii. *Národopisný sborník SAVU* 10: 89–112.

——. 1951b. Niektoré problémy etnografického štúdia národov koloniálnych krajín. *Národopisný sborník SAVU* 10: 201–20.

Profantová, Z. 1988. *Kultúrno-historické a súčasné spoločenské kontexty pranostík.* Bratislava: Národopisný ústav SAV.

Sárkány, M. 1978. Some Questions of Social Anthropological Approach to the Decline of Folk Culture in Hungary. In A. Pranda (ed.), *Premeny ľudových tradícii v súčasnosti: Socialistické krajiny*, pp. 290–300. Bratislava: Veda.

Sergejev, M. A. 1951. Malé národy Severu v epoche sozializmu. *Národopisný sborník SAVU* 10: 221–62.

Slivka, K. 1958. Dosť už vulgarizovania. *Kultúrny život* 13 (20): 4.

Stalin, J. V. 1950. *O Leninovi.* Bratislava: Pravda.

Šimút, Š. 1958. Kam s ním? *Kultúrny život* 13 (20): 4.

Števček, P. 1958. Proti zatemňovaniu diskusie. *Kultúrny život* 13 (21): 6–8.

Švehlák, S. 1958. Ruky preč od folklóru. *Kultúrny život* 13 (20): 4.

Tokarev, S. A. 1951a. Engels a súčasná etnografia. *Národopisný sborník SAVU* 10: 53–70.

——. 1951b. Prínos ruských učencu do světové etnografické vědy. *Národopisný sborník SAVU* 10: 121–50.

——. 1951c. Hlavné vývinové etapy ruskej predrevolučnej a sovietskej etnografie. *Národopisný sborník SAVU* 10: 151–74.

——, and N. N. Čeboksarov. 1951. Metodológia etnogenetického skúmania etnografického materiálu vo svetle prác J. V. Stalina o otázkach jazykovedy. *Národopisný sborník SAVU* 10: 175–200.

Tolstov, S. P. 1951a. Význam prác J. V. Stalina o otázkach jazykovedy pre vývin sovietskej etnografie. *Národopisný sborník SAVU* 10: 25–52.

——. 1951b. V. I. Lenin a aktuální problémy etnografie. *Národopisný sborník SAVU* 10: 71–88.

——. 1951c. K otázce a periodisaci dějin prvobytné společnosti. *Národopisný sborník SAVU* 10: 113–20.

Urbancová, V. 1995. Etnografia. In J. Botík and P. Slavkovský (eds.), *Encyklopédia ľudovej kultúry Slovenska*, pp. 125–27. Bratislava: Veda.

Chapter 16
Historicity in Hungarian Anthropology

Klára Kuti

What does historicity mean in anthropology? Many understandings are possible. Here historicity refers to a reading of the past and, more specifically, to the ways in which anthropologists have dealt with changes in their subject matter over time.[1] In Hungarian anthropology (néprajz), scholars have approached the past in a variety of ways. It is possible to link the different approaches to different historical epochs, but to some degree they have persisted simultaneously, side by side. In this chapter I outline the main conceptions of historicity which have been deployed in Hungarian anthropology from its beginnings, before showing the position of today's historical anthropology within this theoretical repertoire.

Most scholars in East-Central Europe have always viewed anthropology as an historical discipline, because even projects concerned with the present must necessarily locate the phenomena under investigation within an historical frame of reference. Yet despite monotonous repetition of this basic point, many Hungarian anthropologists seem to forget it. Fundamental principles of methodology, including the basis of historicity, have repeatedly been called into question.

Let us begin by considering the statement that there exists a close relation between history and anthropology. Sometimes this is little more than an affirmation of a need for cooperation between the disciplines. Anthropologists and historians can work together closely in any number of fields, from archaeology to local history studies. In Hungary it has long been the custom of mainstream political historians—those who narrate a history of events—to pass on the topics they themselves could not address to anthropologists, who were supposedly more competent in such matters, thanks to their traditional specialisation in 'folk culture' and its authentic representatives, the peasants. In this way a division of intellectual labour took shape in which the history of the masses, especially in the countryside, came to depend heavily on

[1] The research on which this chapter is based was funded by an OTKA Postgraduate Grant (D 45928).

anthropology. Thus the borderline between the disciplines was drawn according to the object of research, and not according to the approach or method applied.

But this was problematic if anthropology itself lacked a dynamic concept of time. For example, the monumental four-volume *Magyarság Néprajza* (Ethnography of the Hungarians) (Czakó 1933-37) portrayed the Hungarians (or rather those domains of their popular culture for which documentation existed) as having enjoyed some uniform existence in the past, which was disintegrating or becoming extinct in the present. It was believed that at some point in the past this culture was authentic and constant, even though by the 1930s only traces and memories of it were recoverable. This is what I call a selective or ahistorical concept of time. It prevailed during the emergence of Hungarian anthropology in the nineteenth century, when the search was on to ground a national identity in the Hungarian-speaking rural population. This nationalist agenda was still strong when anthropologists were invited to produce their four volumes in the inter-war period.

Only a few years after it was published, the shortcomings of this work were critically examined, and the following generation demanded a new synthesis, a 'new Hungarian anthropology'. The new approach to the past demanded that attention be paid to historical changes in peasant culture. Laying the groundwork for this new synthesis took almost three decades (the full set of publications, in eight volumes, is due to be completed in 2005). But how has the concept of folk culture itself changed in recent decades? I answer this question by addressing the formal, institutional, and ideological conditions which have led to more nuanced uses of the concept, all in the context of increased interest in history.

The story begins in 1949, when the chair of the Magyar Néprajzi Társaság (Hungarian Ethnographical Society), Gyula Ortutay, delivered a speech which can be seen as an ideological turning point (see Sárkány, this volume). The speech, published in the society's journal, *Ethnographia,* in the same year, contained everything a communist speech had to contain at the time: grief over the casualties of war, a rejection of pre-war ideology and a call for its replacement by the new ideology of Marxism-Leninism, some self-criticism, and harsh criticism of works by colleagues, including allegations of a lack of professional or ideological competence. The new slogans attributed considerable significance to history by emphasising that all the phenomena anthropologists studied were closely linked to social and productive relations; indeed, the former were to be deduced from the latter. Ortutay gave an example to highlight the new results to be expected from an historical anthropology that would base itself on Soviet science and, in particular, on historical research into ethnicity and ethnogenesis. The historical investigation of ethnic differences remained at the centre of research for many decades. László Kósa has commented that 'even though further particulars are unknown, the speech of 1949 was most probably unavoidable at that time. This is shown by the fact that Ortutay never revoked his theses, though he never repeated them either' (Kósa 1989: 247).

The speech was not merely symbolic. Historical anthropology was indeed given a more prominent role from then on. The first clear sign was the appointment in 1951 of István Tálasi to a new chair for material culture research at Budapest's Eötvös Loránd University (ELTE). A careful evaluation of his work in the 1950s and 1960s gives us valuable insight into the connection between the rise of historical research and the imposition of a new ideology. We need to examine how far, if at all, the methodological basis of Tálasi's historical research can be considered Marxist. Was there a Marxist anthropology in Hungary at all?

Historical Anthropology with a Materialist Foundation

István Tálasi's main thesis was that 'material culture was an expression of the productive conditions' (the identical phrasing is found in many of his works). Citing Pavel Ivanovich Kushner (1949), he insisted on defining culture through a materialist concept of history, which located the ultimate causes of change in the economy. According to Tálasi (1955: 9),

anthropology is an historical science, and therefore explanations of contemporary folk culture must be investigated with great attention to historical determinants. We can reach an understanding of today's folk culture only by carrying out ethnographic analyses of the antecedents. The historical dimension not only leads to a more accurate specification of the age and chronology of the phenomena under review but also enables us to explain their rise, modification, and fall by analysing the connection between social relations and relations of production. Thus the morphology of objects and the history of work processes are based on concrete facts, the comparative analyses of which must be made more scientific and reach a higher standard.

Note, however, that the object of anthropological research—folk culture—has not changed in this formulation. On the other hand, Tálasi argues that it is not only the origin of individual phenomena that must be studied but also the entire process of their rise, modification, and eventual decay.

Tálasi promoted this basic thesis under institutional conditions that had already undergone socialist restructuring. Ortutay had called in 1949 for close cooperation, under a five-year plan, among all anthropological institutions: the ELTE department in Budapest, the Hungarian Ethnographical

Society, and the Museum of Ethnography and similar institutions on the countryside. This was a typically socialist vision:

> PhD and MA dissertation topics are to be allocated in specified fields according to a plan. So far more than one hundred closely related topics have been decided upon. The Hungarian-speaking regions have been divided up among the various institutions. ... The work and schedule of this five-year plan have also been worked out. I would like to emphasise again that the professional competence of each researcher is to be judged by his or her contribution to the fulfilment of our five-year plan. (Ortutay 1949: 23)

In 1951 the Néprajz Committee of the Hungarian Academy of Sciences founded ten study groups and nine research teams, many of which addressed the history of material culture. Tálasi himself headed a group charged with studying farming and livestock breeding during the ages of feudalism and capitalism, while László Kardos's group investigated the emergence and development of classes in Hungarian rural society from the end of feudalism to the liberation (i.e. 1945). Lajos Szolnoky's research team concentrated on the economic development of traditional crafts and the evolution of tools and techniques. The team studying nutrition, headed by Judit Morvay, focused on two basic foodstuffs, meat and dairy products, and their connection to livestock breeding (Morvay 1951). Material culture in the fifteenth century was the main subject of Márta Belényesy's team, and finally, Tálasi was given an additional team to edit the works of the eighteenth-century economist Mátyás Bél. This ambitious research programme was too fragmented to succeed, as Tálasi himself noted many years later. The numerous teams were brought together as a single 'team for economic research', based from 1952 onwards at the department in ELTE. In addition to team members and university staff, museum staff, students, and lay people all collaborated (Tálasi 1976/78: 3–15).

The thematic structure used in teaching material culture in Budapest can be inferred from the curriculum, which underwent only minor modifications between 1956 and 1976. It covered the following topics:

* Traces and remnants of agricultural, forest, and pasture communities; types and organisation of communal labour

* Cereal, maize, and potato cultivation; tools, techniques, work groups, changes in tool use, animal labour, and machines; the emergence of special classes of labourers and producing strata

- Viticulture and fruit growing; regional specialisations; the organisation and functioning of wine-growing communities; peasant wine production in comparative perspective

- Historical and anthropological data on extensive cattle breeding throughout Europe; herding in a farming society

- Cattle breeding by peasants, with special reference to draught animals and nutrition; marketing

- Foraging: gathering, beekeeping, hunting, fishing; collection, cataloguing, and analysis of data on these topics in historical and anthropological monographs; the relevance of foraging in comparison with other sectors of production and with present forms of the economy

- Peasants' nutritional culture and food in the context of the development of production and social relations; the analysis of basic foodstuffs (bread, milk, and dairy products)

- Historical development of rural settlements; changing legal regulation of forms of settlement in relation to modes of production

- Origin of the Hungarian-style farmhouse, typology using medieval archaeology, internal development and interethnic influences; structure and function of the house given local and global development at the end of feudalism and during capitalism

- Monographic accounts of rural and small-town crafts (e.g. processing of iron, leather).

In his 1976 comments, Tálasi took pride in the breadth of the programme and its associated publications. He again emphasised the historical focus of his work, while noting that 'cultural-morphological analysis is also used' (Tálasi 1976/78: 8ff., 15). The publications reflecting this perspective were indeed numerous, including monographs on tools (ploughs, tools used for flax processing) and a series on plants cultivated with the hoe (maize, pota-

toes, tobacco, peppers) which always included a description of their introduction, expansion, commercialisation, and social aspects. Extensive treatment was also devoted to cattle breeding, haymaking, cereal cultivation,
harvesting, storage, land use, and the history of bread and milk processing.

Although the centralised research agenda was typical of the socialist
era, whether those involved actually changed their historical perception in a
Marxist direction as a result of it is doubtful. Tálasi's contemporaries do,
however, emphasise his organisational dynamism. Following his retirement
in 1976 the curriculum was reorganised, though the aforementioned topics
were not dropped. In the 1980s two approaches were pursued: while one
teaching unit focused on the description of ethnic groups in the Carpathian
Basin, the other sought to investigate folk culture chronologically, on the
basis of a strict historical frame. Unfortunately, this frame did not turn out to
be particularly appropriate for investigating changes in folk culture.

Varieties of Historical Anthropology

How can one speak about *the* methods of historical anthropology? Some
have seen the dividing line between history and anthropology in the way
data are analysed: whereas historians are expected to analyse written source
materials from the past, it has typically been the privilege and duty of anthropologists to analyse oral tradition and contemporary materials (Barabás
1971). Some writers have attempted to specify a temporal divide beyond
which the anthropologist should not venture (e.g. Péter Morvay, cited in
Vargyas 1961: 12). Tálasi made his own position clear in his oft-quoted
work of 1955:

> We need the rapid and systematic collection of data, and we will
> continue to do so. Everyone familiar with the local situation of mate
> rial culture research knows how the work of our predecessors was
> impeded by a lack of available data and sources. Without knowledge
> of the subject, Hungarian folk culture, its status and significance in
> world culture cannot be adequately explained. ... In the last few
> years we have made progress in discovering and analysing the
> sources. Many of our colleagues have worked in local, regional, or
> national archives. The use of historical data helped them to explain
> their subjects more thoroughly, and these studies resulted in syn
> thetic historical anthropological works giving valuable overviews of
> the material culture of a particular epoch (Tálasi 1955: 10–11).

It is clear here that the ultimate aim of collecting anthropological materials
was to promote the status of Hungarian culture. Anthropological and historical materials were distinguished from each other indirectly by using the
labels 'oral' and 'written', respectively. The analysis of written sources was

seen as a prerequisite for an historical anthropological analysis of material culture, and the activity of data collection was potentially without limits.

Historicity figured in a debate in 1954 in the pages of the journal *Ethnographia* (Bodrogi 1954; Vajda 1954; Vargyas 1954; see also Vargyas 1961). László Vajda offered a sharp formulation of the Soviet position previously endorsed by Ortutay:

> The particular aspect of historical processes which is exclusively to be grasped through anthropological studies is the ethnic differentiation of historical reality. ... Thus the central question of anthropological research is the demonstration of ethnically specific features of historical phenomena through the various epochs, in the different spheres of social and cultural life (Vajda 1954: 6–7).

He went on to argue that this anthropological knowledge rested on data collection and analysis. This method could be supplemented by an analysis of written sources, but 'our work will become non-anthropological if we start concentrating on phenomena that are connected to written records or some sort of writing' (Vajda 1954: 16).

Tibor Bodrogi polemically opposed drawing contrasts between the historical and social sciences, and also between culture and society. 'The topic of anthropology is not only culture as a social product, but society itself. Since every cultural phenomenon is a social phenomenon at the same time, we can assert that the object of anthropology consists of social phenomena' (Bodrogi 1954: 584). Anthropology and history differed fundamentally in the nature of the social systems they examined—that is, 'primitive societies' and 'peasant societies', respectively. (The term *primitive societies* was borrowed from E. E. Evans-Pritchard; see Bodrogi 1954: 584n.) Anthropologists relied heavily on 'direct observation', and their descriptions, based on such observation, could later be treated as historical sources. According to Bodrogi, historicity in anthropology depended on the object of the study and not the age of the sources. The analysis of written sources was necessary if it would lead to a deeper insight into data collected through direct observation. In his conclusion, Bodrogi called for reinforcing research into the social context, which he believed should always serve as a backdrop for interpretations of culture.

Some years after this discussion, Lajos Vargyas returned to the question of what made anthropology an historical discipline. He answered:

> Néprajz is an historical discipline because it outlines all phases of development from primitive society to European farming societies. It determines the laws of that development, places phenomena within a process of development, connects them to separate stages in the his-

torical process of development, and is able to discover the process of development in recent phenomena (Vargyas 1961: 16).

Development (*fejlődés*) is obviously the keyword here. Vargyas discussed four methods—ethnographic description, comparative research, comparisons with historical data, and actual historical research—which, combined, yielded historical results. Development was determined by socio-economic factors, and its epochs could be reconstructed by combining these four methods. Accumulated stores of knowledge in Hungarian and European anthropology and historical research would help researchers discover those aspects of rural cultures of which they could have no direct observation. In this sense, historical anthropology remained anthropological as far as its object of research was concerned, but it was historical in its method—that is, it was a complex discipline. Vargyas argued that the exploration of rural culture and society involved reconstructing, without a strict concern for chronology per se, all the phases and epochs of a particular historical line of development. In the case of Hungarian néprajz, the prime such line was of course the development of Hungarian peasant society.

This opening to historical research did not really modify the object of néprajz, which continued to be vaguely specified as 'rural culture' or 'rural tradition'. Historical research did, however, extend the temporal framework of the discipline. Researchers had to learn some techniques of source analysis in order to interpret early written documents. The basic assumption of an original, authentic essence, that which existed in the past but had by now disappeared, was not called into question. The expansion of historical research helped to push back the ahistorical concept of time, but it never disappeared completely. On the other hand, the influence of a Marxist conception of history led at least some scholars to investigate folk culture as embedded in the context of socio-economic relations.

In order to demonstrate the opposition of various currents of research in the 1970s, it is appropriate to cite a short article by Mihály Sárkány (1976/78), who discussed the influence of Marxist theory and outlined the differences between research in Hungarian economic anthropology (*gazdálkodás néprajza*) and the equivalent subdiscipline as practised internationally (*gazdasági antropológia*). Within the Hungarian tradition Sárkány distinguished between cultural-morphological and historical orientations. While the first took current data as its starting point, the second began from the origin of a phenomenon and sought to trace it through all its phases of development, presupposing this to be the outcome of a dialectical relationship. According to Sárkány, the latter type of research should also illuminate connections with other domains of culture.

By contrast, international economic anthropology had developed as a subdiscipline of socio-cultural anthropology with an emphasis on a conception of society and culture as a functioning whole and on intensive fieldwork as the principal method. There was a Marxist variant of this international economic anthropology, which placed the concept of mode of production at the centre of the analysis. It was assumed that 'the mode of production is a reality which is not directly available to the observer in the data. It is a reality that should be reconstructed and reconstituted mentally in the entire process of scientific research'. Sárkány characterised the Hungarian anthropology of economic activities as 'an historical project, since it explores individual phenomena diachronically from their origin to the present day. It provides data to determine the processes and laws of the development of culture.' In economic anthropology, on the other hand, 'the same features are interesting as components of a subsystem of the social system, and from their relations generalisations and laws may be ascertained with regard to the structure and function of the given subsystem and of the society as a whole' (Sárkány 1976/78: 23ff.).

Sárkány's distinction between two types of economic anthropology seems very useful. Historical studies of the kind undertaken in Hungarian néprajz could in principle make possible the formulation and testing of evolutionary laws of development based on material causality. However, mere data collection, as exemplified by the extensive works of participants in the *Atlas of Hungarian Folk Culture* project, could not illuminate long-term changes in modes of production. Economic phenomena (tools, work processes, etc.) had to be considered in the context of social relations (this was the point stressed earlier by Bodrogi, Sárkány's senior colleague at the academy institute).

The question raised at the beginning of this chapter about whether the attention Hungarian anthropologists paid to the history of material culture allows us to claim them as representatives of a Marxist anthropology must be answered negatively. In spite of an expansion of historical research, only a few researchers placed the peasant (or working) classes in a wider social context. Most Hungarian anthropologists (including those with an historical focus) doing research into 'rural culture' or 'rural tradition' did not and still do not consider it their task to analyse social and economic relations. The historical method has become bowdlerised in the interest of a 'pure' chronology that has not changed significantly since it was first formulated in the nineteenth century.

Conclusion

Finally, let me connect this discussion of historical orientations in anthropology in socialist Hungary to the new historical anthropology, whose appearance on the Hungarian scene was symbolised by a 1983 conference of the Cultural Anthropological Committee of the Hungarian Academy of Sciences. The thematic foci of the conference were the interaction of rural, elite, and popular cultures, family and household structures, kin relations, and the analysis of social stratification and way of life. Both the anthropologists and the historians in attendance asserted the renewal of their disciplines. Tamás Hofer (1984) discussed recent historical research by anthropologists in Germany and Scandinavia, which had led to revisions of long-established definitions of such basic terms as *people* and *popular culture*. It was necessary, he argued, to engage in new ways with everyday reality, actual events, and individual actions. The 'people,' previously considered to be homogeneous, were henceforth differentiated into groups and strata, even within the peasantry. Gábor Klaniczay described the influence of the socio-historical approach of Peter Burke and how the French 'Annales' school had stimulated a reappraisal of the dichotomy between folk culture and elite culture. According to Klaniczay, the essential features of 'historical anthropology' lay in its method, adopted from cultural anthropology, and in the need to recognise another culture, alien to the researcher: 'historical anthropology is well on the way to fulfilling an old need of history, namely, to illuminate complex connections and phenomena through the synchronic examination of ecological, social, cultural, and religious aspects' (Klaniczay 1984: 34).

It was no coincidence that Hofer, an anthropologist, cited examples from the German-speaking and Scandinavian countries, whereas Klaniczay, an historian, cited French and British research. Both parties were keen to rejuvenate social historical research and reunite subjects whose paths had diverged as a result of the evolution of the social sciences since the nineteenth century. Indeed, basic differences between the major European regions—east and west of the Rhine—have not yet disappeared completely. Eastern European anthropology, preoccupied with studying the roots and identity of its own society and nation, is the intellectual product of Eastern Europe's long nineteenth century. During that same era the social scientists of the world powers were exploring other cultures all over the world. The study of the lower strata, all those who for the most part endure the consequences of politics passively, came to the fore in Western Europe only when the hitherto dominant power structures began to fragment in the course of the twentieth century. This was the moment of crisis when, in Western Europe, historians began to take up the study of *mentalités* and everyday behaviour (including crisis behaviour). This school of historians was later ripe for cross-fertilisation by the accumulated methodological insights gained by anthropologists on alien terrain. The outcome has been the widespread use of oral history methods to shed new light on the pasts of advanced societies.

When these trends reach Eastern Europe, the local anthropologists are not sure how to react. Some might protest that they have been doing historical anthropology all along, before it became a fashionable phrase—but I have tried to show that in fact the anthropologists of néprajz have been doing something very different. I cannot hope to repair in this chapter all the theoretical and methodological shortcomings of the discipline. In conclusion, it might be said that the entire field still suffers as a result of a basic and longstanding deficiency: until we can arrive at agreed-upon definitions of key terms, including both *culture* and *society*, a comprehensive (and yet differentiating) historical anthropology will remain impossible.

References

Barabás, J. 1971. Tér és idő a néprajzi kutatásban. *Népi kultúra—népi társadalom* 5–6: 331–44.

Bodrogi, T. 1954. A néprajzi adatgyűjtés módszere és jelentősége: Megjegyzések Vajda László tanulmányához. *Ethnographia* 65: 581–92.

Czakó, E. (ed.). 1933-37. *Magyarság néprajza.* Budapest: Királyi Magyar Egyetemi Nyomda.

Hofer, T. 1984. Történeti fordulat az európai etnológiában. In T. Hofer (ed.), *Történeti antropológia: Az 1983. április 18–19. tartott tudományos ülésszak előadásai,* pp. 61–73. Budapest: Magyar Tudományos Akadémia Néprajzi Kutatócsoport.

Klaniczay, G. 1984. A történeti antropológia tárgya, módszerei és első eredményei. In T. Hofer (ed.), *Történeti antropológia: Az 1983. április 18–19. tartott tudományos ülésszak előadásai,* pp. 23–61. Budapest: Magyar Tudományos Akadémia Néprajzi Kutatócsoport.

Kósa, L. 1989. *A magyar néprajz tudománytörténete.* Budapest: Gondolat.

Kushner, P. I. 1949. Uchenie Stalina o natsii i natsionalnoi kulture i ego znachenie dlya etnografii. *Sovetskaia Etnografiya* 30 (4): 3–19.

Morvay, J. S. 1951. Munkaközösségek és munkacsoportok. *Ethnographia* 62: 226–29.

Ortutay, Gy. 1949. A magyar néprajztudomány elvi kérdései (A Magyar Néprajzi Társaság 61. közgyűlésének elnöki megnyitó beszéde. Elhangzott 1949. június 22-én.). *Ethnographia* 60: 1–24.

Sárkány, M. 1976/78. A gazdálkodás etnográfiája és a gazdasági antropológia. *Dissertationes Ethnographicae* 2: 18–30.

Tálasi, I. 1955. Az anyagi kultúra néprajzi vizsgálatának tíz éve (1945–1955). *Ethnographia* 66: 5–56.

——. 1976/78. Kutatási törekvések a Tárgyi Néprajzi Tanszék negyedszázados fennállása alatt. *Dissertationes Ethnographicae* 2: 3–15.

Vajda, L. 1954. A néprajzi adatgyűjtés módszere és jelentősége. *Ethnographia* 65: 1–19.

Vargyas. L. 1954. Vajda László cikkének néhány megállapításához. *Ethnographia* 65: 240–44.

——. 1961. Miért és hogyan történeti tudomány a néprajz? *Néprajzi Értesítő* 43: 5–20.

PART FOUR

WIDER HORIZONS

In this final section we have included not only chapters describing some of the accomplishments of East-Central European anthropologists in extra-European comparative anthropology but also two contributions which compare the objectives, pedagogical practices, and organisation of anthropological research in East-Central Europe with their Western counterparts.

Zofia Sokolewicz shows how it was possible under socialism for Polish teachers and their students to maintain traditions of fieldwork dating back to the nineteenth century. After beginning with modest summer camps at home, anthropologists initiated numerous foreign expeditions and were able in many cases to maintain long-term links through cooperation agreements. Though far removed from the standard Western model of individual participant observation, these expeditions also differed from the Soviet model, and they generated solid contributions to the discipline. Sokolewicz's account also gives insights into the workings of the educational bureaucracy during the socialist era and into informal networking in Polish society in general; it was crucial to know the right people in order to obtain permission and financial support. She also touches on the political problems that sometimes gave rise to friction with local partners.

Other countries seem to have been less flexible than Poland, both in the composition of anthropological syllabi and in the scope afforded to researchers to organise fieldwork abroad. The Africanist Ulrich van der Heyden reviews the achievements of Africanist anthropology in the German Democratic Republic, where traditional Völkerkunde was discredited through its association with colonialism. The new institutional framework was shaped to a considerable extent by the GDR's foreign policy goals and emphasised interdisciplinarity. The scholars themselves had little or no autonomy to initiate foreign projects, and a single political misjudgement could mean disaster for one's academic career. Yet van der Heyden shows that, despite these practical and ideological impediments, much important work was accomplished. Anthropologists also contributed significantly to a weakening of stereotypical views of Africa in German society. None of this was enough to prevent their work from being brusquely dismissed after 1990.

Bea Vidacs, too, was determined to become an Africanist, but the only discipline institutionalised in her native Hungary was néprajz, where the syllabus was dedicated overwhelmingly to Hungarian folk culture. Vidacs compares her experiences as an undergraduate in Hungary with those during a brief sojourn in London and then her later path as a graduate student in the United States. In the case of Hungarian 'national ethnography' (a concept she adapts from Tamás Hofer) she was required to absorb a national canon based on the findings of research oriented towards reconstructing the Hungarian peasantry of the nineteenth century. The Hungarian curriculum stressed consensus rather than argument, whereas in the United States the emphasis was placed on criticism, theory, and systematic comparison. Yet the programme in néprajz afforded Vidacs the opportunity to read quite a lot about Africa, even in her undergraduate years, and did provide some insights into other kinds of anthropology. Although there was little concern at the time in Hungarian néprajz with contemporary social processes, the programme had enough flexibility to allow Vidacs to carry out extended fieldwork in Hungary for her master's thesis. Her attempts to address issues of reflexivity in this work were criticised as an irrelevance by most of her Hungarian teachers.

Hungary also provides the main context for the volume's final chapter. Tamás Hofer chose to base his contribution not on the engaging reminiscences he narrated at the Halle workshop but on a classic contribution, first published in 1968 in *Current Anthropology*, which pays almost no attention to the effects of socialism but instead focuses on a quite different East-West encounter. The customs of American cultural anthropologists are compared with those of Central European 'native ethnographers', as if they were two distinct tribes. Hofer is a scholar who enjoys a unique 'dual citizenship' and has devoted much of his career to building bridges between these different research traditions. The essay republished here is an example of those bridge-building contributions. Hofer's position, then and now, is that Hungarian néprajz and the equivalent disciplines in other European countries should not lose their identity by being merged into the larger enterprise of international anthropology, driven by the law-seeking aspirations of a social science. He shows that each of these two research traditions has its own 'professional personality' and its own role in academia.

Much has changed in the decades since Hofer's witty comparative observations were first published. The national and international branches of anthropology in East-Central Europe have converged. Both traditions nowadays cultivate a wide range of contacts in both the social sciences and the humanities, including cultural studies, and both have become reflexive and self-critical. Yet to some extent the 'tribes' have preserved their separate identities, and this cannot be explained entirely by institutional inertia. The socialist period ultimately protected and even privileged the nation-centred strand of the discipline—even in the case of the GDR, where, as we saw earlier, the attempt to forge a unified anthropological science was irresolutely pursued. National ethnography weathered the storm brought by Marxism-Leninism. It remains to be seen whether, in the postsocialist era, increasing exposure to Western social sciences, including social and cultural anthropology, will lead to more radical changes in the disciplinary traditions of East-Central Europe.

CH

Chapter 17
Polish Expeditions Abroad, 1945–1989

Zofia Sokolewicz

The Polish anthropological community in the early years after the Second World War was relatively small: in the entire country, fewer than 20 scholars held university posts. After the destruction caused by the war, which included significant human losses, university chairs and institutes were rapidly re-established (see Jasiewicz, this volume). By the 1980s, in addition to seven university departments of etnologia, anthropologists were also employed at the Institute for the History of Material Culture of the Polish Academy of Sciences, both centrally and at its regional branches, and at a great number of museums.

The socialist authorities did not treat anthropologists as political reactionaries, even during the period of the people's democratic revolution (1948–56). Nevertheless, according to the theory of class struggle, intellectuals were less trustworthy than workers. In the eyes of the party, therefore, regional enthusiasts such as rural teachers, who were positioned closer to the 'healthy' rural working classes, were better placed to offer a guarantee of the proper ideological line than were the discipline's full-time professionals. Among the latter, hardly any joined the Communist Party or took any interest in a political career. As Aleksander Posern-Zieliński argues (this volume), anthropologists posed no serious threat to the socialist authorities. Etnografia found a quiet niche for itself in the shadow of its more powerful partners, history and archaeology. In cultural politics it was assigned the task of upholding folk culture (*kultura ludowa*), which was taken to be the core of national culture; the latter was defined as folk in form but socialist in content. Although in the 1980s most anthropologists, like other Polish intellectuals, supported the Solidarity movement, there was little spontaneous activity; more activism was found in neighbouring disciplines. On the other hand, among students of anthropology political opposition was conspicuously strong from the beginning of the 1970s onwards, out of all proportion to their numbers.[1]

Students were attracted to anthropology because of the way it was taught and because the topics studied gave cause for reflection on both existential and social issues, such as social justice, freedom, and equality. The works of Mircea Eliade, Carl Jung, and Erich Fromm offered opportunities to talk about the meaning of life, about the possibilities which existed for self-realisation despite the socialist system, and about the sense of that system.

Young people were also stimulated to reflect by the design of their curriculum, especially by the emphasis given to comparative studies of cultures throughout the world. Foreign expeditions, which became a particularly significant part of academic life in the 1970s, played an important role in broadening the horizons of teachers and students alike.

Indeed, the tradition of fieldwork dates back to the beginnings of Polish anthropology in the nineteenth century and has never been interrupted. In the early years research was often linked to educational work among rural people: the educated elites who wished to document folk culture travelled from manor house to manor house, or from presbytery to presbytery, and later from school to school, collecting folklore. They contributed to what Eric Hobsbawm (1983) was later to call the invention of tradition: their work substantiated the notion of a national culture and the mythology of this culture in the era when the territory of the Polish state was divided among three great powers, Russia, Prussia, and Austria. Particular mention should be made of those political opponents of the tsarist empire who were exiled to Siberia or to Central Asia. Spending many years among local people, some of them wrote pioneering descriptive monographs. This tradition was continued following the re-emergence of a Polish state in 1919. During the inter-war period, field trips sometimes involved a relatively short stay, perhaps a few weeks, either in a single village or in several sequentially, but it could also mean lengthy residence and repeated return visits.[2]

---

[1] Consequently, students of anthropology, together with history students, who were both more numerous and more revolutionary, fell under the surveillance of the secret services from 1975 onwards.

[2] Long-term field research is exemplified by the work of Kazimiera Zawistowicz-Adamska (1948), who spent more than a year in the Polish village of Zaborów in the 1930s. Józef Obrębski conducted research in Macedonia in 1932; only a small part of his ensuing writings has been published (1972).

Foundations

Those responsible for relaunching anthropology in Polish universities after 1950 were always keen to maintain the strong emphasis on fieldwork. The authorities, in a sweeping reform of university education in 1950, did away with the principle that students should be allowed to choose both main and subsidiary subjects freely. Instead, a list of subject areas was established with a clearly defined programme, within which certain subjects and examinations were obligatory. Anthropology (etnografia) was no longer available as a subsidiary subject to students of history, sociology, geography, or history of art, because it was not included in the programme of studies set up by those departments. It was, however, available to students of archaeology. Fieldwork was an important feature of the curriculum in anthropology. It took the form of inter-university ethnographic camps (*Międzyuczelniane Obozy Etnograficzne*; Szyfelbejnová 1957) and summer holiday trainee camps, usually designed to meet the needs of regional museums or of a given university department. These camps gave students and staff from different universities the opportunity to work together, and students learned important research skills such as interviewing peasants (although this did not resemble participant observation) and documenting artefacts. This curriculum was already innovative, because such fieldwork had not figured officially in any pre-war programme for students of the subject then popularly known as *ludoznawstwo*.

These camps served as an important foundation for future fieldwork expeditions. Although research was necessarily confined initially to Poland, after 1956, under the pretext of organising such camps, it was possible to establish valuable contacts with young academics from other communist countries, including Yugoslavia. Individual contacts were strengthened also by cooperation promoted by the Polish Ethnological Society (Polskie Towarzystwo Ludoznawcze). The need to conduct comparative studies, and even to investigate other continents in order to gain a new perspective on Polish issues, led to the organising of expeditions outside Poland from 1958 onwards. The political thaw under the regime of Władysław Gomułka made this possible and enabled further initiatives to proceed during the 1960s, even after the turmoil caused by political events in 1968.

The very term *expedition* was probably taken from Soviet terminology, although it had also been used earlier in Polish. The travels of the Prince of Mecklenburg in the Nile-Congo region, in which Jan Czekanowski took part in 1907, were termed *expedycja* (see Czekanowski 1917–27).[3]

---

[3] Jan Czekanowski's work formed part of the Deutsche Zentral-Afrika-Expedition of 1907–8, under the leadership of Adolf Friedrich, Prince of Mecklenburg. It is important to stress,

Thus it was not a word that sounded foreign to the spirit of the Polish language. It could mean a number of different things, but in Polish anthropology it primarily denoted research conducted outside Poland. Usually it was work involving a group that lasted from a few weeks to a few months, and it was organised mainly during the summer holidays (particularly when the organiser was an academic centre). Data collection was typically repeated over a few seasons, or even many years, most often by the same group of people.

In the academic world, the same principle of Communist Party responsibility applied as in other fields of life. In principle, an institution's director and party organisation were responsible for all political aspects of its expeditions. Some decisions, however, could be taken only higher up, at the level of the Central Committee's Research Department. For example, long-term international cooperation between Academies of Science or Ministries of Education or Culture had to be managed centrally, although agreements at this level might then specify by name those institutes in Poland which were responsible for implementing the cooperation. Some decisions were politically sensitive, such as the establishment of a Centre for American Studies at the University of Warsaw. Often, however, especially when an international agreement was already in place, decisions were taken by directors and party officials at a lower level. Competition between institutions—for example, concerning project coordination and the division of funds—was common. Researchers often suspected that scientific considerations were playing second fiddle to informal connections and distortions caused by inter-institutional rivalries. The extent of such practices remains unclear, but there is no doubt that rivalry between the Polish Academy of Sciences and other institutions was a recurrent source of tension.

The full extent of informal links and networking in Polish anthropology during the socialist era may never be known. Anyone wishing to organise a foreign expedition, in addition to going about it in the normal, official way—by applying straight to the director of his or her institution—would also look for support somewhere higher up the ladder. It is still remembered today that Premier Piotr Jaroszewicz intervened personally to allocate additional funds for a Mongolian expedition in 1964.[4] Until the mid-eighties the

---

however, that an expedition (Russian, *ekspediciya*) as an organised trip for a group of people, whatever the length of time involved, was very common in the Soviet Union after 1917. It was probably encouraged by the socialist authorities at all levels because it was easier to maintain control over a trip organised in this way.

[4] Another example is the conviction that Hieronim Kubiak, a Central Committee member and professor of sociology at the Jagiellonian University, was able personally to decide that the hotel for the Institute of Polonia Studies at the university's Przegorzały campus would be financed from the central budget, simply by putting his signature of approval on the architec-

University of Warsaw's budget included a certain sum for the inter-university ethnographic camps. The original agreement was negotiated in 1953 by Witold Dynowski, then holder of the chair at Warsaw University, with highly placed officials at the Ministry of Higher Education whom he happened to know well from the times when they had worked together at the University of Vilnius before the Second World War. There is no doubt that the central authorities regularly interfered to support certain projects or people, sometimes assigning additional funds from the central budget. Could detailed archival research shed further light on such practices and the extent to which they influenced the decisions taken by research institutions? I am unsure, but in the meantime we must rely on oral tradition and on what the organisers of expeditions themselves have volunteered concerning their sources of funding. The information available is plausible inasmuch as it is consistent with what is known about the workings of informal networks under socialism in general, and in the Polish case in particular (see Wedel 1992).

This manner of organising expeditions differed from those known to us from the USSR, and it seems that no attempt was made to emulate Soviet models. At Polish universities it was difficult to combine expeditions with teaching, and researchers were constrained by the periods for which they could apply for permission to be in the field. Both in higher education and in the Academy of Sciences, foreign expeditions had to compete for money with fieldwork projects in Poland. After 1970 the universities were more active in organising expeditions than was the academy, a result largely of student initiative (which, after the events of 1968, the authorities were ready to heed for reasons of political calculation). The Academy of Sciences, on the other hand, with its more rigid profile of long-term agreements, often fell victim to changing political circumstances. For example, tension arose between Polish and Bulgarian partners concerning a joint expedition to the village of Gramada. With the benefit of hindsight it seems likely that the inquisitiveness of Polish researchers concerning, for example, the religiosity of local people aroused political suspicion and that this lay behind the Bul-garians' decision not to publish any of their own results. (Ostensibly the reason given by the Bulgarian side for ending the project was that the Poles had broken an agreement by publishing first; see Kopczyńska-Jaworska 2003.) Such joint projects with socialist 'brotherly nations' were always beset with delicate concerns about what exactly should be observed or pursued in interviews.

---

tural design and budget of the investment. He was not the minister of finance or even a member of the government; his position within the party was sufficient for him to have the right to act in this way.

Examples of Expeditions

Let us now consider in greater detail some of the more important expeditions of the socialist period.

The Carpathian Commission was established in 1958, following agreements between the eastern-bloc scientific academies, to conduct field-work in the Carpathian Mountains. It was administered by a team of re-searchers from all the countries participating. The purpose of the research, initiated in 1959, was to establish the interdependence of technology and the organisation of upland dairy farms. The project also involved research into regional cultures which crossed state boundaries, the co-existence of multi-ple ethnic groups within the same area, and the direction of cultural diffu-sion. The results of the research were presented at regular conferences and published independently (see Gladysz 1981; *Etnografia Polska* 1989, no. 2 [special issue]).

Systematic research was begun in Mongolia in 1966, after two years of planning and a pilot project (1965). Apart from an intermission in 1975–76 this work has continued until today. The initial research goal was to investigate the adaptation of pastoralist culture to the requirements of con-temporary civilisation and the model of the so-called people's democratic republics. The first task was to reconstruct a picture of Mongolian pastoral-ism as it had existed before the revolution. This was followed by a compara-tive analysis of the situation of young shepherds in communist countries. Prior to 1989 the research was carried out under the auspices of an interna-tional agreement between the Academies of Science in Mongolia and Po-land. The Polish partner was the Institute for the History of Material Culture (see *Etnografia Polska* 1975, no. 1, and 1980, no. 1; Dynowski 1976; Szynkiewicz 1984). After 1989 the basis for the research was changed and it took on commercially driven dimensions.

In Bulgaria, ethnographic research was completed in the village of Gramada, Vidin, between 1967 and 1970. It focused on village development within the communist system, particularly changes of socio-cultural micro-structures within that system (especially architecture). This project was carried out on the basis of an agreement between the Bulgarian Ethnographi-cal Institute and the Polish Institute for the History of Material Culture. According to the agreement, the issues to be dealt with included the role of powerful leaders in village transformation, the role played by national heri-tage and group memory, and possible disharmonies in cultural development. In practice, however, sensitive questions were not posed, owing to reserva-tions on the part of the Bulgarians. Following the publication of the Polish researchers' report, their Bulgarian colleagues brought the cooperation to an end (Nizińska and Markowska 1972).

Expeditions to Mexico, Peru, and Guatemala were mounted in the 1970s, growing out of the American seminars conducted by Maria Frankowska since 1963. The first expedition to Peru (Cayash Valley) took place in 1978; its main fields of interest were archaeology, ethnohistory, and ethnology. It was financed by four museums (Poznań, Szczecin, Warszawa, Kraków), which had obtained permission to use special funds to expand their anthropological collections. Close cooperation with the State University of San Marco and the National Institute of Culture and all contacts and preparations were facilitated by local circles of Polish emigrants, in particular Professor Maria Rostworowska, a professor at Lima University. The interest shown by the Polish fishing industry in the Peruvian shelf, the involvement of Polish experts in mining and prospecting, and the possibilities for the arms trade were also factors of great importance behind the Peruvian expedition. Apart from short breaks caused by the imposition of martial law in Poland and by civil war in Peru, the project continues in the present day. The expeditions were supported mainly by the Poznań Centre (Frankowska 1978; see also Posern-Zieliński 1982, 1984; *Etnografia Polska* 1985, no. 1). It is worth pointing out that the more detailed results of this research were typically published in *Ethnologia Polona*, in Spanish.

In 1978 an agreement of cooperation was signed between the Folklore Institute in Skopje, Macedonia, and the Anthropology Institute (then known as Katedra Etnografii) of Warsaw University to continue mutual assistance. The idea was to continue the research begun by Józef Obrębski in 1932–33 in an explicitly holistic manner. It was impossible to continue research in Obrębski's original village because of its depopulation. Instead, interrelations between ritual, worldview, and social structure were studied in Jablanica, close to the Albanian frontier. The results of the research were published (*Etnografia Polska* 1985, no. 1; Pokropek and Stronczek 1992; Zadrožinska 1995).

Many expeditions were organised by students. Their history can be divided into two phases. In the 1970s students typically looked for a sponsor among Polish enterprises, such as the truck manufacturers in Starachowice. In exchange, they would advertise the firm's products abroad. One group of students travelled 37,000 kilometres around Africa in STAR trucks (Koziorowska 1976). Similarly, expeditions organised by the University and National Museum of Szczecin made use of transportation and other support offered by the Polish Merchant Navy (Łapott 1984). Sponsors were many and varied—it was all a question of advertising and creating a favourable climate for Polish trade during the period in which Edward Gierek was first secretary (1970–80).

The second phase of Polish student expeditions took place between the declaration of martial law in 1981 and the round-table talks of 1989. During this period the goal of the authorities was to neutralise students' anti-government activism. A special grant for expeditions was established, following pressure from the Polish Students' Association, which turned out to be a breeding ground for Poland's post-communist politicians. This financial support did little to appease the political views of the vocal anthropology students, who, together with young historians, were among the most radical anti-communist activists, but it did make possible countless expeditions to Asia (especially India), Africa (Sudan, Burkina Faso), Mexico, and the Venezuelan Amazon.

The students' expeditions generated much useful documentation, some of it published. They proved to be of the utmost significance for the careers of numerous academics, among them Slawomir Szynkiewicz, Jerzy Wasilewski, Aleksander Posern-Zieliński, and Ryszard Vorbrich.

General Discussion

This description of the expeditions undertaken remains very incomplete.[5] It is clear, however, that organising ethnographic expeditions outside Poland was far from impossible. One needed to know how to play with words and how to touch on every topic which the researcher considered to be of importance without provoking the attention of a censor. It was different for certain partners, such as the Mongolians and Bulgarians, who were more closely controlled by the party. They probably had to accept that members of their security forces participated in their expeditions whenever foreigners were involved, but of course we Poles never had proof of this.

The members of all of these expeditions were, as a rule, Polish citizens, although in the cases of the Polish-Macedonian and Polish-Bulgarian joint projects, groups were mixed. Similar mixed teams sprang up spontaneously as a result of friendships forged between participants in the Carpathian Commission. Although no Western scholars took part in these expeditions, participation often turned out to be a springboard for meeting Western colleagues, either during the fieldwork or at international conferences later on.

Another intended form of international cooperation within the eastern bloc involved the development of vast publications such as *The Peoples of*

---

[5] I am currently embarking on archival research into the implementation of scientific policies and the system of academic institutional linkages which prevailed during the Polish People's Republic. The results may modify the account presented here, which is based on my experiences as a participant and witness from 1950 onwards.

the World and *The Ethnography of Slavonic Nations*. These projects were overseen by the Miklucho-Maklaj Anthropological Institute of the Soviet Academy of Sciences. In reality, they only sparked conflict between the groups that were supposed to be cooperating and proved to be rather uncreative and unproductive.[6]

Among the most popular destinations for individual anthropological trips (and there were many of these, lasting from a few weeks to several months) were India, Afghanistan, Uzbekistan, Iraq, Baluchistan, Iraqi Kurdistan, Tuva, Buryatiya, and—less often—Siberia. Individual research was also carried out in Africa, among the Dogon and Tuareg peoples. Individual trips differed from expeditions mainly in having a less complex field of research. Polish missionaries (notably the Divine Word Missionaries [*Zgromadzenie Księży Werbistów*]) carried out research throughout the world. The one region where it was impossible to conduct research individually was the European part of the Soviet Union. Even photographing the wooden architecture of old Moscow could prove risky.[7]

What light do expeditions, and international contacts in general, shed on the way the scholarly world functioned in Poland between 1945 and 1989? We must bear in mind that, following the Second World War, Polish anthropologists were required to shift the focus of their research away from the eastern borderlands (Żmudź, Auksztota, Polesie, Wołyń) to the western and northern parts of the country. It was also necessary to change their subject matter. Instead of searching for the archaic, anthropologists were now expected to study migrations and the manner in which people had been forcibly relocated from the east to the lands newly acquired by Poland on the basis of the Yalta agreement and the Potsdam Treaty. A little later they began to investigate the great changes taking place in the Polish countryside as a result of urban migration and the socialist variant of industrialisation. The influence of Soviet science expressed itself in the acceptance of the approach known as historical materialism, which presented traditional folk culture as an expression of the historical development of the peasant class. In

---

[6] For example, although the author of the section 'Poles' in the series *Narody Mira* (Peoples of the world) was praised in Poland, she was also criticised for accepting certain political assumptions concerning, for example, the homogenisation of Polish culture. In another example, it appeared impossible to accomplish a comprehensive study of Slav nations, because the Bulgarian partners, after a disagreement with the Macedonians, went ahead and published a separate volume entitled *Bulgarians*, which entirely disregarded the standpoint of the international editorial board.

[7] Marian Prokopek was interested in the wooden architecture of Great Russia, but as a foreigner he could not travel freely outside Moscow. His efforts to photograph the old wooden part of the city led to his being interrogated by the Moscow police, and the Polish Ministry of Higher Education was advised that he should not apply for permission to enter the USSR for the next ten years.

agreement with Marx's theory, the material foundations of peasant existence and the role of this class in society had to be emphasised. The most important contribution of the peasantry to progress was the folk culture itself, the acknowledged source of the national culture, as Soviet ideology never ceased to proclaim.

As early as in the mid-1950s, however, Polish anthropologists began searching for an altogether different system of reference. The iron curtain deprived them of access to Western literature and forced them to work in Poland, even when it was obvious that certain phenomena could be studied only by crossing political borders. These restrictions explain why some researchers turned their attention to so-called tribal societies and why in university curricula the 'world panorama of cultures' was introduced as a backdrop to the study of Polish folk culture. This is the context in which the Carpathian Commission and research on highland pastoralism became so important—they gave Polish anthropologists the opportunity to study outside their own country. Later expeditions to Africa, Asia, South America, and Mexico were facilitated by the government's foreign policy, which proclaimed solidarity with peoples of the Third World, who were exploited by international imperialism. Many anthropologists had links to Polservice, an organisation which sent Polish specialists to newly independent African and Asian countries. Some university professors (a minority) took the opportunity to travel and conduct research but did not return to Poland. Overall, the contributions from the Third World proved highly significant for the development of anthropology in Poland.

As for studies carried out in neighbouring 'Second World' countries, there was an increase in cooperation between Poland and Czechoslovakia and Hungary in the 1960s, but ties to Romania and Bulgaria remained more limited, in part because of the more difficult political conditions there.

Two phases can be distinguished concerning choices of research topics and types of arguments used. The first was characterised by reference to Marx's theory of basis and superstructure; the subject matter was economy, or, more precisely, traditional subsistence technologies, agriculture, animal breeding, crafts, and so forth. The importance of studying traditional implements derived from Marx's theory concerning the development of the relations between the means and the forces of production. These topics figured prominently in the studies by the Carpathian Commission and the Bulgarian expedition (Nizińska and Markowska 1972). In the second phase, according to the theory of development from people's democracy to socialism, priority was to be given to investigating social and economic changes. This agenda shaped the work of both the Bulgarian and the Mongolian expeditions. After 1980 these priorities seem to have been forgotten: it was not the proposed topic of the expedition but the loyalty of its members towards the government which was evaluated.

The Polish authorities took remarkably little interest in the choice of issues researched by anthropologists. Undoubtedly, subjects such as religiousness, rituals, and the spiritual sphere were avoided. Applications for permission to organise foreign expeditions had to be written in official jargon that often included a large dose of ideology. Of course this was no reflection of the convictions of the participants. A frequently used phrase in such applications was 'research on social and economic changes', which could cover virtually anything.

For example, the transition from a nomadic economy to a socialist one in Mongolia was researched in this way, with increasing attention being paid to young herdsmen and their aspirations in life. The enquiries were conducted through conversations and questionnaires. Quite unexpectedly, in the 1970s the Mongolian side started to cause trouble. They were interested in applying modern research methods, by which they clearly meant statistical studies, and were suspicious of qualitative research. They claimed that they did not want to be studied 'as if they were Kaffirs'. We found similar evidence for the existence of an unfavourable image of anthropology in Africa when, in the 1960s, we were refused permission to study the Pygmies in the Congo, for fear that we would depict them as a 'bad example' of Congolese civilisation.

Every expedition had its positive and its negative side, not to mention its own way of conducting research. Both themes and methods depended heavily on those who took the decisions in the host countries. Even international agreements could prove fragile. A personal conflict between the leader of the Mongolian expedition and the secretary of the academy in Warsaw lay behind the suspension of that expedition for two years. It could be resumed only under a new leader, an outcome which clearly demonstrates the supremacy of party officials over the academics.

The curtailing of research in the Bulgarian village of Gramada supports this point. Some of our Bulgarian colleagues were annoyed at the interest we showed in everyday matters, particularly in the religious life of the inhabitants. They tried to convince us that ceremonies such as family life-cycle rituals had a purely administrative character, and it became impossible to conduct conversations that would provide us with qualitative data. Permission to record ceremonies was also refused. As noted earlier, the excuse given for terminating the research was the publication of the Polish studies, allegedly in contravention of the agreement, which assigned the Bulgarians priority in the matter of publication. During this acrimony, it is important to stress, the political opinion of the head of the Institute of Ethnography of the Bulgarian Academy of Sciences was not shared by all the Bulgarian members of the team, but they were helpless to protest. Similarly, in the Mongolian case, questions about rituals were criticised on the grounds that this was religion. Questions about animal breeding were, according to our guides, matters of economy. Neither set of questions could be an anthropological problem.

The expeditions were thus never independent of politics. They were supposed to prove the existence of cooperation and friendship between communist countries, to channel aid towards developing countries, and to prove that one was committed to opening up towards the world. Their organisation often depended on important party officials, who were ready to support those who were not openly opposed to the authorities or those whom they wanted to appease, especially students. It was always crucial to use informal connections and to be able to use the right language when writing the project proposal. Organisers also had to know which subjects to avoid and, sometimes, to take the views of the host country into consideration. Overall one can conclude that, despite their many limitations, these anthropological expeditions really did facilitate international cooperation. The Mongolian expedition brought Poles into contact with Mongolists and Altaists from all over the world. The same applies to research on Carpathian pastoralism and to the other studies mentioned here. Each of them offered a window on the world.

References

Czekanowski, J. 1911–27. *Forschungen im Nil-Kongo Zwischengebiet.* Vol. 1, 1917; vol. 2, 1924; vol. 3, 1911; vol. 4, 1922; vol. 5, 1927. Leipzig: Klinkhardt und Biermann.

Dynowski, W. 1976. *Mongolia współczesna.* Wrocław: Ossolineum.

Frankowska, M. 1978. Ludowy synkretyzm religijny w Meksyku. *Etnografia Polska* 22 (1): 57–81.

Gladysz, M. 1981. Kultura Ludowa Karpat i Bałkanów. *Etnografia Polska* 25 (2): 27–220.

Hobsbawm, E. 1983. Introduction. In E. Hobsbawm and T. Ranger (eds.), *The Invention of Tradition*, pp. 1–13. Cambridge: Cambridge University Press.

Kopczyńska-Jaworska, B. 2003. Badania a obraz zapamiętany: Uwagi na marginesie badań w Bułgarii. In J. Kowalska, S. Szynkiewicz, and R. Tomicki (eds.), *Czas Zmiany Czas Trwania: Studia etnologiczne*, pp. 97–105. Warszawa: Polish Academy of Sciences.

Koziorowska, J. 1976. Polish Expeditions in Africa, 1972–1974. *Ethnologia Polona* 2: 226–30.

Łapott, J. 1984. Ethnological Studies and Africanistic Collections of the National Museum in Szczecin. *Ethnologia Polona* 8: 261–63.

Nizińska, J., and D. Markowska. 1972. Podstawowe zajęcia ludności wsi Gramada: Rolnictwo i hodowla. *Etnografia Polska* 16 (1): 11–54.

Obrębski, J. 1972. Obrzędowa i społeczna struktura wsi macedońskiej. *Etnografia Polska* 16 (1): 201–13.

Pokropek, M., and T. Stronczek. 1992. *Sporedbena monografija na makedonskoto selo Jablanica i polskite sela Pjentki i Tvarogi.* Skopje: Institut za Folklor 'Marko Cepenkov'.

Posern-Zieliński, A. 1982. Polish Ethnographic Fieldwork in the Peruvian Andes. *Etnografia Polska* 26: 186–90.

——. 1984. Los efectos culturales de la expansión del protestantismo en los communidades indígenas de America Latina: El caso andino. *Ethnologia Polona* 8: 143–220.

Szyfelbejnová, Z. 1957. K. Výchovnej metode v etnografickom ustave varsavskej university. *Slovensky Národopis* 5 (3–4): 417–24.

Szynkiewicz, S. 1984. Polish Studies on Mongolian Ethnology. *Ethnologia Polona* 10: 211–21.

Wedel, J. R. (ed.). 1992. *The Unplanned Society: Poland during and after Communism.* New York: Columbia University Press.

Zadrožinska, A. 1995. *Semejni obredi: Sporedbena monografija na polskite sela Pjentki i Tvarogi i makedonskoto selo Jablanica.* Skopje: Muzej na Makedonija.

Zawistowicz-Adamska, K. 1948. *Społeczność wiejska.* Łódź: Polski Instytut Służby Społecznej.

Chapter 18
Africanist Anthropology in the German Democratic Republic

Ulrich van der Heyden

A comprehensive history of anthropology in the German Democratic Republic has yet to be written.[1] Within the field, the representatives of Volkskunde have paid more attention to disciplinary history than have those on the Völkerkunde side. I cannot make good this deficit in this chapter, which I restrict to Völkerkunde studies concerning sub-Saharan Africa (for a fuller account see van der Heyden 1999).

Africanist anthropology was in many ways exemplary for the discipline in the GDR. It was also among the most developed branches, since the reorientation of the discipline in the 1960s coincided with the independence of many African states, some of which looked to the GDR for development aid and political solidarity, including close scholarly ties (Engel and Schleicher 1998). Indeed, in many fields, anthropology among them, tertiary education in the GDR was a major focus of development policy (van der Heyden n.d.). In the following account I concentrate on university anthropology. Although the ethnographic museums in Leipzig and Dresden also played a significant role, it was strongly shaped by the specifics of their institutional histories, and these details cannot be examined here.

A New Beginning

No less than in the field of Volkskunde, general anthropology in Germany stood in need of a completely new beginning when the era of Nazi barbarism was finally brought to an end in 1945. As Wolfgang Jacobeit noted, 'Volkskunde and Völkerkunde found themselves left with nothing in 1945; a new foundation and completely different conditions had to be developed in order to rebuild teaching and research activities' (1986: 15). German anthropolo-

---

[1] The only general overview is that by Ulla Johansen (1983), from a West German perspective. This contribution can be contrasted with the distorted description of GDR anthropology in Leipzig provided by Bernhard Streck (1997).

gists were deeply implicated in the racial and chauvinist theories of the Third
Reich (Fischer 1990; Linimayr 1994; Hauschild 1995). The entanglements in
fascist ideology were no doubt greater on the Volkskunde side, but Völkerkundler, too, had compromised their scientific integrity by supporting Nazi
colonialist ambitions (Schlenther 1959–60; Mischek 1996).[2]

Behind the propaganda rhetoric lay a genuine conviction among
young anthropologists in the GDR that it was their duty 'to serve international peace' (see Lips 1961: 13f.) The prioritising of peace and understanding among nations was understood in an explicitly political sense in debates
on the raison d'être of anthropology in the GDR. Ursula Schlenther, an
Americanist who moved to the GDR from West Germany in 1956, defined
the discipline as 'an historical science [that] can serve the Asian, African,
and Latin American peoples' struggle for independence. Contemporary
society and its culture ... are to be studied on the theoretical basis of historical materialism as the object of a modern anthropology, a complex science
not to be subsumed under other disciplines' (Schlenther 1959–60: 79).[3] To
say that this anticolonialism was 'contrived, dictated, and adopted only to
curry favour', as was alleged some years after German unification by a
scholar of West German origin now teaching in Leipzig, demonstrates little
familiarity with the historical facts (Streck 1997: 66).

The existence of the discipline was justified not through ideological
pronouncements but in terms of its scientific objectives, as expressed in
research publications, textbooks, encyclopaedias, and other popularising
works. This breadth is all the more remarkable in that the discipline kept its
illusory appearance of dealing with the exotic, the foreign, and the remote.
Evocations of the wide world of anthropology outside Europe were not
exactly in the interest of the authorities, who needed to accustom the population to the Wall and very limited opportunities for travel. Yet in one popular
introduction to the discipline, the reader was told of the necessity of fieldwork: 'Knowledge of foreign countries is already widespread and will be
deepened through first-hand experience in the future. Scientists, skilled
craftsmen, artists, and tourists will find a home beyond the borders of their
own countries and carry their sense of international understanding [Völker-
verständigung] from continent to continent' (Treide 1967: 9).

Anthropology's new start took place within the theoretical frame of a
unified discipline of Ethnographie (see Noack and Krause, this volume).[4]

---

[2] See Scholze 2001 for an incisive analysis of the relaunching of Volkskunde in the Soviet
Zone after 1945; see also Jacobeit, this volume.
[3] For more details of Schlenther's life and work see Rusch 1979; Krause 1991.
[4] The widespread opinion among West German colleagues that the term *Ethnographie* was
chosen simply because the discipline was called *etnografiya* in Russian (Elwert 1987: 140;

The primary goals of Marxist anthropology were seen from the beginning of its institutionalisation in the GDR as the 'triumph over all racist and fascist thought' and the 'overcoming of the division of Volkskunde and Völkerkunde and a historification of the discipline'. The focus was placed on socio-economic relations, both past and present, as well as on ethnogenetic processes (see Rusch [and Winkelmann] 1987: 295). Among the most influential theoreticians was Günter Guhr, whose conceptual triad of way-of-life, culture, and ethnicity was understood dynamically, 'to include moments of development and historical change in every individual nation and in all the nations of the world' (1976: 124).

But this adaptation of historical materialism emerged only later. Let us look first at the slow process of institution building. In a sense this began in January 1946 when Richard Thurnwald, an anthropologist of international fame, was named full professor in the Philosophical Faculty of the Humboldt University in Berlin (Scholze-Irrlitz 1991: 43). Thurnwald's attempts to found his own institute, however, were a failure. They met with the interest of a senior figure in the Soviet military administration, Lieutenant-General Petr Vasilyevich Zolutukhin, who in civilian life was a professor of ethnography and rector of the University of Leningrad (Lönnendonker 1988: 64), but it seems probable that Thurnwald's close ties to colonial planning and propaganda in the Nazi period precluded a continuation of his career. Political responsibility for employing 'compromised personnel' was assumed not only by the Soviets but also by proven anti-fascists. Thurnwald's case was assessed by Ernst Hoffmann, who had just returned from English exile and who later became professor of history at the Humboldt University, and by the Africanist Dietrich Westermann. The eventual outcome was that Thurnwald moved to West Berlin, where he was involved in the founding of the Free University.[5]

An anthropological institute was eventually founded at the university in East Berlin in 1952, thanks primarily to the Finno-Ugrist Wolfgang Steinitz (Kubitscheck 1996: 23; Jacobeit, this volume). Two years earlier, the Julius Lips Institute for Anthropology and Comparative Legal Sociology had been founded in Leipzig (Treide, this volume). Lips has been unjustly denigrated by his West German successor as a 'producer of ideology' (*Ideologieproduzent*; Streck 1997: 70). After his untimely death, his work was continued, with a strong focus on economic anthropology, by his

Streck 1997: 64) is incorrect. This terminology was rather a return to the differentiation developed in the nineteenth century between descriptive Ethnographie and comparative Ethnologie; see Fischer 1988: 22f.; Kohl 1993.
[5] For more detail on Thurnwald see Timm 1977: 617ff.; Melk-Koch 1989. On his 'denazification' see also Rüger 1985: 203f.

widow, Eva Lips. It proved to be more difficult to build up the discipline in
Berlin, a problem exacerbated by a lack of staff possessing any Marxist
anthropological training. This deficiency was addressed through the appointment of Sergey Aleksandrovich Tokarev, from the Lomonosov State
University in Moscow, who taught in both Berlin and Leipzig and provided
'essential advice for the development of a Marxist Ethnographie', according
to an internal report in Berlin at the beginning of the 1960s.[6] His volume on
the anthropology of religion became a classic, even if not all East German
academics agreed with its contents (Tokarew 1968; revised edition 1976).
His lecture manuscripts were, for reasons unknown, never published in the
GDR, but they were archived in the Ethnographie Division of the Humboldt
University until its disappearance in 1990, and they served as an important
reference for generations of students (Winkelmann 1986: 281f.). Tokarev's
work was well grounded in the discipline and, while it certainly had an effect
in communicating a historical materialist approach, it was by no means
designed exclusively to promote the political goal of the 'sovietisation' of
anthropology (Nikitin 1997).

When the first group of Marxist anthropologists had been trained, research was resumed in traditional areas of speciality, notably material culture
(see Rusch 1987: 303). Wide-ranging comparative studies were not undertaken—or at least not published. Eva Lips, in spite of her regional focus on
North America (her popularising 'Indian books' were frequently reprinted),
also influenced work on other regions, including Africanist research (e.g.
Schinkel 1970; Liedtke 1975; Mirreh 1976).

The Africa expertise of the Karl Marx University was concentrated in
economic anthropology and was exemplified by the publication in 1964 of
the article 'Cartographic Description of East African Economic Anthropology' (Liedtke 1964), which went for the first time beyond the confines of
merely describing the forms of subsistence economies.

Areas of Specialisation and Soviet Influence

Since there was little opportunity for GDR anthropologists to do fieldwork
outside their country, it is not surprising that Ethnographie came increasingly
to be considered an 'historical anthropology'. Historical writing was considered an important source for further anthropological analysis. In Africanist
research, studies were completed, for example, on 'Forms of Dissolution of
Ancient Society among the Tswana' (Berger 1961), 'On the Problem of the

---

[6] Archive of the Humboldt University of Berlin (hereafter HUB, A), Faculty of Philosophy,
Akte 55, 'Rechenschaftsbericht des Instituts für Völkerkunde und deutsche Volkskunde', p.
77 (no date).

Revolutionary Triumph over Pre-capitalist Social Conditions in Present-Day Africa' (Herzog 1975), and on 'Class Relationships among the Fulbe before French Colonial Rule' (Kurella 1965; see also Suckow 1973; Rusch 1975; Arnold 1988). Several of the first graduates with a specialisation in Africanist anthropology found employment at the Institute for Oriental Studies of the Academy of Sciences (Irmgard Sellnow, Jürgen Herzog) and at the Institute for African Studies of the Humboldt University (Hildegard Höftmann, Eberhard Berger). In this context it was only natural to combine the teaching of anthropology with that of African philology and history—in other words, to follow what is nowadays termed an interdisciplinary approach (see Krauth 1998a, 1998b). Topics touching on German colonial rule were particularly encouraged as part of the GDR's extensive historical investigations of colonialism (Höftmann 1956; Schulze 1958; Ahmed 1974; Franke 1978; Dolz 1982; van der Heyden 1992). The Central State Archive in Potsdam and other archives provided rich material for these endeavours (Metschies 1990). Work done by Africans themselves, substantial numbers of whom studied in the GDR, was also significant (Treide, this volume). The common pattern was to carry out repeated comparisons of several neighbouring regions and their major centres of population in order to analyse the parallel existence of traditional institutions and new social developments, how they interacted with each other, and how new social groups and classes emerged (Asamoa 1971; Ismail 1975; Mirreh 1978; Löfwander 1983).

In general, representatives of Africanist anthropology in the GDR were not in a position to set the theoretical agenda of the discipline. Irmgard Sellnow, who made an influential contribution in the early 1960s to the 'formations debate' (Noack and Krause, this volume), was the only exception (Sellnow 1961). Her main interest was in the process of state formation among south-eastern Bantu populations and the role of the masses in the precolonial period (Sellnow 1974: 134–45, 1975: 29–38). Like her colleagues from the Central Institute for Ancient History and Archaeology of the Academy of Sciences, she framed her data with a concept of universal human evolution derived from classical Marxist-Leninist writers (Sellnow et al. 1978: 21).

In these debates, and in other discussions with a more contemporary focus that were also highly political in character, GDR scholars did not shy away from criticising the 'Soviet sciences' (Müller 2001). Although the latter were treated with near hagiographic respect until towards the end of the 1960s, by the 1980s the position was quite different. The Soviet Union had begun to pay more attention to the African continent in the 1950s, primarily for reasons of foreign policy. The first studies to be published in the

GDR concerning contemporary issues in Africa, notably the 'principle of the collapse of the colonial system', were Russian works in translation, including passages from the Stalinist 'Soviet Encyclopaedia' (*Afrika* 1954; see also Datlin 1953; Stroja 1954; Tjagunenko 1959; Tjulpanov 1959).

This perspective on the development of Africa had a considerable influence on the first Africanists in the GDR. Soviet literature played the role of 'life-support literature' in this period, in the words of the colonial historian Walter Markov (1974: 50). Many GDR scholars were able to make research visits to Soviet universities (although the number of students with Africa as their main specialisation was cut back in the 1980s). Soviet specialists came to the GDR as guest professors, and conferences and other joint projects were organised regularly.

Among the first GDR students to study etnografiya in the Soviet Union was the Africa specialist Horst Stöber, who went on to participate in the controversy over the Asian mode of production (see Oberlack 1994) and to carry out research into the Organisation of African Unity (OAU). Many other young Africanists from Leipzig completed postgraduate studies in the Soviet Union (Brauner, Selter, and Voigt 1974: 759). Numerous linguists studied at the Zhdanov University in Leningrad under the doyen of Soviet African philology, Dmitriy Alekseevich Ol'derogge (Brauner et al. 1985: 541). In 1980 it was estimated that more than a third of all staff members of the African Teaching and Research Section of the Karl Marx University Leipzig had either studied in the USSR or had spent 'long-term sojourns' (*langfristige Qualifizierungsaufenthalte*) there (Stark 1981: 162).[7]

This cooperation was not without its problems, and in the first years of GDR African studies a number of difficulties arose. An internal report of the Communist Party organisation for Asian and African studies at the Karl Marx University Leipzig in 1961 recommended more careful advance planning of stays abroad, but the reasons for the desire to improve scholarly exchanges with Soviet partner institutions can no longer be reconstructed.[8]

Jointly organised conferences of socialist Africanists resulted in a number of publications, but of much greater influence than such edited volumes were translations of major Soviet works, which often became standard works for more than one discipline. One example was the two-volume *The Peoples of Africa*, edited by Ol'derogge and Ivan Izosimovich

---

[7] Regular contacts with colleagues in the Soviet Union were supplemented by cooperation with Africanists in other socialist countries, but such relationships did not develop much beyond personal contacts until the end of the 1980s.

[8] SAPMO, BArch, J IV 2/9.04/232 (o.P.): 'Zusammenfassender Bericht über den Stand der Verwirklichung der Empfehlung der UPL zur Entwicklung der Asien- und Afrikawissenschaften, Leipzig, den 27.9.1961'.

Potechin (Potekhin), which was the first attempt 'to illustrate the history and anthropology (Ethnographie) of the peoples of Africa on the basis of Marxist-Leninist methodology' (1961: xi). The work was intended to provide, 'with a view to the inevitability of the triumph of national liberation movements in Africa, a comprehensive description of the then current knowledge of the history, economy, languages, and cultures of the African peoples on the basis of Marxism-Leninism, imbued by the spirit of amity among peoples and a deep respect for African social and cultural achievements' (Brauner 1987: 942). While the breadth of the books was impressive, many parts remained somewhat superficial. Nonetheless, these volumes were still used in teaching in GDR universities in the 1980s. It is curious to note how the German translators of this Marxist overview added footnotes with additional data of older, 'bourgeois' German or Anglophone provenance.

In addition to Russian Africanist literature, works of English or French origin, provided they were Marxist or at any rate useful for Marxist science in their renunciation of racist or Eurocentric points of view, were also translated. Examples included the internationally recognised work of the Frenchman Jean Suret-Canale (1966), the overviews of the American Victor Perlo (1953, 1960), publications of the British journalist and trade unionist Jack Woddis (1963), the work of Basil Davidson (1962), and, very late in the day, a series of essays by Frantz Fanon (1986). 'Africa literature' from Hungary (Keszthelyi 1981), Poland (Domarańczyk and Wójcik 1976), and Czechoslovakia (Hanzelka and Zikmund 1954) was also translated on occasion; these books tended to be not scientific works in the strict sense but rather popular overviews intended for a wide readership.

The Pressure to Conform Politically

As far as political conformity is concerned, it is necessary, first, to recall that many of those who taught anthropology in the 1950s and 1960s had returned only recently from exile in countries such as Australia, the United States, and Sweden. By far the largest number, however, came from West Germany. Second, scholars such as Günter Guhr (e.g. 1969), concerned to develop the theoretical foundations of Marxist anthropology, were working on shifting sands. Even today, little is known about how anthropology was affected by official ideology and how far scholars 'themselves influenced the strategic, tactical, and propaganda game'; as Lothar Steinbach noted, quite a number of them were 'not just passive figures on the chessboard of the SED-leadership' (1999: 666).

Günter Guhr was denounced by his colleagues in the Section for History at the Humboldt University, who accused him of revisionist tendencies. The scandal led to Guhr's leaving Berlin to take up a position at the Museum für Völkerkunde in Dresden. After this, greater care was taken to ensure that manuscripts were vetted for political correctness before their publication. Guhr's book (1969) had already been printed and partly distributed before the ideologists realised its errors. All remaining copies were confiscated, and they are stored to this day in the basement of the Museum für Völkerkunde in Leipzig.

Political considerations certainly had an effect on the topics studied by GDR anthropologists. Among the enduring 'safe' fields were socio-economic development throughout history, material culture, and the relationship between material production and social evolution. Research into the last topic contributed to the formations debate (see Noack and Krause, this volume). Especially in the 1980s, methodological questions came in for close scrutiny in the GDR (Treide 1981). Anthropologists were encouraged to use interdisciplinary approaches. This led to studies of new topics such as nation-building and the development of ethnicity, particularly among the socialist, or at least non-capitalist, states of Africa. Ethiopia was well studied as the consequence of a request by the revolutionary Ethiopian government for assistance in the development of a museum network, which of course had to be built upon on careful scholarly foundations (Escher and Treide 1985). Reinhard Escher was the leading figure in this research. He was able to travel to Ethiopia on numerous occasions and to publish his dissertation (1983) in instalments in the journal *Ethnographisch-Archäologische Zeitschrift*, which was most unusual (Escher 1985a, 1985b, 1986a, 1986b, 1986c, 1987a, 1987b). His final report also appeared in the journal (Escher and Helmboldt 1988). In general, however, the work of GDR specialists abroad, especially in 'exotic Africa', was not extensively documented in any home medium.

Questions of nation-building were also discussed at many international conferences. In 1980 a conference titled 'The Development of Nations, National Languages, and National Cultures in Africa' was held in Leipzig (Escher and Stark 1981). It can be seen as an accommodation on the part of GDR anthropologists to their political regime. How far was this reorientation towards current politics voluntary on the part of the scholars? Bernhard Streck was right to speak of a 'pressure for practicality' (*Verwertbarkeitsdruck*; Streck 1997: 67). And some scholars judged, at least in hindsight, that their high levels of engagement had indeed been elicited in the name of the state; at any rate, attempts to escape such pressures were apparently few and far between.

In the founding session of the Anthropology Workgroup (*Arbeitsgemeinschaft Ethnographie*) of the GDR Historical Society, Dietrich Treide spoke in his keynote address of the contribution anthropology could make to the study of revolutionary processes in the Third World. 'The anthropology of non-European regions', he stressed, 'contributes in unison with the Marxist-Leninist social sciences to the study of world revolutionary processes today, and in particular to the study of anti-imperial, democratic independence movements in Asia, Africa, and Latin America. It has a part to play above all in the study of the increasing differentiation and polarisation of social forces and the formation and growing role of the working class and its allied classes.' Treide went on to specify four research priorities:

1. The evolution of classes and the establishment of the state; this would feed into the international discussion of pre-capitalist social forms
2. The study of processes of ethnonational evolution, ethnic assimilation, and national consolidation, processes that gain in political importance with state independence
3. Study of the factors corroding or sustaining traditional tribal and family ties and the role of such traditional social institutions in independence movements
4. A strong critical response to bourgeois social and cultural anthropology, which had to be incorporated into all research and teaching in Ethnographie (see Herzog 1974)

Many publications attest to the fruitfulness of this new, more politicised anthropology (e.g. Hutschenreuter and Treide 1981; Escher, Treide, and Hutschenreuter 1985). Leipzig was at the forefront of this rapprochement with GDR foreign policy interests. Previously, Klaus Hutschenreuter, Hans Dieter Kubitscheck, and Klaus Timm (1974) had contributed a chapter dealing with ethnic processes of nation-building in Asia and Africa to the volume *Socialism in the Liberated States*. The publication of these volumes marked the opening of a new era in GDR anthropology, in which the discipline was more directly entangled in the foreign policy of the state.

Investigations into pre-colonial social relationships in African societies were still undertaken in the last phase of the GDR, even though government support was now directed primarily towards contemporary, politically relevant topics. Continuities with colonial institutions were explored, and the colonial archives were utilised, not only to reconstruct ethnic history and nation-building but also—a particular concern of the Africanists in Leipzig—increasingly to illuminate the origins of underdevelopment in Africa. In this way 'traditional GDR Ethnographie' could adapt readily to new political demands. The major problem, as Treide admitted, was the lack of opportunities to study contemporary nation-building processes through fieldwork.[9]

---

[9] Archive of the University of Leipzig: ZM 4812 [o.P.]: letter from Treide to Kück, 6 November 1985.

Despite this deficiency, Africanist anthropology in the GDR received international attention (see Rusch 1994). This was true for both the work of native Germans and the research undertaken by African guest scholars. There was little working contact with anthropologists in West Germany, but a basic similarity existed in the way in which anthropology was increasingly seen as tightly connected to the social sciences (Johansen 1983: 271).

Teaching Anthropology in the GDR

In the teaching programmes in Leipzig and Berlin, university anthropologists were regularly assisted by guest lecturers, primarily members of the Academy of Sciences but also foreign guests. Again, the difficulty of doing fieldwork was a handicap, as was the case for all institutions working on 'foreign problems'.[10] A virtual ban existed on personal contacts (i.e. contacts outside of the scientific relationship) with students and scholars in Western countries, and it was very difficult to acquire up-to-date literature. The contents of Africanist anthropology courses were determined centrally in guidelines laid down by the ministry and the research plans of the Communist Party. In the end, however, implementation depended on the scholar giving the course, and not on the hierarchy of university organs, deans, rectors, and section heads above him.

African Studies, especially in Leipzig, was designed to communicate to students a broad anthropological knowledge base, supplemented by a variety of neighbouring disciplines. In fact 'a close interweaving of anthropology with other disciplines' (Schlenther 1959–60: 67) could be traced back to the pre-war period in Berlin, and this tradition was continued. In the 1970s, however, the teaching staff and the responsible functionaries recognised that it was necessary to give more priority to the 'primary scientific disciplines' (*tragende gesellschaftswissenschaftliche Disziplinen*). This category comprised economics, history, philology, literature, and cultural sciences (where anthropology would presumably be included). At a later stage sociology, philosophy, and ideology were to be incorporated, in both their general and their regionally relevant aspects. This policy was tied to the 'communication of Marxism-Leninism according to needs' and to a solid introduction to relevant regional and international languages (Brauner et al. 1985).

Anthropology (Ethnographie) students were accepted as majors (*Direktstudenten*) not every year but only every four or five years (Jacobeit 1986: 13); the number of students in one cohort seldom exceeded ten. The

---

[10] Yet it is an exaggeration to claim that fieldwork was altogether impossible for GDR scholars. See, e.g., Escher and Stark 1981; Rusch (and Winkelmann) 1987: 304.

'social relevance' of the discipline thus remained limited (Mohrmann and Rusch 1991: 64). This often led to critical comments and protests by the teaching staff, since their capacities were much larger than the demands put on them. In 1969, for example, a complaint was made that the Ethnographie Division at the Humboldt University 'has for two years not had a single German major but only guest listeners, minors, and a few foreign students'.[11] This meant that the small number of students admitted received very close attention from staff. All were able to complete at least a part of their studies abroad, particularly at the Universities of Moscow, Leningrad, Budapest, Prague, and Sofia (Mohrmann and Rusch 1991: 67).

Beginning in the fall of 1972, the Humboldt University began a combined history-Ethnographie programme which allowed students to specialise in anthropology to a greater extent than had been possible previously. The graduate was known as a *Diplom Ethnograph*, with either Völkerkunde or Volkskunde specified as a specialisation. The very fact that the Ethnographie programme at the Humboldt University was linked to history reveals that as in the Soviet model, the discipline was considered to be an historical science (Stöber 1957–58).[12]

The strong official ties between anthropology and history dated back to 1960–61, after which all Ethnographie students had to enrol first as students of history. In reality, however, the two subjects always maintained their separate identities (Mohrmann and Rusch 1991: 65). The following definition of Ethnographie was given in 1971: 'Ethnographie in its two branches, Volkskunde and Völkerkunde, is integrated into the system of Marxist-Leninist social sciences as an historical cultural-historical discipline [*historisch-kulturhistorische Disziplin*].[13] The same memorandum included a detailed list of other relevant disciplines in order of importance. It stated: 'The Diplom Ethnograph with a Völkerkunde specialisation well acquire expertise in

- modern world historical evolution, with special attention to the evolution of the socialist world system and its constantly growing influence on the global revolutionary process, the experience of the struggle of the international working class, and the anti-

---

[11] Private Archive: Akte 'Institut Vö/Vo III': 'Rechenschaftsbericht der Parteigruppe Ur- und Frühgeschichte, Alte Geschichte, Mittelalterliche Geschichte und Ethnographie. Berichtsperiode 27. Februar bis 21. März 1969'.
[12] Some of those affected by the 1968 reform believe that the grounds for linking anthropology to history were actually pragmatic: an affiliation with *Kulturwissenschaft* and *Asienwissenschaften* was also considered (Walter Rusch, interview 3 October 1996).
[13] Humboldt-Universität zu Berlin, Sektion Geschichte/Bereich Ethnographie (ed.), 1971.

imperial struggle of the peoples of Asia, Africa, the Americas, and Australia/Oceania as one of the primary elements of the global revolutionary process

- the cooperation of the socialist community of states with the countries of Asia, Africa, and Latin America

- the history and culture of the German people, especially that of the labour movement in the GDR

- the international relations of the GDR, above all with the states of Asia, Africa, and Latin America

- the deformation and dissolution of pre-capitalist social forms under the conditions of capitalism

- the beginning of their planned restructuring under non-capitalist evolutionary conditions and their revolutionary restructuring under socialism

- the historical and contemporary evolution of ethnic communities in particular regions and the historical development of specific traits in culture and way of life [*Kultur und Lebensweise*] of the regional population

- processes of national consolidation and the development of national consciousness on the basis of a knowledge of historical processes in the formation of ethnic units

- knowledge of Marxist-Leninist doctrine on the national and colonial question, and the theory and practice of Leninist nationality politics

- the history of anthropology, in particular with respect to the theory and methodology of Marxist-Leninist anthropology and the critique of bourgeois-imperial anthropology

- a language pertinent to the regional specialisation'[14]

The extent to which teaching staff actually followed this official declaration of requirements depended on the individual. As far as Africanists were concerned, these requirements 'from on high' played hardly any role at all. Gerd-Rüdiger Hoffman, for example, was adamant that no one ever intervened in his classes in Leipzig (Hoffmann 1993: 550).

Anthropological Publications in the GDR

Three journals were of particular significance for GDR anthropologists under socialism. These were the quarterly *Ethnographic-Archaeological Journal* (EAZ), the *Proceedings and Reports of the State Ethnographic Museum Dresden*, and the *Yearbook of the Ethnographic Museum Leipzig*. The last, founded in 1926, resumed publication in 1951. Publication of the 'Proceedings' from Dresden was resumed only in 1962, after a 75-year interruption (Guhr 1985: 274). The Museum für Völkerkunde in Leipzig also published an irregular series reserved for monographs and thematic anthologies. Both museums published regular brochures of around 50 pages in which the results of Africa-oriented research were presented to the wider public (Arnold 1981; Escher 1982; Dolz 1988; Bruyninx 1990). These publications also reported new acquisitions and exhibits and gave accounts of field trips (Svobodova 1977; Lange 1983; Escher 1985c; Neuwirth 1986; Herms 1989). The Berlin journal *Asia Africa Latin-America* seldom accepted articles by anthropologists.

The quarterly EAZ provided a forum for discussion of new research in virtually all fields of anthropology and prehistory. It included reports on conferences and fieldwork as well as book reviews. Over the years it expanded its coverage well outside the two disciplines named in its title, a symptom of increasing interdisciplinary cooperation (Rusch [and Winkelmann] 1987: 302). Anthropology and archaeology dissertations accepted in the GDR were listed with short summaries. A careful study of the journal's 'introductory essays' and the changing composition of its editorial board reveals that it was more 'a venture of the pre-historians than [of] the ethnographers' (Johansen 1983). Indeed, the proportion of anthropological contributions, especially those dealing with non-European issues, shrank markedly in the 1980s.

Publication in Western journals was difficult if not impossible for GDR scholars. One exception was Klaus Ernst, whose study of the structure and dynamics of social relationships in an African village, one of the first

---

[14] Ibid., pp. 3-4.

and most important studies on this topic, based on extensive fieldwork in
Mali, was published in London in an English translation (Ernst 1973, 1976).
Publication in journals appearing in Africa was also rare, and many African-
ists were confined to presenting their results in Eastern Europe. Even pre-
senting an article or a review in a Russian journal could prove difficult, since
the Soviet Union had plenty of Africanists of its own. The only journal in
Eastern Europe which published materials in German was the Czech journal
Archiv Orientalni.

    In principle, with a few exceptions based on specific profiles, any
publisher in the GDR could accept a manuscript on African issues. The print
runs were relatively high as a rule, and the prices heavily subsidised. In
terms of scholarship, the best work was published by the Akademie-Verlag.
At least in the 1950s and 1960s, 'authors from the GDR could present their
work to the public more quickly than [could] their colleagues in the Federal
Republic' (Dammann 1999: 169). The case of Ursula Hintze (1959) is a
good illustration. The Akademie-Verlag and also other publishers accepted
manuscripts from scholars who were not citizens of the GDR, such as the
linguist Johannes Lukas (1953), G. S. P. Freeman-Grenville (1962), Basil
Davidson (1962), Jack Woddis (1963), and Gerhard Kubik (1988). In comparison with the relatively small numbers of scientific monographs published, the GDR publishing industry was generous in presenting the interested reader with views of the world outside Europe. It is beyond the scope
of this chapter to summarise these efforts to popularise anthropological
knowledge, which found recognition among colleagues in the Federal Republic (Johansen 1983: 282f.).

Ideology in African Studies

Marxism-Leninism determined the horizons of anthropological perception,
as it did for other social sciences in the GDR. Within this ideology, there
was much room for manoeuvre, provided that what took place in this 'ma-
noeuvring room' (*Ausgestaltung*) could somehow be justified with reference
to Marxism-Leninism. As Franz Ansprenger, dean of African political
science in West Germany, wrote when the GDR had already been eliminated, Karl Marx left an analytical methodology 'with which it is no disgrace
to work. This is valid for the study of Africa in general' (Ansprenger 1991:
71).

    In fact, dogmatism did not severely affect African studies in the GDR.
As Jürgen Kocka confirmed for the historical and social sciences in the GDR
as a whole, works on Africa did not 'suffer from too much Marxism.' Their
Marxism—and this was certainly true for much of the anthropological
work—:

was often reduced to conformity to a politically dictated Marxist-Leninist historical and social model, which determined the existing socialist system as the apex of history to date and thus legitimised the present leadership. The premises of this model existed outside the academic discussion, claimed a monopoly, and as such were dogmatic and scientifically dysfunctional. The Marxism-Leninism of East German historians was often discernible in their forewords and afterwords, in the broad tendency of their interpretations, in their moral and political assessments, and in their polemics against the 'class enemy' in the West; their detailed methodology was hardly influenced by it. The latter often remained conventional and 'bourgeois'. Nevertheless, they were often successful in applying the productive potential of Marxist theory and came to conclusions which also generated attention outside the Marxist-Leninist system and advanced scholarship (Kocka 1992: 14).

Africanists in the GDR can be subdivided into two groups. Judging from their writings, some scholars worked with original sources, produced solid work within the limits laid down by Marxist theory, and presented their answers to questions about the African past and present in an explicit reflection of their Marxist orientation. Such work, above all in the fields of history, anthropology, literature, and linguistic studies, was generally well received by colleagues in the GDR and abroad. On the other hand, some scholars thought it more important to produce 'fundamental Marxist-Leninist research' for the countries of Africa. Their work was based on 'revolutionary-theoretical overviews' which forced all the regional, social, political, and ethnic characteristics of Africa into a Marxist-Leninist straitjacket. Some members of this group dedicated themselves professionally to combating bourgeois ideology. For the most part they merely identified 'an increasing divergence between bourgeois-imperial and socialist ideologies in the national independence movements in Africa' (Büttner and Rachel 1970: 241). While they often identified themselves as the ideologists of a discipline or even as philosophers, their undifferentiated point of view showed that their prime affiliation was to the dogmatic tradition of the Communist Party (Leonard 1994).

Africanist Anthropology during and after Socialism ✦

Africanist anthropology was only one small element of GDR Ethnographie. It always remained understaffed in Berlin, where its most significant representative was Walter Rusch (1936–2000).[15] In retrospect, it appears that from the early 1970s onwards Völkerkunde in Berlin came increasingly to be dominated by Volkskunde. This is evident in the scant attention paid to the former in historical analyses of the development of the discipline as a whole (Mohrmann and Rusch 1991: see especially p. 64; Jacobeit 1984, 1986).

Aspirations to unify Völkerkunde and Volkskunde had a strong appeal (Steinitz 1953). But this unity could never be fully realised because Völkerkunde could never escape from the shadow of the politically more important Volkskunde. In any case, their convergence was also criticised and refuted by numerous significant GDR scholars (cf. Jacobeit 1986: 17f.)

Anthropology in Berlin under socialism, concluded several representatives of the discipline after the turning point of 1989, was of marginal importance. 'This led to a certain complacent isolation, but it also opened doors to relatively independent scientific work' (Mohrmann and Rusch 1991: 66). When obliged to undertake an intensive, self-critical inquiry into research and teaching practices and to face the threat of closure, two of the most important representatives of Ethnographie in Berlin argued for retention of the historical orientation: 'To negate the benefits of historicity and contemporary relevance would be to step away from a consciousness of the origins of the discipline, away from a coming to terms with the past [*Aufarbeitung*] and towards repression' (Mohrmann and Rusch 1991: 68).

The worst fears of the Ethnographie community became reality at the Humboldt University when their subject was promptly eliminated from the teaching programme after 1989, to be replaced by a chair for European ethnology (*Europäische Ethnologie*). At the Academy of Sciences many researchers at the Central Institute for Ancient History and Archaeology practised a methodology approaching that of anthropology. There was even a research area designated 'Archaeology and Anthropology', which dealt with practical applications of natural science methods to archaeological and cultural-historical research (Scheler 2000: 141). Yet the German Unity Agreement dictated that every institute of the Academy of Sciences be closed.

Meanwhile, the research units at the ethnographic museums in Leipzig and Dresden were preserved, along with most of their staff.[16] Their journals

---

[15] Rusch alternated with Ute Mohrmann as chair of the Ethnographie Division between 1984 and 1990. See the obituary by Schlüter and Scott (2001).

[16] For more detail on Africa-related work at the Dresden museum which specialised in the arts and crafts of Africa, see Guhr 1985: 274f.; Arnold 1991: 276ff., 1995: 15ff. Unfortunately, we have no comparable analysis concerning the Leipzig museum, even though its coverage of Africa was much more extensive (but see Drost 1971; Blesse 1994). In addition to their exhibits and publications, museum staff organised many public lectures and conferences. They played a major role in changing popular images of non-European peoples among the

have survived and are nowadays published by LIT Verlag in Münster. Völkerkunde is still taught at the University of Leipzig. The new holder of the chair in the country's oldest department of anthropology is Bernhard Streck, a West German.[17] The scholars who once taught Ethnographie in Berlin or Leipzig, like the great majority of East German university scholars, will never have the chance to teach at a university in Germany again (Bollinger and van der Heyden 2002; Bollinger, van der Heyden, and Kessler 2004). Yet the great majority of museum professionals in eastern Germany today received their education under the phased-out scholars. And if one visits the library one can readily find scores of monographs bearing witness to the breadth and competence of GDR scholarship. All in all we can conclude that anthropologists played a significant role both in advancing their discipline and in creating and disseminating a relatively realistic image of Africa in the GDR.

References

Afrika (Große Sowjet-Enzyklopädie, Reihe Länder der Erde). 1954. Leipzig: Rütten and Loening.

Ahmed, K. 1974. *Die Entwicklung der sozialökonomischen und ethnisch-kulturellen Verhältnisse der Bevölkerung Westkameruns von der deutschen Kolonialzeit bis zur Erlangung der staatlichen Unabhängigkeit*. Thesis, Karl-Marx-Universität Leipzig.

Ansprenger, F. 1991. Zur Wiedervereinigung der deutschen Afrikawissenschaft. *Internationales Afrikaforum* 1: 71–77.

Arnold, B. 1981. Frauendarstellungen in der 'Touristenkunst' Westafrikas. *Kleine Beiträge aus dem Staatlichen Museum für Völkerkunde Dresden* 4: 9–13.

———. 1988. Fragen des Übergangs vom Mutterrecht zum Vaterrecht bei Völkern Südwest-Tansanias. In J. Herrmann and J. Köhn (eds.), *Familie, Staat und Gesellschaftsformation: Grundprobleme vorkapitalistischer Epochen einhundert Jahre nach Friedrich Engels' Werk „Der Ursprung der Familie, des Privateigentums und des Staats"*, pp. 262–67. Berlin: Akademie-Verlag.

GDR population. Other museums, though less important in terms of research, also had African holdings (see Germer 1982: 6ff.) and contributed to the dismantling of old stereotypes.

[17] On the basis of a single individual who was allowed to hold onto his position (Wolfgang Liedtke), Streck asserts that there was continuity in the institute he heads (1997: 66).

——. 1991. 'Afrika' am Staatlichen Museum für Völkerkunde Dresden: Zu Kontinuität und Wandel der afrikaspezifischen Sammel-, Ausstellungs- und Publikationstätigkeit. *Ethnographisch-Archäologische Zeitschrift* 2: 269–78.

——. 1995. *120 Jahre Völkerkundemuseum Dresden*. Afrikabezügliche Übersichten des Forschens und Publizierens sowie des Sammelns, Bewahrens und Ausstellens (unpublished manuscript). Dresden.

Asamoa, A. 1971. *Die gesellschaftlichen Verhältnisse der Ewe-Bevölkerung in Südost-Ghana*. Veröffentlichungen des Museums für Völkerkunde zu Leipzig 22. Berlin: Akademie-Verlag.

Berger, E. 1961. *Formen der Auflösung der Urgesellschaft bei den Tswana*. Diploma thesis, Humboldt University, Berlin.

Blesse, G. 1994. Daten zur Geschichte des Museums für Völkerkunde zu Leipzig (1869–1994). *Jahrbuch des Museums für Völkerkunde zu Leipzig* 40: 24–71.

Bollinger, S., and U. van der Heyden (eds.). 2002. *Deutsche Einheit und Elitenwechsel in Ostdeutschland*. Berlin: Trafo-Verlag Dr. Wolfgang Weist.

——, ——, and M. Kessler (eds.). 2004. *Ausgrenzung oder Integration? Ostdeutsche Sozialwissenschaftler zwischen Isolierung und Selbstbehauptung*. Berlin: Trafo-Verlag Dr. Wolfgang Weist.

Brauner, S. 1987. Personalia: Dimitrij Aleksevič Ol'derogge. *Asien-Afrika-Lateinamerika* 5: 941–42.

——, G. Sclter, and M. Voigt. 1974. Die Sektion Afrika- und Nahostwissenschaften der Karl-Marx-Universität Leipzig im 25. Jahr der Deutschen Demokratischen Republik. *Asien-Afrika-Lateinamerika* 5: 755–66.

——, et al. 1985. Karl-Marx-Universität Leipzig: Schwerpunkt afrikawissenschaftliche Lehre und Forschung. *Wissenschaftliche Zeitschrift der Karl-Marx-Universität Leipzig. Gesellschaftswissenschaftliche Reihe* 6: 530–48.

Bruyninx, E. 1990. Eisenplastik aus Tansania. *Kleine Beiträge aus dem Staatlichen Museum für Völkerkunde Dresden* 11: 3–9.

Büttner, K., and C. Rachel. 1970. Die Bedeutung des Marxismus/Leninismus für den ideologischen Klassenkampf in Afrika. In W. Markov, *Asien-Afrika-Lateinamerika 1970. Bilanz-Berichte-Chronik Zeitraum 1969*, pp. 223–43. Leipzig: Deutscher Verlag der Wissenschaften.

Dammann, E. 1999. *70 Jahre erlebte Afrikanistik: Ein Beitrag zur Wissenschaftsgeschichte*. Berlin: Reimer.

Datlin, S. 1953. *Afrika unter dem Joch des Imperialismus*. Berlin: Verlag Neues Leben.

Davidson, B. 1962. *Alt-Afrika wieder entdeckt*. Berlin: Akademie-Verlag.

Dolz, S. 1982. *Die Entwicklung der gesellschaftlichen Verhältnisse der bäuerlichen Bevölkerung im zentralen und östlichen Simbabwe unter den Bedingungen der Kolonialherrschaft bei besonderer Berücksichtigung des Standes und Charakters der Erforschung dieser gesellschaftlichen Verhältnisse*. Diploma thesis, Karl-Marx-Universität Leipzig.

———. 1988. Der Afrikaforscher Emil Holub: Seine Dresdner Sammlung und seine ethnographischen Forschungen. *Kleine Beiträge aus dem Staatlichen Museum für Völkerkunde Dresden* 9: 6–13.

Domarańczyk, Z., and T. Wójcik. 1976. *Vorhof der Hölle: [im Brennpunkt: Südafrika]*. Leipzig: Brockhaus.

Drost, D. 1971. *Wegweiser durch Geschichte und Ausstellungen: Museum für Völkerkunde in Leipzig*. Leipzig: Museum für Völkerkunde.

Elwert, G. 1987. Ethnologie. In T. Buddensieg, K. Düwell, and K.-J. Sembach (eds.), *Wissenschaften in Berlin*, vol. 2, *Disziplinen*, pp. 135–41. Berlin: Technische Universität.

Engel, U., and H.-G. Schleicher. 1998. *Die beiden deutschen Staaten in Afrika: Zwischen Konkurrenz und Koexistenz 1949–1990*. Hamburg: Institut für Afrika-Kunde.

Ernst, K. 1973. *Tradition und Fortschritt im afrikanischen Dorf: Soziologische Probleme der nichtkapitalistischen Umgestaltung der Dorfgemeinde in Mali*. Berlin: Akademie-Verlag.

———. 1976. *Tradition and Progress in the African Village: The Noncapitalist Transformation of Rural Communities in Mali*. London: C. Hurst.

Escher, R. 1982. Einheimische Schriftsysteme im subsaharischen Afrika. *Kleine Beiträge aus dem Staatlichen Museum für Völkerkunde Dresden* 5: 8–12.

———. 1983. *Grundtendenzen der ethnischen Entwicklung und Nationsbildung in Äthiopien: Studien zur ethnischen Geschichte der Völker Nordost-Afrikas von den Anfängen bis 1974*. Thesis, Karl-Marx-Universität Leipzig.

———. 1985a. Ethnische und ethno-soziale Hauptglieder, Makro- und Mikroeinheiten der altorientalischen Klassengesellschaft in Äthiopien: Versuch einer Typologisierung ethnischer Gemeinschaften von ihrer Entstehung bis zum 1. Jh. *Ethnographisch-Archäologische Zeitschrift* 4: 569–87.

———. 1985b. Ethnische und ethno-soziale Hauptglieder, Makro- und Mikro-einheiten der Vorklassengesellschaft in Äthiopien: Versuch einer Typologisierung ethnischer Gemeinschaften von ihrer Entstehung bis zum 1. Jh. *Ethnographisch-Archäologische Zeitschrift* 3: 417–32.

———. 1985c. Studienreise zu den Völkern des großen Grabenbruchs (Äthiopien). *Kleine Beiträge aus dem Staatlichen Museum für Völkerkunde Dresden* 7: 24–31.

———. 1986a. Ethnikos und ethno-sozialer Organismus in der altorientalischen Klassengesellschaft Äthiopiens: Analyse ihrer Verhältnisse am Beispiel der Amhara vom 14. bis zum 19. Jh. *Ethnographisch-Archäologische Zeitschrift* 2: 177–96.

———. 1986b. Ethnikos und ethno-sozialer Organismus in der feudal-kapitalistischen Klassengesellschaft Äthiopiens: Analyse ihres Verhältnisses unter besonderer Berücksichtigung der Amhara vom 19. Jh. bis 1974. *Ethnographisch-Archäologische Zeitschrift* 4: 623–40.

———. 1986c. Faktoren und Bilanz ethnischer Prozesse in der vor- und altorientalischen Klassengesellschaft Äthiopiens: Untersuchungen ethnischer Veränderungen am Beispiel ethnisch-sprachlicher Prozesse von ihren Anfängen bis zum 19. Jh. *Ethnographisch-Archäologische Zeitschrift* 3: 385–404.

———. 1987a. Faktoren und Bilanz ethnischer Prozesse in der feudal-kapitalistischen Klassengesellschaft Äthiopiens. *Ethnographisch-Archäologische Zeitschrift* 3: 379–92.

———. 1987b. Zum Stand der ethnischen Entwicklung und Nationbildung in Äthiopien vor der nationaldemokratischen Revolution von 1974. *Ethnographisch-Archäologische Zeitschrift* 4: 615–24.

———, and R. Helmboldt. 1988. 'Wallaga-Museum' öffnet seine Türen: Bericht über die wissenschaftliche Beratertätigkeit beim Aufbau des Museums der Verwaltungsregion Wallaga in Naqamt, Äthiopien, 1987. *Ethnographisch-Archäologische Zeitschrift* 3: 489–504.

———, and K. Stark. 1981. Die Entwicklung von Nationen, Nationalsprachen und Nationalkulturen. *Asien-Afrika-Lateinamerika* 2: 352–56.

———, D. Treide, and K. Hutschenreuter. 1985. Ethnische Situation und Nationalitätenpolitik. In G. Brehme et al., *Sozialistische Orientierung national befreiter Staaten: Grundprobleme, Hauptprozesse*, pp. 165–79. Berlin: Staatsverlag der Deutschen Demokratischen Republik.

Fanon, F. 1986. *Das kolonisierte Ding wird Mensch.* Ausgewählte Schriften. (Ed. by Rainer Arnold.) Leipzig: Reclam.

Fischer, H. 1988. Anfänge, Abgrenzungen, Anwendungen. In H. Fischer (ed.), *Ethnologie: Einführung und Überblick*, pp. 6–25. Berlin: Reimer.

———. 1990. *Völkerkunde im Nationalsozialismus: Aspekte der Anpassung, Affinität und Behauptung einer wissenschaftlichen Disziplin*. Berlin: Reimer.

Franke, J. 1978. *Die Dschagga im Spiegel der zeitgenössischen Berichte 1885–1916: Ein Beitrag zur Geschichte der Dschagga während der deutschen Kolonialzeit*. Thesis, Karl-Marx-Universität Leipzig.

Freeman-Grenville, G. S. P. 1962. *The Medieval History of the Coast of Tanganyika, with Special Reference to Recent Archaeological Discoveries*. Berlin: Akademie-Verlag.

Germer, E. 1982. Völkerkundliche Museen und Sammlungen in der Deutschen Demokratischen Republik. *Abhandlungen und Berichte des Staatlichen Museums für Völkerkunde Dresden* 39: 6–53.

Guhr, G. 1969. *Karl Marx und theoretische Probleme der Ethnographie*. Jahrbuch des Museums für Völkerkunde zu Leipzig 26, Beiheft. Berlin: Akademie-Verlag.

———. 1976. Über die Komplexität von Kultur und Lebensweise. *Acta Ethnographica Science Hungaria* 25 (1–2): 124–43.

———. 1985. Ethnographie in Dresden. In G. Guhr and P. Neumann (eds.), *Ethnographisches Mosaik: Aus den Sammlungen des Staatlichen Museums für Völkerkunde Dresden*, pp. 266–75. Berlin: Deutscher Verlag der Wissenschaften.

Hanzelka, J., and M. Zikmund. 1954. *Afrika: Traum und Wirklichkeit*. Berlin: Verlag Volk und Wissen.

Hauschild, T. (ed.). 1995. *Lebenslust und Fremdenfurcht: Ethnologie im Dritten Reich*. Frankfurt am Main: Suhrkamp.

Herms, I. 1989. Safari am Njassasee. *Kleine Beiträge aus dem Staatlichen Museum für Völkerkunde Dresden* 10: 25–27.

Herzog, J. 1974. Ethnographen der DDR beraten gemeinsame Probleme. *Asien-Afrika-Lateinamerika* 2: 313–14.

———. 1975. *Traditionelle Institutionen und nationale Befreiungsrevolution in Tansania: Zum Problem der revolutionären Überwindung vorkapitalistischer gesellschaftlicher Verhältnisse im heutigen Afrika*. Berlin: Akademie-Verlag.

Heyden, van der, U. 1992. Die Afrika-Geschichtsschreibung in der ehemaligen DDR: Versuch einer kritischen Aufarbeitung. *Afrika Spectrum* 27 (2): 207–11.

——. 1999. *Die Afrikawissenschaften in der DDR: Eine akademische Disziplin zwischen Exotik und Exempel. Eine wissenschaftsgeschichtliche Untersuchung.* Münster: LIT Verlag.

——. n.d. *Das internationale entwicklungspolitische Engagement der DDR: Doktrin und Strategien zwischen Illusion und Wirklichkeit.* Münster: LIT Verlag. Forthcoming.

Hintze, U. 1959. *Bibliographie der Kwa-Sprachen und der Sprachen der Togo-Restvölker.* Berlin: Akademie-Verlag.

Höftmann, H. 1956. *Ein Beitrag zur Erkenntnis der Ursachen des Maji-Maji-Aufstandes im ehemaligen Deutsch-Ostafrika 1905–1906.* Diploma thesis, Humboldt Universität, Berlin.

Hoffmann, G.-R. 1993. Afrikawissenschaften. In U. van der Heyden (ed.), *Sichten auf die historische Afrikawissenschaft in der DDR: Ein Rundtischgespräch mit Afrikawissenschaftlern.* In *Asien-Afrika-Lateinamerika* 5: 539–71.

Humboldt-Universität zu Berlin, Sektion Geschichte/Bereich Ethnographie (ed.). 1971. *Information über das 1972 beginnende Studium Geschichte/Ethnographie an der Humboldt-Universität zu Berlin.*

Hutschenreuter, K., and D. Treide. 1981. Die Herausbildung von Nationen in Afrika und die Politik afrikanischer Führungskräfte in Bezug auf ethnisch-nationale Prozesse. *Asien-Afrika-Lateinamerika* 2: 197–212.

——, H. D. Kubitscheck, and K. Timm. 1974. Grundfragen des antiimperialistischen Kampfes in der Gegenwart. In L. Rathmann et al., *Grundfragen des antiimperialistischen Kampfes der Völker Asiens, Afrikas und Lateinamerikas in der Gegenwart*, pp. 376–98. Berlin: Akademie-Verlag.

Ismail, K. 1975. *Die sozialökonomischen Verhältnisse der bäuerlichen Bevölkerung im Küstengebirge der Syrischen Arabischen Republik: Eine Untersuchung im Gebiet von As-Saih-Badr.* Berlin: Akademie-Verlag.

Jacobeit, W. 1984. Zum Verhältnis von Ethnographie und Geschichte. *Jahrbuch für Wirtschaftsgeschichte* 2: 165–77.

——. 1986. Dreißig Jahre Ethnographie an der Humboldt-Universität zu Berlin 1952–1982. *Ethnographisch-Archäologische Zeitschrift* 1: 13–26.

Johansen, U. 1983. Die Ethnologie in der DDR. In H. Fischer (ed.), *Ethnologie. Einführung und Überblick*, pp. 303–18. Berlin: Reimer.

Keszthelyi, T. 1981. *Afrikanische Literatur: Versuch eines Überblicks.* Berlin: Aufbau-Verlag.

Kocka, J. 1992. *Die Auswirkungen der deutschen Einigung auf die Geschichts- und Sozialwissenschaften: Vortrag vor dem Gesprächskreis Geschichte der Friedrich-Ebert-Stiftung in Bonn am 29. Januar 1992.* Bonn: Friedrich-Ebert-Stiftung.

Kohl, K.-H. 1993. *Ethnologie: Die Wissenschaft vom kulturell Fremden. Eine Einführung.* München: Beck.

Krause, M. 1991. Ursula Schlenther (1919–1979): Ihr Beitrag zur Weiterführung der Tradition der Völkerkunde Lateinamerikas an der Berliner Universität. *Geschichte der Völkerkunde und Volkskunde an der Berliner Universität. Zur Aufarbeitung des Wissenschaftserbes. Beiträge zur Geschichte der Humboldt-Universität zu Berlin* 28: 73–80.

Krauth, W.-H. 1998a. Asien- und Afrikawissenschaften. In J. Kocka and R. Mayntz (eds.), *Wissenschaft und Wiedervereinigung: Disziplinen im Umbruch,* pp. 21–78. Berlin: Akademie-Verlag.

——. 1998b. Die Asien- und Afrikawissenschaften in der DDR: Wissenschaftssoziologische Bemerkungen. In W.-H. Krauth and R. Wolz (eds.), *Wissenschaft und Wiedervereinigung: Asien- und Afrikawissenschaften im Umbruch,* pp. 443–66. Berlin: Akademie-Verlag.

Kubik, G. 1988. *Zum Verstehen afrikanischer Musik: Ausgewählte Aufsätze.* Leipzig: Reclam.

Kubitscheck, H. D. 1996. *Das Südostasien-Institut an der Humboldt-Universität zu Berlin: Zur Geschichte der Südostasienwissenschaften.* Berlin: Institut für Asien- und Afrikawissenschaften.

Kurella, S. 1965. *Die Klassenverhältnisse der Fulbe vor der französischen Kolonialherrschaft im Gebiet der Futa-Djallon und Futa-Toro.* Diploma thesis, Humboldt-Universität, Berlin.

Lange, W. J. 1983. Geburts- und Totenfeiern bei den Cheka in Äthiopien. *Kleine Beiträge aus dem Staatlichen Museum für Völkerkunde Dresden* 6: 29–35.

Leonard, W. 1994. Die Etablierung des Marxismus-Leninismus in der SBZ/DDR (1945–1955). *Aus Politik und Zeitgeschichte: Beilage zur Wochenzeitung Das Parlament* 40 (7 October): 3–11.

Liedtke, W. 1964. Beiträge zur Wirtschaftsethnologie (Kartographische Darstellungen zur Wirtschaftsethnographie Ostafrikas. Von einem Kollektiv des Julius Lips-Instituts. Leitung W. Liedtke). *Wissenschaftliche Zeitschrift der Karl-Marx-Universität Leipzig, Gesellschafts- und Sprachwissenschaftliche Reihe* 2: 281–87.

——. 1975. *Analyse der sozialökonomischen Verhältnisse westafrikanischer Völker: Eine Untersuchung der Beziehungen zwischen Produktivkräften und Produktionsverhältnissen bei Völkern Nordghanas,*

Obervoltas und im Hinterland Liberias. Thesis, Karl-Marx-Universität, Leipzig.

Linimayr, P. 1994. *Wiener Völkerkunde im Nationalsozialismus: Ansätze zu einer NS-Wissenschaft.* Frankfurt am Main: Peter Lang.

Lips, E. 1961. Vorwort. In J. E. Lips, *Vom Ursprung der Dinge: Eine Kulturgeschichte des Menschen*, pp. 11–14. Leipzig: Brockhaus.

Löfwander, T. 1983. *Die sozialökonomischen Verhältnisse der bäuerlichen Bevölkerung in der Republik Mali: Ergebnisse einer Feldforschung im Arrondissement Sananleoroba, Region Bamako.* Berlin: Akademie-Verlag.

Lönnendonker, S. 1988. *Freie Universität Berlin: Gründung einer politischen Universität.* Berlin: Duncker und Humblot.

Lukas, J. 1953. *Die Sprache der Tubu in der zentralen Sahara.* Berlin: Akadmie-Verlag.

Markov, W. 1974. Zu einigen Ergebnissen und Problemen der Erforschung der Geschichte der nationalen Befreiungsbewegung. *Wissenschaftliche Mitteilungen: Historiker-Gesellschaft der Deutschen Demokratischen Republik* 2: 49–53.

Melk-Koch, M. 1989. *Auf der Suche nach der menschlichen Gesellschaft: Richard Thurnwald.* Berlin: Reimer.

Metschies, K. 1990. Quellen im Zentralen Staatsarchiv in Potsdam zur kolonialen Politik Deutschlands in Afrika und Nahost. *Archivmitteilungen* 40: 134–41.

Mirreh, A. G. 1976. *Die wirtschaftlichen und gesellschaftlichen Verhältnisse der nomadischen Bevölkerung im Norden der Demokratischen Republik Somalia.* Thesis, Karl-Marx-Universität Leipzig.

———. 1978. *Die sozialökonomischen Verhältnisse der nomadischen Bevölkerung im Norden der Demokratischen Republik Somalia.* Berlin: Akademie-Verlag.

Mischek, U. 1996. Der Funktionalismus und die nationalsozialistische Kolonialpolitik in Afrika: Günter Wagner und Dietrich Westermann. *Paideuma* 42: 141–50.

Mohrmann, U., and W. Rusch. 1991. Vier Jahrzehnte Ethnographie an der Humboldt-Universität zu Berlin: Geschichte der Völkerkunde und Volkskunde an der Berliner Universität. *Geschichte der Völkerkunde und Volkskunde an der Berliner Universität. Zur Aufarbeitung des Wissenschaftserbes. Beiträge zur Geschichte der Humboldt-Universität* 28: 61–73. Berlin: Humboldt-Universität zu Berlin.

Müller, E. W. 2001. *Kultur, Gesellschaft und Ethnologie: Aufsätze 1956–2000.* Münster: LIT Verlag.

Neuwirth, B. 1986. Mädchensituation bei den Bemba in Sambia. *Kleine Beiträge aus dem Staatlichen Museum für Völkerkunde Dresden* 8: 36–42.

Nikitin, P. I. 1997. *Zwischen Dogma und gesundem Menschenverstand: Wie ich die Universitäten der deutschen Besatzungszone 'sowjetisierte'; Erinnerungen eines Sektorleiters Hochschulen und Wissenschaft der sowjetischen Militäradministration in Deutschland.* Berlin: Akademie-Verlag.

Oberlack, M. 1994. *Das präkoloniale Afrika und die Kontroverse um die 'Asiatische Produktionsweise' in der DDR-Historiographie.* Münster: LIT Verlag.

Ol'derogge, D. A., and I. I. Potechin (eds.). 1961. *Die Völker Afrikas: Ihre Vergangenheit und Gegenwart.* 2 vols. Berlin: Deutscher Verlag der Wissenschaften.

Perlo, V. 1953. *Der amerikanische Imperialismus.* Berlin: Dietz.

——. 1960. *Das Reich der Hochfinanz.* Berlin: Dietz.

Rüger, A. 1985. Rasvitie istoriografii Afrikii juschnee Sachary v GDR (ot vosniknovenija do 1970 g.). In B. B. Piotrovskii and B. M. Tupolev (eds.), *Izucenie istorii Afrikii: Problemij i dostischenija*, pp. 201–38. Moskva: Izdatel'stvo Nauka.

Rusch, W. 1975. *Klassen und Staat in Buganda vor der Kolonialzeit: Über die Entwicklung der Produktionsverhältnisse in Buganda bis zum Ende des 19. Jahrhunderts und die Herausbildung eines Staates, seinen Aufbau und seine Funktionen. Ein Beitrag zur Erforschung der Geschichte der Baganda.* Berlin: Akademie-Verlag.

——. 1979. Ursula Schlenther zum Gedenken. *Ethnographisch-Archäologische Zeitschrift* 2: 193–95.

—— (and I. Winkelmann). 1987. Zur Entwicklung der außereuropäischen Ethnographie in der DDR. Eine Skizze auf Grund ihrer Struktur und ausgewählter Publikationen. *Ethnographisch-Archäologische Zeitschrift* 2: 295–320.

——. 1994. Sichten auf die historischen Afrikawissenschaften in der DDR. In U. van der Heyden (ed.), *Sichten auf die historische Afrikawissenschaft in der DDR: Ein Rundtischgespräch mit Afrikawissenschaftlern.* In *Asien-Afrika-Lateinamerika* 5: 539–71.

Scheler, W. 2000. *Von der Deutschen Akademie der Wissenschaften zu Berlin zur Akademie der Wissenschaften der DDR: Abriss zur Genese und Transformation der Akademie.* Berlin: Dietz.

Schinkel, H.-G. 1970. *Haltung, Zucht und Pflege des Viehs bei den Nomaden Ost- und Nordostafrikas: Ein Beitrag zur traditionellen Ökonomie der Wanderhirten in semiariden Gebieten.* Veröffentlichungen des Museums für Völkerkunde zu Leipzig 21. Berlin: Akademie-Verlag.

Schlenther, U. 1959–60. Zur Geschichte der Völkerkunde an der Berliner Universität von 1810 bis 1945. *Wissenschaftliche Zeitschrift, Humboldt Universität zu Berlin. Beiheft zum Jubiläumsjahrgang* 9: 67–74.

Schlüter, T., and A. H. Scott. 2001. Walter Rusch, 10 july 1936–8 june 2000. *Asien-Afrika-Lateinamerika* 3: 275–78.

Scholze, T. 2001. Anmerkungen zur Frühgeschichte der Volkskunde in der sowjetischen Besatzungszone bzw. späteren DDR. In T. Scholze and L. Scholze-Irrlitz (eds.), *Zehn Jahre Gesellschaft für Ethnographie–Europäische Ethnologie in Berlin: Wolfgang Jacobeit zum 80. Geburtstag*, pp. 149–56. Münster: LIT Verlag.

Scholze-Irrlitz, L. 1991. Richard Thurnwald (1869–1954): Einige Aspekte seiner Forschungs- und Lehrkonzeption. *Geschichte der Völkerkunde und Volkskunde an der Berliner Universität. Zur Aufarbeitung des Wissenschaftserbes. Beiträge zur Geschichte der Humboldt-Universität zu Berlin* 28: 37–46.

Schulze, A. 1958. *Die Auswirkungen der deutschen Kolonisation auf die sozialökonomischen Verhältnisse der Bevölkerung Deutsch-Ostafrikas.* Diploma thesis, Berlin: Humboldt-Universität.

Sellnow, I. 1961. *Grundprinzipien einer Periodisierung der Urgeschichte: Ein Beitrag auf Grundlage ethnographischen Materials.* Berlin: Akademie-Verlag.

——. 1974. Zur Rolle der Volksmassen im Prozeß der Staatsentstehung: Ein Beitrag auf der Grundlage ethnographischen Materials. In J. Herrmann and I. Sellnow (eds.), *Beiträge zur Entstehung des Staates*, pp. 134–45. Berlin: Akademie-Verlag.

——. 1975. Die Überwindung urgesellschaftlicher Traditionen im Prozeß der Staatsentstehung: Dargestellt am Beispiel südafrikanischer Bantustämme. In J. Herrmann and I. Sellnow (eds.), *Die Rolle der Volksmassen in der Geschichte der vorkapitalistischen Gesellschaftsformationen: Zum XIV. Internationalen Historikerkongress in San Francisco*, pp. 29–38. Berlin: Akademie-Verlag.

——, et al. 1978. *Weltgeschichte bis zur Herausbildung des Feudalismus: Ein Abriß.* Berlin: Akademie-Verlag.

Stark, K. 1981. 20 Jahre Afrika-Institut an der Karl-Marx-Universität Leipzig: Bericht über die Festveranstaltung am 13. Oktober 1980 in Leipzig. *Asien-Afrika-Lateinamerika* 1: 161–62.

Steinbach, L. 1999. Wer und was blieb von der DDR-Geschichtswissenschaft? Unterschiedliche Forschungsschwerpunkte, kontroverse Bewertungen. *Archiv für Sozialgeschichte* 39: 663–91.

Steinitz, W. 1953. *Die volkskundliche Arbeit in der Deutschen Demokratischen Republik: Vortrag gehalten auf der Tagung der Sektion für Völkerkunde und Deutsche Volkskunde der Deutschen Akademie der Wissenschaften zu Berlin vom 4.–6.9.1953.* [Leipzig]: Zentralhaus für Laienkunst.

Stöber, H. 1957–58. 40 Jahre sowjetische Ethnographie. *Wissenschaftliche Zeitschrift der Humboldt-Universität in Berlin, Gesellschafts- und Sprachwissenschaftliche Reihe* 1: 119–23.

Streck, B. 1997. *Fröhliche Wissenschaft Ethnologie: Eine Einführung.* Wuppertal: Edition Trickster im Peter-Hammer-Verlag.

Stroja, L. 1954. *Studien über die Krise des Kolonialsystems im Imperialismus.* Bukarest: Staatsverlag für wissenschaftliche Literatur.

Suckow, C. 1973. *Die Bantu- und Khoisan-Bevölkerung Südafrikas unter den Bedingungen der europäischen Kolonialexpansion von der Mitte des 17. Jahrhunderts bis zur Mitte des 19. Jahrhunderts im Spiegel der Berichte deutscher Reisender.* Thesis, Humboldt-Universität, Berlin.

Suret-Canale, J. 1966. *Schwarzafrika.* Berlin: Akademie-Verlag.

Svobodova, J. 1977. Im Busch- und Savannenland der Fulbe von Senegal. *Kleine Beiträge aus dem Staatlichen Museum für Völkerkunde Dresden* 1: 31–37.

Timm, K. 1977. Richard Thurnwald: 'Koloniale Gestaltung'. Ein 'Apartheids-Projekt' für die koloniale Expansion des deutschen Faschismus in Afrika. *Ethnographisch-Archäologische Zeitschrift* 4: 617–50.

Tjagunenko, V. 1959. *Kriege und Kolonien: Der Einfluß des Zerfalls des Kolonialsystems auf die kriegswirtschaftliche Basis des Imperialismus.* Berlin: Dietz.

Tjulpanov, S. 1959. *Das Kolonialsystem des Imperialismus und sein Zerfall.* Berlin: Verlag der Wirtschaft.

Tokarew, S. A. 1968. *Die Religion in der Geschichte der Völker.* Berlin: Dietz.

Treide, D. 1967. Was will die Völkerkunde? In R. Habel et al. (eds.), *Völkerkunde für jedermann*, pp. 9–13. Gotha: Hermann Haack.

——. 1981. *Zur Methode der Formationsanalyse: Das Erbe der Klassiker des Marxismus-Leninismus und gegenwärtige Untersuchungen zu urgesellschaftlichen Verhältnissen, ihrer Auflösung und der Heraus-*

bildung von Klassen unter verschiedenartigen historischen Bedin-gungen. Thesis, Karl-Marx-Universität Leipzig.

Winkelmann, I. 1986. Sergej Aleksandrovic Tokarev zum Gedenken. *Ethno-graphisch-Archäologische Zeitschrift* 2: 281–82.

Woddis, J. 1963. *Afrika: Kontinent im Morgenrot.* Berlin: Dietz.

Chapter 19
An Anthropological Education: A Comparative Perspective

Bea Vidacs

The following is a partial comparison of my education as a 'national ethnographer' (néprajzos) at the Eötvös Loránd University (ELTE) in Budapest, Hungary, between 1975 and 1981 with my subsequent experiences as a graduate student in cultural anthropology in the United States, where I received a PhD in 2002 from the City University of New York (CUNY) Graduate Center. I focus my reflections on Hungary, because I imagine that the nature of American education is better known to most readers. Some might think that the main differences would spring from the fact that socialism was still in full swing in Hungary in the 1970s, whereas in the United States a free market of 'bourgeois' ideologies has prevailed all along. However, I argue that most of the differences between the two experiences spring not from ideologies but from differences between the two societies, differences in the purpose and nature of the two disciplines, and differences in university education and in intellectual traditions.

I have chosen to adopt the terminology which Tamás Hofer adapted from Alfred L. Kroeber and used to such good effect in his 1968 article in *Current Anthropology*, which is republished in this volume (chapter 20). Hofer was the first to offer a systematic discussion of the differences between 'national ethnography' as practised in Hungary and other European countries and the generalising cultural anthropology practised in America. I refer to néprajz, the discipline I studied in Hungary, as ethnography and to the subject I studied in the United States as anthropology. Two further preliminary distinctions are necessary. The Néprajz Department at ELTE was actually subdivided into a Department of Material Culture and a Department of Folklore. In order to earn a degree as an ethnographer, a student had to take classes in both departments. The whole discipline concentrated on documenting Hungarian traditional peasant culture, while the study of cultures outside Europe was designated etnológia. Hofer presented an accurate assessment of the main differences between European ethnography and

American anthropology, and these differences were reflected in the training students received.

Scholars in Training: Joining the Néprajz Community

I began my university studies in Hungary in 1975 at ELTE, the country's premier university. The other major Hungarian university where néprajz degrees were conferred at the time was the Lajos Kossuth University in Debrecen, which was thought to be more fieldwork oriented. Because I have no personal knowledge of the training offered in Debrecen, my remarks apply only to the Budapest department. Hungary was and remains a highly centralised country, and the Budapest department was undoubtedly considered to be the flagship department, certainly by its students and professors.

Having spent three years in Nigeria as a teenager, I entered the university with the express goal of becoming an Africanist. I thought I wanted to study ethnography, unaware that what I was really interested in was anthropology. I recognised this when, after my second year at ELTE, I had the opportunity to spend a full year at the School of Oriental and African Studies (SOAS) in London. Even before this experience, however, I had been ever more dissatisfied with the atomistic, empirical, historical reconstructionism which dominated ethnography. I was more interested in social processes.

At the time there was no separate social or cultural anthropological programme in Hungary; there was only néprajz. University entrance was highly competitive, depending on both the results of the baccalaureate and an entrance examination. Subject quotas were centrally decided. Most students in the Faculty of Humanities were expected to have a dual major: the possible combinations were announced in advance, and one had to select accordingly. In the year that I applied, English, which was going to be one of my majors, was offered only in conjunction with either library science or adult education (népművelés). I chose the former, since the materials for the entrance exam were less ideologically charged (no Marxist theory). All students were expected to gain some kind of vocational training, mostly as high school teachers, and therefore they were obliged to supplement their majors with pedagogical courses. These courses involved an element of practical classroom experience.

Néprajz (and a few other disciplines, including archaeology and art history) constituted an exception to this rule. Graduates of this programme did not receive teaching diplomas (though they were entitled to lecture at universities) but were rather trained to become museologists. Néprajz majors were also exceptional in that direct admission to the department was impossible. Rather, potential students were obliged to take courses, write papers, and pass exams in néprajz, in addition to their existing majors, for two semesters. Upon completion of these, the department decided whether or not to admit them. Upon admission into the Néprajz department, most of us dropped one of the two majors we had started with, but we were expected to retain the other major, which was usually a subject that would give us a qualification as a high school teacher. Despite this, most students took their néprajz training more seriously than their other subject and hoped to become professionals in the field.

Indeed, the department trained us to be scholars and researchers from the outset. The community of scholars we had joined extended beyond those actually teaching in the department, because through informal channels we could establish working relations with many other members of the profession. In practice the formal and informal training that students underwent was more akin to graduate studies in the English-speaking countries. Given our small numbers, the experience was a kind of total immersion. Whereas in the United States a graduate student is exposed to only a fraction of the discipline as it happens to be represented in that particular department, we in Budapest had good reason to think that we knew the entire field of Hungarian néprajz, of which we were the centre.

In keeping with the idea that students of néprajz were being trained to be academics, even in the first, preparatory year we were taught research methods and techniques and were expected to read articles in scholarly journals and monographs, with minimal reliance on textbooks. During the preparatory year there were two exercises which stand out in my recollection with special clarity. The first was to compile a bibliography for one region of Hungary on the basis of the major Hungarian ethnographic journals. (The most venerable of these, *Ethnographia*, has been continuously published since 1889.) Even just to handle each volume, skim the contents page, and perhaps browse through one or two articles was enough to give us an overall sense of changes in the concerns of the discipline over time. The other exercise, equally demanding of time and effort, required us to prepare a two-minute (!) presentation on a Hungarian village of our choice, based on the data we could gather from statistical sources. We were given a list of all available sources, which ranged from the earliest medieval inscriptions (*összeírás*) to the most modern censuses. I still have my copy of this list, and when I came to do my fieldwork for my master's thesis I relied on it to orient myself in choosing a field site. Both exercises were meant to prepare students for an academic career by acquainting them with some of the main tools of the discipline.

Other assignments during that preparatory year included writing reviews of articles and books. For the examinations we were expected to have acquired an overview of traditional Hungarian folk culture, including settlement patterns, the evolution of peasant architectural forms, folklore genres, and so on. In subsequent years our lecture courses investigated these topics in much more detail. There were separate courses on subjects such as animal husbandry, food, and costume (all in the realm of material culture) and on ballads, poetry, tales, and beliefs (*hiedelmek*), in the realm of folklore. We had a memorable seminar on witchcraft with Tekla Dömötör in which each student wrote a paper about a different aspect of witchcraft using the recently published body of Hungarian witch trials as our primary source material (Schram 1970). Because I was interested in West African secret societies at the time, I wrote about associations of witches as they appeared in the trial transcripts. In addition, we took courses on non-European cultures, and some anthropological courses were also compulsory, including an introduction to social anthropology. Nonetheless, the bulk of the training was concerned with acquiring an encyclopaedic knowledge of traditional Hungarian folk culture. Since the avowed primary purpose of the education we received was preparation to work in a Hungarian museum, the courses were entirely appropriate. They were accompanied by internships, which typically took the form of a one-month sojourn at a provincial museum and a course on museological methods.

Even as students we were encouraged to attend conferences, at any rate those organised in Budapest, and the more advanced and ambitious students participated with papers. We had relatively easy access to staff at the three main institutions in Budapest (the ELTE department, the Museum of Ethnography [Néprajzi Múzeum], and the institute of the Hungarian Academy of Sciences), and we often consulted them unofficially when following up our particular interests. In fact some of our lecturers were formally full-time employees of the museum or the institute. In this way, from their second year onwards students could consider themselves part of the discipline. I remember the contrast when I spent a year studying social anthropology at SOAS in London, and the president in his address to launch the academic year in essence advised us to enjoy dabbling in our respective disciplines but warned us that we should not expect to spend the rest of our lives working in this field. Expectations in Hungary at the time were entirely different.

Such a small-scale operation also meant that one had to tread lightly. We understood of course that only so many jobs could be supported in each particular area. The need for a reasonable division of labour dovetailed neatly with the general tenor of Hungarian intellectual life and social traditions, in which competition and controversies were avoided and it was untoward openly to challenge authority. As Hofer (this volume) points out, most controversies were confined to subtle asides, footnotes, and off-the-cuff remarks. To what extent this was a continuation of feudal patterns rather than a consequence of the top-down nature of the socialist regime is open to debate, but it seems to me that past and present reinforced each other and resulted in an intellectual attitude in which holding a strong opinion was deemed unscientific and unbecoming to a serious scholar. An American would have received the impression of a community in complete unison. When I showed my research proposal for funding in the United States to colleagues and friends in Hungary, I felt obliged to apologise for some of the overly ambitious claims and the generally boastful tone and to explain that this was how it had to be done in America.

In 1976, in my second year, the ELTE students 'challenged' the two other institutions (i.e. the staff of the ethnographic museum and the academy institute) to a mock competition modelled on a TV quiz show that was popular at the time. This took the form of a Mardi Gras party, and it was held in the museum because its physical layout was more suitable than that of the university. We, the ELTE students, organised the event, but it was well attended by members of the other two institutions. For me, this event epitomised our strong links and sense of belonging to an intellectual community.

While the field of néprajz was intimate enough, within it the attention paid to non-European cultures (etnológia) was minuscule. I had met all of its representatives even before completing my preparatory year. They advised me not to mention that my real ambition was to become an Africanist, for fear of jeopardising my chances of admission to the department. Nonetheless, whenever I had an opportunity, I chose to read something on Africa, usually in English, so that although most of my training was based on Hungarian materials I also acquired some knowledge of Africa and of socio-cultural anthropology. In this respect I differed from the average student. This 'community within a community' included Tibor Bodrogi, Luiz (Lajos) Boglár, Csaba Ecsedy, Mihály Sárkány, and Gábor Vargyas. They made me feel welcome and encouraged my efforts. Given their regional interests, they were much more attuned to socio-cultural anthropology than were their colleagues dealing with Hungary. These scholars thus provided important bridges between the two disciplines, even though it was next to impossible at this time for them to do fieldwork in their regions of specialisation.

Learning the Canon and Challenging It

What was clearly lacking in this training was any serious attempt to theorise social processes. The material culture part of our studies, especially, was an eminent example of 'butterfly collecting.' Hungarian ethnography was in large part a salvage operation, although some were concerned with reconstructing patterns of material culture and folklore which had fully disappeared. Virtually all research focused on territory where the Hungarian language was spoken. Since its origins the discipline had been intimately involved in the creation and maintenance of Hungarian national identity (Niedermüller 1989; Hofer 1994; Taylor 2004). However, there was actually very little overt nationalism in our lectures, and many lecturers took pains to locate their materials within larger historical contexts, both Western and Eastern.

The emphasis on historical reconstruction was no doubt one of the factors which caused Hungarian ethnographers to shy away from theoretical generalisations and rigorous comparisons. The present was for the most part ignored. In part this was due to a wish to avoid political trouble that might result from presenting Hungarian socialist society in an unfavourable light. As Chris Hann (2004) has pointed out, this would have been foolhardy, and not just for the individual researcher. Negative commentaries could have endangered the entire discipline. But I do not think the caution can be attributed entirely to politics. It seems to me that many ethnographers thought it somehow improper to make ambitious theoretical claims in their published works, because model-making was insufficiently scientific.

For me, a student interested in social processes, this refusal to draw conclusions, together with the atomistic, encyclopaedic bent of Hungarian ethnography, was frustrating. We did read some of the 'sociographic' literature from the pre-socialist period, which was politically engaged and critical of social conditions. I found this very exciting, especially the work of Ferenc Erdei. However, we were given little insight into the political climate that produced this literature. Altogether, and somewhat paradoxically, given the supposed permeation of the socialist world in general and the social sciences in particular by Marxism, virtually no attention was paid to power relations. I discovered this dimension of anthropology only when I came to study in the United States. At the CUNY Graduate Center I was exposed to more Marxism and political economy than I ever had been in Hungary. Like all other university students in Hungary, I was obliged to take courses in so-called scientific socialism, but few of us took these seriously, and it was obvious that often the professors did not take them seriously either. In short, the official Marxist stance of the discipline, like every other discipline in the humanities and social sciences, could not be challenged, but it could in practice be largely ignored.

We were inducted into the field of ethnography in a much more comprehensive way than can happen in an undergraduate department of anthropology in the United States. The focus was on teaching the canon, and we were not expected to critique the methods or theories of our elders and betters. Current research, either by our professors or by other members of the discipline, was not discussed; it was almost as if it did not exist. This might seem unsurprising in a firmly backwards-looking discipline, yet it was just as true for the then fledgling field of social anthropology (*társadalomnép-rajz*), which did set out to study the present. Rarely did anyone mention the Varsány studies that were being written up during the years I studied at ELTE (see Sárkány, this volume; Tamás Hofer, the best known Hungarian anthropologist internationally, did not start lecturing in the department until later). Like students elsewhere, we were eager to challenge the status quo and hungry for debate, but our curriculum offered little access to controversial or new research. I remember the sense of excitement when one of the 'young Turks' of the institute, following a special invitation from the students, gave a provocative talk, making broad and exciting claims. But this was a rare occurrence; it took place outside the official curriculum and had an air almost of subversion. I recall nearly getting into an argument over it with one of my professors, who insisted that conjecture and 'empty' theorising had no place in the curriculum.

It goes without saying that graduate education in cultural anthropology in the United States puts far greater emphasis on novelty and debate. This may be seen as being due at least in part to cultural factors: it is a truism to say that American culture is obsessed with the new and thrives on competition. In writing articles or research proposals one is always expected to take account of the newest research and the newest theoretical trends. If one fails to do so, it is taken as a sign of insufficient scholarship, of 'not having done one's homework'. All the practitioners of a discipline are forced to keep up with the literature and engage with the newest ideas, and thus they drive the discipline forward by continuously calling established paradigms into question. Yet being always 'on the cutting edge' carries its own dangers. Foremost among them is that chasing the newest trends often means neglecting the results of the past and hence reinventing the wheel. The tremendous emphasis on originality inherent in the American approach sometimes leads to specious arguments without much substance. The pressure to publish is such that one often has the feeling that an article has been recycled, and some papers have little valuable content of any kind.

Breaking Out of the Mould: Fieldwork and Reflexivity

The fieldwork we Hungarian students undertook was very much along the lines described by Hofer (this volume). We made day trips or spent at most a few days at a time in a particular village, usually interviewing members of the older generation (aged over 70) and collecting artefacts. Implicit in this approach was the idea of an authenticity which only the older generation possessed, by virtue of age. Given the goal of ethnography this was not an unreasonable assumption, but I could not help thinking that Béla Bartók, who did fieldwork at the turn of the century, would at that time have rejected the same interviewees as too young and ignorant. This strategy meant that what was going on in the present was irrelevant or of only anecdotal interest to the researcher. In fact, many of our colleagues were indeed interested in the present, and no doubt they took mental notes, but they did not see this as part of their job as ethnographers.

It is my understanding that earlier cohorts participated in more field trips organised by the department, but my class officially did little more than one week's worth of fieldwork during the entire five-year programme. Unofficially, however, many students collected data as volunteer research assistants. This contributed in many cases to their master's theses, which had to be based on original research.

My first trip to a village took place during my second year. I had begged a more advanced fellow student to take me along because I wanted to see how fieldwork was carried out. Five or six of us descended on a western Hungarian village. I recall the leader of our group, a folklorist, interviewing a former swineherd who had seen a dragon with his own eyes and who was able to describe its appearance in vivid detail. This was exciting stuff for a novice, and I was enchanted. Our informant lived in a dilapidated house on the outskirts of the village. We wanted to spend the night and had arranged to stay at various houses. While we were waiting to find our lodgings, a young woman walked up to us in the centre of the village and asked what we were doing there. We explained that we were ethnographers. She asked who we had been talking to, and when we named our swineherd she had a hard time recalling who that might be. When eventually the identity of our 'exotic' informant dawned on her, she expressed her disdain for him quite clearly. This episode stayed in my mind because it made me realise that, although for us he was an important informant, he was not a figure of significance in the contemporary village.

After completing my second year as a néprajzos I was able to study social anthropology and the Hausa language for a year at SOAS. Upon returning from England I continued my studies at ELTE. In my fourth year I had to carry out the one week of obligatory fieldwork in the village of Etyek, near Budapest. As was the custom, we took day trips to the village. On one occasion we missed the bus back to the city and stayed longer than usual at the house of one of our elderly informants. The woman's daughter happened to drop by and made a remark which, though it was not part of any official interview, gave me a clue to understanding the larger social implications of what I was studying (see Vidacs 1984). This sort of chance event will come as no surprise to anyone who does fieldwork, but for me it was the first time I fully appreciated the need to go beyond the interview situation. I recognised the shortcomings of the scattered sort of research that was customary in Hungary at the time.

Later I was hired to do some data collection using questionnaires. I took this on with the express purpose of gaining more field experience. Although I was expected to spend a day, or two at the most, going through the questionnaire in six households, I ended up staying for a week. The questionnaire was an ambitious one, aimed at gaining a comprehensive image of the pre-war state of the village. It began with questions about the pattern of landholding prior to collectivisation. I soon recognised that, in order to gain the confidence of my informants, it was advisable to reverse the order of the questions and start with the more 'innocent' cultural information. The tougher, more sensitive questions could be posed only after establishing some rapport. It was in the course of this work that I came to understand the anthropological truism (new to me at the time) that when people reflect on the past they do so through the filter of the present.

These experiences in the field, together with my social anthropological training at SOAS, led me to try my hand at anthropological-style fieldwork for my master's thesis. I dropped my plan to write a thesis on an African topic based on library research and instead set out to do participant observation in an eastern Hungarian village. My topic was strategies for choosing godparents. This attempt to break out of the mould of Hungarian ethnography was accepted by the department at ELTE. I was allowed to realise my plan and received support from a variety of quarters. In particular, Professor Jenő Barabás praised my work in Etyek and made useful suggestions about where I might find a suitable field site for my very own attempt to do 'anthropology at home'. Despite the rigidity of the administrative system, I was granted permission to take a semester off in order to carry out the field study (had I been able to take off an entire year I probably would have done so, but that was considered absolutely impossible).

Tibor Bodrogi was my advisor for this project. At the time he was the senior social anthropologist in the country and the successor to Gyula Ortutay as director of the academy institute. He did not raise an eyebrow when I presented him with the plan and merely asked mildly how I proposed to finance my stay. When I said that I planned to sublet my apartment and might also be able to rely on my parents, he replied that if I didn't ask, then he couldn't give me any money himself. Naturally I did ask, and I was rewarded with the standard per diem paid to all researchers, regardless of their discipline, who were called out of town for work-related purposes. This was a derisory sum, unchanged since the early 1950s, intended to cover out-of-pocket expenses. If the assignment lasted for more than 30 days it was assumed that some kind of domicile would be established, and therefore the amount of the per diem was automatically reduced by half at that point. In the usual fashion of finding slightly irregular solutions for the idiocies of bureaucracy, I was advised to return to Budapest once a month in order to be able to continue to receive the full amount. Since protracted fieldwork was not a requirement for students, there was no official mechanism for funding such research, but the institute had the flexibility to support a wide array of data collecting activities. In any case I was the only student who requested such financial aid. I was also granted the luxury of secretarial support in transcribing my notes. In return I had to deposit my data and a copy of my thesis in the archives of the institute.

My initiative met with bemused approval among many of my colleagues, both students and more senior researchers. Some questioned the need to stay away so long, and all seemed to think that what I was undertaking involved unusual hardship. I received remarks such as, 'I really respect you for doing this', but no one rushed to follow my example. (I understand that this situation has changed a lot in recent years, especially since the introduction of cultural anthropology at ELTE in 1990, as a result of which more and more students are conducting extended fieldwork, both inside and outside Hungary.)

During my village research I became fascinated with the way one's methods shape the data and the way people's perceptions of me influenced what they might or might not tell me. Driven by these concerns and the awareness that my methods were unusual in Hungarian ethnographic practice, I liberally sprinkled my ethnographic account with asides about how my observations might have been influenced by my own presence. I was not yet aware of the concept of reflexivity, but it seemed to me to be self-evident, and I automatically discussed this factor whenever it seemed relevant for my analysis. To my great surprise this turned out to be the most controversial aspect of my thesis. People who otherwise had no quarrel with its findings and premises, or who even thought highly of it, almost all deemed this irrelevant, an unnecessary personal intrusion, something which had no place in scholarly work. I was asked to extract these passages before my study was published in *Ethnographia* and instead to summarise the methodological implications in an appendix (Vidacs 1985). I was convinced that these methodological asides were an essential part of my work, but I complied; this was, after all, my first publication in Hungary.

The United States: A Different Kind of Community

Despite the advice received at the beginning of my studies not to mention my wanting to become an Africanist, nobody in the néprajz department tried to dissuade me from this plan. I explored African work whenever it was possible to do so, and I was lucky enough to receive a job as an Africanist upon graduation. A few years later, when I joined the Anthropology Program of the CUNY Graduate Center, I was met with a surprising attitude (I suspect the same would have happened in most departments in the United States). Professors, fellow students, and even the departmental secretary all assumed that I was going to do my dissertation research in Hungary. I had to repeat time and again that I wanted to work in Africa. Eventually I succeeded in convincing people, but I realised in the process that there is a widespread assumption in American universities that natives of the United States are free to choose whatever world area takes their fancy, but non-native PhD students in anthropology will want to go back to their home countries and study their own. Although I can see the possible explanations for this attitude, I can't help thinking that it contains an element of unconscious imperialism and double standard. In any case, I ended up doing fieldwork on processes of identity formation and the nature of political culture in Cameroon by examining the practice and symbolic construction of football (soccer). By the time I came up with this project the department had accepted my choice of area and fully supported my efforts.

The community I joined at CUNY differed greatly from the one I left in Hungary. Because of the lack of funding, most students work during their graduate studies, which delays completion of the PhD. Students at the CUNY Graduate Center are given the opportunity to teach their own courses at the various colleges of the CUNY system, and the department encourages students to give conference papers. Nevertheless, until receiving the PhD, unlike in Hungary, students are not really part of the profession as such; rather, they identify much more strongly with the department. This is partly due to the size of the discipline in the United States, but it is also a conscious policy on the part of the programme, which explicitly fosters cooperation rather than competition among the students. In addition, this particular department has a strong sense of self (being part of a public university and being politically engaged have a lot to do with this), and the notion of being 'special' is perpetuated among the students.

The education I experienced in the United States differed radically from what I had been through in Hungary. It was not just that the research sites did not coincide with the location where the training took place. Much more emphasis in our courses was placed on theoretical issues and social problems than on acquiring in-depth ethnographic knowledge. Even in the area courses we were encouraged always to adopt a comparative perspective rather than to analyse ethnographic details for their own sake. As for fieldwork, the CUNY department has recently built up a strong group of researchers who study American society. Students with this interest of course find it easier to get their feet wet in the field prior to their dissertation research than do the majority, who wish to do their research 'elsewhere'. Although the latter are encouraged to travel to their prospective field sites for a reconnaissance trip, financial constraints often make this impossible. Many students enter the field only following protracted theoretical preparation in the form of course work and examinations, when they have received funding from an outside agency.

However, unlike their Hungarian counterparts in the late socialist era, once American students go to the field, they stay for a long time.

References

Hann, C. M. 2004. Két tudományág összemosódása? Néprajz és szociálantropológia a szocialista és posztszocialista időszakokban. In B. Borsos, Z. Szarvas, and G. Vargyas (eds.), *Fehéren, Feketén Varsánytól Rititiig: Mihály Sárkány Festschrift*, pp. 45–63. Budapest: L'Harmattan.

Hofer, T. 1968. Anthropologists and Native Ethnographers in Central European Villages: Comparative Notes on the Professional Personality of Two Disciplines. *Current Anthropology* 9: 311–15.

———. 1994. Construction of the Folk Cultural Heritage in Hungary and Rival Versions of National Identity. In T. Hofer (ed.), *Hungarians between 'East' and 'West': Three Essays on National Myths and Symbols*, pp. 27–52. Budapest: Museum of Ethnography.

Niedermüller, P. 1989. National Culture: Symbols and Reality. *Ethnologia Europaea* 19 (1): 47–56.

Schram, F. 1970. *Magyarországi boszorkányperek, 1529–1768*, vols. 1–2. Budapest: Akadémiai Kiadó.

Taylor, M. 2004. Nineteenth- and Twentieth-Century Historical and Institutional Precedents of the Hungarian Dance-House Movement. *Fulbright Student Conference Papers*, pp. 95–103. Budapest: Hungarian-American Commission for Educational Exchange.

Vidacs, B. 1984. Food as Ethnic Identity in Etyek, Hungary. *Journal of Folklore Research* 21 (2–3): 226–28.

———. 1985. Komaság és kölcsönösség Szentpéterszegen. *Ethnographia* 96: 509–29.

Chapter 20
Comparative Notes on the Professional Personalities of Two Disciplines

Tamás Hofer

Preface: 2004

The republication of an essay which dates back almost 40 years calls for some retrospective contextualisation on the part of its author.[1] At the level of international politics it was clear at the time to both Hungarian and American scholars that officially they belonged to opposed political camps, a fact which severely constrained scholarly contacts. In comparison with the harsh restrictions of the Stalinist years, however, the 1960s brought signs of a thaw. After the defeat of the 1956 revolution in Hungary the authorities did not reinstate the full strictures of the earlier 'ideological discipline'. Space opened up in science, including néprajz, to experiment with methods used abroad and to establish personal links with foreign scholars.

---

[1] The first version of this paper dates back to 1967. I wish to express my gratitude to participants in the conference 'Central and North-Central European Peasant Cultures', among them George Nellemann, Holger Rasmussen, and Eric Wolf. The conference was held in Chicago on 9–13 January 1967 by the Wenner-Gren Foundation for Anthropological Research. I am especially indebted to conference chairman John Honigmann, who invited me to prepare a paper summing up my own contributions in the course of the debate. It was published with the conference papers in 1970 in a special issue of *Anthropologica* edited by Honigmann (new series, vol. 12, no. 1, pp. 5–22). A preliminary publication appeared in *Current Anthropology* in 1968 (vol. 9, pp. 311–15). I returned to this essay recently, and an amended version was published in Hungarian in a Festschrift for Mihály Sárkány (Hofer 2004). The version published here is based on this Hungarian paper (the opening preface was translated by Chris Hann and corrected by me). Its 'experimental basis' remains unchanged: it was, as I explain in this preface, the community study prepared by Edit Fél and myself of the Hungarian village Átány (Fél and Hofer 1969). In that volume we tried to balance and reconcile approaches which I characterise as anthropological (referring primarily to the comparative discipline of American cultural anthropology) and ethnographic (referring primarily to the discipline of Hungarian national ethnography, i.e. néprajz). I thank the late Professor Sol Tax for his encouragement and advice during this experiment as well as later, during my stay in Chicago in the winter of 1966–67.

In 1965 the Ford Foundation took the opportunity to make available 25 scholarships annually for Hungarian researchers in various disciplines.[2] My stay in Chicago of almost a year in 1966–67 stimulated me to reflect on the differences between American anthropologists and Hungarian 'national ethnographers' (a phrase I borrowed from Alfred L. Kroeber) concerning their basic understandings of their respective disciplines and methodologies. My original lecture was based on my self-understanding as a Hungarian ethnographer, that is, a *néprajzkutató*, but it was prepared for an audience of American anthropologists, and therefore I adapted some of their concepts in order to render intelligible the ways in which European scholars thought, their research strategies, and their selection of topics and methods. As far as I know, no such comparison of anthropology (antropológia) and Hungarian national ethnography (néprajz) had been attempted previously, and such discussions have remained rare.[3]

I recall being influenced in my discussion by the way in which Bernard Cohn (1962) at the University of Chicago had compared and contrasted the vantage points and strategies of the anthropologist with those of the historian. A further opportunity to draw such comparisons arose in the course of my collaboration with Edit Fél in Átány, which resulted in the monograph *Proper Peasants* (Fél and Hofer 1969). Most of the fieldwork for that study was carried out between 1954 and 1958, on the eve of collectivisation. Well aware of the precariousness of their traditional way of life, the villagers were able to articulate its components with exceptional clarity. For reasons that were never explained to us, it was decided in 1961 that our work could not be published in Hungary, despite a signed contract with the Akadémiai Kiadó. In a spirit of obstinacy we decided to try our luck with

---

[2] To the best of my knowledge no comparable scheme was implemented at this time in any other socialist country. In 1966 about 2,000 applications were received and processed by the Cultural Relations Institute, Budapest, which functioned under the direct control of the government. We were briefed on how one could bring home information that might be contrary to US regulations (I am not aware of any such cases) and on how to respond if approached by the secret services (again I am unaware of any such case). Eventually 50 candidates were nominated, of whom 25 were selected by the committee which represented the foundation. The Hungarian side insisted that half of those selected come from the natural sciences and technical branches, from which one might expect long-term benefits to the economy. The American side, however, wanted at least half the scholars to be from the humanities and social sciences, with the expectation that these would be better able to communicate the merits of the 'American way of life'. Many of my fellow scholars rose to prominent positions after their return to Hungary, in politics as well as in academic life.
[3] The counterpart to this lecture in Chicago was the plenary presentation I gave in September 1967 to the Hungarian Ethnographic Society in Budapest, in which I outlined the research profile of the Chicago department and introduced the growing American interest in 'peasant studies' to my Hungarian colleagues.

foreign publishers, taking advantage of foreign visitors to Hungary to establish contacts. (For the entire period between 1948 and the mid-1960s it was virtually impossible for us, as for the great majority of Hungarian citizens, to travel to any Western country.) We divided the voluminous manuscript into three parts and then rewrote and supplemented it for our imaginary foreign readers. While negotiations in Germany and Denmark dragged on, the Wenner-Gren Foundation decided to support publication (based on a recommendation from Sol Tax, following a visit to Budapest). I was able to help polish the English translation during my stay in Chicago. In the introduction we discussed the differences which form the subject of this chapter and presented the volume as an experiment in bringing the two disciplines together. In that sense the monograph serves as an illustration of the motivations behind this essay, even though our knowledge of international anthropology was rather incomplete at the time.

The main task of the paper republished here was to provide a solid basis of information about the character of European (Hungarian) national ethnography, its role and its historical background, for American anthropologists, to whom the discipline was almost unknown. Some Americans had begun to undertake research in Europe after the Second World War and had published community monographs, but they had at best taken only superficial notice of the fact that the Europeans themselves had a research tradition which was in many ways comparable to the American one. This uncertain orientation is well reflected in Robert Anderson's (1965) overview of the expanding field of 'studies in peasant life'.

The main title of the original essay was 'Anthropologists and Native Ethnographers in Central European Villages', and the rural setting exemplified the differences I was addressing. The underlying issues were more general, however, and for this republication I have therefore promoted the original subtitle to the status of main title. I adapted the term *professional personality* (*szakmai személyiség*) to refer to a complex of factors comprising primarily national variations on the theoretical premises of a discipline, its choice of subjects and methods, its habitual research practices, the form and structuring of its publications, and so forth. Such details constitute the distinctive features of a discipline's 'personality type'.

I tried to draw attention to the divergent ground rules of néprajz and anthropology in terms of the classical distinction between the humanities and the natural sciences, between an 'interpretive science in search of meaning' and an 'experimental science in search of laws'. I did not ask which discipline was right, or even which was more right, but rather explored which was more appropriate for answering different types of questions. The coexistence of various disciplines with disparate competences within one and the same 'intellectual field' seemed to me to resemble a network in what we would nowadays term 'multi-sited ethnography'.

It was important to me, then as now, to establish the continued scientific validity of Hungarian néprajz as a discipline in the humanities tradition. I sought to build up links to the enterprise of comparative anthropology, but I had no wish to see my own discipline swallowed up by it. Many far-reaching changes have taken place in Hungarian and other European national ethnographies since the 1960s. The distance to the social sciences has diminished, boundaries have become blurred, and crossing them has become common. Nevertheless, the two traditions which I identify in this essay continue in many places to be institutionalised separately, each maintaining its own university chairs and research organisation.

Even though there is much in the following pages that I would express differently today, I have not changed my earlier opinion: anthropology and national ethnography are two complementary scholarly pursuits, and each should be accorded scientific legitimacy in its own way. In 1982 historian of anthropology George Stocking speculated that the days of sociocultural anthropology were numbered, though it would be possible to continue 'business as usual' until the year 2000 (1982: 186). In 1992 he corrected this forecast: 'institutional inertia, if nothing else, will maintain anthropology until well into the twenty-first century' (Stocking 1992: 372). I am not aware of any comparable prognoses for European 'national ethnographies', but they might perhaps be expected to fade from the scene one or two decades sooner. It is of course possible that a general reconfiguration will render all such predictions inaccurate.[4]

***

---

[4] The text which follows is largely but not quite identical to the version published in *Current Anthropology*. I have taken the opportunity to correct some minor errors which crept into the original editing of my text and to reinsert some sentences that were erroneously omitted. I cannot be held responsible for the fact that the semantic field of certain terms has shifted significantly since the 1960s.

American Anthropologists and European Ethnographers Compared: 1968

A growing number of American anthropologists are coming to Europe to study European peasant or post-peasant villages. These same villages have been explored for 100 or even 150 years by ethnographers who specialised in the study of the folk component of their own cultural heritage. However, contact between the two disciplines is scanty and rather casual. In the United States, ethnography of the European type has been drawn in on the map of the sciences of man with indistinct contours only. Kroeber (1959: 399) identifies 'the folk ethnography of peasantry in civilised countries as it is pursued in Europe' as a branch of anthropology. Yet the *Biennial Review of Anthropology* reviews the studies of European ethnographers in only a haphazard way. In the 1965 volume, Anderson introduces a 'new kind of study' which owes its life to a 'scholarly intercourse with investigators who themselves belong to the subject civilization', since 'the literati of peasant societies have their own traditions of scholarship' (Anderson 1965: 182–83).

Often European ethnographers and ethnologists are treated as one group indiscriminately, whether they study their own or foreign peoples; this composite is then contrasted with American anthropologists (Ishida 1965). In Europe, however, ethnographers studying their own people are considered a separate and different group from scientists who study non-European peoples. Each group has its own chairs at the universities and its own associations and museums, even when some of these scientists and institutions have a 'dual nationality' (cf. Hultkrantz 1967: 38).

A survey of the field is difficult, since interest in these areas of research arose more or less independently in each European country or in larger national areas. Hence there are differences in approach, methods, and knowledge within each of the two disciplines. Even the terms in the national languages for what these researchers do (Volkskunde, *folklivsforskning*, néprajz, národopis, etc.) are not congruous in meaning. These terms can be rendered into circumscribed forms of English only; this Kroeber (1959) has done. The term *folklore* is also current. In a narrow sense it means the study of oral literature; in a broader sense it means the study of all manifestations of traditional culture. Folklore is sometimes regarded in Europe as a field of ethnography and sometimes as an independent branch of knowledge. With the aim of creating a unanimous terminology, an international conference of European 'folk ethnographers' held in Arnhem in 1955 adopted the term *regional ethnology* or *national ethnology* as an international denomination for the discipline which studies European folk culture or a certain national folk culture in Europe (Hultkrantz 1960: 202–3).

Lack of knowledge about one another often makes contact between anthropologists and ethnographers frustrating; they do not take into account each other's differing professional personalities. An anthropologist may consult books written by European ethnographers only to be disappointed when he finds that most of what they have written is irrelevant to his own problems. He may well conclude that ethnographers in Central Europe are underdeveloped anthropologists unable to rid themselves of a narrow-minded, nineteenth-century empiricism and to reach a higher level of generalisation and theorisation.

The case is no better on the other side. In general, the ethnographer can add little to his own knowledge from community studies of Europe done by Americans in the 1950s. He may admire the Americans' fresh approach as well as their capacity to analyse and describe themes too familiar to European ethnographers for them to investigate. However, conclusions about culture, society, and human nature drawn by the anthropologist from the study of a single community dash through the layers where the European ethnographer feels that his problems lie. His own research involves interpretation of processes and patterns of cultures in definite regional and historical frameworks.

As a Hungarian ethnographer I am directly acquainted with the ethnographic research of my fellow countrymen. A grant from the Ford Foundation allowed me, after a period of library research, to acquire knowledge of American anthropologists through participant observation. These two experiences form the empirical basis for this short essay comparing the ways of life and thinking of anthropologists and ethnographers.

The Study of One's Own Culture versus the Study of Other Cultures

Anthropologists devote much attention to specialists (for example, shamans, medicine men, genealogists, and mythographers) who guard traditional knowledge within a given society. However, as far as I know, European national ethnographers have not yet been studied as equivalent figures in their own society. Such a study would help in understanding their writings and perhaps would throw light on some problems of anthropology as well.

The origins of national ethnography, like those of anthropology, may be traced back to the Renaissance. Antecedents of ethnography are to be found partly in essays on national and regional characteristics of European people and partly in the objective studies of rural populations carried out from the beginning of the eighteenth century by government commissions, prompted partly by the zeal of political reformers. However, systematic ethnographic studies began only in the early nineteenth century. The centres of ethnographic growth were those regions where the creation of national states and cultures had become a vital problem (for example, Germany). Johann Gottfried Herder and the Grimm brothers are usually credited as initiators of the new discipline. Generally, Central Europe is considered to be the birthplace of ethnography. In nineteenth-century Europe, two differing sets of notions dominated thinking about society and culture. In Germany the notion of culture was in vogue, stressing moral worth and other internal qualities. In England and France the key concepts were society and civilisation (Wolf 1964: 16–19). National ethnography of the Central European type was clearly associated with areas where 'culture' prevailed.

The birth of ethnography in Central Europe formed part of the revitalisation movement—according to the definition of Anthony Wallace (1956), 'a deliberate, organised, conscious effort by members of a society to construct a more satisfying culture'. Thus, during the first half of the nineteenth century in Hungary the Reform Era began. A reform of the literary language was launched. Attempts were also made to reform economic life, the civil service, law, art, and literature. The poets introduced national metrical structures extracted from folklore and wrote epic poems of the past; these replaced older epics which were felt not to fit in with the political movements for national independence and social reform. The sources of the new national culture were sought in national history and folk culture, or 'small traditions'. The systematic exploration of the 'small traditions' called for a new branch of research; this became the national ethnography. At its birth, the disciplines linguistics, literary history, and national history cooperated. That is to say, ethnography remained closely associated with the humanities.

The new discipline was expected to produce an overall and coherent picture of the folk culture. Meticulous recording of texts and ceremonies and collecting of objects were animated by the conviction that even the slightest piece of information had its own place in the overall picture. As in Jacob Burckhardt's portrayal of Italian Renaissance culture, every historic event, military campaign, work of art, and festivity got a special meaning as a manifestation of the culture of a period; ethnographic facts were looked upon as manifestations of an integrated national culture. The national culture was regarded as a fabric of intertwining subcultures of local and professional groups. Side by side with the exploration of various regional groups, ecological systems, and local styles was the historical trend of interpretation—that is, the study of the origin and history of particular cultural elements, the classification of the elements of folk culture by historical layers, and the study of evidence of historical contacts produced by cultural elements. Research became permeated with the conviction that everything that had been studied (ballads, tools, religious ideas, systems of land tenure) was of interest and value by itself. This interest was some sort of 'sensory, aesthetic interest' which was not alien even to early anthropology (Kroeber 1956).

One has to go to Africa in order to profess to be an Africanist. On the other hand, everyone is born into his own nation and may even believe that he knows it well. Thus, periodically, varying numbers of European amateurs and laymen, clinging to scientific ethnography, focused their attention on small, more local units of folk culture. Local movements of revitalisation with a small sphere of action tried to keep alive or revitalise elements of folk traditions in industrialised societies. (For a discussion of these roots of ethnography and of the secondary, artificial folk traditions, see Bausinger 1961.) Various trends of 'applied ethnography' came into existence in Central Europe; endeavours were made to utilise elements of folk culture in ornamental art, fashion, and architecture. In general, scholars kept away from these endeavours and tried to weed out the romantic opinions of these amateurs.

The relationship of ethnography to national societies and cultures underwent changes because the nations and their political systems were changing. Ethnography, cultivated by a sense of humanism and scientific responsibility, found itself sometimes in opposition to and at other times supported by official cultural policy.

In spite of national concerns, ethnographers from the very beginning transgressed national and linguistic boundaries and sought international cooperation. Nor did they completely ignore the views and procedures of anthropology (or ethnology). Hungarian ethnographers, for example, were led as far as Siberian tribal settlements in their search for the predecessors of the Magyars and for other, linguistically related peoples. Recently, international contacts and cooperation between ethnographers have been developing rapidly, as Holger Rasmussen (1967) has pointed out. Accumulated knowledge and critical comparative and historical methods have indicated that few cultural processes are limited to a single nation. Ethnographers, formerly remaining within the frontiers of their own countries, now frequently embark on study trips abroad. Coordinated projects have been launched for the exploration of such European regions as Scandinavia and the Carpathians, even taking the form of all-European enterprises. (It is characteristic of the personality of ethnography that the most successful international committees include specialists in well-defined partial topics such as folk narratives and legends, proverbs, traditional farming implements, and methods of tillage.) However, this cooperation does not alter the fact that each regional ethnographer has his own country and concentrates his research there. He moves only occasionally from his own country to other regions, and then only, for the most part, for comparative studies. In spite of international cooperation, Swedish ethnography is still normally explored by Swedes, and Hungarian ethnography, by Hungarians.

Hence the question may arise: What drawbacks or limitations and what advantages are implied in this ethnocentricity? Ethnography in Central Europe differs from anthropology in many respects. Is a 'national' or 'regional' anthropology imaginable at all? Are the methods and principles of anthropology applicable exclusively to the study of other peoples, or may these methods and theories be used in studying and understanding one's own people?

Many excellent studies have been written by anthropologists about their fellow countrymen. Nevertheless, in the United States, most of the research into the culture of the nation (except for that into the autochthonous population) is carried out outside the sphere of anthropology. The Central European ethnographer may have the impression that this research is far less unified in both organisational and methodological aspects than are the regional ethnology or 'folk-life' studies in Central and Northern Europe. In the United States, students of folklore, American folk art, colonial antiquities, immigration and immigrant groups, and agrarian history seem to have only scanty contacts with one another and with scientists studying contemporary American Indians. It is almost symbolic that in the Smithsonian Institution, the Museum of Natural History houses collections from all human cultures except that of the 'white man in America', which is displayed in the Museum of History and Technology.

The formerly primitive peoples now on the way to becoming new nations refuse more and more emphatically to remain subject matter for anthropologists. As Claude Lévi-Strauss states, 'the mere fact of being subjected to ethnographic investigation seems distasteful to these peoples' (1966: 125–26). In his opinion, anthropology, in order to survive, has to undergo radical changes:

> For Anthropology is the science of culture as seen from the outside, and the first concern of people made aware of their independent existence and originality must be to claim the right to observe their culture themselves, from the inside. ... Anthropology, progressively taken over by local scholars, should adapt aims and methods similar to those which, from the Renaissance on, have proved fruitful for the study of our own culture. (Lévi-Strauss 1966: 126)

The ethnographies of the Central European peoples can be comprehended as experiments in this direction.

Strategies of Anthropology and Ethnography

It seems that American anthropologists in Europe are surprised by the fragmentation of anthropology into specific fields in university instruction, museums, and institutions (Kroeber 1953; Maday 1966; Arensberg 1967). For instance, physical anthropology is in the medical schools, whereas the folk component of national culture is part of the humanities and does not include the study of folk cultures outside Europe. Similarly, Europeans are astonished at seeing that Americans are capable of grasping the enormous range of anthropology and often doubt whether the human intellect is capable of such a performance at all (Hultkrantz 1965).

The spheres in which anthropologists and ethnographers have to be well versed and those in which they can afford to be naïve differ considerably (see Gluckman 1964). An anthropologist may be at least familiar with all the fields of anthropology, even when he does not explore them. His European colleague lacks this familiarity and is naïve where an anthropologist ought not to be. On the other hand, the ethnographer's sphere of competence extends to regions where an anthropologist will be naïve. He has been brought up as a member of the culture he is studying. He has received a thorough training in the culture, literature, and history of his country; in addition, because of his profession, by the time he becomes a middle-aged man, he has spent many years studying his fellow countrymen. These two types of specialisation may complement one another. However, serious consequences may result when each discipline stresses the naïvety of the other.

F. G. Bailey (1964) examined the extent to which knowledge of national culture and literary tradition was necessary in order to understand the social system of a small Indian community. In his opinion, in some types of studies it was possible to be naïve of Sanskrit literature and national history. Ely Devons and Max Gluckman went even further:

> To import too much knowledge of Hinduism would indeed be a dangerous solecism. ... We would indeed contend that knowledge of South American and European villages might be more useful for the analysis of Indian villages than is knowledge of Sanskrit. (Devons and Gluckman 1964: 194–95)

Nevertheless, they admitted the possibility of research of another type.

In the case of India, Milton Singer (1961) expressed a similar contrast by juxtaposing text and context. He did not question the justification of the trend represented by Devons and Gluckman but went on to investigate the potentialities of the anthropological approach on the other side, where 'texts', history, 'the great tradition', and 'the textual approach' are involved.

This comparison between basically different but complementary approaches looks rather similar to the comparison between the approaches of anthropology and Central European ethnography. The ethnographer does much 'textual' analysis, and his work habits are in many respects similar to those of a 'textual' scholar. (I think that objects, houses, clothing, and formalised behaviour can be treated 'textually' equally well.) The ethnographer is inclined to look at the social organisation of tradition, which, according to Bailey, is the alternative to internal structural explanation (Bailey 1964: 60–65; see also Redfield 1956).

To all appearances, at least in the case of India, the two approaches can hardly be united in a single person. As Devons and Gluckman (1964: 195) point out, 'the study of Sanskrit and the sacred texts is a lifetime's work in itself'. Interdisciplinary cooperation is needed, as in the case of Singer's Krishna volume (1966). The European native ethnographer is unlikely to be familiar with villages in India or Central America (such intimate knowledge of the society cannot in practice be acquired even through a lengthy period of fieldwork). On the other hand, he/she is socialised in a 'great tradition'. For such a textualist, the problem is how to free oneself of the habits and prejudices of one's own society, in order to achieve a degree of objectivity. By contrast, the American anthropologist is generally unable to invest a lifetime's work in the study of a single European national culture and is therefore obliged to rely upon local, *contextual* studies.[5]

In a book review, Anthony Wallace (1966) made the observation: 'Theory in cultural (or social) anthropology is like slash-and-burn agriculture: after cultivating a field for a while, the natives move on to a new one and let bush take over—then they return, slash and burn, and raise crops in the old field again.' This statement, I think, expresses the extreme mobility of American anthropologists, which is perhaps characteristic not only of their theories but of their entire way of life. The theoretical orientation of the discipline as a whole, coupled with a continual search for the new, makes too long a cultivation of fields unproductive and forces the anthropologist to slash and burn.

---

[5] The terms textual and contextual may no longer convey the clear contrastive meanings which they expressed in 1968. They were used, especially in the anthropology of religion, to designate alternative approaches in scholarship. According to Singer, in the case of Hinduism there was a cleavage between, on the one hand, the scholars of texts and 'scriptural philosophy' and, on the other hand, the scholars of the 'web of functional connections', where one could observe the impact of religious ideas on the life of the society (Singer 1961). Textuality and contextuality do not necessarily correspond to whether a scholar is working at home or in a foreign land, although in the great majority of cases Hungarian ethnographers have done their research at home.

These traits are in general missing from European ethnography. European ethnographers are not as mobile as their American colleagues. Geographically, their activities are confined for the most part to a single country, or perhaps only to a specific area of a country. They tend to make fewer theoretical statements, usually of a more limited range, than the anthropologists do. Scholars earn recognition with voluminous works that systematise great bodies of data. The period before scientific publications reach obsolescence is far longer than seems to be the case with anthropological literature. National ethnography may be compared to a granary in which generations of ethnographers, one after the other, hoard and preserve their knowledge. Ethnography is a cumulative discipline, like history (Cohn 1962).

The divergent strategies of investigation in the two disciplines result in different career patterns for their members. In general, the life cycle of the American anthropologist consists of several rather short periods of changing affiliations, of participating in a number of different government projects and international commissions, and of well-delineated periods of fieldwork lasting a year or two in different parts of the world. This variegated career is held together by a peculiar approach or personal point of view.

It is by far more difficult to offer a general picture of the lives of European ethnographers. They expend considerably more effort in collecting data. In the United States, the authors of books or monographs are presented to readers through biographical notes, so that external observers may conveniently follow their careers by comparative methods. In Europe, it is not customary to add biographical data to an article (perhaps because few European biographies are as colourful as American ones are).

There are fewer scientific institutions, with more stable personnel, in Europe than in America. Ethnographers are more 'settled' than anthropologists. Careers often begin in the service of a museum or institution and end with retirement from the same institution. Fieldwork can easily be integrated into such a career; the field is nearby and easy to visit, and field visits are usually short. The personal career of an ethnographer is also cumulative.

As soon as an anthropologist has passed the initiation of fieldwork and has formulated generalisations or hypotheses of his own, he can qualify for a frontline position in his science (see Cohn 1962). The period of maturation of his European colleague is longer, and his recognition depends to a greater extent on the knowledge and experience he has accumulated, and so in fact on his age. Some of his themes will mature into a book only after many decades.

Differences between Anthropological and Ethnographical Publications

From what has been set forth above, it follows that there are essential differences between the books of European ethnographers and those of anthropologists. The differences are evident even in the choices of titles. Recently, Charles M. Leslie (1960) wrote of the naming customs of anthropologists and determined which muses must have cooperated to create titles such as *Argonauts of the Western Pacific, New Lives for Old, The Chrysanthemum and the Sword*, and *Nomads of the Long Bow*. To a European reader these titles themselves sound like the shouts of returning argonauts or successful hunters informing those awaiting them of their booty. European titles, on the other hand, are prosaic and flat but describe the contents of the book. These titles read like the communiqués of a slow-moving army in an occupied area or like items in an inventory of a scientific storehouse. Often titles are understatements. It is considered ill mannered for an author to call attention to the significance of his discoveries. Richard Weiss, for example, investigated the relations of regional subcultures to both linguistic and religious boundaries and to historical territorial divisions in Switzerland and established the independent system of the variation of culture in space. He published his results under the title *The Brünig-Napf-Reuss Line as a Cultural Boundary-Line between East and West Switzerland on Swiss Ethnographical Maps'* (Weiss 1947). István Györffy discovered that until the middle of the nineteenth century the dwelling houses and farm yards (with all their related outbuildings) were located in two different zones within the settlements of the villages and peasant towns in the Great Hungarian Plain. This discovery threw new light on the family and community structure of the Hungarian peasantry, on the organisation of peasant farms, and on certain historical processes. His study bears the title, *The Settlement Pattern of Hajdúböszörmény* (Györffy 1926; cf. Den Hollander 1960–61).

The European ethnographer's modesty is not confined to the titles of books and papers. In general, ethnographers devote far less energy to elaborating general statements and theoretical conclusions than do their American colleagues (see Hultkrantz 1967). If theoretical conclusions are drawn, they are often concealed, so to speak, in the studies. Monographs are generally written for colleagues who are thoroughly familiar with the country being discussed and with the accumulated knowledge of their specialised branch of science. For them the wink of an eye or an allusion between the lines is sufficient to convey the theoretical significance of a newly described fact.

The books of ethnographers may be compared to icebergs: besides the facts on the printed page, there is much which does not emerge above the level of the water. In the United States, on the contrary, the glittering hypotheses and theories are on top, and most of the factual material is forced below the water level. The facts serve the theory. Facts are 'marshalled towards an objective, like ranks of privates that are there to make Gen. Principle win a campaign' (Kroeber 1956: 306; see also Wolf 1964: 16).

This difference does not merely express divergence in the rules of literary form; it also touches on the essence of the two approaches. According to Eric Wolf (1964: 92): 'In a true humanistic sense an individual life or even the sum of lives, interlaced in a common fate, are entities irreducible to general statements.' For the humanist there is no doubt that Homer's poetry, or Rembrandt's paintings or even those of lesser masters, is more valuable, more important, and more outstanding than the humanist's theories about it. The ethnographer harbours about the same modesty with regard to his subject. On the other hand, the anthropologist, humanistically minded and sympathetic as he may be to the people he studies, is a natural scientist, for whom peoples and cultures are only limited cases and arguments in his search for laws. According to Lévi-Strauss (1966: 126), it is exactly this objectivity which irritates the sensitivity of the new nations. It recalls a 'state of affairs in which one part of mankind treated the other as an object'.

The major portion of ethnographic literature is arranged by factual categories. Manning Nash studied the seasonal fluctuation of pottery production in a Mexican village and the reasons for this fluctuation. The title of his article (Nash 1961) is *The Social Context of Economic Choice in a Small Society*. Had he written this paper as a European ethnographer (ethnographers have, in fact, studied the same phenomena), it would probably have carried the title 'Pottery Production in Amatenango del Valle'. In indices and bibliographies it would be listed under categories such as 'domestic industries' and 'pottery'. The anthropologist looking for data on the topics of 'decision making' or 'economic choice' would stumble upon the paper only after perusing an enormous mass of irrelevant ethnographic monographs on pottery.

The cumulative growth pattern of ethnography presents further difficulties. In general, scholars disclose only what adds to the fringes of knowledge. Hence, the overall picture of the cultural process varies continually and lives only in the general consciousness of the ethnographers. Only rarely is it expressed in summarising studies.

An enormous mass of information has been accumulated in the ethnographic literature on a number of topics that are of interest to anthropologists. From its beginnings European ethnography focused its attention on the peasantry and other groups of 'ordinary people'. The concept of peasantry has recently entered anthropology to indicate a general social and cultural type in the history of humanity. Those nations and ethnic and regional groups studied by European scholars provide the framework for anthropologists wishing to research processes of cultural integration and differentiation in the contemporary nation-state. It must be admitted that the great majority of ethnographic studies has concentrated on material culture topics such as buildings, clothing, furniture, types of economic implements, and folklore texts, songs, and dances. But some ethnographers have also investigated the social organisation of tradition, networks and centres of cultural integration, revitalisation movements, the unfolding of local peasant styles, and their florescence and exhaustion. Even if one takes only the Hungarian case, an anthropologist who is interested in such questions would have to consult dozens of sources, many of them articles in periodicals. Given the absence of textbooks or convenient compilations, the foreign scholar will have a hard task tracking down the relevant materials.

In Central Europe, or at least in Hungary, the skills needed to handle the literature and to obtain data are taught to the student ethnographer in his preparatory courses. In ethnographic publications, the text often reverts to footnotes. Often footnotes cover a larger portion of the page than the text itself. Good and exact footnotes are appreciated by fellow ethnographers as indispensable guideposts in the scattered data. This is also a consequence of the affiliation between ethnography and the humanities. As Kroeber wrote (1953: 358): 'Now humanists unquestionably operate evidentially. They not only cite evidence, it was they who invented the footnote.' In American books, the notes in general cover the back pages or are missing altogether.

The anthropologist using the ethnographic literature embarks on a long and tiresome work and, as John Honigmann said at the conference 'Central and North-Central European Peasant Cultures' (Chicago, 1967), will have to perform some sort of 'footnote gymnastics'. However, ethnographic literature was made for this kind of use, so a cursory examination of a random sample of studies yields little insight into the knowledge of the ethnographers.

Alan P. Merriam, when criticised for neglecting the European and Latin American contributions to his topic, answered, 'One chooses from the materials he has at hand and knows best' (Merriam 1966: 230). This reasoning is fully justified in anthropology, where the author uses a more or less random sample of facts to prove his theoretical proposition. In Central Europe this position is unacceptable; anybody making a new statement is expected to do so in full command of all the previous contributions to the subject, citing all of the evidence which is available.

Conclusion

If this essay has any predictive character, it will in all probability earn only displeasure. Anthropologists, like a developing nation awakened to self-consciousness, prefer to study their culture from the inside. Joseph Berliner, an indigenous American and a professional in a related branch of science, visited anthropologists to study them and was censured for choosing the wrong informants and for misunderstanding their writings (Berliner 1962). With this essay I could be exposed to such censure for a better reason.

The nature of comparison is to minimise the differences between the two things being compared. Yet I am not unaware of the differences in the order of magnitude of the societies compared or of the complexity of their ideologies. This awareness is expressed in the apologetic character of my opinion for the side of ethnography.

Nor can this article be expected to evoke a more favourable reaction from ethnographers. As I have tried to make clear, theorising is not as customary in European ethnography as in American anthropology and is generally reserved for the elders of the science. It is considered a sign of bad manners when one pronounces his opinion of his branch of science with a levity of this sort.

In the Scandinavian countries, where contact between ethnographers and American anthropologists is both intensive and long established, it has been recognised that the adoption of a number of anthropological concepts and theories might benefit ethnography (Hultkrantz 1960: 12, 1967: 39). On the other hand, it has been declared openly that a wholesale adoption of American anthropology would be a step backwards (Hultkrantz 1965: 18). In such commentaries, a certain anti-missionary zeal is implied, together with complaints against the missionary attitude of American anthropologists. I have never read a proclamation in which anthropologists have invited ethnographers to abandon the gods of their ancestors and join the anthropological universal church. Yet from anthropologists' writings, the conviction may be formed that they have discovered the general science of man, which will become a new humanistic creed of mankind (cf. Hultkrantz 1965: 5–6). This may arouse in the ethnographer uncomfortable doubts about his right to exist. If the net of the anthropologists were in fact as large as the lake itself, this would mean not only that not a single fish could escape but also that the situation of all other fishermen would become hopeless (cf. Tax et al. 1953: 353).

Anthropology is a vigorous, expanding discipline which continually conquers new territories. The national ethnographies of Central Europe also appear to be thriving, if not at the same rate as North American anthropology. There are no symptoms of a depletion in research themes, nor are the ethnographers under a compulsion to repeat themselves.

I am inclined to believe that this situation is good, and that both anthropologists and ethnographers have their own tasks in the exploration of Europe. It is regrettable that the picture of the European countryside formed by anthropologists is more or less confined to what the community studies of recent years (i.e. between 1950 and 1967) have grasped, namely, the oppressive post-peasant morals of vanishing villages and backward societies. I believe it would be expedient to insert into this picture the colourful, rich, intricate fabric of cultural processes which the ethnographers have explored and described in a language differing from that of the anthropologist.

References

Anderson, R. T. 1965. Studies in Peasant Life. *Biennial Review of Anthropology* 176–210.

Arensberg, C. M. 1967. *Report to the American Council of Learned Societies*. The Study Committee, East European Studies. Manuscript.

Bailey, F. G. 1964. Two Villages in Orissa. In M. Gluckman (ed.), *Closed Systems and Open Minds: The Limits of Naïvety in Social Anthropology*, pp. 52–82. Chicago: Aldine.

Bausinger, H. 1961. *Volkskultur in der technischen Welt*. Stuttgart: Kohlhammer.

Berliner, J. S. 1962. The Feet of the Natives Are Large: An Essay on Anthropology by an Economist. *Current Anthropology* 3: 47–77.

Cohn, B. S. 1962. An Anthropologist among the Historians: A Field Study. In B. S. Cohn, *An Anthropologist among the Historians and Other Essays*, pp. 1–17. Delhi: Oxford University Press.

Den Hollander, A. N. J. 1960–61. The Great Hungarian Plain: A European Frontier Area. *Comparative Studies in Society and History* 3: 74–88, 155–69.

Devons, E., and M. Gluckman. 1964. Conclusion: Modes and Consequences of Limiting a Field of Study. In M. Gluckman (ed.), *Closed Systems and Open Minds: The Limits of Naïvety in Social Anthropology*, pp. 158–261. Chicago: Aldine.

Fél, E., and T. Hofer. 1969. *Proper Peasants: Traditional Life in a Hungarian Village*. Chicago: Aldine.

Gluckman, M. (ed.). 1964. *Closed Systems and Open Minds: The Limits of Naïvety in Social Anthropology*. Chicago: Aldine.

Györffy, I. 1926. Hajdúböszörmény települése. *Föld és Ember* 6: 177–210.

Hofer, T. 2004. Amerikai antropológusok és hazai néprajzkutatók közép-európai falukban: Összehasonlító jegyzetek két tudományág szakmai személyiségéről. In B. Borsos, Zs. Szarvas, and G. Vargyas (eds.), *Fehéren feketén, Varsánytól Rititiig*. Budapest: L'Harmattan.

Hultkrantz, Å. 1960. *International Dictionary of Regional European Ethnology and Folklore*, vol. 1. Copenhagen: Rosenkilde and Bagger.

———. 1965. Anthropology as a Goal of Research: Some Reflections. *Folk* 7: 5–22.

———. 1967. Some Remarks on Contemporary European Ethnological Thought. *Ethnologia Europea* 1: 38–44.

Ishida, E. 1965. European vs. American Anthropology. *Current Anthropology* 6: 303–18.

Kroeber, A. L. 1953. Concluding Review. In S. Tax et al. (eds.), *An Appraisal of Anthropology Today*, pp. 357–76. Chicago: University of Chicago Press.

———. 1956. History of Anthropological Thought. In W. L. Thomas, Jr. (ed.), *Current Anthropology: A Supplement to Anthropology Today*, pp. 293–311. Chicago: University of Chicago Press.

———. 1959. The History of the Personality of Anthropology. *American Anthropologist* 61: 398–404.

Leslie, C. M. 1960. *Now We Are Civilized: A Study of the World View of the Zapotec Indians of Mitla, Oaxaca*. Detroit: Wayne State University Press.

Lévi-Strauss, C. 1966. Anthropology: Its Achievements and Future. *Current Anthropology* 7: 124–27.

Maday, B. C. 1966. *Anthropology in Hungary*. Paper presented at the Sixty-fifth Annual Meeting of the American Anthropological Association, Pittsburgh.

Merriam, A. P. 1966. Review of *The Anthropology of Music*. *Current Anthropology* 7: 217–30.

Nash, M. 1961. The Social Context of Economic Choice in a Small Society. *Man* 61: 186–91.

Rasmussen, H. 1967. *Some Central Points of View of European Ethnology*. Paper prepared for the conference 'Central and North-Central European Peasant Cultures', January 9–13, University of Chicago Center for Continuing Education.

Redfield, R. 1956. *Peasant Society and Culture*. Chicago: University of Chicago Press.

Singer, M. 1961. Text and Context in the Study of Contemporary Hinduism. *Adyar Library Bulletin* 25: 274–303.

—— (ed.). 1966. *Krishna: Myths, Rites and Attitudes*. Honolulu: East-West Center Press.

Stocking, G. W., Jr. 1982. Afterword: A View from the Center. *Ethnos* 47 (1–2): 172–86.

——. 1992 *The Ethnographer's Magic and Other Essays in the History of Anthropology*. Madison: The University of Wisconsin Press.

Tax, S., L. C. Eiseley, I. Rouse, and C. F. Voegelin (eds.). 1953. *An Appraisal of Anthropology Today*. Chicago: University of Chicago Press.

Wallace, A. F. C. 1956. Revitalization Movements. *American Anthropologist* 58: 264–21.

——. 1966. Review of *The Revolution in Anthropology*, by I. C. Jarvie. *American Anthropologist* 68: 1254–55.

Weiss, R. 1947. Die Brünig-Napf-Reuss Linie als Kulturgrenze zwischen Ost- und Westschweiz auf volkskundlichen Karten. *Geographica Helvetica* 2: 153–75.

Wolf, E. R. 1964. *Anthropology*. Englewood Cliffs, N.J.: Prentice Hall.

Contributors

Chris Hann (b. 1953) is a Director of the Max Planck Institute for Social Anthropology, Halle.

Tamás Hofer (b. 1929) is retired Director of the Néprajzi Múzeum, Budapest.

Wolfgang Jacobeit (b. 1921) is Emeritus Professor of Ethnographie, Humboldt University, Berlin.

Zbigniew Jasiewicz (b. 1934) is Professor at the Institute of Ethnology and Cultural Anthropology, Adam-Mieckiewicz-University, Poznań.

Josef Kandert (b. 1943) is Professor at the Department of Sociology, Faculty of Social Sciences, Charles University, Prague.

Gabriela Kiliánová (b. 1951) is Director of the Institute of Ethnology, Slovak Academy of Sciences, Bratislava.

Martina Krause (b. 1963) is Director of the *Selbsthilfeinitiative für Alleinerziehende* (SHIA) organisation in Berlin.

Klára Kuti (b. 1969) is Lecturer in Néprajz, Janus-Panonnius-University, Pécs.

Petr Lozoviuk (b. 1968) is Research Fellow at the Institute for Saxon History and Volkskunde, Dresden.

Ute Mohrmann (b. 1938) is Emeritus Professor of Ethnographie, Humboldt-University, Berlin.

Dagmar Neuland-Kitzerow (b. 1953) is Curator at the Museum of European Cultures, Berlin State Museums, Prussian Cultural Heritage Foundation.

Karoline Noack (b. 1961) is Research Fellow at the Latin America Institute of the Free University, Berlin.

Juraj Podoba (b. 1958) is Senior Research Fellow at the Institute of Ethnology, Slovak Academy of Sciences, Bratislava.

Aleksander Posern-Zieliński (b. 1943) is Professor at the Institute of Ethnology and Cultural Anthropology, Adam-Mieckiewicz-University, Poznań.

Mihály Sárkány (b. 1944) is Senior Research Fellow at the Institute of Ethnology, Hungarian Academy of Sciences.

Peter Skalník (b. 1945) is Lecturer in Social Anthropology at the University of Pardubice.

Olga Skalníková (b. 1922) is retired Senior Research Fellow of the Institute of Ethnography and Folklore, Czechoslovak Academy of Sciences.

Zofia Sokolewicz (b. 1932) is Emeritus Professor of Etnologia, Institute of Ethnology and Cultural Anthropology, University of Warsaw.

Dietrich Treide (b. 1933) is Emeritus Professor of Ethnologie, University of Leipzig.

Ulrich van der Heyden (b. 1954) lectures at the Humboldt University and is also a Privatdozent of the Free University, both in Berlin.

Bea Vidacs (b. 1955) is Fulbright Visiting Lecturer at the Department of Cultural Anthropology, Eötvös Loránd University, Budapest.

Index

299-300, 306, 329, 350, 353n, 355
revolution 10, 55, 70, 74-6, 79-80, 88, 96, 135, 145, 160, 186, 252, 262, 289-90, 294, 307, 310-1, 313-4, 317, 322-3, 343, 361
Robek, A. 66-7, 74-6, 78, 80, 83-4, 227, 230-1, 235, 239-40, 242
romanticism 7, 71, 88, 99, 186, 191, 193, 198, 203, 245, 248, 250, 252, 262, 350
rural, groups 3, 71, 88, 202-3, 274, 290, 321, 348; Hungary 22, 99, 276; life 88, 111, 203-4, 232; research 2, 4, 8, 95, 111, 114, 176n, 232; society 7, 87-90, 95-6, 99-101, 111, 165, 186, 193, 239, 250, 276, 280-2; workers 62, 70, 76, 111, 239, 289, *see also* peasant
Russia 8-9, 12, 30, 35, 38, 41n, 46, 57, 67, 70, 80, 91, 119, 135, 160, 166, 172n, 259, 261, 290, 292n, 297n, 304n, 308-9, 316

Sárkány, M. ix, 1-20, 22, 87-108, 194, 242n, 259, 270, 274, 280-1, 283, 335, 337, 342-3, 363
Scheffel, D. 80, 84-5, 179-80, 230n, 233, 235, 238, 243, 249, 255
Second World War 8-9, 12, 21, 55, 58, 87, 109, 112, 116, 133, 142, 148, 150-1, 159, 211n, 228, 231n, 239, 263, 289, 293, 297, 345
Sellnow, I. 14, 37-8, 47, 51-2, 144n, 148n, 151, 157-8, 307, 328
semiotics 100, 121, 237, 264, 266
Siberia 7, 22, 29n, 35-6, 63, 66, 68n, 90, 98, 107, 120, 290, 297, 350
Skalník, P. ix, 1-20, 21-2, 55-86, 105, 179, 228-9, 235, 237n, 242, 246n, 253, 363
Skalníková, O. 4, 14n, 59, 62-3, 65, 70-4, 80, 85, 129-30, 171-81, 228, 230, 232-5, 239-40, 249, 364
Slav 7-8, 29-30, 55n, 58-9, 70, 73, 75, 84, 146, 159n, 162-3, 166,

173-6, 214, 235, 237, 246n, 253, 255, 265, 297
Slovakia 3-4, 6, 9, 12, 21-2, 30, 55, 57-8, 61-2, 64, 67, 73-4, 76-7, 80-1, 172n, 176-8, 193, 233n, 237, 242, 245-55, 257-67, 269, 363
social, condition 8, 32n, 36n, 64, 92n, 137, 143, 245, 257, 307, 336, 356, 360; development 12-3, 36n, 39, 94, 97, 147, 198, 214, 307; group 185, 203, 264-5, 307; integration 15, 40, 71; life 13-4, 41, 116, 167, 191, 196, 263, 279; organisation 13, 43, 85, 97, 116, 146, 152, 353, 357; phenomena 3, 39, 91-2, 97, 114, 124, 144, 278-9, 290, 317; problems 30, 161, 341; process 13, 42-4, 75, 101, 248, 259, 286, 332, 335-6; reality 2, 76, 122; relations 13, 41, 72, 74n, 94-6, 165, 176, 194, 197, 242, 253n, 274-5, 277, 281, 311, 315; stratification 3, 69, 81, 88, 92, 156, 282; system 148, 232, 279, 281, 352
Social Democratic Party (SPD) 134, 141, 175
social science 10, 152, 237, 245, 259, 264, 282, 287, 344; and anthropology 22, 36, 72, 110, 112-4, 124-5, 155, 165, 233, 279, 286, 312-3, 316, 336, 346; Faculty of 133, 136, 145, 363; and socialism 87, 110n, 112, 119, 124, 133, 165, 203, 246, 260, 311
socialism, anthropology under 109, 124, 191, 211, 228, 230, 233, 238, 251-2, 257, 261, 267, 285, 293, 314-5, 318; construction of 12-3, 59, 62, 65, 91, 124, 162, 165, 172, 232, 239, 255, 260; end of 2, 21, 100, 124, 187, 266, 317; as era 1, 9, 11-2, 16-7, 22-3, 89, 91-2, 103, 112-3, 122, 131, 193, 239, 252, 262; scientific 13-5, 112, 135, 191, 298, 336; as system 1, 17-8, 21, 70, 80, 145, 331

Halle Studies in the Anthropology of Eurasia

General Editors: Chris Hann, Richard Rottenburg, Burkhard Schnepel and Shingo Shimada

Chris Hann and the "Property Relations" Group
The Postsocialist Agrarian Question
Property Relations and the Rural Condition
"... anthropology needs a broader vision. It needs to shake off its strong association with the primitive and the exotic and become genuinely global in its comparisons. From this perspective, more sustained attention to Eurasia and a renewed focus on its underlying unity might launch the transformation of our parochial scholarly traditions into a mature cosmopolitan science." – Chris Hann, in his Preface to this series This is an age of neo-liberalism, in which the advantages and virtues of private property are often taken for granted. Postsocialist governments have privatized and broken up state farms and socialist cooperatives. However, economic outcomes and the social insecurity now experienced by many rural inhabitants highlight the need for a broader anthropological analysis of property relations, which goes beyond changes in legal form. A century after Kautsky addressed 'The Agrarian Question' in Germany, it is therefore necessary to address a postsocialist Agrarian Question throughout Central and Eastern Europe, the former Soviet Union and China. The studies collected here derive from the first cycle of projects at the Max Planck Institute for Social Anthropology. They are prefaced by a substantial Introduction by Chris Hann, a Founding Director of the Institute. Contributors: Susanne Brandtstädter, Andrew Cartwright, Barbara A. Cellarius, John Eidson, Patty A. Gray, Chris Hann, Patrick Heady, Deema Kaneff, Alexander D. King, Carolin Leutloff, Liesl L. Gambold Miller, Gordon Milligan, Mihály Sárkány, Florian Stammler, Wolde Gossa Ta-

desse, Davide Torsello, Aimar Ventsel, Lale Yalçın-Heckmann, John P. Ziker
Bd. 1, 2003, 488 S., 30,90 €, br., ISBN 3-8258-6532-0

Hannes Grandits; Patrick Heady (eds.)
Distinct Inheritances
Property, Family and Community in a Changing Europe
Questions about the respective roles of private and state property have been at the center of European political life for the whole of the past century. Much less publicity has been given to the ways in which rights to property are transmitted over time and how different inheritance traditions have affected European societies. The chapters in this book draw on historical and anthropological research to show how inheritance practices connect the intimate organization of domestic life with questions of economic development, political structure and religious belief. The book traces the story from the coming of Christianity, through the imposition and dissolution of different forms of feudalism, to the development of the modern economy. Several chapters deal with the impact of communism and its collapse - and demonstrate how ideas about the inheritance of property and status are continuing to shape, and be shaped by, economic and social changes in a continent that is moving beyond the ideological dichotomies of the Cold War. Contributors: Ulf Brunnbauer, Nevill Colclough, John Cole, John Eidson, Jack Goody, Hannes Grandits, Patrick Heady, Karl Kaser, Margareth Lanzinger, Robert Layton, Carolin Leutloff-Grandits, Hans Marks, Michael Mitterauer, Frances Pine, Andrejs Plakans, David Warren Sabean, Tatjana Thelen, Davide Torsello, Oane Visser, E.A. Wrigley
Bd. 2, 2004, 440 S., 29,90 €, br., ISBN 3-8258-6961-x; 39,90 €, gb., ISBN 3-8258-7334-x

LIT Verlag Münster – Berlin – Hamburg – London – Wien
Grevener Str./Fresnostr. 2 48159 Münster
Tel.: 0251 – 62 032 22 – Fax: 0251 – 23 19 72
e-Mail: vertrieb@lit-verlag.de – http://www.lit-verlag.de

Davide Torsello
Trust, Property and Social Change in a Southern Slovakian Village
Slovakia is a young and little studied country of the former socialist bloc. As in all postsocialist Eurasia, continuing transformations of everyday practices are still inadequately understood. This study combines anthropological and historical methods to search for alternative ways of "reading postsocialism" in the rural community. More specifically, it applies the notions of trust and property to map the outcomes of over a hundred years of turbulent social change, but not in the way that mainstream economists and political scientists have used these concepts. Trust and property acquire analytic significance only when contextualised into the practices and ideologies of the actors. This allows the observer to grasp the nuances of apparently ambivalent behaviour and "uttered mistrust" in other villagers and local institutions. Ambiguity veils subtle strategies for keeping up with the instability of the times and obtaining the best one can from the present. By providing a theoretically grounded ethnographical account of historical transformation the book makes an original anthropological contribution to the classic theme of social change in rural societies, while at the same time engaging constructively with other social science approaches to postsocialism.
Bd. 3, 2004, 264 S., 29,90 €, br.,
ISBN 3-8258-6962-8

Frances Pine; Deema Kaneff;
Haldis Haukanes (eds.)
Memory, Politics and Religion
The Past Meets the Present in Europe
This collection of essays focuses on the haunting themes of religion, politics and remembering the past. Spanning Europe from Ukraine to Spain, the authors consider ways in which memory is used, at the local level, both to legitimate and to contest claims to power, status, and social and cultural capital. The result is a rich and innovative set of texts on memory and silence, on the place of the past in the present, and on the ideologies and practices which constitute memory at the local level.
Bd. 4, 2004, 320 S., 29,90 €, br.,
ISBN 3-8258-8051-6

Joachim Otto Habeck
What it Means to be a Herdsman
The Practice and Image of Reindeer Husbandry among the Komi of Northern Russia
Habeck takes the reader to the tundra in the Far North of the Russian Federation, describing and interpreting the practice of reindeer herding on the land. His vivid account of the everyday life of Komi reindeer herders and their family members as they interact with their bosses, the town, the market and oil companies, reveals both the reach of their agency and its limitations. Through a meticulous analysis of each of these domains, Habeck shows how public discourse about reindeer husbandry as a traditional life-style derives from outside the Komi reindeer-herding communities, yet it has powerful effects on the local actors' ability to frame their own existence. He argues that the concept of tradition, despite its many positive connotations, places Komi reindeer herders in a „golden cage" which leaves no space for acknowledging their drive to innovation and flexibility.
Bd. 5, 2005, 296 S., 29,90 €, br.,
ISBN 3-8258-8045-1

LIT Verlag Münster – Berlin – Hamburg – London – Wien
Grevener Str./Fresnostr. 2 48159 Münster
Tel.: 0251 – 62 032 22 – Fax: 0251 – 23 19 72
e-Mail: vertrieb@lit-verlag.de – http://www.lit-verlag.de